Global Changes and Theoretical Challenges

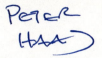

Series Editors' Foreword

As world affairs become ever more complex and dynamic, so have those in the field of international studies become increasingly innovative. There is no alternative. New approaches, methods, findings, and theories are needed just to keep up with the changing foci and concerns of international relations. The Issues in World Politics series, of which this volume is but one entry, is designed for serious students who are open to rethinking basic premises and pondering new insights.

Each volume in the series addresses a major dimension, problem, or dynamic of the expanding field of international studies. Each of them is also innovative in both content and method, thereby providing an opportunity to stay abreast of the changes in world politics and the changing modes of comprehension. At the same time, the series is not intended to advance a particular theoretical, methodological, or value perspective. Rather, its unity derives from the readiness of all its contributors to think afresh and creatively about the subject domain with which they are concerned.

James N. Rosenau
William C. Potter

Global Changes and Theoretical Challenges

Approaches to World Politics for the 1990s

Edited by

Ernst-Otto Czempiel
J.W. Goethe Universität
  Frankfurt am Main

James N. Rosenau
Institute for Transnational Studies
  University of Southern California

Lexington Books
D.C. Heath and Company/Lexington, Massachusetts/Toronto

This book is published as part of the Lexington Books *Issues in World Politics* series, James N. Rosenau and William C. Potter, consulting editors.

Library of Congress Cataloging-in-Publication Data

Global changes and theoretical challenges : approaches to world politics for the 1990s / edited by Ernst-Otto Czempiel, James N. Rosenau.
    p.   cm.

    Includes index.
    ISBN 0-669-17877-2 (alk. paper). ISBN 0-669-17878-0 (pbk. : alk. paper)
    1. International relations. I. Czempiel, Ernst-Otto, 1927–   . II. Rosenau, James N.
JX1391.G52   1989   88-28282
327—dc19   CIP

Published simultaneously in Canada
Printed in the United States of America
Casebound International Standard Book Number: 0-669-17877-2
Paperbound International Standard Book Number: 0-669-17878-0
Library of Congress Catalog Card Number: 88-28282

The paper used in this publication meets the minimum requirements of American National Standard for Information Sciences—Permanence of Paper for Printed Library Materials, ANSI Z39.48-1984. ∞™

89 90 91 92 8 7 6 5 4 3 2 1

Contents

Preface

T his book has its origins in a transatlantic dialogue between the editors that began in the early 1980s and continues to the present. Whether it ensued in Los Angeles, Frankfurt, or through the mails, we found ourselves sharing a concern for the state of theorizing in the study of world politics. So much change seemed to be unfolding in international affairs, and yet so little attention seemed to be addressed to its implications. It might well be, we reasoned, that currently available paradigms and perspectives for comprehending world politics are sufficient to meet the challenges posed by the continuing processes of change but that the only way to reach this conclusion is by testing it, by focusing thoughtful minds on the question of whether new approaches and concepts are needed to probe the unfamiliar and often anomalous developments that arrest attention. Put differently, the more we communicated, the more were we struck by the discrepancy between the amount of empirical work done in the field and the relative paucity of coordinated efforts to locate this work in a more encompassing theoretical context. What coordination exists among international relations analysts, moreover, tends to be along national lines—within countries rather than between them. Indeed, it can be fairly said that the cooperation among politicians in the Atlantic Community exceeds by far that which can be found in the community of American-European community of scholars.

These considerations led to a call for collaboration in a series of workshops, the first of which resulted in this book and the second of which is now in the planning stages. Chapter 1 outlines the reasoning that underlay the first workshop and the specific foci that came within its purview. Chapter 14 undertakes a summary evaluation of the proceedings and the chapters that arose from the workshop.

We are pleased to acknowledge our appreciation of the several individuals and organizations whose generosity enabled the workshop to be held and its proceedings to unfold in a relaxed and yet organized fashion. Birgit Hasselbach, a senior at the University of Frankfurt, shouldered most of the technical burdens of convening a transatlantic conference, and she did so with a zest and effectiveness that made a huge difference. The workshop itself was held at the conference site of the Werner-Reimers-Stiftung in Bad Homburg, West Germany, and we are indebted to that organization for providing facilities that were especially conducive to the exchange of complex ideas. And we gratefully note that financial support for the occasion was provided mainly by the Deutsche Forschungsgemeinschaft, with additional help from the Esther A. and Joseph Klingenstein Fund, William and Jane Rosenau, and Harold C. Mayer.

We are also grateful to members of the staff of the Institute for Transnational Studies at the University of Southern California—E. Martha Decker, Lilia Amezcua, and Christine Kralovansky—for their help in preparing the index.

Our thanks go, too, to Jaime Welch-Donahue, Robert D. Bovenschulte, and their colleagues at Lexington Books who recognized that these essays would make a fine first entry in the new series on Issues in World Politics. It is a series designed to enable students to come to terms with the challenges of the 1990s, and for that purpose this book could hardly be more suitable.

Lastly, as editors we feel a particularly keen sense of gratitude to our colleagues who attended the workshop and revised their papers for this book. In the end our effort at transatlantic intellectual cooperation was so successful precisely because they took on the awesome task of rethinking the nature of world politics so seriously and so creatively.

1

Global Changes and Theoretical Challenges: Toward a Postinternational Politics for the 1990s

James N. Rosenau

Though the chapters of this book touch upon a number of substantive and conceptual issues, at their core is a concern with theory and transformation. In turn, these core concepts are linked by more than alliterative nuance. Theory and transformation are not separate spheres, with the former designating an activity of observers of world affairs and the latter referring to developments in the world itself. Rather the two are inextricably intertwined. Just as one can hardly appreciate and comprehend the nature of the transformations without an appropriate theoretical perspective, so is it extremely difficult to evolve and maintain appropriate theory without a sense that seemingly stable features of the world scene are undergoing such severe strains as to be transformed into new and unfamiliar patterns.

Nor is this close link between the theoretical and actual worlds only a matter of academic concern. Leaders and publics, no less than their compatriots in the universities, conduct themselves in terms of some notions of why and how the issues and situations of world politics unfold as they do. These notions may be crude, vague, and contradictory, and as such they may often be subject to wide fluctuations and gross distortions; but, still, there can be no action in the public arena without prior expectations of what the parties to a situation seek and what the outcomes are likely to be. And thus, too, there can be no meaningful accommodations to change (or, for that matter, to constancy) without a sense that it is under way.

The fact that theory and transformation go hand in hand for actors as well as for observers highlights the potential contribution that academics and intellectuals—and, I like to think, this book—might make to the course of world affairs. For leaders and publics evolve their criteria for sensing and evaluating the tensions between change and constancy from somewhere. Their theories are not mere responses to what happens. The world does not say to them, in effect, "Look, things have changed and you must adjust!" Rather, the changes have to be perceived and interpreted, and it is in the processes of perception and interpretation that the formulations of professional theorists can be relevant. It is not, to be sure, an immediate relevance, as politicians, foreign offices, opposition spokespersons, and the mass media are the prime interpreters of meaning and definers of current issues. From a long-term, indirect, and more encompassing perspective, however, those in the public arena acquire at least some of their conceptual tools and competing value systems for assessing world affairs from the insights and ideas that emerge from the formulations and debates of those for whom the study of world affairs is a full-time occupation.

The processes whereby ideas make their ways from the halls of academe into the foci and discourses of leaders and publics are, of course, circuitous and slow moving. Some of the communications channels may involve direct interaction as the actors turn to academics for their expertise on technical questions. But for the most part the channels are marked by twists and turns, from those that are as irregular as the long-run influences of education to those that are as haphazard as the ways in which the milieu of public affairs evolves to shape the political agenda for each generation. Thus the connection between those ideas that get introduced into the communications system as a consequence of controversy and consensus among intellectuals and those that emerge as the orientations of citizens and their leaders often seem tenuous, oversimplified, and misapplied. But, whatever their emasculation and distortion, the connections are nevertheless there—as any quick appraisal of the impact of Marxist ideas on history would readily demonstrate.

If this assessment of the long-term links between abstract theories and concrete transformations is accurate, and if a number of global trends may be converging to induce worldwide transformations which, in turn, may throw the world's images of political institutions and its conceptions of political processes into flux, redefinitions of political life are likely to develop and, along with them, respecifications of the norms, habits, and practices of global politics. Hence it is time for intellectual leadership, for students of world politics to offer new understandings that are consistent with the emergent patterns and that thus shape how the world's politicians, journalists, and publics perceive the processes in which they participate. In the absence of such leadership, global political institutions may change faster than the world's capacity to comprehend them, and at that point orderly mechanisms for resolving conflict will surely be more unobtainable than ever.

Postinternational Politics

Given a focus on the pervasive presence of transformations in global life, it seems awkward to continue referring to the field in which they occur as "international politics." Even the notion of "international relations" seems obsolete when so many of the interactions that presently sustain world politics do not unfold directly between nations or states. So a new term is needed, one that clearly denotes the possible advent of new structures and processes while at the same time allowing for still further structural development. An obvious label quickly springs to mind: *postinternational politics*. If the social sciences are now marked by analyses of postcapitalist society, postcivilized era, postcollectivist politics, posteconomic society, posthistoric man, postideological society, postliberal era, postliterature culture, postmarket society, post-Marxists, postmaterialistic value system, postmaturity economy, postmodernism, postorganization society, post-Christian era, postscarcity society, postsocialist society, posttraditional society, and postwelfare society, as well as postindustrial society, surely it follows that profound changes in world affairs can be regarded as constituting postinternational politics (the foregoing concepts are discussed in Bell [1973]).

But use of this label involves more than conforming to a trend. Postinternational politics is an appropriate designation because it clearly suggests the decline of long-standing systemic patterns without at the same time indicating where the changes may be leading. It suggests flux and transition even as it implies the presence and functioning of stable structures. It allows for chaos even as it hints at coherence. It reminds us that matters international may no longer be the dominant dimensions of global life, or at least that other dimensions have emerged to challenge or offset the interactions of nation-states.[1]

The Workshop on International Theory

Sensitive to both the positive and negative potentials of a newly emergent global politics, it was with a special sense of urgency that the Workshop on International Theory was convened on 31 May 1987. Not that the three days were conducted in the crisis-like atmosphere that can envelop those who seek solutions to immediate policy problems. Quite to the contrary: the relaxed, quiet setting of the Werner-Reimers-Stiftung in Bad Homburg, fifteen miles southwest of Frankfurt, Federal Republic of Germany, was conducive to a contemplative mood of exploration and critical exchange. At the same time, like those who see ominous clouds on the distant horizon, the workshop participants shared a sense of restless urgency with respect to the viability and adequacy of the theoretical enterprise. Their widely shared concern that the gap between theory and transformation in world politics may be widening was an ever-present undertone of the deliberations.

Indeed, it was precisely this deep preoccupation with the growing gap between practice and theory, between world politics as it is and as it is understood, that underlay the convening of the workshop and the distinguished quality of its participants. The case for a return to theoretical drawing boards was made by the organizers of the workshop (and the editors of this book) in the invitations to prepare a paper for the occasion, and seventeen of the eighteen invitees were quick to accept and take on the assignment. (For a variety of reasons, however, only thirteen of these papers were revised for inclusion in this book.)

But, because the organizers were far from certain as to the proper directions new theorizing should follow, the invitations allowed plenty of leeway for diverse approaches to the task. In order to provoke a readiness to theorize afresh, ten guidelines (noted below) that might serve as possible foci for the papers accompanied the invitations and, in addition, I circulated in advance two preliminary papers along these lines (summarized below). At the same time it was emphasized that both the guidelines and the preliminary papers were to be treated as points of departure—a delineation of problems—rather than as a framework for the working papers. That only a few of the ensuing chapters take direct note of these previously circulated materials, that they pursue thirteen different lines of theoretical inquiry, is a measure both of how seriously the participants view the need for theorizing afresh and how diverse the responses to this need can be. The pages that follow are eloquent testimony to how pluralistic and disparate approaches to the field have become since those now distant decades when most analysts organized their work around one or another form of the realist paradigm.

Stated differently, the contributors to this book share an aspiration to broadening theoretical horizons and, in so doing, to deepening sensitivity to the potentials for global change. Clearly, however, they do not share a conception of how and why world politics are undergoing change and what are the most fruitful theoretical orientations to bring to bear on the changes. Indeed, at least four of the chapters question whether fundamental transformations are at work. Still, the consensus around the need to theorize afresh is manifest and thoroughgoing. None of the ensuing chapters argues for a politics-as-usual approach to the subject.

It might be said that the workshop would have been more productive if the invitations had listed a strict set of perspectives and/or hypotheses to which the participants had to conform. Though a more unified book would have doubtless resulted, in our view such a collection would also have been misleading. It would have conveyed the presence of a consensus about the appropriate lines of theoretical development at a time when creative and thoughtful theorists are not in agreement as to how to interpret the dynamics of change at work in the world. The central lesson of this book is precisely that the fluidity and pluralism of postinternational politics is matched by a diversity of approaches to understanding the deeper structures that may or may not be emerging from the change.

Theoretical Challenges

In short, readers will find here ample opportunities for engaging their own theoretical impulses. So that they may start from the same point as did the contributors, the ensuing paragraphs reproduce the challenge contained in the invitations to the workshop. From the very first sentence on, the stress was on the interaction between theory and transformation.

> There are numerous signs that global politics is, at all levels, undergoing enormous change. New economic, social, and political structures are emerging and old ones are being transformed as technology becomes ever more dynamic. At

best, however, the development of theory to comprehend this change has been piecemeal. Most analysts have been so fully preoccupied with the problems of policy analysis that their theoretical efforts tend to be either sketchy or narrow in scope.

Some scholars, to be sure, have recorded theoretical progress in the areas of linkage politics, complex interdependence, transnational relations, world systems analysis, long-cycle dynamics, dependency theory, and regime formation. Compelling critiques of the limits of realist theory have also been published. This forward movement, however, has been at the cost of fragmentation. Huge gaps remain. Work since the pace of global change quickened in the 1960s has resulted in islands of theory, but few bridges to connect them have been identified, much less built. Perhaps most notable in this regard is the persistent scarcity of theorizing addressed to the interaction of domestic and international politics. Most theorists agree that such interaction is considerable, but for a variety of reasons students of comparative politics continue to hold international variables constant and those of international politics continue to do the same with domestic variables. Rare indeed are those who have attempted formulations in which the operation of variables within and between nation-states are hypothesized to be functions of each other.

To a large degree, in short, much of what passes for theory in international relations today was designed for an era now passing into oblivion. The state-centric structure of world affairs, in which actions and interactions are dominated by nation-states, is now rivaled by a more complex, less symmetrical set of patterns whereby international issues arise and are managed. Many of today's crucial problems—such as currency crises, environmental pollution, and the drug trade—are transnational in scope, with the result that governments are less and less able to be effective within their own domains and must, instead, contend with a multiplicity of issues sustained in part by external dynamics.

It follows that activity in the global community today is the result not only of nation-states striving for goals, but also of a number of varied transnational collectivities—from multinational corporations to professional societies to international organizations to terrorists, and so on through a vast range of new kinds of actors—engaging in pursuits that are not confined by national boundaries. Furthermore, the growing interdependence of the world economy is transforming the capacity of states to maintain independent policies. One need only ponder the emergent role of the IMF with respect to debt-ridden societies in the Third World to appreciate the extent to which long-standing patterns of world politics are undergoing change.

But how to cope with the pervasive change? One way is to patch up existing theoretical formulations so that they can accommodate the emergent structures. Increasingly, however, it is clear that such efforts have limited potential and that new, more encompassing endeavors to construct theory rooted in the emergent patterns need to be undertaken. Increasingly it is clear that the elevation of economic issues to the realm of "high politics" on the global agenda is requiring theoretical syntheses that focus on the interplay of international politics and the world economy. Increasingly it is clear that the breakdown of the old inter-state system is necessitating reformulation of how domestic and international processes sustain each other.

In addition, even if the turbulence of world affairs is conceived more as continuity than as change, unmistakable signs of crisis bearing on the authority and competency of the state are readily discernible in the sharpening debate about its centrality as the pivotal subject of international history. And, as is often the case in crises, polarization is occurring: analysts are moving away from an unquestioning, often implicit, commitment to the state as an organizing concept to opposite poles. At one extreme is an orthodoxy that celebrates the state as the true vantage point around which all analyses must eventually converge. At the other extreme is a heterodoxy that involves various challenges to the state's claim to centrality, from Marxist and neo-Marxist alternatives through those founded on transnationalism and complex interdependence. Absent from this debate is theorizing in which the crisis occasioning the polarization can be comprehended.

The document accompanying the invitation to the workshop then turned to enumerating the ten guidelines that were suggested as a point of departure for writing the papers. More specifically, the invitees were

asked to consider the implications of the hypothesized global authority crisis in the process of including some or all of the following foci in their theoretical formulations:

(1) the implications of widening and/or narrowing gaps presently at work on a global scale (e.g., between publics and governments, between haves and have-nots, between nuclear and nonnuclear powers, between technologically advanced and technologically stagnant allies and/or adversaries, etc.);

(2) the consequences of increasingly ineffective governments;

(3) the significance of the simultaneity of coherence and breakdown within and between national states;

(4) the political learning curves inherent in the ever greater exposure of publics to the products of the microelectronic revolution;

(5) the relevance of conspicuous, rapid, and extensive global shocks (such as famines, currency crises, runaway inflation, large-scale migrations, etc.);

(6) the emergence of an often volatile, sometimes fragile, world economy;

(7) the growing tendency at every system level to challenge authority and question legitimacy;

(8) the conceptualization of crisis and how authority, economic, and geopolitical crises might differ;

(9) the differential circumstances of various strategies and practices of revolution, adaptation, and resistance;

(10) indicators of the foregoing dynamics (i.e., how can the processes set forth in subparagraphs 1–9 be detected and measured?).

These guidelines were subsequently followed up by the circulation of two preliminary papers designed to provide the workshop participants with additional materials for pondering the potential and direction of change in global politics. In one of these, henceforth called the micro formulation, I proposed that, for a variety of reasons, the skills and orientations of people in all parts of the world have undergone such an extensive transformation as to have important consequences for the conduct of global politics. Nine attributes of citizens, five involving their analytic capabilities and four their orientations toward authority, legitimacy, and control, were hypothesized to have been expanded to the point where the coherence and structures of macro systems can no longer be taken for granted.

Crucial to the micro formulation are the processes by which the postulated changes in individuals get translated into consequences for collectivities and structures at the macro level. There is nothing magical about these processes, no mystical force that converts micro tendencies into macro outcomes. Rather, the conversion occurs through specifiable processes of aggregation that lie at the heart of any political process. Accordingly, the micro formulation devoted considerable attention to elaborating on these processes, with a primary distinction being drawn between those aggregations in which people are mobilized for particular purposes and those in which they are unaware of their actions as forming parts of a larger whole. The difference between a protest march and a population explosion is illustrative of these two basic types of aggregation.

If the micro–macro links inherent in the several types of aggregation are not adequately conceptualized, the micro formulation argued, it seems unlikely that theory adequate to comprehending the changing nature of world politics can be developed. In the past it may have been possible for realists to assume that macro structures so fully shape the micro level as to justify ignoring the latter in their explanatory schemes; but the worldwide tendencies toward decentralization have gained such momentum in recent decades that it is questionable whether such an assumption about the irrelevance of micro phenomena is still tenable. Indeed, the micro formulation unqualifiedly asserts that the causal flows between individuals and their collectivities go in both directions, with the former being in part shaped by their macro cultures and institutions even as the latter are in part a product of the skills and orientations that predominate among their members.

But it is misleading to presume that the theoretical challenges inherent in global changes can be fully met by specifying the aggregative processes through which micro–macro interactions unfold. If it is the case that the skills and orientations of people are changing and having macro consequences, then it is incumbent upon the theorist also to identify both the macro consequences and the emergent macro structures with which the micro dynamics interact. This is what my second paper circulated in advance of the Bad Homburg workshop sought to accomplish. Referred to here as the macro formulation, it explicitly followed up on the first paper by focusing on changes at the macro level of international structures and process through which states and other collective actors seek to manage global affairs.[2]

The prime hypothesis set forth in the macro formulation is that since World War II, world politics has undergone a bifurcation into two worlds. One of these is the state-centric world that has existed for some three hundred years and is dominated by the state system; the other is an emergent multicentric world that is composed of nongovernmental and governmental transnational actors whose decentralized structures and processes constitute a highly pluralistic system in which no single actor or groups of actors are dominant. The actors in the state-centric world are conceived to be endlessly faced with a "security" dilemma even as their counterparts in the multicentric world must contend with a continuing "autonomy" dilemma. At the same time the rules underlying the conduct of the actors in each world accept the existence of the other and allow for considerable interaction among them.

This macro formulation posits several prime dynamics as having given rise to both centralizing and decentralizing tendencies which, in turn, have fostered the bifurcation of global politics. One involves the fast-moving technological developments that have greatly intensified the flow of ideas, peoples, and goods across national boundaries. The world is thus rendered ever more interdependent, and a number of new public issues—such as debt crises and terrorism—signal the advent of an era of postinternational politics in an expanding and transnationalized global agenda. A second dynamic at the macro level is the obverse of these centralizing tendencies: the very same technologies are conceived to have made it increasingly difficult for states and governments to resolve major public issues on their political agendas and, as a result, they have been sufficiently weakened by decentralizing tendencies as to raise doubts about their authority and legitimacy. This "crisis" in the authority of whole systems is, in turn, hypothesized to have fostered a strengthening of subsystems and a surge of "subgroupism" that has begun to challenge the premises of the "nationalism" around which the orientations and loyalties of people have long been organized. The final dynamic viewed as promoting the bifurcation of macro structures and processes involves the feedback of the new technologies, weakened states, and strengthened subsystems at the micro level: individuals, both officials and citizens, are postulated as having enlarged their analytic skills as a consequence of exposure to the new technologies and having to cope with the challenges posed by the expanding interdependence.

Figure 1–1 offers a diagrammatic summary of these dynamics and the interactive ways in which, through time, they have culminated in a bifurcation of global politics. The sequence depicted in figure 1–1 culminates with a question mark because neither the micro nor the macro formulation anticipates whether the bifurcation is a transitional or an enduring characteristic of global life.

Alternative Perspectives

As previously indicated, none of the ensuing chapters were provoked by the initial guidelines and the two preliminary papers. In his or her own way, however, each

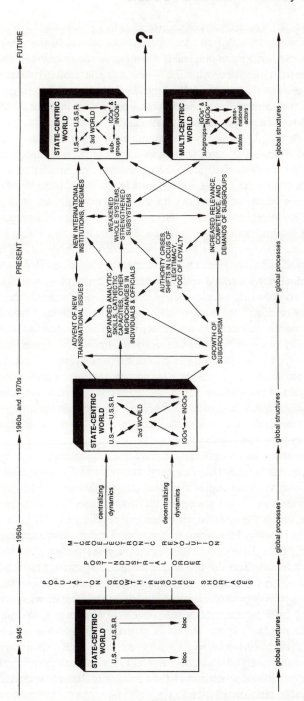

Figure 1-1. The Two Worlds of World Politics

* IGOs – International Governmental Organizations

** INGOs – International Non-governmental Organizations

contributor does address the question of change and, to a lesser extent, a concern for the micro–macro problem can also be discerned in several of the essays.

Because he focuses on epistemological dimensions of the question—"on how to think about international transformation"—perhaps the most thoroughgoing discussion of change in world politics is developed by John Gerard Ruggie (chapter 2). He argues that an understanding of fundamental global transformation can only be acquired if the analyst employs an appropriate conceptualization of international structures, that meaningful change occurs through such structures, and thus can only be recognized if one's notion of structures allows for their transformation. He contends that the conventional use of the concept, a "physicalist" construction, inhibits the recognition of change and suggests that a "third image" or "structuration" approach is better suited to the tracing of transformation. Indeed, he challenges his readers to generate ways of testing for the presence of international structures, arguing that the existing conceptual equipment is so "incapable of capturing" structural transformations as to render "the continuity thesis . . . no firmer a scientific footing than its opposite, that fundamental change is taking place."

Although he does not specifically address the possibility of a bifurcation of the essential structures of world politics, Ruggie's analysis does point in the direction of a multiplicy of power centers, not all of which are dominated by nation-states. Such a conclusion derives from a perspective in which power is conceived not in the physicalist sense of possessed capabilities, but as the possession of a perceived right to undertake action in global affairs, a right that has "shifted toward some actors, and away from others" through history and that is presently possessed by actors in "that part of the world which is nonterritorial and globalized" as well as by states that are territorial and internationalized. As my own macro formulation distinguished between the state- and multicentric worlds, so does Ruggie differentiate the global from the international subset of social interactions.

It is also noteworthy that in the conclusion of his chapter Ruggie makes reference to micro phenomena but he does that in a very different way from the aforementioned notion of micro as consisting of the behavior of individuals. For Ruggie a focus on the micro level involves a concern with "micro cases" and "micro practices," by which he means the specific situations and conflicts in which decisions get made. Viewed in this way he appears to conceive of micro–macro interactions as flowing essentially from the macro to the micro level, since "only the appropriate macroperspectives can elucidate the full significance . . . of micro practices."

Although writing independently of Ruggie's assessment, Robert W. Cox (chapter 3) responds to Ruggie's challenge that global transformations cannot be grasped without a proper formulation of the concept of structure. Cox also links the question of international change to that of structural transformation and explores it by, first, distinguishing between a perspective he calls "structuralism" that treats structures as innate and immutable and a "historical structures" approach that conceives of international structures as the products of history, as cumulative results of innumerable repetitive actions in which micro–macro interactions are seen, following Marx, as being "in balance." Then, after rejecting structuralism and adopting the historical structures approach, he identifies three interrelated "levels" of structures as being "most relevant to change in world order . . . (1) the organization of production, (2) the form of state, and (3) the structure of world order." The functioning of these structures is subjected to scrutiny with respect to world politics late in the nineteenth century and all three are deemed to have undergone transformation. In his conclusion Cox applies this paradigm of inter-related structural change to the contemporary period and finds several indications—the decline of U.S. hegemony is one and the "massive restructuring of production processes" is another—that processes of basic global change are under way.

Still another innovative approach to the problems of structure in world politics is developed by Alexander Wendt and Raymond Duvall (chapter 4). They offer a "structurationist" perspective that they regard as providing a more incisive understanding of the nature of international institutions, hierarchy, and order than do the various realist and neorealist theories. At the core of a structurationist approach is a concern with how structures and systems get reproduced and a premise that the reproduction occurs through the "codetermination" of the agents comprising the structures and systems that result from the regular interaction of the agents—that is, the agents both shape and are shaped by their own structures and systems. For Wendt and Duvall, therefore, the dynamics of change are continuously operative as the "constitutive" elements of states and international institutions are endlessly in flux in the processes of reacting to each other and reproducing themselves. Thus, as they put it, "there are neither state actors and practices nor international system structures apart from international institutions." The Wendt–Duvall chapter concludes with a challenging research agenda that outlines four suggestions for pursuing the numerous theoretical implications inherent in their approach.

Chapters 5, 6, 7, and 8 share a premise that is treated as a hypothesis in the Ruggie, Cox, and Wendt–Duvall formulations. Where the latter regard the onset of profound global transformations as a theoretical challenge, the contributions of Wolf-Dieter Eberwein, Werner Link, Ernst-Otto Czempiel, and James A. Caporaso take as given that world politics have undergone such transformations. For them the problem is not how to determine the extent and direction of the changes, but how to analyze the considerable interdependence that has become so central to the international system.

Wolf-Dieter Eberwein (chapter 5) for example, accepts the development of complex and global interdependence "as a structural fait accompli," but argues forcefully that there is lack of adequate theory to grasp these changes. His approach to overcoming this problem is to view "understanding the dynamics of a theoretical system" as "a problem of method." As Eberwein sees it, the ever greater interdependence of the world is founded on an elaborate "feedback structure" that cannot be sufficiently understood unless its components can be simulated and its dynamics thus observed. The bulk of his chapter then illustrates this approach with some of the results generated by a computer simulation model, GLOBUS, designed to assess long-term political and economic trends on a global scale. Among the insights and conclusions derived from this form of inquiry, perhaps the most useful is that though there is variation from state to state, for all nations "a loss of control is inevitable given the level of international interdependence."

Werner Link (chapter 6) addresses the problem of theory building from a perspective in which the task is to explain global changes that have already unfolded rather than to assess whether they have occurred. In contrast to Eberwein's simulation approach, however, Link relies on historical analysis to probe what he regards as the three main paradigms of the international system presently claiming the attention of analysts—the decentralized anarchic system of states, the quasi-institutionalized society of states, and the transnational relations system. More accurately, he regards the differences between the first two and the third paradigms as crucial and uses two empirical case studies, German–U.S. relations in the 1920–33 and 1945–75 periods, as the basis for an exploration of them. In so doing he finds that though the multicentric transnational system does have a significant impact upon relations in the anarchic world of states, it is nonetheless a subordinate system, a "complementary" set of arrangements rather than an "emergent new world order." His cases suggest, in other words, that the bifurcation that has occurred in the international system is of a limited kind and does not amount to an alteration of the central place of states in world politics. Moreover, by comparing the German–U.S. cases with the findings of an inquiry into Canadian–U.S. relations (Nye 1974), his analysis comes to the valuable conclusion that the interaction of international and transnational relations in a particular setting can have different internal and external consequences for the parties to the relationships.

Ernst-Otto Czempiel (chapter 7) agrees that world politics has undergone pervasive transformations, but in contrast to Link he seeks to develop a synthesis of, rather than trace a complementarity among, the realist, neorealist, and transnational paradigms. His goal is nothing less than a single scheme that encompasses the whole range of activities within and between societies that bear upon world politics. This effort leads him to adapt Easton's (1965) formulation of politics as the authoritative allocation of values to the circumstances of a highly interdependent world, an adaptation he refers to as "internationalizing politics." It also focuses his attention on the concept of the state and the various ways it is unsuitable to the analysis of a rapidly changing world in which values are allocated at all levels of society.

Like Eberwein, Link, and Czempiel, James Caporaso (chapter 8) presumes that world politics have experienced extensive transformation, but he applies still another approach, that of microeconomics, to the problem of theorizing about the international system as it is presently structured. It is an approach that by its very nature leads to an insightful discussion of micro–macro interactions and a useful comparison of how two major research programs—the "new institutional history" and "evolutionary" perspectives on political economy—serve to link micro dynamics to macro outcomes. Irrespective of whether one is led to focus on individuals as basic units of analysis because of an interest in neoclassical economics, or vice versa, Caporaso's chapter is distinguished by its preoccupation with the nature of the individuals whose actions are consequential in world politics. He finds that the world of microeconomics is "not composed of free-floating individuals," that rather they are joined to a "particular institutional environment," the market, which is in turn subject to the institutional setting in which it operates. As a consequence of these constraints, microeconomics treats individuals as asocial, rational actors who seek to maximize their gains and whose behavior across time is best understood in the context of the history of the institutions in which they are embedded. Caporaso finds this approach wanting in comparison to the evolutionary perspective, which allows for the intervention of nonrational norms, "sociality," and actions that are not necessarily power-maximizing.

In contrast to the inclination of Ruggie, Cox, and Wendt and Duvall to develop means of explaining global transformations, and contrary to the readiness of Eberwein, Link, Czempiel, and Caporaso to explore the implications of change, four chapters share a tendency to discount the degree to which world politics have undergone meaningful alteration. Those by Susan Strange, Bruce M. Russett, Janice E. Thomson and Stephen D. Krasner, and Erich Weede differ in key respects, but they have in common a presumption that it is all too easy to exaggerate the rate and direction of global changes.

Susan Strange (chapter 9) begins with a discussion of the nature of theory—what it is and what it is not. She emphasizes that viable theories of world politics are those that attempt to explain aspects of the international system not easily understood through the application of common sense. This leads her to outline a theory of "structural power" as a means of comprehending the disorder apparent in the world economy, a perspective that in turn leads to the hypothesis that the developments others see as manifestations of structural change in world politics stem from a distortion of existing structures. It is not that the world has undergone profound transformation, she argues in effect, but rather that its prime center of power, the United States, is conducting itself unwisely. More specifically, and explicitly in opposition to hegemonic stability theory, she contends that the epitaphs for the American Century are premature, that the course of events is a consequence not of U.S. hegemonic decline but of "the misuse of American hegemonic power in a unilateralist manner."

Bruce M. Russett (chapter 10) also addresses the question of whether there has been a decline in U.S. hegemony, but his focus is on nuclear weapons rather than economic resources as the bases of hegemonic power. The result is a provocative and complex analysis in which he reaffirms doubts about the U.S. decline insofar as nonmilitary sources of dominance are concerned. At the same time he records a "carefully nuanced" analysis of the changing role of nuclear weapons in world politics. Noting some limited ways in which such weapons have proved useful in the past, he offers data pertaining to a number of situations since 1945 in which nuclear deterrence has been a relevant factor to suggest that the utility of these weapons is increasingly questionable and that "the doubts have grown substantially, and with good reason, over the past two decades." In his conclusion Russett stresses that it is unclear whether the world will seize the opportunities or succumb to the dangers inherent in this diminution in the relevance of nuclear weapons.

Where Strange and Russett question the premise of underlying change through an assessment of hegemonic stability theory, Janice Thomson and Stephen Krasner directly challenge the proposition that "micro processes driven by exogenous technological innovations are fundamentally altering macro structures." Using a vast amount of systematic data on international transactions and the survival rate of national states, they seek to demonstrate that world politics is still very much a state-dominated system, that hegemonic powers still serve to promote international stability, that states have always encountered difficulties in controlling the decentralizing tendencies on which interdependence rests, and that in some issue areas states are still consolidating their sovereignty. Perhaps most innovative in this regard are their data on the consolidation of sovereignty, a process they examine through evidence on the operation of foreign mercenaries and pirates in the eighteenth and nineteenth centuries. Their finding that it was not until the nineteenth century that the state "achieved the exclusive right to deploy violence beyond its borders" may come as a surprise to many students of international politics. Despite their evidence of continuity in world politics, however, Thomson and Krasner conclude by acknowledging that change may lie ahead for world politics; but if it does, they assert, it "will not be accomplished by the burrowing from below of microprocesses."

Erich Weede (chapter 12) also discounts the extent to which fundamental change is presently under way in international politics and, accordingly, focuses his analysis on what he perceives as "the permanent features of politics." These consist of both "goods" and "bads"—authority, order, and property rights are the goods and international competition, rivalry, and war are the bads—but his analysis suggests that it is a mistake to draw this distinction too rigidly, that there is some good in the bads and some bad in the goods. Thus, for example, the tendencies toward pluralism in global life are beneficial in the economic sphere but dangerous insofar as their impact on international security is concerned. After all, he notes, international rivalries and wars (bads) were among the dynamics that contributed to the development of limited government (a good), thereby facilitating the emergence of the authority, order, and property rights (more goods) that have allowed for the growth of economies and the overcoming of "mass poverty as the ordinary condition of man." In effect, Weede's chapter, by highlighting the ways in which what seem like welcome indicators of change in world politics may be neither welcome nor change, is a refreshing demonstration of the virtues of caution in approaching the question of whether basic transformations are at work in international life.

The last two chapters are distinguished by having been written in response to stimuli other than the initial guidelines and papers circulated in advance of the

Bad Homburg workshop. Subsequent to the workshop Richard K. Ashley decided to replace his original contribution to the deliberations (a lengthy presentation on the ways in which postmodernist and poststructural perspectives are relevant to the study of world politics) with an entirely different paper addressed to an entirely different paper that I subsequently drafted. The latter was written exclusively as a response to the workshop's last session in which it was concluded that the endeavor to explore the theoretical challenges of global change should continue but that its focus should be narrowed to problems associated with authority and rule in international affairs. Accordingly, by way of anticipating subsequent workshops, I drafted "notes for a collaboration" under the title, "Governance without Government: Systems of Rule in World Politics," and it is this paper to which Ashley responds in chapter 13. Happily, in so doing he gives voice to the same postmodernist perspective on theorizing that underlay his original paper even as his chapter can also be regarded as a transition between the work represented in these pages and the efforts to come to terms with the possibilities for and implications of global change that still lie ahead.

In chapter 14, Peter J. Katzenstein carries out a commitment to respond, not to the original materials circulated in advance of the Bad Homberg workshop, but to the papers and discussions that marked the occasion. In effect, his chapter is an evaluation and assessment of the problem of theorizing about a changing world as it was considered by the workshop and as it is presently confronted by the international relations field as a whole. Put more strongly, Katzenstein provides a succinct and yet thorough summary of this book and where it fits in the ongoing conflicts and dialogues that are likely to underlie approaches to world politics in the 1990s.

The Concept of Change

One obvious explanation for why the participants responded so differently to the idea of international system transformation is that the concept of change did not have a common meaning for them. Little wonder! It is a difficult and elusive concept, pervaded with ambiguity and marked by a deceptive simplicity. All too often we delude ourselves into presuming that fundamental social and political changes are self-evident, as if there is an objective reality to the differences we perceive at two or more points in time. But changes, and continuities too, are not objective phenomena. Their existence acquires meaning through conceptual formulation and not empirical observation. It is not history that dictates whether change has occurred, but rather the interests of observers—those scales of time and space in which they seek to trace transformations in the past and to evaluate those that may lie ahead in the future. Consider the differences between a macro system and any of its micro subsystems. What may be a sea change for the latter, may be merely another instance of a recurrent tendency for the former. The birth of a first child, for example, involves a monumental transformation for the family, but this same event is only another data point for the demographer concerned with population growth. Similarly, the advent of a new government that seizes power may have enormous consequences for that society, but for the global system this development may be simply another case in the endless process whereby the personnel of states periodically changes.

Before becoming engaged with the chapters that follow, therefore, readers may be well advised to pause and ponder what they mean by change and how they would know it when they see it. Indeed, there are at least seven reasons that argue for pausing to clarify the concept. One is that change, transformation, and the other descriptors of dynamism take on meaning only as they can be clearly delineated from the statics of continuity. A second is that it is all too easy to speak loosely of global change—to call attention to its presence if today's events seem overwhelming or to stress its absence if the same events appear as just another of the conflicts in which people regularly embroil themselves. The past offers an endless supply of events with superficial resemblances to those of the present if one is predisposed to see current affairs as subject to rapid obsolescence and history as essentially repetitive. Contrariwise, the past seems barren of guidance if one is inclined to treat the dynamism of technology as endlessly creating new plateaus from which human affairs evolve.

Third, pausing to conceptualize the dynamics of change is a means of disciplining inquiry. The raw premise that change is under way offers no guidelines as to where to look for it and how to assess it. And, indeed, its identity can be difficult to trace. As one thoughtful observer puts it, "The trouble with change in human affairs is that it is so hard to pin down. It happens all the time. But while it happens it eludes our grasp, and once we feel able to come to grips with it, it has become past history" (Dahrendorf 1986, 5). Hence, without a conception of what constitutes meaningful changes, as distinguished from temporary or minor fluctuations, we are likely to be overwhelmed by the welter of activities that sustain world affairs. Without a conception of when the complexities and dynamism of world politics give rise to enduring changes and when they merely reinforce existing continuities, we may too readily presume that nothing remains constant and thus overlook how the endless tensions between past and present can often result as much in stalemate as in transformation.

A fourth reason to pause concerns the possibility that turbulent events may not always be reflective of change. Because the complexity and dynamism of most political issues involves swiftly moving flows of activity—flows that often gather in strength and surge irregularly in diverse directions—the constant flux conveys the impression of endless change, of individuals, officials, collectivities, and institutions being caught up in the course of events and adjusting to them by altering their ways. Yet, all the commotion and activities of present-day social systems need not always result in change. They can form repetitive patterns that are marked by constancy. Both people and societies can be on the move, only to converge back on their starting points as their changes encounter constraints that redirect them back to where they began, a circular process that is distinguished by both short-term changes and long-term continuities.

Still another reason for pausing is that the presumption of pervasive change is, as these chapters clearly suggest, open to dispute. Because the prospects for social transformation can feel as threatening as those for continuity can feel reassuring, assertions about change can spark intense debate. What is new for one person can be more of the same for another, depending in good part on how each feels about the present situation and the prospects for future progress. Such arguments over the degree of change frequently founder on a failure to recognize that the differences are rooted as much in conceptual orientations as in empirical realities.

Accordingly, self-evident as it may be to many observers, myself included, that the world is in a period of profound and irreversible change, such a process ought not be taken for granted. Those who regard history's continuities as immutable may not be persuaded by even the most elaborate case for the pervasiveness of change, but their argument needs to be acknowledged and compared with the view that underlying transformations are at work. If nothing else, the case for stressing continuities serves as a useful reminder that even the most pronounced changes have antecedents, that the past cannot be ignored, and that there is always a danger of mistaking the appearance of upheaval for the dynamics of transformation and, thus, exaggerating the depth and breadth of change.

Sixth, pausing to sort out the controversy over present-day transformations also serves as a cogent reminder of the possibility that one's posture toward change may be a matter of temperament. Perhaps for a variety of reasons, some analysts derive comfort from feeling that the present is but a continuation of the past, while others are uncomfortable with the idea that new departures do not occur in history. Although there may be no way to suspend one's temperament, its relevance to analysis is better recognized than denied. For, obviously, in the absence of the constraints imposed by explication, our temperamental impulses can get out of control. Those who adhere to a strict historical perspective may reject out of hand any evidence that change is under way; those who are inclined to look for transforming dynamics may flatly dismiss any signs that underlying historical tendencies are shaping the course of events. Such extreme responses are unfortunate because they blind us to the more viable position that change and continuity are both operative in history, that the tensions between them are the foundations from which both progress and retrogression evolve.

Lastly, even if our temperaments are successfully put aside, we often rely on guidelines for discerning and assessing change that remain implicit and that can surely benefit from explication and close inspection. It can even be said that wherever there are expectations of what lies ahead, so may there be implicit notions of change, its pace, direction, and problems. Scratch any conception of the human condition and notions of change and continuity (and the tensions between them) soon become a central focus. Why? Because we ponder problems in a time context, endlessly comparing current conditions with those experienced, cherished, and/or hated in the past and those anticipated, feared, and/or desired in the future.

An example will suffice to illustrate the pervasiveness of our assumptions and hypotheses about the nature of change. Consider the present situation in South Africa and how widespread is the presumption that "only time will tell" before the confrontation of blacks and whites in that strife-torn society erupts into wide-scale violence and change. Embedded in this expectation is a series of notions that express a philosophical perspective on change and time. One is that under certain conditions change is more likely than continuity; another is that at certain points in the course of history the ability to insure continuity is beyond the control of any actors; a third is that time is not neutral, that it cumulates pressures for the resolution of confrontations; a fourth is that certain kinds of change cannot simply evolve but, instead, are bound to culminate in upheaval; a fifth is that knowledge of the first four is not sufficient to insure success on the part of those who have the will to prevent the dynamics of change from unfolding along their historic path.

Explicating our underlying assumptions about change, in short, is an extraordinarily challenging task. It requires us to go well beyond conventional conceptions of causality and to think, instead, in terms of cause-and-effect dynamics that unfold through time. As Robert O. Keohane put it in a paper presented at the workshop (1987) but not included in this book, "We have a hard enough time analyzing causal relationships within a particular international system, since so many factors impinge on key events. Explaining change is much more difficult, since shifts in technology, domestic political coalitions and institutions, or the attitudes of policy elites can alter not merely the weights of variables but the relationships among them as well."

The Absence of Contention

Despite their diverse responses to the theoretical challenges posed by global transformations, the chapters that follow are marked by one common dimension worthy of note. Unlike earlier attempts to assess the state of theory in world politics, here there is a minimum of concern with and conflict over epistemological and methodological issues. As if propelled by the urgency of the need for substantive understanding, none of the chapters dwells exclusively on questions pertaining to the philosophy of knowledge. In the corresponding symposia on international theory that commanded attention in each of the last several decades—say, those organized by Fox (1959) in the 1950s, Knorr and Verba (1961) in the 1960s, Tanter and Ullman (1972) in the 1970s, and Oye (1986) in the 1980s—a preoccupation with the analytic problems of theorists tended to take precedence over the substantive dilemmas of actors on the global stage.[3] For better or worse, and for diverse reasons ranging from battle fatigue to a growing acceptance of diversity, today the epistemological and methodological issues have turned quiescent, or at least an appreciation of the need for theory has come to be widely shared, thus giving rise to a readiness to live-and-let-live that has enabled theorists to focus on the subject matter itself, on the patterns that may be evolving and the habits that may be attenuating as the world's actors struggle to achieve goals and cope with challenges.

Viewed in this way, the current book, like its predecessors that sought to clarify the issues for their respective decades, can be seen as seeking to illuminate the way for the 1990s and the advent of a new millennium. And if the light thereby cast seems excessively diffuse, that may well be the best, even the only, way to grasp the expanding interdependence and pluralism of a decentralizing world.

A Transnational Dialogue

One other background note may facilitate evaluation of this book, namely, that the workshop was explicitly designed as a transnational event. One of the organizers of the workshop (Czempiel) has spent his professional life in three West German universities, while the other (Rosenau) has been on the faculty of three U.S. universities. In collaborating we sought to enlist scholars, like ourselves, from both sides of the Atlantic. Given a scarcity of theory appropriate to a transforming world, it was reasoned that much could be gained—if not theoretical breakthroughs, then at least an expanded dialogue—by bringing together colleagues from diverse traditions of inquiry. Such interaction seemed especially compelling for North American and West European scholars in the world politics field, since previously this has occurred haphazardly through the journals and occasionally at meetings of professional societies.

Generalizations about the distinctions between theorists in different national settings are at best risky, but different perspectives do exist and it is surely reasonable to presume that beneficial consequences will flow from a systematic and focused effort to share them. Those who participated in the workshop discussions all came away agreeing that this presumption was well founded. Indeed, it may be that one of the surest indicators of the advent of a postinternational politics is that increasingly analysts from different countries are sharing their expertises and seeking to integrate their perspectives.

Notes

1. That postinternational politics may evolve in either chaotic or coherent directions needs to be underlined at the outset. It is not conceived here as the political side of those versions of the postmodernist philosophy which assert, on the basis of unsystematic evidence, that the expiration of the modern industrial age has resulted in a postmodern epoch wherein humankind will be unable to manage its affairs and thus sink into unmitigated disarray, perhaps even extinction. Rather, the postinternational politics perspective treats ultimate outcomes as an open question, as a set of issues to be explored empirically. It allows, in other words, for a variety of outcomes, the gloomy one anticipated by the postmodernists no less than the more upbeat expectation of surviving modernists who believe that somehow,

perhaps when the nuclear, resource, and management crises become acute, humankind will get its act together and successfully cope with the turbulent conditions presently unfolding. (For a succinct summary of the several postmodernist versions of what lies ahead for world politics, see Nelson 1987, 3–4).

2. The macro formulation was subsequently revised and published (Rosenau 1988a); the micro formulation, originally titled "Micro Sources of Macro Global Change," was later revised (Rosenau 1988b) and is now available by writing to the Institute for Transnational Studies, 3708 Figueroa Street, Los Angeles, CA 90007. Both an elaboration and synthesis of the two papers has been undertaken in a book-length manuscript (Rosenau forthcoming).

3. For other symposia that are also illustrative of the theoretical concerns of earlier generations, see Farrel (1967), Knorr and Rosenau (1969), and Maghoori and Ramberg (1982).

References

Bell, Daniel (1973). *The Coming of Post-Industrial Society: A Venture in Social Forecasting.* New York: Basic Books.

Dahrendorf, Ralf (1986). "The Europeanization of Europe." In *A Widening Atlantic? Domestic Change and Foreign Policy,* edited by A.J. Pierre. Pp. 5–56. New York: Council on Foreign Relations.

Easton, D. (1965). *A Framework for Political Analysis.* Englewood Cliffs, N.J.: Prentice-Hall.

Farrel, J.C., ed. (1967). "Theory and Reality in International Relations." *Journal of International Affairs* 21, no. 2.

Fox, William T.R., ed. (1959). *Theoretical Aspects of International Relations.* Notre Dame, Ind.: University of Notre Dame Press.

Keohane, R.O. (1987). "Changes in Patterns of International Cooperation and the Valuation of Sovereignty." Paper prepared for the American–German Workshop on International Relations Theory, Bad Homburg.

Knorr, K., and J.N. Rosenau, eds. (1969). *Contending Approaches to International Politics.* Princeton: Princeton University Press.

Knorr, K., and S. Verba, eds. (1961). *The International System: Theoretical Essays.* Princeton: Princeton University Press.

Maghoori, R., and B. Ramberg, eds. (1982). *Globalism versus Realism: International Relations' Third Debate.* Boulder, Colo.: Westview Press.

Nelson, John S. (1987). "Postmodern Meanings of Politics." Paper presented at the annual meeting of the American Political Science Association, Chicago.

Nye, J.S., Jr. (1974). "Transnational Relations and Interstate Conflicts: An Empirical Analysis." *International Organization* 28:961–96.

Oye, K.A., ed. (1986). *Cooperation under Anarchy.* Princeton: Princeton University Press.

Rosenau, James N. (1988a). "Patterned Chaos in Global Life: Structure and Process in the Two Worlds of World Politics." *International Political Science Review* 9 (October):357–94.

—— (1988b). "Post-International Politics: The Micro Dimension." Paper presented at the fourteenth World Congress of the International Political Science Association, Washington, D.C. (August 28 to September 1).

—— (Forthcoming). *Turbulence in World Politics.* Princeton: Princeton University Press.

Tanter, R., and R.H. Ullman, eds. (1972). *Theory and Policy in International Relations.* Princeton: Princeton University Press.

2

International Structure and International Transformation: Space, Time, and Method

John Gerard Ruggie

The chapters in this book seek to enhance our collective understanding of the phenomenon of international transformation. My concern in this essay is less with the question of whether or not international transformation is occurring, than with the methodological issue of how to ask that question, of how to frame it so that it yields analytically interesting research and empirically telling insights.

By definition, the study of transformation is the study of structure. This is so because structure imparts organization, disposing and constraining effects, on domains of social discourse and action. A change of structure makes possible, and is indicated by, a fundamental rupture in previous patterns and the emergence of new patterns—a transformation, in short. Structure has a specific reality, its own characteristics; it is not merely the sum total of unit-level attributes and behaviors. The study of structures therefore imposes upon the analyst a specific research program, one designed to give expression to phenomena deeper than everyday reality and to capture movement of a slower tempo. That much is agreed to by most students of international politics. However, the implications of this research program by and large are either little understood or ignored in the literature, especially on the part of those who are most persuaded by the idea that there has been relatively little change in the history of international politics and that there is little in the offing (see Waltz 1979). An obvious question that arises immediately is to what extent the perceived continuity is an artifact of the intellectual apparatus with which it is studied. I raised that query in passing in an earlier article (Ruggie 1983). My task here will be to spell out some of the neglected dimensions in the study of international structure and its transformation, and to indicate what kind of research is demanded if we take them seriously.

I proceed as follows. In the first section, I briefly examine the core concept in the study of international transformation: international structure. In the second

I acknowledge with thanks the helpful comments on an earlier draft by Hayward Alker, Peter Cowhey, Ernst Haas, Robert Keohane, and members of the Colloquium on International Institutions at the Harvard University Center for International Affairs.

section, I illustrate by means of concrete example why the prevailing approach to structural theory won't get us very far in understanding the possibility of international transformation. In the third section I generalize from the stylized case to theoretical argument, and suggest that in the standard usage the concept of international structure shares a peculiar attribute with and is subject to the same limits as Newtonian physics. What is needed in the study of international transformation, I contend, is a conception of structure that is more space/time-contingent. In the final section I briefly indicate how we might profitably apply such a conception of international structure in the empirical study of one area of possible international transformation: the effects of globalization on several domains of international activity.

Structural Theory

It stands to reason that in a system characterized by the absence of central authority, issues pertaining to the power of units loom very large indeed. If no one can be counted on to take care of anyone else, the capacity of each to fend for itself assumes a special significance. Therefore, as an attribute of international structure no factor has been considered more crucial than the configuration of power among states—whether it is concentrated or diffuse, stable or changing rapidly, relying directly on force or institutionalized through other means. Despite its centrality, however, the concept of international power remains a highly "contestable concept" (Conally 1983), and its cognate, the balance of power, remains deeply mired in ambiguity.[1] Clear specification of usage, it goes without saying, must precede any analysis that employs these concepts (see Baldwin 1985).

But my purpose here differs from restating this all-too-familiar obiter dictum. My purpose is to draw attention to an underlying epistemological dimension of the configuration of power as a "structural variable." When configurations of power are conceived in this manner, ultimately they are anchored in the possession of material capabilities: the means of force, the means of production, the resource base fueling both. Depending on the preferences of the theorist, one, or another, or some combination of these factors is employed to depict such positional arrangements as polarity, hegemony, center, and periphery. These positional arrangements, in turn, are presumed to structure patterns of outcomes, including the incidence of system-wide wars, the extent to which international economic orders are open or closed, and the more prosaic question of who gets what, when, and how. Structure, in short, is defined as the configuration of power, and the configuration of power in turn serves as the "independent variable" of structural theory.

Consider Waltz's formulation (1979) as an exemplar of this genre—though mutatis mutandis everything said about it applies equally well to its chief systemic competitor, the "world system" perspective of Wallerstein (1974, 1979).[2] As is well known, political structure in Waltz's formulation actually consists of three component parts: the organizing principle of a system, the functional differentiation of its units, and the configuration of power among them. International political structure is defined by the configuration of power only because the organizing principle—anarchy, or self-help—is assumed not to vary, and functional differentiation of units apart from that imposed by their capabilities is said not to exist. The rest is easy. As Waltz describes the nature of the enterprise (1979, 99): "In defining international political structures we take states with whatever traditions, habits, objectives, desires, and forms of government they may have. . . . We abstract from every attribute of states except their capabilities. . . . What emerges is a positional picture, a general description of the ordered overall arrangement of a society written in terms of the placement of units rather than in terms of their qualities." The only task that remains is to count: "Market structure is defined by counting firms; international-political structure, by counting states. In the counting, distinctions are made only according to capabilities."

How far does this approach take us in understanding the possibility of international transformation? The answer is, as we will see, not very far. But rather than arguing it in the abstract, let us first explore that question in a concrete case and then draw some general theoretical implications from it. The case I have in mind is the governance of the world's oceans, and specifically the transformational significance of the recent invention and incorporation into state practice of the Exclusive Economic Zone (EEZ).

The Governance of the Oceans

Why raise the issue of the oceans? I do so because it is analytically interesting given the purposes at hand. From the beginning, the governance of the oceans has posed a puzzle to statecraft. Consider the situation in the seventeenth century. The newly emerged territorial states defined their essence, their very being, by the *possession* of territory and the *exclusion* of others. But how does one possess some thing one doesn't own? And, still more problematical, how does one exclude others from it? Contiguous waterways could be shared, administered jointly, or, more than likely, split down the middle. But the oceans were another matter. It was not for lack of trying that states were unable to extend their dominion over the oceans; claims to that effect abounded until well into the seventeenth century. Spain and Portugal tried a bilateral deal, whereby Spain claimed a monopoly of ocean trade routes with "the West" and Portugal with "the East". All such unilateral and bilateral attempts failed, however. In the end, a multilateral solution was instituted. Beyond the territorial sea, initially set at three miles—the range of land-based cannons at the time— the oceans were declared a *public* waterway.

Individual solutions failed for the simple reason that it is not possible in the long run to vindicate *any* property right that is not recognized as being valid by the relevant others in a community. Attempts to do so lead to constant challenge and recurrent conflict. Once a property right is socially recognized, however, the institutional context of the exercise of power is transformed. Those who transgress the property right then are put in the position of having to defend their transgression while others can attack them with impunity because they do so in behalf of the collectivity of states. By this means—a process that Ashley (1984) has described as "social empowerment"—the collectivity adds to or diminishes from the material capabilities of individual actors.

Now let's turn to the 1980s, to the institution of the Exclusive Economic Zone, and to the question of what, if anything, it illuminates about international transformation. The relevant facts about it are these (United Nations 1983). Each coastal state now has the right to establish an EEZ beyond its territorial sea, up to two hundred nautical miles from its coast or baseline. Jurisdiction within the EEZ is by activity, however, not by area. The coastal state has exclusive sovereign rights for the purposes of exploring, exploiting, conserving, and managing all natural resources of the waters, seabed, and subsoil; and with regard to any other economic exploration and exploitation, such as the production of energy from the water, currents, and winds. The coastal state has the right to control all installations as well as the dumping of wastes by other states, the latter coupled with safeguards for the accused. The coastal state also has the right to be informed of and participate in proposed scientific research, or to withhold its consent under specific circumstances. The coastal state has the duty to protect the marine environment, to ensure the conservation of living resources, to determine their maximum sustainable yield, and to grant access by other states to any surplus. Land-locked and geographically disadvantaged states have special rights to such surpluses. All states have the freedom of navigation, overflight, the laying of submarine cables and pipelines, and other internationally lawful uses of the sea related thereto. Each state must exercise its rights with "due regard" to the rights and duties of others. And if the Law of the Sea Treaty takes effect, all states are obliged to work within its dispute settlement provisions.

What if anything does the EEZ imply for change in international political structure? That is to say, does this new component of the world's oceans regime exhibit any kind of discontinuity in the prevailing mode of ordering political relations among states? Apparently, it all depends on how one looks at it. There are at least three contending interpretations.

One position focuses on the extent of offshore national jurisdiction. It views the EEZ as a massive land-grab, favoring coastal states in general and industrialized coastal states in particular; as a Pyrrhic victory for developing countries who advocated the EEZ but by the luck of the resource draw ended up with a minor share of its wealth; and as a rout for the international community as a whole, in whose name the concept of the "common heritage of mankind" (which catalyzed the entire Law of the Sea negotiations) was advanced in the first place (see Oxman et al. 1983).

A second and quite different view holds that the EEZ is a reflection of "the contemporary thrust for economic development" (Puri 1980, 39), and that it "will place the developing countries in a better position in their relations with the developed world and make a basic change in the directions of overall development leading to greater ultimate economic gains for all the developing countries" (Alam and Khan 1983, 35). The focus here is not simply on the extent of national jurisdiction. More importantly, it is believed, this extension enclosed in part the high seas from which the Third World derived few benefits in any case; the share of the enclosure that now accrues to the developing countries gives them greater standing and bargaining power in the future governance of the oceans; and because the enclosure is functional, not territorial, the developing countries now have some rights they did not have before in the richer EEZs of the industrialized world.

Yet a third and perhaps the most radical position contends that the ultimate winner from the existence of the EEZ is the international community at large. In this view, the EEZ represents nothing less than one instance of a new form of international governance. It holds that the EEZ comprises a "horizontally shared zone between the coastal state and other states," in which the coastal state "must have due regard" for the rights of other states, and in which the "unfettered freedom" of the past has been replaced by "delegated powers" that are exercised by the coastal state in behalf of international society (Allott 1983, 15). Consequently, the EEZ is said to exemplify a deeper change in the constitutive principle of international governance, "involving states more and more not only in the mystical composite personage of the international legislator but also in performing the function of the executive branch of their own self-government" (Allott 1983, 24).[3]

Ignore for the sake of the argument the possibility that any or all of the three interpretations may be wide of the mark. The points I wish to explore are methodological, not substantive; therefore it doesn't much matter for my purposes what the correct answer is. Treat the interpretations as stylized facts. Two features about them stand out.

First, because they take seriously the possibility of international transformation, each of the three interpretations treats international structure as a *dependent*, not an independent, variable. And there is nothing strange about that. If international political transformation means change in international political structure, then the extent to which that structure is or is not changing must, ipso facto, constitute the focus of inquiry. Due to this duality of structure, Anthony Giddens has formulated what he calls a theory not of *structure*, but of *structuration*:

> According to the theory of structuration, all social action consists of social practices, situated in time-space, and organized in a skilled and knowledgeable fashion by human agents. But such knowledgeability is always "bounded" by unacknowledged conditions of action on the one side, and unintended consequences of action on the other. . . . The structured properties of social systems are simultaneously the medium and outcome of social acts [Giddens 1981, 19].

The conventional understanding of structures in international theory encompasses solely the "unacknowledged conditions" of action: the sediments of the past, the constraints of the present.

Waltz has addressed this issue explicity, first in his original formulation (1979), and then again in his response to his critics (1986). In both places, he contends that treating structure as a dependent variable—endogenizing structure into the theory, rather than taking it as exogenously given—simply does not belong within his realm of discourse because it is inherently reductionist in character. That is to say, the sources of structural change, he maintains, reside in the units and unit attributes, not in systems and systemic factors. Therefore for Waltz they have no place in systemic theory. But our simple oceans example suggests otherwise. A *claim* for the ownership of ocean space may be an attribute of an individual state. But the *structure* of ownership of ocean space surely is an attribute of the system of states—it is a social fact no less than is the configuration of power among states. Indeed, it is a social fact that can affect the efficacy of the configuration of power.

As for the second point, each of the three interpretations of the EEZ focuses on a different component of international structure. What is more, the three look remarkably like the three components of Waltz's general definition of political structure! And they suggest an interesting pattern of possible variation.

From the vantage point of the first position, the "land-grab" view, the EEZ exhibits no structural change: states moved out into the oceans, and the haves got more while the have-nots got less. Here structure is viewed much as the conventional structural theories see it—and the evidence suggests that it was simply replicated in the new context of the EEZ.

In the second assessment, that the place of the Third World has been enhanced, the EEZ is measured not only in miles and isobaths. The relevant facts that are adduced by the analysts we cited—Third World analysts, we might note—include progress in the political efficacy and collective self-concept of a group of states who in many instances until recently were, and in some cases continue to feel themselves, dispossessed of autonomous international identity. Seen in this light, it is not unreasonable to entertain the notion that the Third World gained from the EEZ, that there was a change in their relative status even if not in their actual allocation of resources. After all, in large measure they authored this particular chapter of history. But where is structure here? Structure is conceived of as *differentiation* among states based on *status*—not material capability, but status. Such a differentiation is not unheard of historically. Each civilization, including the West, has systematically differentiated between its members and outsiders, and has treated them differently in peace and war (Wight 1977). Has that practice ended? When did it end? Could it return? Are there other modes of differentiating among states beyond their material capabilities that still remain in place and that systematically affect international outcomes? What if groups of actors believe and behave as though such modes of differentiation exist and are important—as Krasner (1985) seems to suggest in his study of North–South relations? Then we have variation in a second component of international structure, a component apart from the distribution of capabilities.

When we shift to the third position, the international community view, what matters about the EEZ is the balance of rights and obligations that determines how states stand in relation to one another in it—not only as coastal versus maritime versus landlocked states, industrialized versus developing states, or capitalist versus socialist states, but as states qua states. The argument is advanced that, though states did indeed move into the oceans, the principled bases legitimizing their actions in doing so—the institutional context—now express broader community norms and processes than before. This of course speaks directly to the issue of anarchy or self-help, the "deep" structure of the international polity. And it suggests that a variety of forms of nonhierarchical rule should be explored systematically—not merely short of but fundamentally different from the domestication of international politics on the one hand, and the emergence of a universal "socialist commonwealth" on the other, which are the only kinds of "ultimate" transformation recognized by the two major branches of conventional structural theory, realism and Marxism respectively.

In sum, the three interpretations of the EEZ offer two suggestions for the study of international transformation. First, that structure be treated simultaneously as dependent as well as independent variable, that the appropriate formulation in fact would combine this duality of structure in a theory of *structuration*. Second, that the one component of international structure that is permitted to vary in the prevailing structural theories shows no variation, but it may be that change is taking place precisely in those other components of international structure that are assumed not to vary at all!

Before going on, let me repeat a point I made above: my aim has been not to "test" the three interpretations of the EEZ, but to use them as stylized facts in order to raise the more important theoretical issue of whether the way in which we conceptualize international structure in the mainstream of our field is appropriate if our concern is to explore the possibility of international transformation.

Beyond Physicalist Structure

Doing better involves more than merely turning structure around and treating it as a dependent variable, together with turning into variables several components of structure that now are held constant. If our concern is international transformation, then there is something more profoundly wrong with conventional structural theory. An analogy will help describe it.

In its epistemological assumptions, the prevailing conception of international structure is not unlike the corresponding views of Newtonian mechanics: "Newtonian mechanics by itself did not attempt to explain what forces might exist in nature, but rather described how motion occurred when the force was known"

(Feinberg 1978, 9). In point of fact, Newton's contemporaries were quite explicit in drawing on this analogy, especially in their rhapsodies about the balance of power. The Peace of Utrecht (1713) enshrined the self-regulating equilibrium as a venerable institution of European society. And for theorists of the day, "The sovereign states followed their ordered paths in a harmony of mutual attraction and repulsion like the gravitational law that swings planets in their orbits. Perhaps no statesmanship was needed. As Grotius had said that natural law would be binding even if God did not exist, so Rousseau said that the balance of power was self-regulating whether or not anybody troubled to maintain it" (Wight 1973, 98). The parallel with Waltz's treatment of the balance of power is striking (1979, chaps. 3 and 6)—and ironically also Wallerstein's (1974). Let us call theirs the physicalist conception of international structure. It is a conception of structure as "being," not of "becoming" (Prigogine 1980).

Now, Newtonian mechanics served well enough in situations of ordinary human experience: day-to-day life in the palpable here-and-now. However, once Newtonian mechanics was pushed up against the limits of ordinary experience, in the form of the speed of light, for instance, or the behavior of subatomic particles, it no longer sufficed. It had to yield to relativity and quantum mechanics. I would suggest that similar kinds of limits exist for the physicalist conceptions of international structure. Those limits too appear when the basic "field of forces," as it were, begins to shift.

Periods of fundamental political transition—of transformation—are characterized by a generalized loss of predictability and control among social actors. The reestablishment of an effective system of rule once again fixes parametric conditions. The world then returns to the realm of "ordinary experience," albeit often of a radically different kind than it knew before. The disarticulation of the medieval system of rule, and the emergence of the modern international state formation, constituted such an instance (Wight 1977; Ruggie 1983). It transformed the prevailing system of rule in European society. The issue that was up for grabs during the transformation was not who had *how much power*, but who had *the right to act as a power* (cf. Ashley 1984). From the vantage point of models of structure that are defined solely by the configuration of power, the outcome is not merely anomalous; it has to appear as being positively bizarre. For when all was said and done, Europe ended up with numerous political entities, beginning with many of the more than two hundred German "states," which simply could not have vindicated their right to act as constitutive units of the new European state system had their fate depended on their possession of material capabilities, while far more powerful actors disappeared from the political landscape.

The explanation is that their fate rested on more than physicalist structure: the "field of forces" was changing—or, in a formulation that I prefer, the institutional context for the exercise of power was changing. The right to act as a power shifted toward some actors, and away from others; some types of units were socially deemed to be legitimate wielders of authority, others were delegitimized. To understand that transformation on the grand scale, or the transformation of property rights in ocean space on a smaller scale, it is not enough therefore to describe "how motion occurs when the force is known." It becomes necessary "to explain what forces might exist in nature." Completing the analogy, doing that in turn requires introducing space/time into the "equation."

But what does it mean to introduce space/time into our analysis of international structure? If we go back and reexamine the three interpretations of the EEZ, we find that though they all look at the same thing, each sees a different reality, not only substantively but also epistemologically. Each in fact is embedded within a different space/time complex.[4]

The "land-grab" view exemplifies physicalist structure. It sees the reality of the EEZ in terms of separate and distinct actors; palpable, discrete, and infinitely divisible properties; and discontinuous events. The actors are individual states. The properties in question are miles, isobaths, tons of fish and barrels of oil. The "shadow of the future" may be longer or it may be shorter and thereby affect outcomes (Oye 1985). But time itself is a succession of discrete temporal increments. And if history plays any role in this view, it is *l'histoire événementielle*, the history of the event (Braudel 1980): a battle, a conference, a new technology, a move, a countermove. Understanding this level of reality involves straightforward empirical research using "objective" indicators—at the extreme, Waltz's simple act of counting heads.

In the second interpretation, history weighs more heavily, and it is the history of a conjuncture—of which an appropriate example might be what Barraclaugh (1967) called "the revolt against the West." The socially relevant universe is visualized in terms of groupings and their collective destinies, and temporality as the unfolding of some dynamic movement or process that acts through a succession of events. Understanding this level of social reality requires that we probe beyond the palpable here-and-now until we come to see the historicity—the historically contingent subjectivities—of the pertinent social groupings as they see it themselves.

When we reach the third position, the international community view, social totalities comprise the units of analysis. The focus here shifts to the "constitutive structures" of such totalities, those inclusive frameworks of social discourse and practices that give meaning to the social totality and to behavior within it. History in this context is the history of *la longue durée* (Braudel 1980) which, as Jacques Le Goff (1980, xi) has made clear, should be regarded not simply as lasting a long period of time but as having the quality of a system.[5] Constitutive structures form such a deep level of social reality that, at any particular moment, they may seem a *rule* rather than a *regularity* of social life. Moreover, any given change in the elements of such structures may be imperceptible or may seem insignificant at any particular point in time. Only over the entire lifespan of a social totality will their historical contingency become apparent. Finally, the relevant facts for analysis here are institutional facts, and institutional facts inherently are intersubjective facts, not "brute" or palpable facts (Kratochwil forthcoming).[6] As Garrett Mattingly found in his magisterial study of the transition from medieval to modern diplomatic practices, the outward appearances of institutions changed less and more slowly than people's understanding of and expectations about them (Mattingly 1964).

In sum, the three interpretations of the EEZ not only focus on different substantive attributes of international structure. They also are premised on different epistemological grounds. Most importantly, they are grounded in three very different space/time complexes. Fundamental international transformation—the medieval to modern shift, for example, or a shift from the modern to some postmodern form of organizing political space on this planet—is well beyond the grasp of physicalist conceptions of structure. It *is* in the province of the third perspective. With due apologies to Waltz, let us term it the "third image" of structure.

The Third Image

There is a lively debate going on in European social thought over the issue of modernity versus postmodernity. It began in the arts, spread to culture more generally, and now encompasses the social realm as well. Among the leading protagonists are Jürgen Habermas, upholding the virtues of what he calls the project of modernity (Habermas 1981), and Jean-François Lyotard, making the case for postmodernity (1984). What is intriguing about this debate are some of the terms used to convey the essential features of postmodernity: detotalized, decentered, and fragmented discourses and practices; multiple and field-dependent referents in place of single-point fixed referents; flow-defined spaces and the simultaneity of temporal experiences as opposed to place-defined spaces and sequential temporal experiences; the erosion of sovereign or macro powers over society coupled with the diffusion of disciplinary or micro powers within society.

To the student of international political economy these terms sound a great deal like descriptions of certain recently emerged global systems of economic transaction: the global markets in currencies, for example, or in credit and even equities; to a somewhat lesser but still considerable extent global production; and in several of the institutional arrangements that have emerged in the global commons, including the oceans and the biosphere. But the economic realm isn't the only one in which such changes have taken place. Brian Jenkins of the RAND Corporation has studied the global infrastructure that sustains international terrorism and new modes of low-intensity warfare. He concludes: "With continuous, sporadic armed conflict, blurred in time and space, waged on several levels by a large array of national and subnational forces, warfare in the last quarter of the twentieth century may well come to resemble warfare in the Italian Renaissance or warfare in the early seventeenth century, before the emergence of national armies and more organized modern warfare" (1983, 17).

If they are visible anywhere, we ought to be able to find the contours of a postmodern international system in these increasingly globalized domains of human behavior. Hence it is here that we should begin to look. It seems to me that an appropriate research program consists of three steps.

The first is to specify and operationalize the notion of "global." Perhaps the best way to put it is that the globe itself has become a *region* in the international system, albeit a *nonterritorial* one. Thus, global does not mean universal. Instead, the concept refers to a subset of social interactions that take place on the globe. This subset constitutes an inclusive level of social interaction that is distinct from the *international* level, in that it comprises a multiplicity of integrated functional systems, operating in real time, which span the globe, and which affect in varying degrees what transpires elsewhere on the globe. As Emory and Trist (1973, 11) have put it: "Any person or group is at any instant in many 'presents'," each corresponding to the different space/time complexes in which they are embedded. Simply put, the globe is one such "present." And it has changed radically since the time when it first made sense to speak of a global factor in world politics—as Sir Halford Mackinder did, for example, at the outset of this century (Mackinder 1904).

The second step is to study the process of political structuration in this global present. Some of those employing conventional structural approaches have already dismissed the case. They have concluded—with only a little element of caricature in my characterization—that the superpowers are still the superpowers, and the United States is still stronger than anybody else, therefore no structural change of significance is occurring.[7] I am highly dubious about that proposition, but this is not the place to quarrel with it. I merely point out that the work testing it simply has not been done. All the tests of which I know employ a conception of international structure that, for the reasons suggested in this chapter, are epistemologically incapable of capturing the phenomenon. The continuity thesis, therefore, has no firmer a scientific footing than its opposite, that fundamental change is taking place. Unless the "third image" of structure is operationalized and employed in empirical research, no firm conclusion can be reached. And what it means to operationalize the "third image" of structure is, as we have seen, to specify and examine appropriate institutional facts that are suggestive of authority relations in various global contexts. We must note how states see themselves in relation to one another; how they stand in relation to private actors; the principled bases of state behavior; the extent to which both states and private actors are socially empowered to act as they do or merely reflect their respective material capabilities; the extent to which relations differ when the resource at stake is knowledge and information rather than material things; the shared mental imageries actors bring to bear in organizing their relations when time is telescoped and space is temporalized—in short, how the structures of disjoint territoriality are faring in that part of the world that is nonterritorial and globalized.

The third and most critical step will be to see to what extent the modal patterns of structuration in the global arena, if they are different, affect behavior in the other areas of contemporary international life. Several possibilities exist: that the global domains enjoy no ontological autonomy and are strictly dependent on the familiar structures of modernity, which would be the conventional structural expectation; that global domains do enjoy relative autonomy but are encapsulated and have little effect beyond their bounds, which is a view I would expect some of the so-called "modified structural realists" among us to hold; that global domains are relatively autonomous and have increasing spillover effects on other domains, which amounts to a liberal or functionalist view; or, finally, that global domains enjoy a degree of autonomy and are growing more important relative to other domains of international relations even though they are not fundamentally reshaping them—which would be my own hunch. But choosing among these scenarios given our current ignorance of the facts of the matter amounts to no more than acting out our most deeply held "themata"—defined by Robert Merton (1975, 335) as "tacit cognitive imageries and preferences for or commitments to certain kinds of concepts, certain kinds of methods, certain kinds of evidence, and certain forms of solutions to deep questions and engaging puzzles." The exercise can be fun, but it's not yet social science.

Conclusion

This has been an essay in thinking about how to think about international transformation. There surely is more such thinking to be done, but enough has been said to establish my basic points: how we think about transformation fundamentally shapes what we look for; what we look for obviously has an effect on what we find; if we look for signs of transformation through the lenses of the conventional structural approach of our discipline we are unlikely to conclude that anything much is happening out there; but we cannot say whether or not that conclusion is correct because the epistemological biases of that approach are such that it is ill-equipped to detect signs of transformation.

I used a micro case to help illustrate my argument because the fabric of international life is made up of micro cases: policymakers generally do not get to choose on the future of the state system; they confront choices on exchange rates, trade deficits, arms-control treaties, hostile acts against international shipping, terrorist attacks on airport lobbies and embassy compounds, and garbage that floats down a river or is transported through the air. If change comes it will be the product of micro practices. Hence if we want to understand change or help to shape it, it is to these micro practices that we should look.[8]

I also used an analogy from physics to illustrate my argument because only the appropriate macro perspectives can elucidate the full significance and signification of micro practices. Like Newtonian mechanics, conventional international structural approaches are simple, powerful, elegant, and useful for many things. But just as Newtonian mechanics does not have much of a grasp on transformation of the palpable forces in nature—because the universe comprised by the theory presupposes their stability—so too it is with conventional structuralism in international relations. As a result, the processes of international transformation are among its voids.

Notes

1. Note Waltz's observation (1979, 117): "If there is any distinctively political theory of international politics, balance-of-power theory is it. And yet one cannot find a statement of the theory that is generally accepted. Carefully surveying the copious balance-of-power literature, Ernst Haas discovered eight distinct meanings of the term, and Martin Wight found nine. Hans Morgenthau, in his profound historical and analytical treatment of the subject, makes use of four different definitions."

2. By and large, my critique does not apply to the unconventional Marxist approach of Robert Cox (1986, 1987), who is extremely sensitive to most of the issues I raise here and from whom I have learned a great deal. My problem with his approach is that an interesting argument is grounded in what I consider to be a highly problematical base: the priority of production.

3. It is interesting to note that Allott was a member of the U.K. delegation to the Law of the Sea negotiations.

4. For a more extended discussion of social time on which I draw here, see Ruggie (1986).

5. Bolingbroke, writing in the early eighteenth century, had much the same idea when he differentiated epochs by the chain of events being so broken "as to have little or no real or visible connexion with that which we see continue. . . . the end of the fifteenth century seems to be just such a period as I have been describing, for those who live in the eighteenth, and who inhabit the western parts of Europe." Similarly, Creighton, in his 1902 introductory essay to the *Cambridge Modern History,* defined the beginning of the modern era as "the period in which the problems that still occupy us came into conscious recognition, and were dealt with in ways intelligible to us as resembling our own." Both citations are from Wight (1977, chap. 4).

6. John Rawls long ago spelled out the significance of this distinction, but he seems to have had little impact on political scientists who study institutions: "One may illustrate this point from the game of baseball. Many of the actions one performs in a game of baseball one can do by oneself or with others whether there is a game or not. For example, one can throw a ball, run, or swing a peculiarly shaped piece of wood. But one cannot steal a base, or strike out, or draw a walk, or make an error, or balk; although one can do certain things which appear to resemble these actions such as sliding into a bag, missing a grounder and so on. Striking out, stealing a base, balking, etc., are all actions which can only happen in a game. No matter what a person did, what he did would not be described as stealing a base or striking out or drawing a walk unless he could also be described as playing baseball, and for him to be doing this presupposes the rule-like practice which constitutes the game. The practice is logically prior to particular cases: unless there is the practice the terms referring to actions specified by it lack a sense" (Rawls 1955, 25).

7. Indeed, at least one practitioner of this genre has recently concluded that the United States if anything is strengthened by such developments and that any discussion of fundamental change is ideologically inspired, in part to obfuscate the continuing power of the United States (Strange 1987).

8. In this connection, I have always been puzzled why some critical theorists, including Ashley (1984) and Cox (1986), refer to the conventional structural approach as "problem solving." How would any policymaker solve problems with it? What would he or she do? Alter the international configuration of power? Modify anarchy? Tell the weak to get stronger, the poor richer?

References

Alam, Md. Shah, and Mizanur Rahman Khan (1983). "The Exclusive Economic Zone—Developing Countries' Quest for a New Law of the Sea." *BIISS Journal* [Bangladesh Institute of International and Strategic Studies] 4 (January).

Allott, Philip (1983). "Power Sharing in the Law of the Sea." *American Journal of International Law* 77 (January).

Ashley, Richard K. (1984). "The Poverty of Neorealism." *International Organization* 38 (Spring).

Baldwin, David A. (1985). *Economic Statecraft.* Princeton: Princeton University Press.

Barraclough, Geoffrey (1967). *An Introduction to Contemporary History.* Harmondsworth, Middlesex: Penguin Books.

Braudel, Fernand (1980). *On History.* Translated by Sarah Matthews. Chicago: University of Chicago Press.

Conally, William (1983). *The Terms of Political Discourse.* 2d ed. Princeton: Princeton University Press.

Cox, Robert W. (1986). "Social Forces, States, and World Orders: Beyond International Relations Theory." In Robert O. Keohane, ed., *Neorealism and Its Critics.* New York: Columbia University Press.

—— (1987). *Production, Power, and World Order: Social Forces in the Making of History.* New York: Columbia University Press.

Emory, F.E., and E.L. Trist (1973). *Towards a Social Ecology: Contextual Appreciation of the Future in the Present.* London: Plenum.

Feinberg, Gerald (1978). *What Is the World Made Of? Atoms, Leptons, Quarks, and Other Tantalizing Particles.* Garden City, N.Y.: Anchor.

Giddens, Anthony (1981). *A Contemporary Critique of Historical Materialism.* Berkeley: University of California Press.

Habermas, Jürgen (1981). "Modernity versus Postmodernity." *New German Critique* 22 (Winter).

Jenkins, Brian (1983). *New Modes of Conflict.* Santa Monica, Calif.: RAND Corporation.

Krasner, Stephen (1985). *Structural Conflict: The Third World against Global Liberalism.* Berkeley: University of California Press.

Kratochwil, Friedrich (Forthcoming). *Rules, Norms, and Decisions: On the Conditions of Practical and Legal Reasoning in International Relations.* New York: Cambridge University Press.

Le Goff, Jacques (1980). *Time, Work, and Culture in the Middle Ages.* Translated by Arthur Goldhammer. Chicago: University of Chicago Press.

Lyotard, Jean-François (1984). *The Postmodern Condition.* Minneapolis: University of Minnesota Press.

Mackinder, H.J. (1904). "The Geographical Pivot of History." *Geographic Journal* 23.

Mattingly, Garrett (1964). *Renaissance Diplomacy*. Baltimore: Penguin Books.

Merton, Robert (1975). "Thematic Analysis in Science." *Science* 188.

Oxman, Bernard E., et al. (1983). *Law of the Sea: U.S. Policy Dilemma*. San Francisco: Institute for Contemporary Studies.

Oye, Kenneth A., ed. (1985). "Cooperation under Anarchy." *World Politics* 38 (October; special issue).

Prigogine, Illya (1980). *From Being to Becoming: Time and Complexity in the Physical Sciences*. San Francisco: W.H. Freeman.

Puri, Rama (1980). "Exclusive Economic Zone: A New Dimension in the Law of the Sea." *The Indian Political Science Review* 14 (January).

Rawls, John (1955). "Two Concepts of Rules." *Philosophical Review* 64.

Ruggie, John Gerard (1983). "Continuity and Transformation in the World Polity: Toward a Neorealist Synthesis." *World Politics* 35 (January).

—— (1986). "Social Time and International Policy." In Margaret P. Karns, ed., *Persistent Patterns and Emergent Structures in a Waning Century*. New York: Praeger.

Strange, Susan (1987). "The Persistent Myth of Lost Hegemony." *International Organization* 41 (Autumn).

United Nations (1983). *The Law of the Sea: Official Text of the United Nations Convention on the Law of the Sea with Annexes and Index*. New York: United Nations.

Wallerstein, Immanuel (1974). "The Rise and Future Demise of the World Capitalist System." *Comparative Studies in Society & History* 16 (September).

—— (1979). *The Capitalist World Economy*. New York: Cambridge University Press.

Waltz, Kenneth (1979). *Theory of International Politics*. Reading, Mass.: Addison-Wesley.

—— (1986). "Reflections on *Theory of International Politics*: A Response to My Critics." In Robert O. Keohane, ed., *Neorealism and Its Critics*. New York: Columbia University Press.

Wight, Martin (1973). "The Balance of Power and International Order." In Alan James, ed., *The Bases of International Order*. London: Oxford University Press.

—— (1977). *Systems of States*. Hedley Bull, ed. Leicester: Leicester University Press.

3

Production, the State, and Change in World Order

Robert W. Cox

International relations are part of a continuum of political-economic activity that extends from the power relationships experienced directly by people in everyday life, through the form of state, to the structure of world order. Theory is less concerned with international relations per se than with the structure within which these relations take place. The concept of world order designates this structure. If conventional wisdoms about international relations are now in question then it is probably because of a sense that theory grounded in obsolescent structures is not entirely adequate to explain the emergence of new structures. Any fresh approach to theory should, accordingly, confront the question of change in world order structure; and changes in world order structure have to be understood in relation to changes in structures at other levels of power relations.

On Theorizing about International Relations

Let me begin by contrasting two basic approaches to theory. The one that has been most characteristic of political science is based on actors and interactions. The focus is on individual actors, whether those individuals are conceived as persons (normally of high political or administrative status), bureaucratic entities, associations, or states. The theory reasons about the calculations and motivations that determine what these individuals do and the consequences (often unintended) of their actions.

Another approach focuses on the structures that constitute the framework or parameters for action and that shape the characters of the individual actors. The first approach takes the actors and interactions as given; the second tries to explain why both are as they are. Actors are conditioned by the resources, norms, expectations, and institutions of the societies in which they grow up. They are limited by the social-economic and military-political pressures of their environment. They are products of history.

The structural approach is not so much an alternative to the actor-interactions approach as a logical priority in relation to it. But a logical priority is not always a practical priority: at times when the parameters seem to hold steady, they are taken for granted, unquestioned, and the structural approach yields ground to the actor-interactions approach. When the parameters appear to be in mutation, then the structural approach may be more appropriate in order to explain how and why they are changing. Marx held the two approaches in balance when he wrote: "Men make their own history, but they do not make it just as they please; they do not make it under circumstances chosen by themselves, but under circumstances directly encountered, given and transmitted from the past" (Marx 1852, 1969).

I would make a cautionary distinction between what I prefer to call the historical structures approach and structural*ism*. Structuralism assumes the existence of innate, immutable structures. In this sense, at least one current form of realism in international relations is a structuralism, when it posits a certain immutable type of power-maximizing human nature and the existence of states differentiated only by their relative capabilities in a perpetually unstable balance-of-power relationship. The historical-structures approach (which I trace to Vico) sees human nature and the other structures that define social and political reality—from the structure of language through those of laws, morals, and institutions, and including the state and world-order structures like the balance of power—as being themselves products of history and thus subject to change (Vico 1744, 1970). Thus the conditions not chosen by themselves are also made by people, though in a different and slower-moving kind of time than the events of politics. To take over Fernand Braudel's distinction, events history is the realm of the actors–interactions approach; the *longue durée* is the realm of the historical-structures approach (Braudel 1958, 1980).

Historical structures, the cumulative result of innumerable often-repeated actions, are discoverable through the common understandings and common expectations of behavior that provide the common framework for actions. Another way of saying this is that historical structures are revealed as intersubjectivity. Language; patterns of response to stimuli considered as normal behavior; institutions like the family and the state; as well as less formally defined but nevertheless recurrent practices of personal morality and international behavior—all are constituted by intersubjectivity. Intersubjectivity does not mean approval or consensus, just common recognition of the existence of these things (Taylor 1976). Intersubjectivity makes them objective independently of individual wills. This is not a statement of idealism, that is that the objective world is constituted by ideas. It is consistent with historical materialism, insofar as the behavior patterns that give rise to intersubjectivity are human responses to the material environment, responses that in turn act upon and transform that environment.

In adopting the historical structures approach, two preliminary questions call for an answer. What kinds of structures are most relevant to change in world order? How are the specific structures of these kinds located in time, that is, how are they periodized as to beginnings and endings?

With regard to the first question, I am positing three levels of structures as being necessarily interrelated: the organization of production; the form of state; and the structure of world order. (I do not use world order in a normative sense but in the sense of the way things usually happen.)

There can be little controversy as to the relevance of the last two levels. As regards the first of these levels, it seems to me plausible to take the production of the material conditions of existence for a fundamental human activity. This activity affects the way people relate to one another in society and how they conceive the reality of their world, and it also creates the resources that become transformed into various components of power at the levels of state and world order. Production here is to be understood in the broadest sense. It is not confined to the production of physical goods used or consumed. It covers also the production and reproduction of knowledge and of the social relations, morals, and institutions that are prerequisites to the production of physical goods.

With regard to the second question—the placing of historical structures in time—I shall argue that there is a common periodization of the three levels of structures that results from their interrelatedness. There have been eras of relatively rapid transformation in all three kinds of structures, followed by eras of relative stability. This leads to the proposition that the present may be an era of structural change, and that the historical-structures approach should accordingly serve as a guide to a research program that would help understand the sources of change.

What follows is divided into three parts: conceptual tools for grasping the three levels of production, state, and world order; a paradigm of interrelated structural change in the three levels derived from the late nineteenth century; and aspects of structural transformation in the present suggested by this paradigm.

Conceptual Tools

The Level of Production

Production is both a social process and a power relationship. Different patterns or types of power relations in production, what I call modes of social relations of production, can be derived from empirical historical evidence. For example, in both subsistence agriculture and domestic household production, the power relations have been those of the patriarchal family. Peasants produce under the domination of landlords who appropriate a part of the product. In putting-out production, in self-employment, and in wage employment in a self-regulating labor market without any institutional or collective protection for labor, the power relations are those of the market. Varieties of institutionalized relationships have been devised: bipartite and tripartite; state corporatism; central planning; and the enterprise corporatism of large corporate entities from universities and state bureaucracies to the staffs of corporations in the private sector. Each of these is a distinctive type of relationship with a distinctive balance of power between the dominant and subordinate elements in the production process. Each is associated with characteristic technologies, institutions, norms and expectations, and rationalities—all of which aspects form a distinctive coherent whole in each mode.

These various types or patterns emerged in specific historical circumstances and then continued to evolve as other types came into being. Various types coexist in clusters of dominant and subordinate modes. Thus, relatively unprotected migrant workers in an unregulated labor market situation do jobs that help sustain more securely employed workers covered by collective bargaining or make inputs for enterprises that employ more secure workers. Household production sustains both kinds of workers and thus indirectly subsidizes their employers. This relation of dominant to subordinate modes of social relations of production is present in noncapitalist as well as capitalist development. In China, nonestablished rural-industry workers constitute a flexible adjunct to urban-based industries that employ a core of established permanent workers, and small-commodity producers (both rural and urban) provide goods and services for both.

The social map of the world can be plotted as a hierarchy of interconnected modes of social relations of production. There are country clusters characteristic of different paths and levels of development. There are also transnational clusters formed by the internationalizing of production.

Modes of social relations of production should be analytically distinguished from modes of accumulation. (This is where I differ from those Marxist analyses that tend to confuse production with accumulation.) It is convenient to distinguish two modes of development or accumulation as ideal types: capitalist and redistributive. In capitalist development, investments and output are determined by anticipations of what the market will make profitable. In redistributive development, these decisions are determined by politically authoritative redistributors according to political criteria and priorities. The accumulation processes in each of these two modes of development in practice work through distinct yet changing clusters of production-relations modes. Production-relations modes that historically emerged in capitalist development have reemerged within redistributive development, for example, self-employment and small enterprises, without this implying a shift toward capitalism. (This is one of the problems with some current speculation about China.)

States preside over the accumulation process, whether capitalist or redistributive, and it is ultimately the state that determines the particular clustering of modes of social relations of production through which accumulation takes place.

The Level of the State

Neorealists make an abstraction of *the* state, implying that all states are more or less identical so far as international relations are concerned in serving their own particular understanding of national interest (Keohane 1986). The historical-structures approach orients attention to different historical *forms* of state derived from historical-empirical evidence. Forms of state are to be defined in terms of the apparatus of administration, regulation, coercion, and conformity (police and education); and the historic bloc or class configuration that defines the effective content and limits of what a particular form of state does—the intersubjective awareness of what is possible and what is excluded, or, in other words, the historical definition of political reality or *raison d'état* for that form (Cox 1983).

Examples of distinct forms of state in the post-Westphalian period conceived in political-economy terms are: mercantilist, liberal, welfare-nationalist, neoliberal, neomercantilist or state capitalist, and redistributive or central planning. These various forms came into existence in specific historical circumstances, shaped by particular combinations of pressures, and have performed different functions in relation to the world orders within which they existed.

Forms of state are conceived both teleologically and genetically. Most definitions of the state are in teleological or functional form: The state exists in order that certain necessary functions be performed, that is, functions of public order, the organization of cooperation among individuals for the production of material or cultural goods, the collective security of citizens, and so on. The distinctive forms are designated by their functional characteristics. Functional characteristics, however, cannot account for origins. Each form of state came into existence through a historical process of conflict and realignment of social groups. Teleological and genetic explanations complement one another, but the genetic has priority in the search for an understanding of structural change.

The Level of World Order

The state mediates between the levels of production and world order. As regards production, the state determines the particular cluster of modes of social relations of production conducive to accumulation. The liberal state created the self-regulating market by a series of legislative and administrative acts (Polanyi 1944). The welfare-nationalist state, as I shall suggest, created the corporatist structures of tripartism. The fascist state created state corporatism; and the Bolshevik state, central planning. Each form of state encouraged, permitted, or regulated the relationship between these dominant modes of social relations of production and the subordinate modes clustered around them.

States also determined how these various patterns of production relations fitted into the world economy, sometimes shielding domestic production from external pressures and sometimes encouraging domestic production to adjust to world market conditions. Whether it was the one or the other depended upon the nature and phase of the world order.

I distinguish hegemonic from nonhegemonic world orders. In the first category, I place the Pax Britannica of the mid-nineteenth century and the Pax Americana of the mid-twentieth century. There is a semantic problem with this terminology, because many people use hegemony to mean the dominance of one power in the world system (or in a group of states). I use hegemony to mean not just the dominance of one power but a special kind of dominance that involves some concessions to the interests of other powers such that all (or most) can regard the maintenance of the order as being in their general interest and can define it in terms of universality. Insofar as it involves common norms and ways of thinking about world order, a hegemonic order transcends a purely inter-state arrangement to become a social order. Individuals and associations and schools of thought as well as states identify with it. Hegemony includes dominance, but dominance can exist without hegemony.

Structural Transformation: Late Nineteenth Century

The late nineteenth century provides a case of simultaneous transformation in structures of production, forms of state, and world order. In production, it saw the displacement of craft manufacture by mass production. In forms of state, the liberal state gave way to the beginnings of the welfare-nationalist form, and during the early twentieth century to other forms, Bolshevik and fascist. In world order, Pax Britannica gave place to an era of rival imperialisms—a hegemonic world was transformed into a nonhegemonic world.

Identifying the salient features of this transformation at three levels may serve heuristically to point towards sources of transformation in the present.

The apogee of the liberal era may be dated from the Universal Exhibition in London of 1851 to the Universal Exhibition in Paris of 1866—both symbols of material progress and world economy. From the 1870s through the 1890s, there was discontinuity in structures, a series of changes leading cumulatively to a new phase of world history.

In the first place, there was a change in the relative power of states. This is the explanation that appears to be sufficient in realist theory. Both Germany and Italy became unified, and emerged as new major powers. Britain, after Palmerston (1865), withdrew from the European balance under the influence of Cobdenite foreign policy. A process of polarization between two alliance systems took the place of the European balance. When Britain returned more actively to European politics after 1900, it was as a member of an alliance. The rising importance of the United States and Japan inaugurated a shift toward the Pacific and the beginning of an era of world politics—a shift confirmed by the Anglo-Japanese alliance of 1902. Germany's bid for world power status, initially through its naval construction, remained the salient theme of this period, extending through two world wars, until a new world order structure emerged after World War II in which the United States played the leading role.

In the second place, underlying the shift in relative military-political potential of states was the uneven spread of industrialization. Britain lost its erstwhile monopoly of industrial leadership. Economic history determined changes in the relative power of states. Weapons costs rose, so that only the front-runners in industrialization could have modern weapons, especially naval power. The launching of the *Dreadnought* in 1906 gave Britain immediate advantage but at the same time narrowed and equalized the competition by making older ships obsolete. Steel production was a critical index of industrial (and hence military) power. In 1873, Germany passed Britain in steel produced, and as early as 1890, the United States was in first place. By the end of the century, British monopoly of industrial leadership gave place to a competition among powers of which Britain had become the least dynamic.

In the third place and concurrent with the industrial changes were major changes in societies. The balance of population in Europe swung from rural to urban during the last decades of the nineteenth century. Urbanization was accompanied by the spread of mass literacy, the coming of a popular press for the newly literate masses, and a general extension of political participation through the right to vote and the organization of mass political parties, including socialist parties. Governments, mainly under conservative leadership, responded to their perception of the "labor problem" and the negative social consequences of the liberal self-regulating market (Polanyi 1944) by initiating social measures: factory legislation and the legalization of trade unions in Britain; the factory inspectorate in France; social insurance in Bismarck's Germany.

In the fourth place, underlying these social changes was the emergence of a new social structure of accumulation (Gordon 1980; Gordon et al., 1982). The social structure of accumulation includes all the institutions and practices involved in the accumulation process, but the most critical changes at this time were in social relations of production. When the modes of social relations of production (and the hierarchical relationships of subordination among modes) are restructured, the ways in which surplus is extracted and accumulated are changed.

During the mid-century period, a differentiation in the labor force appeared in the more advanced industrial areas between established and nonestablished workers, the former relatively more skilled and more stably employed. The nonestablished work force, which increased with the urbanization of the late nineteenth century, was swollen by immigrants from rural areas. This shift in the composition of the labor force coincided with the downswing of the Kondratieff cycle in the long depression of 1873–96. The depression brought concentration of capital, and the replacement of the competitive-entrepreneurial businesses characteristic of the liberal era by corporate-bureaucratic capital. The new concentrated forms of capital were characteristic of the new industries that grew out of the depression era—steel, electricity, chemicals, and the internal combustion engine. These industries pioneered new production technologies that required new social relationships in the production process (Taylorism and the assembly line).

The new technologies shifted power over the work process from labor to management. The control over the pacing of work by the skilled worker who built a complete unit gave place to the machine-paced actions of the semiskilled operative. The semiskilled, recruited from among the burgeoning ranks of the nonestablished labor force, in turn developed a new form of trade unionism. Skilled-worker trade unions had been concerned with controlling the supply side of the labor market, and had been attracted by antistate doctrines of syndicalism. The semiskilled had little effective control over either the labor market or the work process because they were drawn from a large pool of undifferentiated labor; because management had restructured the work process so as to deprive workers of that control. These workers created industrial unionism. They looked to political influence and state action as well as collective bargaining to gain their objectives. Politicians, recognizing a new political force, brought the new labor movements into dialogue over state policies. The germs of corporatism, visible already in the last decades of the nineteenth century, generated institutional precedents during World War I.

As a fifth aspect of this composite of structural changes, new historic blocs emerged and with them a new form of state: the welfare-nationalist state. This form of state was built in a gradual process extending from nineteenth-century beginnings with Bismarck and Disraeli and culminating in the welfare state planned during World War II. A crucial part of this process was the bonding of industrial workers to the state, initially through labor protective legislation (factory acts and the like), the legalizing of trade unions and their functions, and state protection (in the form of health, old-age, and disability insurance) against the principal occupational risks, and later extending to state intervention to promote an economic environment conducive to worker welfare, especially through measures to maintain employment levels.

The new historic blocs, encompassing both national industry and labor, discovered the common interest of these groups in protectionism, economic nationalism, and overseas imperialist expansion. Tariffs and immigration restrictions protected industrialists and national labor. Imperial expansion channeled outward energies that might otherwise have fired domestic social conflict (Carr 1945; Wehler 1972; Borkenau 1942). Experiments with corporatism in Britain and Germany during World War I became a model for transcending social conflict that later found expression in the Keynesian social contracts of the post–World War II period. Bismarck's heritage evolved into the welfare state: class conflict was transcended through a combination of nationalism and welfare.

The final aspect was that change in the form of state was at the same time a change in the structure of world order. The shift in relative power of states made for a greater diffusion of power. The world order became more conflictive, but at the same time it was more permissive. There is an analogy here with the post–Congress of Vienna settlement. The Restoration it brought about and the doctrine of legitimacy underpinning it were powerless to prevent the emergence of liberal states as Britain neutralized the interventionist proclivities of the Holy Alliance. When liberalism became hegemonic in the Pax Britannica (I am using "liberalism" in the European and not in the U.S. sense here) the order tolerated varieties of political regime but embodied orthodoxy as regards the rules of a liberal world economy. That orthodoxy was shattered in the world order that followed the demise of Pax Britannica. In the scramble for shares of the world product, two new forms of state emerged: a fascist state that superimposed a command economy upon capitalist accumulation; and a socialist redistributive state. Both were designed to catch up with and surpass the leading industrial powers. Both introduced new forms of production relations—state corporatism and central planning. The world order proved to be as powerless to suppress the new forms (despite a major attempt against Bolshevism) as the Holy Alliance had been to suppress liberalism.

Change in World-Order Structure at Present?

Loss of Hegemony?

The weakening of the hegemonic world order has become a major point of discussion among international relations specialists in recent years and is probably the single most important issue underlying the questioning of the adequacy of conventional theory in the field—a questioning of which this book is an instance and a record.

I shall not enter into the discussion of indicators in the relative power of states. The issue, in my view, is not so much whether a relative decline in U.S. power has resulted in loss of hegemony, as whether there is less disposition outside the United States to believe the United States to be acting in the general world-order interest. Susan Strange (1985, 256) quotes the late Hedley Bull: "The problem America presents for us is not, as so many Americans appear to think, the relative decline of its power, but the decline of its capacity for sound judgment and leadership." Insofar as this is the case, hegemony, in the sense in which I have used the term, recedes, leaving a state of conflict among powers in which one may still retain a preponderance of force.[1]

Economic Crisis

Is there a parallel between the economic crisis following 1973–74 and that inaugurated by the long depression beginning in 1873? The use of the term "crisis" implies something more than one of the cyclical downturns of capitalist economy; it implies that recovery will require structural changes to be made in the economy.

Inflation (which at moderate levels had been a stimulus to business during the 1960s) generated, at high levels during the 1970s, a crisis of confidence. Profits in manufacturing were squeezed between higher wages (which rose dramatically after 1968), higher raw materials costs (which were not confined to oil), and more intensive international competition. Investment declined and unemployment increased.

The concern of governments in advanced capitalist countries shifted from employment creation through stimulating the economy (which now seemed to produce more inflation without producing more jobs) to the creation of conditions favorable for business to invest—which included reducing inflation but also (though officially unavowed) the creation and tolerance of high levels of unemployment. Other countries, notably the more rapidly industrializing Third World countries and socialist countries of Eastern Europe, were less immediately affected, because the excess liquidity of western transnational banks found in them an outlet for loans. The crisis caught up with these countries in the 1980s in the form of a debt crunch that forced them too to confront problems of structural economic change. The economic crisis became a world crisis affecting all forms of state.

A New Social Structure of Accumulation

The way out of the crisis, as in the late nineteenth century, involves the putting into place of a new social structure of accumulation. The ultimate shape of the emerging structure is by no means clear. Indeed, conflicting tendencies are apparent. It will involve a massive restructuring of production. Some of the tendencies apparent in production processes of the advanced capitalist countries are displacement of human labor by equipment (robotics), a continuation of a long-term trend; more systematic use of cheaper labor both within advanced capitalist countries and by shifting production to Third World countries; and adjustment of production to more differentiated demand, that is, shorter production runs, a reversal of the tendency of the Fordist era.

Tendencies vary by country, by industry, and by technologies within an industry. Mass production in manufacturing seems to be in decline in the advanced capitalist countries, but growing in newly industrializing countries. Taylorist methods are less evident in the manufacture of the more sophisticated goods, but growing in services (for example, in office work, retail trades, and fast food). Large-scale production is stalled with overcapacity in steel, but minimills using different technology and specialty steels are doing well.

Employers seek to stabilize permanent work forces at the lowest level consistent with continuous production and also seek maximum versatility to meet changing market demand. This leads to the structuring of a work force with fixed and variable elements: a core of versatile employees with employment security that have in effect become part of fixed capital; and a periphery consisting of a variable work force of semiskilled workers. The core workers become integrated into the firm through enterprise corporatism, a variety of measures linking their interests and career development with membership in the firm's staff.

Periphery workers fall under a variety of types, segmented and with different outlooks and orientations: (1) downgraded skilled workers, many of them union members with full-time but less secure jobs, who are the most likely source of conflict, but have been placed by high unemployment rates in a defensive posture; (2) part-time or short-term employees, mostly nonunion and often satisfied with flexibility of employment, for example, women with family responsibilities; (3) outworkers and subcontractors' employees, often doing jobs such as cleaning and maintenance in plants staffed by permanent employees; (4) underground economy workers, equivalent to the so-called "informal sector" in Third World countries, and estimated to produce 25–30 percent of official GNP in some industrialized countries, a growing proportion of both labor force and total product since 1973–74; and (5) informal and extended-family exchange of services plus household production of use-values that have most probably expanded since the onset of the crisis.

Overall, the trend has been toward greater segmentation of the labor force, with the burden of uncertainty placed upon the periphery workers.[2] Core–periphery, once a geographical expression, is becoming more a social distinction based on relationship to the production process. It retains something of its geographical connotation insofar as production processes become more internationalized and a substantial segment of the peripheral workers are employed in Third World countries. At the same time, there is a marked phenomenon of peripheralization of segments of the work force in what have been regarded as core countries (Ross and Trachte 1983). A pattern can be discerned in the variety of tendencies restructuring work in the late twentieth century. This variety includes, for example, a movement toward Taylorism in fast-food production; and a movement away from Taylorism in some more sophisticated industries, with the introduction of techniques like self-regulating multiskilled work groups to replace assembly line production. The pattern is that Taylorism-Fordism is shifting to the periphery, both social and geographical, while more adaptive production methods become characteristic of the core.

The implications for production relations of these tendencies are: a decline of bipartism and tripartism, together with a weakening of trade unions and reduction in the traditional blue-collar labor force; a consolidation of enterprise corporatism among core workers; an increase in the proportion and the varieties of nonestablished workers, segmented into different categories including part-time, temporary, outworkers, self-employed with a single contractor, and underground-economy workers.

New Forms of State?

Such a massive restructuring of production processes is not without political consequences. The destructive aspect of these consequences has been the more apparent: an end to the social contract that was the linchpin of postwar historic blocs. These historic blocs underpinned the Keynesian demand-management form of state. Formerly unions were able to represent themselves as acting on behalf of the working class as a whole and they could credibly think of their interest as consistent with the general interest of society for economic expansion and welfare. Now the interests of different worker groups have been turned against one another, and the identity of union interests with society's welfare has been challenged.

The enterprise-corporatist sector of employees is relatively satisfied. Wages in this sector have risen despite high unemployment levels for other workers. State-sector workers have become divided from private-sector core workers by the fiscal crisis of the state. Governments trying to trim state budgets do so by cutting back on services and holding back wages of state workers. State-sector workers are under pressure to accept this reversal of their previous (and quite recent) gains in economic strength under pressure of public opinion, including the opinion of blue-collar workers who in this case may think of themselves more as taxpayers than as members of a working class. The instrumental view of work that is characteristic of peripheral workers does not make for working-class cohesion. Much of the power that the working class gained through bipartism and tripartism in the welfare state has ebbed away.

The consequences these structural changes may have in a longer term are far less clear at this time. In the advanced capitalist countries, alternative historic blocs are only dimly apparent. Most visible has been the Reagan–Thatcher populism that substitutes ideology for a stable social coalition. The ideology (patriotism, traditional values, anticommunism) obscures the division of society into broadly satisfied and excluded elements roughly equal in numbers but not in social power. In Gramscian terms, it is a form of Caesarism, that is, the attempt to arrest a crisis of representation by temporary suppression or avoidance of conflict without dealing with the sources of conflict in any lasting way.

Less visible in the present political context of Western countries, but nonetheless evident in some policy initiatives and policy thinking, is the alternative of state capitalism, that is, a new corporatism with an industrial policy geared to competitiveness in world markets (Katzenstein 1983; Rohaytn, 1984; Stoffaes 1978). Such a state capitalism presupposes the reconstruction of a historic bloc capable of creating a reasonably broad social base to sustain its policies. Some countries seem to be better equipped than others by their institutional structures, their prevailing ideologies, and the nature of their elites to undertake the state capitalist road successfully (Katzenstein, ed., 1977; Zysman 1983).

The key to the future may lie in the orientation of social groups now being structured by changes in production. At present, these orientations are still in the making. No coherent alternative in policy or in base of political support has been put together in advanced capitalist societies. The left, which once played an important role in the social contract, is in disarray. The traditional working class that had been the basis for the welfare state is being weakened and fragmented. Newer nonclass movements have gained a political following—the peace, ecology, and feminist movements. A major question for the left is whether these clusters of nonclass issues can be given a firm enough basis in emerging social reality, and combined with issues derived from the segmentation of labor, to become the expression of a new historic bloc.

Conclusion

The argument set forth in outline above can be stated in the following propositions. The emerging world order will be largely determined by the forms of state that compose it. Forms of state will be decided by dominant configurations of social forces and the ability (or inability) of these to achieve some new social compact or internal hegemony. The social forces that will be available for combination into new historic blocs (that is, the possible basis for internal hegemony) are those emerging in the ongoing restructuring of production—in the genesis of a new social structure of accumulation. Therefore, the key to future world order is to be sought, not so much in the sphere of international institutions or "regimes," as in the political leadership that may be able to consolidate a socio-political base from the mutations now going on in production.

Notes

1. Susan Strange (1987) argues that the problem some have attributed to a decline of U.S. power is more accurately to be attributed to the "inconsistent, fickle and unpredictable" conduct of U.S. policy. There is, I think, no difference of substance between us but only a difference in semantics. Strange adopts the vocabulary of the U.S. theorists of hegemonic decline in equating hegemony with the dominance of a great power, whereas I am using the term in a Gramscian sense of coercion accompanied by consent expressed in universalistic principles of conduct. In the latter sense, inconsistent, fickle and unpredictable conduct by a dominant power would be destructive of hegemony, leaving only a preponderance of power—dominance without hegemony.

2. There is a growing literature about labor market segmentation of which the following works are indicative: Gordon et al., 1982; Sabel 1982; Piore and Sabel 1984; and Wilkinson, ed., 1984.

References

Borkenau, Franz (1942). *Socialism, National or International?* London: George Routledge and Sons.

Braudel, Fernand (1958, 1980). "History and the Social Sciences: The *longue durée.*" [Translation of an article that originally appeared in *Annales E.S.C.*, no. 4 (October-December 1958).] In Braudel, *On History.* Translated by Sarah Matthews. Pp. 25–54. Chicago: University of Chicago Press.

Carr, Edward Hallett (1945). *Nationalism and After.* London: Macmillan.

Cox, Robert W. (1983). "Gramsci, Hegemony and International Relations: An Essay in Method." *Millennium: Journal of International Studies* 12, no. 2 (Summer):162–75.

Gordon, David (1980). "Stages of Accumulation and Long Economic Cycles." In Terence K. Hopkins and Immanuel Wallerstein, eds., *Processes of the World System.* Beverly Hills, Calif.: Sage.

Gordon, David, Richard Edwards, and Michael Reich (1982). *Segmented Work, Divided Workers: The Historical Transformation of Labor in the United States.* Cambridge: Cambridge University Press.

Katzenstein, Peter, ed. (1977). "Between Power and Plenty: Foreign Economic Policies of Advanced Industrial States." *International Organization* 31, no. 4 (Autumn; special issue).

Katzenstein, Peter (1983). "The Small European States in the International Economy: Economic Depedence and Corporatist Politics." In John Gerard Ruggie, ed., *The Antinomies of Interdependence: National Welfare and the International Division of Labor.* New York: Columbia University Press.

Keohane, Robert O., ed. (1986). *Neorealism and Its Critics.* New York: Columbia University Press.

Marx, Karl (1852, 1969). *The Eighteenth Brumaire of Louis Bonaparte.* English text. New York: International Publishers.

Piore, Michael J., and Charles Sabel (1984). *The Second Industrial Divide: Possibilities for Prosperity.* New York: Basic Books.

Polanyi, Karl (1944). *The Great Transformation.* Boston: Beacon Press.

Rohaytn, Felix (1984). *Restoring American Competitivenss: Proposals for an Industry Policy.* Washington, D.C.: Center for National Policy.

Ross, Robert, and Kent Trachte (1983). "Global Cities and Global Classes: The Peripheralization of Labor in New York City." *Review* 6, no. 3.

Sabel, Charles (1982). *Work and Politics: The Division of Labor in Industry.* Cambridge: Cambridge University Press.

Stoffaes, Christian (1978). *La grande menace industrielle.* Paris: Calmann-Levy.

Strange, Susan (1985). "Protectionism and World Politics." *International Organization* 39, no. 2 (Spring).

—— (1987). "The Persistent Myth of Lost Hegemony." *International Organization* 41, no. 4 (Autumn).

Taylor, Charles (1976). "Hermeneutics and Politics." In Paul Connerton, ed., *Critical Sociology.* Harmondsworth, Middlesex: Penguin.

Vico, Giambattista (1744, 1970). *The New Science of Giambattista Vico.* Translated by Thomas Goddard Bergin and Max Harold Fisch. Ithaca: Cornell University Press.

Wehler, Hans-Ulrich (1972). "Industrial Growth and Early German Imperialism." In Roger Owen and Bob Sutcliffe, eds., *Studies in the Theory of Imperialism.* London: Longman.

Wilkinson, Frank, ed. (1984). *The Dynamics of Labour Market Segmentation.* New York: Academic Press.

Zysman, John (1983). *Governments, Markets, and Growth: Financial Systems and the Politics of Industrial Change.* Ithaca: Cornell University Press.

4

Institutions and International Order

Alexander Wendt
Raymond Duvall

T he discourse of international relations theory in the 1980s has been marked by the frequent use of terms such as "regime," "structure," and "cooperation." Signaling at least a partial shift away from the preoccupation of international relations scholarship in the 1970s with "event," "behavior," and "conflict," these concepts represent the currently appreciable concern of theorists with the institutionalization of systemic *orders* in international relations in an otherwise anarchic context. Told sometimes in terms of the "problem" of "cooperation under anarchy" (to use the title of a recent [1986] volume edited by Kenneth Oye)[1] and sometimes in terms of an "anarchical society" (to refer to the felicitous oxymoron that is the title of Hedley Bull's [1977] now classic book), the story of contemporary international relations theory seems to be nearly as much about international institutions and order as about behavioral relations of hostility among power-maximizing or security-pursuing states in a Hobbesian state of nature.

Almost paradoxically, this refocusing on international institutions and order has occurred simultaneously with the ascendancy of neorealism, the late-twentieth-century reformulation of realpolitik as a theory of self-interested choice by state actors interacting in a context of international anarchy. However, the predominance of neorealism in contemporary international relations theory, with its focus on the conscious choices of self-interested state actors, has meant that the story of international institutions and order is currently being told overwhelmingly in terms of the strategic problem of constructing "cooperation under anarchy" rather than in terms of an international society, albeit an essentially anarchical one.

Such an imbalance, we believe, is unfortunate. We do not mean to suggest by this that cooperatively constructed order is unimportant. On the contrary, collective action and coordination "regimes" are central to the functioning of the contemporary international system. What we do want to argue, however, is that the state-centered, choice-theoretic formulation of the problem of creating international institutions and order blinds scholars to some equally important, if not even more

The authors would like to thank Cindy Kite, Mark Laffey, Jennifer Milliken, David Sylvan, and Jutta Weldes for helpful comments on previous drafts.

fundamental, processes of "ordering" in the international system. To see these alternative processes of international systemic ordering, we believe, one must adopt a different perspective. This perspective recognizes that the international political system is not only a *system* of states but also a *society* of states.

We pursue this argument in this chapter. Specifically, employing a structurationist viewpoint, we have two basic objectives. First, we seek to elucidate and critique the foundations of the "new institutionalism" of neorealism that stands as the now-dominant approach to thinking about international institutions and systemic order. For this purpose, we first contrast the assumptions and problematique of this tradition with those of the "old institutionalism" of British international relations theory, and then draw on some of the lines of criticism of the new institutionalism previously set forth by Richard Ashley, John Ruggie, and others. In this part of the chapter, then, we plow relatively familiar ground. Second, we attempt, in a more original fashion, to develop an alternative framework for the analysis of international institutions and order that subsumes the problematiques of both the new and the old institutionalism within a "structurationist" conception of the international system.

Neorealism and the New Institutionalism

The New and the Old Institutionalism

The "new institutionalism" of neorealism is not the first tradition in modern international relations theory to emphasize the role of institutions in structuring and organizing international relations. What we will call the "old institutionalism" of the principally British school of international relations theory, for example, evinced quite similar concerns several years before the emergence of "regime theory."[2] Despite their common interest in international "institutions" and "order," however, these two traditions of institutional analysis differ, and indeed mirror one another, in at least three important respects. These differences in turn shed light on what we believe are two interdependent but irreducible aspects of international institutions. Thus an examination of them provides a convenient vehicle with which to work up to our argument about how international institutions should be defined and their role in contributing to international order understood.

The first, and most fundamental, difference between the two traditions is in their underlying pictures of the nature of the states system and international life. The old institutionalists, with their communitarian approach to social order, take an ultimately Grotian view of the international system that emphasizes normative integration and order among state actors. The new institutionalists, with their contractarian approach to social order, in contrast, take an ultimately Hobbesian, or at least Lockean, view of the international system that emphasizes anarchic competition and conflict among states.[3] When put baldly this difference parallels the distinction between what Tonnies (1887, 1940) calls "Gemeinschaft" and "Gesell-schaft," or between what Lockwood (1964) calls "social integration" and "system integration." Taylor (1968, 85) summarizes the former distinction in the following terms:

> Gemeinschaft is translated as community, and Gesellschaft as society. Society, Ton-nies suggested, is characterized by competitiveness and the transactions within it are based on contract. Community, on the other hand, describes a sense among the individuals forming it of belonging together, of having common loyalties and values, of kinship; and tasks performed within a community are not performed because of reciprocal arrangements such as contracts, but because of a feeling of duty, a sense of contributing something worthwhile to the good of the whole. An example of society . . . is the firm; an example of community is the family, the church, or the nation.[4]

Gesellschaft, in other words, is characterized by self-interested and typically conflictual interaction that is "systemically integrated" by the "functional interlacing of unintended consequences"; Gemeinschaft is characterized by normatively driven and typically cooperative interaction that is "socially integrated" "by an underlying intersubjective consensus about norms, values, and ends" (Benhabib and Cornell 1987, 6).[5] An emphasis on one or the other of these two types of integration is manifested respectively in the two traditions' preferred characterizations of and methods for studying the international system—as a *"community* of states" to be studied in "sociological" terms on the one hand, and as a *"system* of states" to be studied in "economic" terms on the other. Admittedly neither school dispenses entirely with the insights of the other. But their tendency to polarize the social and systemic aspects of international life produces characteristic biases and blind spots in the analysis of international institutions; we will argue later that these can only be overcome by recognizing and theorizing explicitly about the interdependence of these two modalities of ordering in international life.

These different conceptualizations of international life relate to a second difference between the two schools, one in the *kinds* of institutions with which they deal. Old institutionalists generally focus on what might be called the "fundamental" institutions of international society: a standard list includes the balance of power, international law, and diplomacy (James 1978), to which others have added war and the concert of Great Powers (Bull 1977) and spheres of influence (Keal 1983). These institutions represent the shared intersubjective understandings about the (not necessarily uncoerced) preconditions for meaningful state action.[6] Put into the discourse of structuration theory, these institutions constitute state actors as subjects of international life in the sense that they make meaningful interaction by the latter possible.[7]

This emphasis on the institutions that embody the collective conditions of possibility for meaningful state action—on "social integration" in international society—contrasts markedly with the kinds of institutions upon which the new institutionalists have usually focused. These institutions are the generally intended artifacts of hegemonic or collective action created by preexisting state actors, and as a result they tend to be located at a less fundamental level of structuring in the international system than those of concern to the old institutionalists—economic or security "regimes" rather than balance of power or diplomacy. This reflects the concern of new institutionalists with inter-state conflict and "system integration," with understanding the conditions under which preexisting state actors in a competitive anarchy can overcome their naturally conflictual condition and create, through social contract or hegemonic dominance, relatively enduring international institutions.

This in turn relates to a third and for our purposes crucial difference between the two traditions, one that concerns the *role* of international institutions in "ordering" the practices of state actors. The old institutionalists are concerned primarily with the ways in which international institutions *structure* those practices—with the ways in which they constitute or make possible inherently social and meaningful international practices. The new institutionalists, on the other hand, are concerned primarily with the ways in which international institutions *organize* the practices of state actors—with the ways in which they constrain the choices of preexisting state actors and in so doing select certain courses of action as most likely from among those that are possible in a given institutional context. The new institutionalists' emphasis on the organization and selection of certain actions is reflected in the neorealist definition of international "regime" as a set of principles, norms, rules, and procedures that shape the *expectations* of state actors vis-à-vis other actors (Krasner 1983c, 2), because it is by such a process of expectation formation that interactions are made *predictable* rather than just possible.

The difference between "structuring" and "organizing" as modes of ordering international life, which we elaborate more fully later when we formally define the concept of "international institution," in part reflects the different kinds of institutions upon which the two traditions focus. Because they are the preconditions for sovereign states and meaningful state action rather than consciously chosen artifacts, the "fundamental" institutions of international society will appear to state actors (and scholars) as defining possibilities for, rather than constraints on, state action—as "structuring" the interactions of state actors (in the sense of making those interactions possible). On the other hand, because they are created by preexisting state actors to serve certain purposes vis-à-vis each other, less "fundamental" institutions like monetary and trade "regimes" will appear to state actors (and scholars) as defining constraints on, rather than possibilities for, state action—as "organizing" the interactions of state actors. It is our contention, however, that *all* international institutions, at whatever level of "fundamentality" in the international system, in fact order international life in *both* ways. The tendency of each tradition to ignore one or the other modality of institutional ordering, then, represents a basic problem in the contemporary analysis of international institutions. We develop a framework for solving this problem below, but first we turn to a more detailed examination of the fundamental assumptions and limitations of the new institutionalism.

The Social Ontology of the New Institutionalism

The basic scope of the new institutionalist problematique stems from its fundamental ontological assumptions about the state and the international system. These assumptions are characterized by an at least implicit ontological individualism, in which state actors are treated as the primitive individuals of the international system—the social atoms or constituent units of which the international system is composed.[8] Two important distinguishing features of this social ontology should be recognized.

First, it takes the identities, powers, and interests of states as exogenously given.[9] Because state actors are the social atoms of the international system, their fundamental properties are not determined by the international systemic orders that they, themselves, compose. Their respective positions in the international system may affect their particular preferences or material power capabilities (see Lake 1987b), but shaping or constituting *what they are* at base as social actors—their fundamental identities, powers, and interests—does not itself involve the international system or its ordering and organization. State actors are ontologically primitive.

Second, and related to the first, the structure of the international system is constituted *by,* but not constitutive *of,* its elements. It is constituted by states in the sense that it is defined as an aggregation of the properties of preexisting, given state actors—as the "distribution of capabilities" or "interests".[10] For this very reason, however, the structure of the international system cannot be constitutive of those states, because something cannot be constitutive of something else if it is ontologically reducible to the latter. As a result, in the neorealist view the "structure" of the states system is a constraint on, rather than constitutive of, state action. It defines the incentives facing previously constituted state actors and thereby constrains and "organizes" their practices, but it does not itself constitute or "structure" those actors and practices in the sense of making them possible.

Although social ontologies do not directly dictate the content of substantive theories, they do have conceptual and methodological consequences for how theorists approach those phenomena they seek to explain, and thus for the development of their theories. In this light, and in line with the above two features of its social ontology, the "new institutionalism" of neorealism approaches the issue of international institutions and order strictly from the viewpoint of already constituted state actors. The new institutionalism, in other words, is a fundamentally *choice-theoretic* project. International institutions, regimes, and order exist insofar as they are consciously chosen to serve the interests of the fundamental units of the system, states. International order, then, is constructed or constituted by preexisting state actors, rather than constitutive of them. This view has at least three serious limitations.

Three Problems with the New Institutionalism

The conventional starting point of the new institutionalist approach is the assumption that state actors face a "cooperation problem" in their efforts to create international order (Krasner, ed., 1983; Oye, ed., 1986). On the surface this problem stems from the fact that in an anarchic system there are by definition no formal, authoritative controls to prevent the defection of state actors from international agreements. Although the systemic condition of anarchy is clearly central to the definition of the cooperation problem, however, neorealism also at least implicitly shows that the root of this problem lies not in anarchy alone but also in the nature and distribution of state interests (defined here as "preferences"). Thus, cooperation under anarchy is possible in a world of positive-sum, but not in a world of zero-sum, interactions (Oye 1985), is more likely in "coordination games" than in "cooperation games" (Stein 1983; Snidal 1985a), and more likely still if state actors define their interests in part to include the interests of other state actors—that is, if they are other-regarding rather than strictly self-regarding individuals (Wendt in progress). Despite the importance of the distribution of interests for the possibilities of international cooperation, however, neorealists do not have an explicit theory of state interests with which to analyze these possibilities, and instead take state interests (or at least the real interests that underlie state "preferences") are given.[11]

Notwithstanding its merits for analyzing certain issues in the study of international relations, taking interests (not to mention powers) as given has an important limitation for the analysis of international cooperation, and therefore ultimately of international institutions and order: It fails to provide a theoretically grounded understanding of when or why state actors will face, for example, positive-sum as opposed to zero-sum interaction situations, coordination as opposed to cooperation games, or self-regarding as opposed to other-regarding state actors. In other words, though neorealism's choice-theoretic approach permits an abstract analysis of the potential for cooperation in various kinds of strategic situations, it provides little insight into the determinants of those situations, and therefore into the question of how often or under what conditions international cooperation and order will obtain. In a phrase, neorealists do not "problematize the cooperation problem." In order to do so they would have to develop an explicit theory of the state—a theoretical framework that could explain the powers and interests of state actors in terms of the domestic and international institutions that constitute them as empowered and interested subjects in the first place.[12] But this is precisely what is denied to an analytical approach that starts with the powers and interests of already constituted state actors, that is, to an approach that is fundamentally choice-theoretic.[13] The neorealist failure to problematize the cooperation problem reflects a more general limitation of the choice-theoretic approach to international institutions, namely that it cannot theorize about the *preconditions* of state choice and state action. This problem is manifested in the neorealist literature in two distinct ways. First, scholars within the new institutionalist tradition have almost completely ignored the class of international institutions that is involved in the constitution—in the production and reproduction—of state actors per se. The most obvious of these institutions are those fundamental institutions of the states system that are of concern to the old institutionalists, such as international law and diplomacy, although we would argue that certain institutions of global capitalism, such as monetized cross-national exchange, are equally important in the constitution of state actors (Duvall and Wendt 1988). These institutions are important because they are what makes "states," interest-driven "state action," and inter-state "conflict" and "cooperation" *possible* in the first place. Yet until very recently they have not been part of the new institutionalist problematique. As we suggested above, this is not accidental; given that the choice-theoretic approach takes as its starting point the choices of already constituted state actors, the institutional preconditions of those choices almost inevitably recede from view as a phenomenon of interest to, and therefore to be explained by, a choice-theoretic approach (see Gilham 1981).

We say "almost" inevitably because in just the past year there have been a number of attempts by prominent neorealists[14] to problematize what some of them have termed a fundamental "institution"[15] of international society: sovereignty (Keohane 1987; Lake 1987a; Krasner 1988). Despite important differences among them, these articles seem to embody a collective effort to broaden the scope of the new institutionalist problematique to respond to earlier critiques of neorealism's silences about the conditions of possibility of state action (Ashley 1984). For our purposes what is most interesting about these efforts, however, is the fact that they treat sovereignty essentially as a variable property of previously constituted state actors (as if the concept of "the state" could be separated from the concept of "sovereignty"), in a fashion that is directly comparable to the neorealists' treatment of power capabilities. State actors simply possess sovereignty in greater or lesser degree, and it is this variance that is to be theoretically explained.

This conceptual move means, in effect, a continuing (though varying) reliance on a choice-theoretic perspective, which leads these scholars to treat sovereignty in the same way in which they treat other international institutions, that is, almost entirely as constituted *by* the choices of preexisting state actors, rather than as constitutive *of* those actors.[16] Thus, even if the choice-theoretic approach overcomes its earlier silence on the class of "fundamental" institutions of international society, it cannot recognize the constitutive quality of those (or for that matter, any) institutions.[17] This second aspect of neorealism's silence on the preconditions of state action follows logically from the basic premise of the choice-theoretic approach—that institutions should be viewed from the perspective of the purposive, preexisting actors that are embedded within or seeking to create them. And this inevitably means that institutions can be seen only as constituted by, rather than as constitutive of, the powers, interests, and choices of those actors.

The failures to problematize the cooperation problem and to recognize any constitutive role for international institutions together generate a third characteristic of the choice-theoretic approach to international institutions: a narrow interpretation of what international "order" involves. The new institutionalists' choice-theoretic approach reduces the problem of *order* in an anarchic system to the problem of achieving *cooperation* between already constituted state actors. In effect, this approach reduces the problem and conceptualization of international order to the problems of strategic interaction facing state actors themselves. Though it is an essential element in the study of international order, however, this "systemic" focus on the interactions of preexisting state actors necessarily brackets the "social" aspects of international order, and in particular the role of international institutions in constituting the "society" of states, which make those interactions, and the actors who engage in them, possible in the first place.

In addition to simply ignoring an important—indeed, fundamental—dimension of "ordering" in international life, this silence on social integration in the international system has the effect of making international institutions and order (defined in terms of the "cooperation problem") appear very fragile and politically problematic. This follows from the assumption that international "order" is ultimately dependent on the distribution of capabilities and interests across previously constituted state actors. This means that international institutions, at whatever level of structuring in the international system, must be incentive-compatible to achieve normative force on state actors and, conversely, that (presumably exogenously driven) changes in the distribution of capabilities and/or interests in the system can easily undermine the viability of existing international institutions.[18] If, on the other hand, students of international institutions recognized their socially integrative or constitutive aspects—that is, if they recognized what Giddens (1979) terms the "duality of agency and structure" in institutional analysis—they would be less inclined to view changes in the distribution of capabilities or interests as threats to the fundamental principles of "international order."

In the rest of this chapter we develop an analytical perspective on the state and international system that explicitly recognizes both the social and the systemic aspects of international institutions and order, and which can therefore begin to address some of the limitations of the choice-theoretic approach that we described above. It should be emphasized at the outset that our perspective subsumes rather than replaces the choice-theoretic aspects of neorealism. By limiting their focus neorealists have contributed substantially to our understanding of the "systemic" aspects of international order, and the approach that we develop below seeks to incorporate that contribution. We differ from neorealists, however, in our effort to capture theoretically the "social" aspects of international institutions and order that are of concern to the old institutionalists by developing a framework that can permit an explicit recognition and theorization of the ways in which international institutions are simultaneously constituted by *and* constitutive of state action.

Structurationism and International Order

Structurationism and the States System

Because the basis of neorealism's choice-theoretic understanding of international institutions and order is its individualist ontology of the international system, an approach that would transcend the limitations of that understanding should start with an alternative ontology. This alternative should be a more "socialized" ontology in the sense that it should posit the existence of international political and economic structures that are constitutive of the powers and interests of state actors. One basis for such an ontology lies in the family of new and not-so-new social ontologies that may be called "structurationist" (for example, Bhaskar 1979, 1987; Giddens 1979, 1984; Manicas 1980).[19] The goal of structurationist ontologies is to replace the "dualism" of agency and social structure that pervades individualist and collectivist ontologies with a perspective that recognizes the "codetermined irreducibility" of these two fundamental units of social analysis. Without claiming to adhere to any particular school of structurationism, let us briefly define the three central concepts of any structurationist ontology: *agent, system,* and *structure.*

Agents are conscious, purposive, and socially recognized individual or organizational actors the practices of which intentionally and unintentionally produce and reproduce social structures.[20] State actors, for example, are agents in this sense; they are capable of reflexively monitoring and learning from their actions; they make choices; and they are socially recognized by other state actors as subjects of international life capable of engaging in a whole range of practices.

Systems are sets of regularly interacting agents and their practices. The states system, for example, is a system in this sense; it is a collection of regularly interacting state actors and their practices in relations to one another.

Structures are sets of internal relations among the social structural positions in a system that define the identities, powers, and real interests of the agents that occupy those positions.[21] The social structure of the states system, for example, is the set of internal relations of spatial and political individuation that constitute state actors as empowered and interested subjects of international life (see Ruggie 1983; Wendt in progress; compare Waltz 1979).

The relationship between structures and systems of agents is one of "codetermined irreducibility." The powers and interests of agents, and therefore their systems of interaction, are only possible in virtue of the social structure in which they are embedded, but they are not reducible to that structure. Social structures, in turn, only exist in virtue of the practices of the agents by which they are produced, reproduced, and instantiated, but they are not reducible to those practices. Social systems, then, have and make possible, but are not themselves, social structures. And social structures make possible, but are not themselves, social systems. Put another way, social systems are the regularized practices of agents that make possible the social structures that make those practices, and the agents who engage in those practices, themselves possible.

This type of social ontology does not yield any particular substantive theoretical claims about the states system, and we will not attempt to develop such claims in this chapter.[22] It does lead, however, to a particular conceptualization of that system as *both* a *society* of states and a *system* of states. It is a "society of states" in the sense that the practices of state actors are structured by certain socially recognized principles (sovereignty, nonintervention, international property rights, and so on) that make sovereign "states" and meaningful "state action" possible. It is a "system of states" in the sense that it is made up of regularized interactions that reproduce and transform those structural principles. The states system, in other words, is simultaneously "socially integrated" and "systemically integrated"—both Gemeinschaft and Gesellschaft.[23]

In the rest of this chapter we develop the implications of this perspective for how scholars should think about institutions and order in international relations. In particular, we want to suggest that a structurationist approach leads to a rethinking of two issues central to the study of "ordering" of international relations: the conceptualization of and causal role attributed to international institutions, and the nature of different "levels" of structuring in the international system. We take up each of these issues in turn below.

The Nature of International Institutions

The structurationist emphasis on the codetermination of state action and international system structures points toward a reconstituted institutionalist problematique that combines the central concerns of both the "old" and "new" institutionalism in international relations. We have suggested that the old institutionalism has been concerned primarily with the constitutive or "socially integrative" aspect of international institutions—with institutions understood as the background conditions of possibility for states and state action. The new institutionalism, on the other hand, has been concerned primarily with the choice-theoretic or "systemically integrative" aspect of international institutions—with institutions understood as options or constraints facing already constituted state actors seeking to regulate their interaction or to realize common interests. These two types of integration in international life are, in the structurationist view, conceptually interdependent and as such are both essential elements of the "institutionalist problematique" in the study of international order.

The simultaneously social and systemic nature of international life is reflected in our definition of *institutions: institutions are coherent sets of principles that structure and organize ensembles of practices* (compare Krasner 1983c, 2; Suganami 1983, 2365; Moos and Dear 1986). In other words, all international institutions—at whatever level of structuration in the international system—have both "structural" and "systemic" dimensions that contribute in distinct ways to the production of state (and some nonstate) actors' practices, and thus to the production of international order.[24] We take up and illustrate each of these dimensions and their relationship to the "ordering" of state actors' practices in turn below.

All international institutions have a *structural* dimension, made up of one or more internal relations or *constitutive principles,*[25] that generates socially empowered and interested state agents as a function of their respective occupancy of the positions defined by those principles. In other words, the powers and interests of state actors on a given level of international structuration—in a given international institution—are constituted or made possible by, and are therefore inseparable from, their participation and position in that institution. This contrasts directly with the at least implicit assumption of the choice-theoretic approach that the powers and interests of state actors are exogenous to international institutions.

The "constitutive" character of international institutions is relatively obvious in the case of the "fundamental," virtually unconsciously reproduced institutions of international society upon which the old institutionalists focus—the balance of power, diplomacy, monetized exchange, and so forth. The practices that instantiate these institutions are concerned with and structured by the constitutive principle of sovereignty[26]—by internal relations of spatial and political individuation among states and state actors. The powers, interests, and practices of these actors would not be possible apart from those relations, and it is therefore one of the purposes or functions of these institutions to reproduce those relations as conditions of possibility for state action.

The constitutive character of international institutions is also apparent, however, in the less "fundamental," consciously constructed institutions upon which the new institutionalists typically focus. A "monetary regime," for example, empowers both state and nonstate actors to engage in cross-national monetized exchange, and it empowers specifically state actors to regulate and to monitor the valuation of that exchange, as well as to extract resources based on the determined value—all of which would not be possible in the absence of the regime. And it "interests" actors in policies by other actors that affect the relative value of national currencies, such as employment or price policies. As we have argued, this is not to say that the perceived salience of the constitutive dimension does not vary across institutions, but it does point to the presence of an "empowering" and "interesting" effect of all international institutions that makes certain kinds of practices possible—and others impossible.

All international institutions also have a *systemic* dimension, embodied in certain *organizing principles*,[27] which generates particular practices—those involving calculated rational action—as a function of the incentives facing (already constituted) state actors. Whereas constitutive principles shape international practices by generating the powers and interests, and therefore making possible certain practical dispositions, of state actors, organizing principles shape those practices that are rational actions by defining the choice environment facing agents. This environment will appear to the state actors within it as a set of constraints and possibilities that define the relative attractiveness of different courses of action (an analysis of which is of course the central focus of the choice-theoretic approach to international institutions). Viewing it in terms of the institution, per se, however, the systemic dimension organizes and regulates the interactions of state actors and in the process "selects" (in an evolutionary sense) certain practices, including but not limited to those that are consciously or rationally chosen courses of action, from among the practices that are made possible by the social structure of the institution.[28] The actual practices that are institutionally organized and selected in turn constitute the medium through which the social structural or constitutive side of international institutions is reproduced and/or transformed—thereby completing the circle of structuration (or ordering) of the international system.

The "organizing" character of international institutions is relatively obvious in the case of the consciously created "regimes" upon which the new institutionalists typically focus. A monetary regime, for example, organizes the practices of state actors in part by shaping the environment of conscious choice for, and hence constraining, action that affects the relative value of currencies. A regime entailing fixed exchange rates is typically regarded as creating incentives for fiscal and macroeconomic policies that make more likely a balancing of budgetary and trade accounts. A regime that is a coordinated effort to manage otherwise freely floating exchange rates, in contrast, creates different kinds of incentives and disincentives regarding the stimulation of the domestic economy, the discounting of the future (because of the possibility of volatility in exchange rates), and so forth. In addition, a monetary regime organizes practices in ways other than shaping the environment for conscious policy choices; for example, it selects and routinizes practices involved in the accounting of cross-national economic transactions.

The organizing character of international institutions is also apparent, however, in the "fundamental" institutions of international society of concern to the old institutionalists. The practices of state actors in these institutions are shaped and selected by the organizing principle of "anarchy." This principle contributes to the ordering of international life by selecting for a range of "self-help" practices, such as viewing with suspicion the acquisition of new power capabilities by another state, or scrutinizing the diplomatic signals of an adversary, or attempting to create positions of market advantage in relation to other economies, and so forth (see Waltz 1979). This organizing, as distinct from structuring, of international practices tends to be neglected or overlooked by old institutionalists as they focus on the constitutive character of the fundamental institutions of international society.

All international institutions, then, shape the practices of state actors, and thereby "order" international life, by means of two distinct mechanisms: constitution and selection. Each of these mechanisms plays a distinct, but interdependent, role in explaining and ordering those practices—the former making them possible and the latter making them more or less likely. This distinction reflects our understanding of the difference between "social integration" and "system integration." Social integration refers to the socially constructed background conditions of possibility for meaningful state interaction; system integration refers to the nature and effects of that interaction per se. Both forms of integration are important to an understanding of the contribution of institutions at all levels of social structuration to international "order." Social integration in international society occurs only through the production, reproduction, and instantiation of certain constitutive principles in the "organized" practices of state actors. System integration only occurs in virtue of the constitutive principles that make those practices possible.

This brings us to the last element of our definition of international institutions: the fact that institutions structure and organize *practices*. International institutions do not exist apart from the practices of state (and nonstate) actors. Constitutive principles exist only in virtue of their production by and instantiation in certain practices, and organizing principles exist only in virtue of the organization of those practices. This ontological dependence of international institutions on practices reflects the fundamental importance of agency in the structurationist perspective. The practices of agents *constitute* international institutions (whether or not such constitution is consciously intended by those agents). The analysis of international institutions, then, must ultimately *begin* with the analysis of the practices and self-understandings of those agents. These practices and self-understandings do not themselves comprise international institutions (because institutions are sets of principles that underlie and shape practices rather than those practices per se). However, they are the conditions of possibility for those institutions, and as such they form the raw material for theorizing about the constitutive and organizing principles that define concrete international institutions. Institutions and practices, then, are "codetermined" just as structures and agents are; all practices presuppose institutions (otherwise they would be mere "behaviors" rather than "practices"), and all institutions presuppose practices (otherwise they would not exist at all).

Levels of Structuring of International Institutions

One implication of the argument above is that there is no inherent conceptual difference between different levels of structuration and order in the international system. Each level has corresponding "institutions" with both structural and systemic properties. Thus, the self-consciously cooperative arrangements that neorealists call "regimes" are not intrinsically different from the "deep structural" institutions of the state system. All can and should be viewed as constitutive with respect to the powers and interests—the fundamental identities—of state actors; similarly, all can and should be viewed as also organizing the purposive interactions and other practices of those actors.

That said, theorists of international institutions nevertheless regularly distinguish different *levels* of ordering in the international system. This hierarchical view of international institutions implies that some are more basic, "deeper," or more fundamental than others. On its face this notion certainly seems sound. The "fundamental" institutions of the state system (diplomacy and so forth) and of the world economy (monetized exchange), or what Jackson (1987, 520–24) refers to as "civil regimes," clearly provide a foundation for and underlie the normative institution of "embedded liberalism" (Ruggie 1983). And the latter is in turn a more basic or fundamental international institution than is the broadly encompassing trade regime, formally manifested in the GATT, which regime is itself a foundation for the more specific issue-area regime regulating trade in textiles, and so on.

Yet, the meaning of hierarchical concepts like "higher" or "lower" is not entirely obvious with respect to international institutions. Though the hierarchical ordering presented in the previous paragraph rings true, one must ask, With respect to what is this hierarchy being established? What does it mean to say that one regime or institution is "more fundamental" than another? How do we establish such hierarchy?

The answer implicit in the new institutionalist project of neorealism, lacking as it does a constitutive conception of social structure, must be, we think, that hierarchy among international institutions is a function of, and is given by, the range of state actions that are constrained by the respective institutions. The textile regime constrains a narrower range of practices by state actors than does the trade regime which, in turn, constrains a narrower range of practices than does the institution of "embedded liberalism," and so on. In this view, the institutions that embody the constitutive principle of sovereignty are most fundamental, not because they are constitutive of state actors as interested and empowered subjects of international life, but because they stand as the least limiting international constraints on the actions of previously constituted states. For the neorealist, then, a hierarchy of international institutions results from the scope of choices—the length of the menu of courses of action—consistent with the systemic organizing principles entailed in those institutions.

From our structurationist perspective, however, international institutions are hierarchically ordered also with respect to their structural, constitutive principles. This is a matter of the ways in which "higher" level (or more fundamental) institutions condition the establishment of "lower" (or less fundamental) ones as they enable, make possible, or, in a different vocabulary, create the conditions of existence of, the latter. Higher institutional principles create certain arrangements by constituting the powers and interests of agents occupying certain structural positions. These arrangements, in turn, enable and foreclose possibilities for institutions at lower levels, albeit in a possibilistic rather than deterministic fashion. Thus, the constitutive principle of sovereignty means that lower-level international institutions must be incentive-compatible rather than authoritative, but it does not prescribe any particular kinds of incentive-compatible institutions. The constitutive principles of embedded liberalism that are made possible by the principle of sovereignty, in turn, enable certain kinds of international trade regimes, but foreclose the possibility of other kinds of trade regimes.[29]

In sum, then, a first distinguishing feature of a structurationist view of hierarchy among international institutions is that it guides the international relations researcher to theorize explicitly about, and to analyze empirically, the constitutive relations among institutions through which some create the conditions of existence of others (in a possibilistic sense), rather than simply treating the constitutive foundations of all international institutions as equivalent by virtue of their being the conscious constructions of interest-driven states, as they are treated in the new institutionalism of neorealism.

But there is also a second feature distinguishing a structurationist view of hierarchy among international institutions that is consequential. For the neorealist, each international institution in the hierarchy is a discrete entity, the range of constrained behaviors entailed in each subject to change by the choices of state actors irrespective of change in other international institutions. The recognition by structurationists of the constitutive relations among institutions, by contrast, implies a causal relationship for international institutional change. This is relatively obvious with respect to the impact of changes in the fundamental institutions of the states system or global capitalism on less fundamental institutions like the trade regime; a change in the constitutive principle of sovereignty would clearly alter the foundations of an international trade regime.

It is less obvious, however, but nevertheless crucially important, with respect to the reverse process—the impact of changes in lower-level international institutions on more fundamental ones. Because social structures are not simply given, but rather exist, and hence are reproduced and/or transformed, *only* by virtue of the practices of the agents whose powers and interests they constitute, there is, even for the most fundamental international institutions, an ever-present "reproduction problem." The structural requisites, or conditions of existence, of any institution must be effected through the practices of agents if it is to be reproduced—that is to say, if it is to continue as an institution. The structural requisites, or reproduction requirements, of "more fundamental" institutions are affected, however, not *only* by the practices of the agents constituted by those institutions per se, but also by the practices of agents the powers and interests of which are constituted by less fundamental, or lower-level, institutions, such as an international trade or monetary regime.[30] Some of those effects may be functional for the reproduction of the more fundamental institution, in the sense that they contribute to the meeting of its structural requisites, whereas others may be disfunctional, in the opposite sense. For example, the conduct of cross-national monetized exchange, made possible by an international monetary regime, may contribute to the reproduction of capitalism, but the extraction of resources by state actors through taxation based on the value of that exchange, also made possible by the same regime, *may* work against the realization of the structural requisites of capitalism, while contributing to the reproduction of the fundamental institutions of the states system. If the disfunctional effects of practices shaped by lower-level institutions predominate, the more fundamental institutions may undergo structural transformation—becoming, in effect, different institutions.

Thus, while the structurationist perspective reveals a hierarchy of institutions based on the ways in which the structuring principles of some institutions (the more fundamental ones) make possible the conditions of existence of other, less fundamental institutions, it also directs attention to the ways in which the practical actions of agents constituted by those latter institutions have a causal effect on meeting the reproduction requirements of the former. From this view, the international system is seen not as a collection of discrete institutions constructed intentionally by the component state actors, but rather as an integrated hierarchy of institutions in which some make possible others, while practices shaped by those others in turn contribute to the reproduction and/or transformation of the first.

Conclusion

We opened this chapter with a brief critique of the choice-theoretic approach to institutional analysis in international relations, and in particular of its silence on the constitutive dimension of international institutions. We argued that this silence stems from the fact that the neorealist approach to international institutions is fundamentally *agent-centric*. Its ontology of the international system, and therefore its overall analytical strategy with respect to international institutions, *starts* with the interests, powers, and choices of already constituted state actors—that is, with precisely those things that would be the object of a constitutive analysis. In contrast, the ontology of the international system that underlies the alternative approach to international institutions that we sketched above is fundamentally *institution-centric*, by which we mean focused on both practices and structures. Let us elaborate this suggestion.

Social "institutions," when viewed from a structurationist perspective, embody both the agentic and the social structural dimensions of social life without being reducible to either, and as such they constitute a powerful focal point for dealing analytically with the duality of agency and structure that is so central to the perspective. When applied to international relations, such a focus permits scholars to theorize about the powers and interests of state actors in terms of institutional structures at various levels of structuration in the international system, while at the same time recognizing—and subsequently theorizing about—the dependence of those institutional structures on the practices of those actors. In effect, the problematique that we have outlined subsumes the choice-theoretic perspective while at the same time it permits scholars to problematize issues about which that perspective must remain silent.

It should be emphasized that this is not a substantive argument about the relative importance of states vis-à-vis other agents in the modern international system. Our point is rather that the powers, interests, and indeed identities of *all* actors in the international system—whether states, multinational corporations, or whatever—have social conditions of existence that are embodied in the structural or "socially integrative" dimension of institutions at various levels of structuration in the international system. Conversely, those social conditions of existence are themselves continuously reproduced and transformed by the contingent practices of social actors that are embodied in the agentic or "systemically integrative" dimension of international institutions. Though ontologically and therefore analytically irreducible, these two dimensions of international institutions are nevertheless interdependent or codetermined. And it is because the concept of "institution" so clearly embodies this interdependence that we advocate a shift toward an "institution-centric" approach to the study of international relations: There are neither state actors and practices nor international system structures apart from international "institutions."

This reconstituted and expanded institutionalist problematique has several implications for scholarly research into international relations.

First, it encourages the current wave of research into the choice-theoretic foundations of international regimes. The growing literature, especially from game-theoretic and collective-goods perspectives, on the evolution and maintenance of cooperation under anarchy speaks directly to a central concern of our institutionalist problematique, namely the "systemic" conditions under which state actors will choose to create, reproduce, or transform international regimes.

Second, it also welcomes the recent efforts to apply the choice-theoretic perspective to understanding the development and reproduction of what we have called the "fundamental" institutions of the international system, like those embodying the constitutive principle of sovereignty (see Lake 1987a; Krasner 1988). International relations scholars working from within the choice-theoretic perspective have in the past neglected these institutions. Perhaps this was because the latter were not so clearly the conscious creations of (because they were conditions of existence for) state actors. From our perspective the production and reproduction of institutions at all levels of structuration in the international system should be analyzed in terms of the incentives and constraints facing relevant actors (as well as in terms of less calculated, perhaps habitual, practices).

Third, where our perspective goes significantly beyond existing research, however, is in its emphasis on the constitutive and socially integrative aspects of international institutions. This emphasis calls attention to the role of such institutions in creating *possibilities*, including unrealized possibilities, for state action. Apart from the contributions of the "old institutionalism," very little research exists on the role of institutions at various levels of structuration in the international system in constituting the powers, interests, and identities of actors in that system (an exception is Der Derian 1987). Yet, if our argument in this chapter is correct, analysis of this process, and of the possibilities (and impossibilities) it creates, is central to an adequate understanding of the "structuring" of international relations, and therefore of "order" in the anarchic context that is the international system.

A final implication of our structurationist approach to international institutions and order is the need to investigate theoretically and empirically the relationship between different levels of structuration in the international system. In part because of their focus on only those institutions that preexisting state actors have consciously created, scholars working within the choice-theoretic perspective have not raised the question of the varying fundmentality of or causal relationships between different international institutions. Our suggestion that the nature of the powers and interests that international institutions confer upon actors depends on the level of structuration upon which those institutions exist clearly makes central the issue of the concrete relationships between these levels, and between the *hierarchy of interests and powers* that they create.

These four suggestions for future research are each broad problematiques for inquiry in their own right, and we do not mean to suggest that an adequate understanding of a given international institution must address all of them simultaneously. Indeed, structuration theorists themselves have stressed the need for "bracketing" different aspects of the agent-structure relationship for purposes of actual theoretical and empirical research. The virtue of our approach is that it provides an overarching conceptual framework for integrating analyses of these different aspects of structuration in international relations, and thus for avoiding premature silences on important issues in the study of international order.

Notes

1. Other important works in this tradition include Taylor (1976), Axelrod (1981, 1984), Stein (1983), Keohane (1984), and Snidal (1985a, 1985b).

2. Important contributions to this school include Manning (1962), Northedge (1975), James (1986), and, with some qualifications, Bull (1977). A good overview of the basic assumptions and characteristics of this approach is Suganami (1983). In recent years a newer form of the "old" institutionalism has been emerging in such important works as Nardin (1983), Frost (1986), Der Derian (1987), Fain (1987), and Ashley (forthcoming). Strands of especially this current form of "old" institutionalism are quite compatible with the line of argument we offer below.

3. Classical political realists tend to adopt a Hobbesian conception of international anarchy as a war of all against all; neorealists tend to adopt a Lockean conception as a world of civilized propertied individuals (for example, Oye 1985). This shift, however, has not changed the basic realist concern with conflict and constructed order rather than normative integration and societal order.

4. We use the word "society" differently than it is used in this passage. What Tyalor calls "society" we refer to as "system." Our use of the term "society" comes closer to his "community."

5. Benhabib and Cornell are actually referring here to Habermas's somewhat different distinction between "system" and "lifeworld," but their characterization of this latter distinction is apt for our purposes here.

6. Throughout this chapter we refer to "state actors," "state action," and so forth in order to facilitate dialogue with the new institutionalists, but we do *not* mean by this that states are, themselves, actors. In our view "state actors" should be conceptualized as the governmental agents that are constituted by "the state," which should be seen as a *structure* of authority, governance, and rule. For a fuller exposition of the distinction between the concepts of "state" and "state actor" see Benjamin and Duvall (1985) and Duvall and Wendt (1988).

7. This is a structurationist "reading" of the old institutionalism; scholars in this tradition would probably not themselves talk in such "generative" terms, but we think that such an interpretation is not inconsistent with the basic thrust of their work. For a more explicit discussion of the constitutive role of the institution of the balance of power see Ashley (1984), and of the institution of diplomacy see Der Derian (1987).

8. Although neorealists generally do not say explicitly that such state individualism is their ontological position, and sometimes go out of their way to deny it (Waltz 1986), the silences in their work and the theoretic frameworks they do erect indicate clearly that this is their de facto position. See Ruggie (1983), Ashley (1984), Kratochwil and Ruggie (1986), and Wendt (1987) for interpretations of the neorealist ontology in these terms.

9. By the term "powers" we mean capacities for social action, or "competencies," rather than material "capabilities" in the neorealist sense. Similarly, by the term "interests" we refer to the objective and enduring needs of states, not the conscious, situation-specific, and more ephemeral "preferences" of microeconomic theory that are the "interests" to which neorealists refer.

10. Waltz (1979) initially defines "political structures" in terms of three elements: principles of differentiation, ordering principles, and distributions of capabilities. The first two elements do not discriminate among different international political structures, however, because he argues that states are not functionally differentiated and because the ordering principle of anarchy is common to all such structures. This leaves the distribution of capabilities as the defining element of international political structures. For a Durkheimian reconstruction of Waltz that shows in fact that all three elements are relevant to the study of international politics—and which is consistent with our arguments below—see Ruggie (1983).

11. This does not mean that neorealists have *no* theory of state interests, because an act of interpretation, of theory, is necessary to determine even "given" interests. But it does mean that neorealist theories of state interests are implicit theories.

12. Our criticism here should not be read as calling for neorealists to develop a theory of the historical emergence or global spread of the modern state. It is rather a criticism of the failure to theorize about the *continual* process of producing and reproducing state actors as interested and empowered subjects of international life. The analogue at the level of individual actors within society is that the methodological individualist should not be criticized for failing to theorize about the existence of the individual as a biological organism, but *can* be criticized for failing to theorize about the constitution of that organism as a social actor with certain interests and powers (such as the capability to act as a rational actor).

13. There is a growing awareness within the choice-theoretic tradition of the need to develop theories of preference formation (for example Elster 1984; Roemer 1986). The proposals that have been advanced for such theories, however, typically treat the problem of preference formation in either strictly endogenous terms (in which case the actors whose preferences are endogenously determined are themselves unproblematically *given* social atoms with fundamental identities as interest-guided actors in the first place), or in terms of learning new preferences from a given starting point—neither of which can ultimately capture the inherently social character of actors' preferences. In addition, to "endogenize" preferences is still not to take the step of theorizing about the more fundamental interests of state actors (see note 9 above). Finally, there is as yet no recognition within this tradition of the equally pressing need for theories of actors' social *powers*.

14. We include under the umbrella of "neorealism" scholars such as Robert Keohane who identify themselves as "modified" neorealists.

15. We place "institution" in quotes because in our view sovereignty is a "constitutive principle" rather than an "institution"; on the relationship between these two terms see the section on "The Nature of International Institutions."

16. The presence and implications of this persistent individualism are particularly evident in Lake's paper (1987a). Though he goes farther than the others toward recognizing

the principle of sovereignty as a "constitutive" principle of the states system, he then focuses almost exclusively on the question of how that principle was spread by the choices and practices of state actors, rather than on how that principle was socially "constitutive" of those actors. We do not deny the ontological dependence of sovereignty on the practices of state actors, but we would argue that that principle does in fact have a "constitutive" dimension about which a choice-theoretic approach is inherently unable to theorize (compare Wendt in progress, chapter 3).

17. This is probably least true of Krasner's work, which therefore poses problems for our simple classification of all neorealist research as fundamentally "choice-theoretic." As early as his important conclusion to the first major volume on regime theory (1983b) he had suggested that international regimes might act as "autonomous variables" between the distribution of power and state action—and therefore implicitly suggested that they could in some sense be "constitutive" of state interests. In his recent work (1988) he also adopts a more structural, less choice-theoretic, notion of "institution" than is characteristic of other neorealists. From our perspective, however, the constitutive side of his approach to international institutions is left largely unattended; indeed, what follows in this chapter might be seen partly as an extension of his recent work on sovereignty, although to other institutions as well.

18. Neorealists have adduced various hypotheses to account for the persistence of international institutions in the face of changes in the distribution of power or interests in the system (for example Keohane 1984). Given the unwillingness of neorealists to theorize about international institutions in a constitutive way, however, these hypotheses must ultimately be seen as ad hoc attempts to strengthen the overall approach in the face of inconsistent evidence, rather than as progressive modifications of the choice-theoretic research program.

19. This term is sometimes associated only with the work of Anthony Giddens, but we follow Nigel Thrift's (1983) more inclusive definition to include all social theories that recognize some form of "codetermined irreducibility" of agents and social structures. Used in this broader sense "structuration theory" goes back at least to Marx's claim that "[persons] make history but not under conditions of their own choosing."

20. The practices of agents include, but are not limited to, the calculated, strategically rational actions in which they engage. Agents may, for example, engage in practices purely out of habit (Rosenau 1986). The neorealists' focus on strategic interaction, then, does not include the full range of practices carried out by state actors of relevance to a structurationist viewpoint.

21. Internal relations are *necessary* relations between entities in the sense that the entities depend upon the relation for their existence and causal powers. Standard examples of internal relations are parent–child and master–slave; each entity in these relations presupposes the other.

22. For our own attempts to apply structurationist arguments to the task of substantive theorizing about the international system see Duvall and Wendt (1988) and Wendt (forthcoming).

23. In arguing for such an interdependence we are diverging from the usual treatment of the distinction between social and system integration as mutually exclusive alternatives; in our view all international institutions include both forms of integration.

24. In our view, international institutions and order must be analyzed in terms of the practices of other actors in addition to state actors, such as the agents of capitalist classes.

Here, however, we restrict our attention to state actors in order to facilitate a clearer comparison with neorealism.

25. Waltz (1979) calls these "principles of differentiation." It should be noted, however, that these principles need not differentiate actors *functionally,* as seems to be implied by Waltz's analysis. The differentiation may, for example, be one of spatial individuation, as is the case in the structure of the states system (see Ruggie 1983).

26. Note that this means that, in contrast to the suggestion of some neorealists, "sovereignty" is a constitutive principle of international institutions rather than an institution per se.

27. Waltz (1979) calls these "ordering principles."

28. It is here that Krasner seems to be focusing most of his attention in his recent work on the fundamental institution of sovereignty. His emphasis on the path dependence and punctuated equilibria of institutional development is, in effect, a focus on selection processes.

29. Such a relationship, however, does not seem to us to exist between the trade regime and the textile regime, for example, and we would not therefore say that there is any hierarchical ordering of these regimes beyond that recognized by the neorealist.

30. These actors may be the same actors as those constituted by more fundamental institutions; in this case we would say that those actors have a hierarchy of interests and powers, different levels of which may be inconsistent.

References

Ashley, Richard (1984). "The Poverty of Neorealism." *International Organization* 38, no. 2:225–86.

—— (forthcoming). "Social Will Formation and International Anarchy: Beyond the Domestic Analogy in the Study of Global Collaboration." In Hayward Alker and Richard Ashley, eds., *Anarchy, Power, and Community: Understanding International Collaboration.*

Axelrod, Robert (1981). "The Emergence of Cooperation among Egoists." *American Political Science Review* 75, no. 2:306–18.

—— (1984). *The Evolution of Cooperation.* New York: Basic Books.

Benhabib, Seyla, and Druscilla Cornell (1987). "Introduction: Beyond the Politics of Gender." In Seyla Benhabib and Druscilla Cornell, eds., *Feminism as Critique.* Minneapolis: University of Minnesota Press.

Benjamin, Roger, and Raymond Duvall (1985). "The Capitalist State in Context." In Roger Benjamin, ed., *The Democratic State.* Pp. 19–57. Lawrence: University Press of Kansas.

Bhaskar, Roy (1979). *The Possibility of Naturalism.* Brighton: Harvester.

—— (1987). *Scientific Realism and Human Emancipation.* London: Verso.

Bull, Hedley (1977). *The Anarchical Society.* New York: Columbia University Press.

Der Derian, James (1987). *On Diplomacy.* Oxford: Blackwell.

Duvall, Raymond, and Alexander Wendt (1988). "The International Capital Regime and the Internationalization of the State." Unpublished manuscript; originally presented in 1987 at the German-American Workshop on International Relations Theory, Bad Homburg, Federal Republic of Germany.

Elster, Jon (1984). *Ulysses and the Sirens.* Rev. ed. Cambridge: Cambridge University Press.

Fain, Haskell (1987). *Normative Politics and the Community of Nations.* Philadelphia: Temple University Press.

Frost, Mervyn (1986). *Towards a Normative Theory of International Relations.* Cambridge: Cambridge University Press.

Giddens, Anthony (1979). *Central Problems in Social Theory.* Berkeley: University of California Press.

—— (1984). *The Constitution of Society.* Cambridge, England: Polity Press.

Gilham, Steven (1981). "State, Law, and Modern Economic Exchange." In David Willer and Bo Anderson, eds., *Networks, Exchange, and Coercion.* Pp. 129–51. New York: Elsevier.

Jackson, Robert (1987). "Quasi-States, Dual Regimes, and Neoclassical Theory: International Jurisprudence and the Third World." *International Organization* 41, no. 4:519–50.

James, Alan (1978). "International Society." *British Journal of International Studies* 4:91–106.

—— (1986). *Sovereign Statehood.* London: Allen and Unwin.

Keal, Paul (1983). *Unspoken Rules and Superpower Dominance.* New York: St. Martin's.

Keohane, Robert (1984). *After Hegemony.* Princeton: Princeton University Press.

—— (1987). "Changes in Patterns of International Cooperation and the Valuation of Sovereignty." Paper presented at the German-American Workshop on International Relations Theory, Bad Homburg, Federal Republic of Germany.

Krasner, Stephen, ed. (1983a). *International Regimes.* Princeton: Princeton University Press.

—— (1983b). "Regimes and the Limits of Realism: Regimes as Autonomous Variables." In Stephen Krasner, ed., *International Regimes.* Pp. 355–68. Princeton: Princeton University Press.

—— (1983c). "Structural Causes and Regime Consequences: Regimes as Intervening Variables." In Stephen Krasner, ed., *International Regimes.* Pp. 1–22. Princeton: Princeton University Press.

—— (1988). "Sovereignty: An Institutional Perspective." *Comparative Political Studies* 21, no. 1:66–94.

Kratochwil, Friedrich, and John Ruggie (1986). "International Organization: A State of the Art on an Art of the State." *International Organization* 40, no. 4:753–76.

Lake, David (1987a). "The Expansion of Sovereignty: Imperialism, Decolonization, and the Constitutive Principle of International Relations." Paper presented at the 1987 annual meeting of the APSA, Chicago.

—— (1987b). "Power and the Third World: Toward a Realist Political Economy of North–South Relations." *International Studies Quarterly* 31, no. 2:217–34.

Lockwood, David (1964). "Social Integration and System Integration." In George Zollschan and Walter Hirsch, eds., *Explorations in Social Change.* Pp. 244–57. Boston: Houghton Mifflin.

Manicas, Peter (1980). "The Concept of Social Structure." *Journal for the Theory of Social Behavior* 10:65–82.

Manning, Charles (1962). *The Nature of International Society.* London: G. Bell.

Moos, A., and Michael Dear (1986). "Structuration Theory in Urban Analysis: 1. Theoretical Exegesis." *Environment and Planning A* 18:231–52.

Nardin, Terry (1983). *Law, Morality, and the Relations of States.* Princeton: Princeton University Press.

Northedge, F. (1975). *The International Political System.* London: Faber and Faber.

Oye, Kenneth (1985). "Explaining Cooperation under Anarchy: Hypotheses and Strategies." *World Politics* 38, no. 1:1–24.

——, ed. (1986). *Cooperation under Anarchy.* Princeton: Princeton University Press.

Roemer, John (1986). " 'Rational Choice' Marxism: Some Issues of Method and Substance." In John Roemer, ed., *Analytical Marxism*. Pp. 191–202. Cambridge: Cambridge University Press.

Rosenau, James (1986). "Before Cooperation: Hegemons, Regimes, and Habit-Driven Actors in World Politics." *International Organization* 40, no. 4:849–94.

Ruggie, John (1983). "Continuity and Transformation in the World Polity: Toward a Neorealist Synthesis." *World Politics* 35, no. 2:261–85.

Snidal, Duncan (1985a). "Coordination versus Prisoners' Dilemma: Implications for International Cooperation and Regimes." *American Political Science Review* 79, no. 4:923–42.

—— (1985b). "The Limits of Hegemonic Stability Theory." *International Organization* 39, no. 4:579–614.

Stein, Arthur (1983). "Coordination and Collaboration: Regimes in an Anarchic World." In Stephen Krasner, ed., *International Regimes*. Pp. 115–40. Princeton: Princeton University Press.

Suganami, Hidemi (1983). "The Structure of Institutionalism: An Anatomy of British Mainstream International Relations." *International Relations* 7, no. 5:2361–81.

Taylor, Michael (1976). *Anarchy and Cooperation*. London: Wiley.

Taylor, Paul (1968). "The Concept of Community and the European Integration Process." *Journal of Common Market Studies* 7, no. 2:83–101.

Thrift, Nigel (1983). "On the Determination of Social Action in Space and Time." *Society and Space* 1, no. 1:23–57.

Tonnies, Ferdinand (1887, 1940). *Fundamental Concepts of Sociology: Gemeinschaft and Gesellschaft*. New York: American Book Company.

Waltz, Kenneth (1979). *Theory of International Politics*. Reading, Mass.: Addison-Wesley.

—— (1986). "Reflection on *Theory of International Politics:* A Response to My Critics," in Robert O. Keohane, ed., *Neorealism and Its Critics*. Pp. 322–45. New York: Columbia University Press.

Wendt, Alexander (1987). "The Agent–Structure Problem in International Relations Theory." *International Organization* 41, no. 3:335–70.

—— (In progress). "The States System and the Structuring of Global Militarization." Ph.D. dissertation, University of Minnesota.

5

In Favor of Method, or How to Deal with International Interdependence

Wolf-Dieter Eberwein

This chapter focuses on the problem of theory building in international relations. The major argument is that we are too much preoccupied with the formulation and evaluation of substantive theoretical statements but too little with their dynamic implications. The dynamic properties of any theory are a function of direct and indirect influence relationships operating over time. These relationships are explicitly stated and implicitly contained in the formulations of the scholars of international relations. Yet how these relationships behave dynamically over time cannot be foreseen by the scholar. Even less so can the dynamics of real world relationships be assessed by the practitioners of international politics in the short term or in the long run.[1] For that purpose we need computer simulation. Simulation complements our tool kit for describing and explaining international processes. What these statements entail will be argued in greater detail below and complemented by a set of illustrative results from the simulation model GLOBUS, a global model.[2]

In Need of Better Theory and Method

Are we in need of better theory on international relations as Rosenau (1987) argues? The answer is definitely yes! But is it just better theory or even a new paradigm that we need, as stated by Rosenau in his paper presented to the workshop on international relations theory in Bad Homburg in 1987?[3] In this case my answer is no!

In his book *Against Method* Feyerabend (1975) argued that theoretical anarchism is more likely to encourage (scientific) progress than its law-and-order alternatives.[4] My argument is apparently the opposite of his because I will strongly argue *in favor of method*. As far as the substantive aspect of theories is concerned I am equally as much in favor of "theoretical anarchy" as Feyerabend is. But I strongly reject anarchy when it comes to assessing the dynamic implications of alternative theories.

When speaking of the substantive aspect, I limit myself to the phenomenon of international interdependence and its conceptualization at the macro level of analysis. I think that it is plausible to accept this phenomenon as a structural fait accompli, global in scale, that we still understand too little. What does understanding mean in that specific context? Understanding international interdependence means the scholar's ability to trace through time the (dynamics of the) behavior of the phenomena included in the representation, or conceptualization of, a specific segment of the international system. That behavior is a result of the feedback loops of first and higher order contained in the theoretical statements, or the set of hypotheses. Understanding the dynamics of a theoretical system is a problem of method.

I will address first the substantive aspect of theory building in international relations, and then discuss the methodological one. The proposition I will substantiate is that global modeling is one option at our disposal to evaluate both the substantive aspects of theorizing about the process of international interdependence as well as to analyze its dynamics.

The Substantive Aspect of Theory Building

Evaluating the components and relationships of a theoretical system is a problem of substance. When Rosenau (1987, 21) raises the two fundamental questions why the states have not done a better job in managing world affairs and why world politics seem so often to be out of control, he addresses the substantive issue of theory building.

His answer is that "profound changes are underway on a global scale and the capacity to analyze their consequences has lagged, posing a severe challenge to social scientists" (Rosenau 1987, 2). He calls for a new paradigm to analyze and explain four developments in global politics that account for these fundamental changes (Rosenau 1987, 3):

the coming into being of two interactive worlds, the multicentric actor system and the sovereign state system;

the diminishing utility of coercive force;

the two dilemmas the actors in global politics are confronted with, that is, autonomy versus security; and

the interplay between macro structures and process and micro-level shifts.

I do not have any major problems with these statements. I fundamentally agree with him that the stage of world politics is crowded with numerous actors that have—for whatever reasons—the ability to put their issues on the agenda of world politics (see Rosenau 1987, 33). I agree as well with his dictum that the sovereign nation-states have lost the ability to control the international environment because of the multicentric world in which "actions and reactions originate with a multiplicity of actors at diverse system levels" (Rosenau 1987, 6). Finally, I fully subscribe to the verdict that the concept of international interdependence may have concealed much more than revealed, given the way it has been used (see Rosenau 1987, 5).

And yet, this proposed conceptual expansion may lead to even greater problems in analyzing international interdependence than a nation-as-actor approach.[5] The latter approach does not a priori prevent us from analyzing the loss-of-control issue. I suspect that the loss of control of the national governments is the result of the inherent dynamics of the complex global structural setting in which they are embedded. But from a purely substantive point of view we do not know what the consequences of our theories are when it comes to assessing the loss-of-control issue.

Loss of control results from the dynamics of the structural context in which nations interact. One property of that context is that causes are simultaneously effects (Rosenau 1987, 9), the net result being a "vast interactive system of feedback [the chaos]."[6] That feedback structure cannot be understood meaningfully unless stated explicitly. Once that feedback structure is determined one can simulate it and observe the dynamic behavior it produces.

But that aspect of the substantive theorizing about international interdependence is methodological in nature. Before discussing that problem at some length I do want to draw some conclusions with respect to the substantive aspect of international interdependence first.

First, alternative conceptualizations of the international system exist. A new paradigm of international relations that gives up a state-centered perspective is possibly meaningful, depending on the problems one wants to analyze. But the argument is certainly wrong on logical grounds that a state-centered approach could not explain the loss of control of the nation-as-actor. Loss of control results from the dynamics of the complex structural setting in which the various nations act and interact with each other and with nongovernmental actors. The interaction between the national governments trying to influence, if not control, their environment and the structural setting consisting of a whole set of feedback loops through various policies cannot be inferred from the verbal formulations of any conceptual approach.

Second, national governments, or the states-as-actors, make almost by definition binding decisions for the nation they represent as a whole. Nonnational actors, in contrast, can only make binding decisions for themselves. That does not exclude the fact that decisions of both types of actors will affect some if not all of them. Thus, I would argue that a conceptual approach underestimating the nation-state as actor neglects the fundamental asymmetry existing between governmental and nongovernmental actors.

Third, we therefore have to better understand the processes that determine the degree to which national governmental actors try to influence and control their environment even if that attempt is in vain.

And fourth, it seems obvious that the complex structural setting referred to above is the product of the interdependence between economics and politics and the interdependence between domestic and international processes. That environment need not necessarily be conceptualized in terms of the variety of actors. It might be sufficient to take into account the effect resulting from the behavior of these actors.

It is misleading to assume that the basic substantive alternatives as I have sketched them above could be proven empirically. It is practically impossible to estimate a completely endogenous dynamic system. Standard econometric techniques have not been developed for that purpose.[7] Therefore the standard empirical research methods, as important as they are, will at best provide us with limited information about the feedback loop structure and its dynamic properties.

To fill in the gap in the arguments developed thus far, I will now turn to the methodological aspect of theory building.

The Methodological Aspect of Theory Building

If we have a theoretically determined system consisting of a number of variables, have specified the relationships among these variables, and have defined precisely the system boundaries, we have described its theoretical structure explicitly.[8] But we have only determined implicitly the dynamic potential of that structure. The verbal description will not allow us to draw any inferences with respect to that system's dynamic behavior even if we have stated explicitly the direction of the relationships included. These can be positive or negative.

The reason is that the parameter values will determine the actual behavior of that system. The quantification of the parameters is a precondition for determining the dynamic behavior of that specific system. The standard Richardson two-equation system, for example, explodes, oscillates, or converges to an equilibrium level, depending on the numerical values assigned to its parameters. Thus, dynamic behavior is not just a function of a system's structure but of the actual parameter values as well.

An additional problem arises, however. Intellectually, we are unable to describe the dynamic behavior of such a simple two-equation model over time. That system is already so complex that we either have to mathematically analyze it or use computer simulation. The mathematical analysis of nonlinear complex models including many variables, equations, and parameters is impossible. Therefore computer simulation is required to give us numerical solutions for specific parameter values. We cannot think in terms of a set of simultaneous relationships. Computer simulation allows us to analyze the effects of the build-in feedback structure that otherwise would remain concealed.

Substantive theorizing is the precondition for modeling complex systems. Whereas modeling will never be a substitute for theory, theory will never be a substitute for computer simulation when it comes to analyzing the dynamic implications of our theories. Thus:

1. In order to study the process of global interdependence the representation of the central components and relationships among them in a computer simulation model is necessary.

2. That is the case if we want to understand what global interdependence means in terms of the dynamics, and thus the consequences, for governments trying to control the environment in order to achieve their goals.

3. Once we have such a model we can study the variety of interaction effects determining the degree to which individual national policies do influence their environment. This puts us in a position to analyze how intended policies work out and what their short- and long-term effects are.

The last point just mentioned is crucial for determining the phenomenon described as "loss of control," which itself is a corollary of international interdependence. Only then could we possibly decide that we need an alternative theoretical model, or a new paradigm if one wishes to use that term. As long as this is not the case we are more or less groping in the dark. I do not imply with this argument that global modeling will finally lead to the Newtonian revolution in international relations. But I definitely believe that (global) modeling is a methodological approach we can no longer discard. It has to become a standard tool in the analysis of social processes.

Illustrating the Argument

Let me turn now to the illustration of the argument. For the analysis of the issue of international interdependence we do not just need any model. What we need is a specific type of model: so-called *global models*. At this point there is but one global model available that does allow the systemic study of the various facets of international interdependence: the GLOBUS model. A short overview of that model will be given, followed by a number of illustrative results.

GLOBUS—An Overview

GLOBUS stands for *G*enerating *L*ong-Term *O*ptions *B*y *U*sing *S*imulation. It is the most recent offspring of a whole family of computer simulation models known as global models. The focus of these models is future worldwide developments. These models, the first of which became famous under the name *Limits to Growth* (Meadows et al., 1972) almost two decades ago, opened a new field of research.[9] Among others these models represent aspects of the real world's complex structure and use simulation to analyze the dynamic behavior resulting from these complex structural properties.

GLOBUS was developed at the Social Science Research Center in Berlin in order to evaluate the interdependence between long-term developments in politics and economics, nationally and internationally, on a global scale. The full documentation of the model, including its theoretical assumptions and rationale, the specific equations, the parameter values, and the initial values, has been published (Bremer 1987b). A microcomputer version has been released.[10]

Global models always represent one segment of reality. What segment of reality does GLOBUS address? The major selection criteria determining the structure of the model are listed in figure 5–1 below. The long-term options referred to in the model's name relate to the evaluation of alternative policies with respect to economics and politics. The time horizon is forty years. The model is initialized with real-world data at the year 1970 and runs until the year 2010. Forty years seems fairly long, but not so long as to be irrelevant to the present generations. One of the reasons why the model has been initialized for the year 1970 is related to the purpose of evaluating the model's performance against real-world developments since then.[11]

Substantively, GLOBUS focuses on the interdependence between economics and politics at the national and international levels; it represents the national

Overview of Selection Criteria and Structure	
THE *GLOBUS* MODEL	
Purpose	Evaluation of Alternative Long-Term Policies with Respect to Global Economic and Political Problems
Time Span	1970-2010
Domain	25 nations
Focus	National and International Political and Economic Developments
Issues	◆ Economic Growth and Vulnerability ◆ Governability ◆ Political Stability and Unrest ◆ North-South Relations ◆ International Conflict ◆ East-West Relations
Structure	Modular, Continuous-Time Computer Simulation

Figure 5–1. The GLOBUS Model: Overview of Selection Criteria and Structure

economies and international trade (including arms, manufactured goods, food, raw material, services, and primary energy); it also represents the national political system with government support and opposition as two major dimensions. International politics is incorporated in terms of the balance of military power, (bilateral) international conflict interaction, and (bilateral) international cooperation.

At the heart of GLOBUS is the nation-state-as-actor. The basic assumption is that the sovereign nation-states represented by their respective governments are, and will continue to be, the dominant actors in national and international politics. The national governments are not considered to be omnipotent but decisive in shaping the future. These governments have a fairly detailed budget to manage (including taxation, investment, consumption, and military and social welfare expenditures), with which they determine the degree to which the levels of political stability and welfare will be maintained, raised, or lowered. They intervene in the national economy and international trade with specific policies such as exchange rates and trade partner preference. Politically, the governments try to maintain their power status by spending resources for defense, and engage in conflict and cooperative activities with other nations.

On the basis of these selection criteria, GLOBUS allows the user to address a multitude of relevant issues. Prominent themes are listed in figure 5–1. Research to date has dealt with a variety of questions, some of which are listed in the appendix. In each case major alternative policies were framed and the long-term and indirect consequences of each examined. The model is not considered to be a crystal ball capable of generating unconditional forecasts of what the future holds but rather a laboratory in which it is possible to carry out "what-if" investigations that would be impossible in the real world. A list of the questions which have been investigated thus far is given in the appendix.

How does GLOBUS compare with the real world? The world at present consists of more than 170 sovereign nation states; GLOBUS is limited to twenty-five nations. These nations are subsumed into four regional groups: the East, OPEC (the oil-exporting developing nations), the South (non-oil-exporting developing nations), and the West (figure 5–2).

This seemingly limited number of nations nevertheless is dominant in comparison to the rest of the world. Looking at figure 5–3, one can see that these few nations are in control of 85 percent of the world's arms buildup; that they are in command of 80 percent of the world's production and 68 percent of world trade; and that two-thirds of international conflict occurs among them. As the focus of GLOBUS is on long-term global developments in politics and economics, this subset of nations is so dominant that it permits the assessment of specific aspects of global developments.[12]

The relations between these twenty-five national actors and their national and international environments is shown in figure 5–4, which outlines the basic structure of the model. At the center we find the national government, which is embedded in four specific environments: domestic economic, domestic political, foreign economic, and foreign political. In each of the four fields surrounding the government

The Twenty-Five *GLOBUS* Nations	
EAST	**OPEC**
Czechoslovakia German Democratic Republic Poland Soviet Union	Indonesia Iran Nigeria Saudi Arabia Venezuela
WEST	**SOUTH**
Canada Federal Republic of Germany France Italy Japan United Kingdom United States	Argentina Brazil China Egypt India Mexico Pakistan South Africa Turkey

Figure 5-2. The Twenty-Five GLOBUS Nations

as an actor, we have listed illustrative policy instruments with which it influences specific developments in the respective environment. Tax and spending policies, for example, are means whereby the government attempts to influence, if not regulate, economic growth, employment, and prices of the national economy.

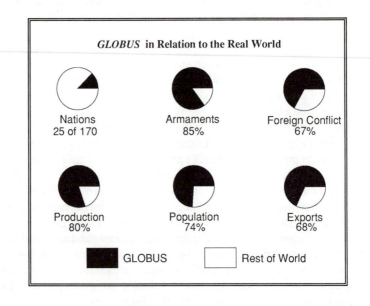

Figure 5-3. GLOBUS in Relation to the Real World

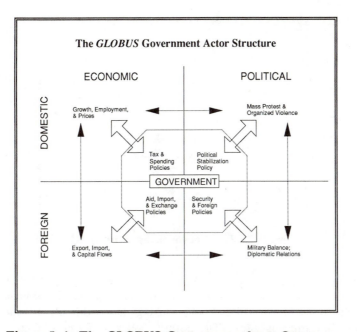

Figure 5–4. The GLOBUS Government Actor Structure

This illustration does not show two additional aspects. First, the twenty-five nations are linked directly and indirectly to one another. In the international political area each government in GLOBUS interacts with each of the others via conflict and cooperative behavior. Direct linkages exist as well in international economics. The twenty-five nations exchange six different types of goods with each other.[13] Finally, there are numerous indirect linkages between the four environments themselves and the governments, such as the effects of national security politics, the international economy, and the national economies.

How is the government as an actor conceptualized in GLOBUS? As in reality, the government acts towards, and reacts to, the different environments as a function of the conditions it perceives and considers necessary to be changed. The fundamental logic is represented graphically in figure 5–5. The GLOBUS government is not conceptualized as a rational actor but rather as an adaptive collective actor. This collective actor has goals it wants to accomplish. By observing the environment, the government assesses and evaluates the state of affairs against the goal(s). If there is a gap, decisions will be made in order to close that gap. These decisions will be implemented and action taken according to standard operating procedures.

One basic assumption of the GLOBUS model is that the ability of the individual nation to influence the environment satisfactorily is very low. Nations differ with respect to their selective perception of reality, their goals, their policies, and their efficiency in implementing policy. In addition, there are the processes taking place within the four environments themselves, which no government can control.

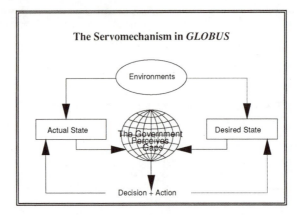

Figure 5-5. The Servomechanism in GLOBUS

Perceptions are related to the nation-specific priorities, and they vary as a function of the changes taking place in the environment and the policies implemented. Goals are adjusted as a function of the changes taking place within the relevant environment.[14] Governments also differ in their policy preferences, that is, deficit-spending policies vs. fiscal-restraint policies, the urgency they see for such policies, and the ability of the bureaucracy to implement such policies quickly and efficiently.

The logic underpinning what has just been explained is explicitly captured in the cybernetic model of behavior, which is represented graphically in figure 5-5 on the servomechanism in GLOBUS. Each government seeks a stable state of affairs, an equilibrium, defined as the situation in which the gap between the goals and the actual states is closed. As in reality, however, that gap can never be closed for good, and a stable equilibrium will never be obtained.

Too many actors and environmental factors try to reach their goals simultaneously. The net effect is that the outcome will always differ from the expectations about that outcome. The major concern is how large the fluctuations around an equilibrium level will be for specific nations or for the system at large, that is, a level where the gap between the goals and the actual state of affairs is negligible. Scenarios can reveal the conditions under which the system is likely to move away from the equilibrium and break down. My assumption is that this aspect determines the structural conditions that are at the root of the process characterized as "loss of control."

Illustrative Results

Having described in general terms the model structure, I want to give a few illustrations of what the concept of international interdependence implies. In the real world policies are implemented. What their effects are is usually debated in political terms.

A real assessment cannot be made because there is no reference base.[15] This is not only true in terms of the more or less immediate impact of specific policies, but even more so in terms of their longer-term consequences.

Computer simulation, in contrast, allows the testing of various policy options and to assess their relative impact, both in the short and long term. Such tests are scenarios in which specific policy options are described and then implemented. Scenarios are controlled experiments. Comparing the results of scenario runs and evaluating them against the base run of the model will reveal how much of a difference the assumptions implemented do make. They will also allow us to trace these effects over time.

The year of this writing, 1988, is the last year of Ronald Reagan's administration. When he took office a strong shift in policies occurred: for example, the fiscal policies at the national level seemed to have flourishing effects at first, but later turned more or less into a disastrous breakdown of the dollar. At the international level a number of developments took place that only a few foresaw at the time Reagan took office, among them the disarmament talks and the agreement on the double-zero option between the two superpowers.

Reagan's policy towards the Soviet Union resulted in a significant change of U.S. behavior in two respects: first, in an increase of the defense budget of about five to eight percent, and second, in a change in the foreign policy towards the Soviets, from less cooperation to more hostility. Of course, there were other changes as well. Yet these policy changes cannot be exactly simulated as precisely as the two aspects mentioned, defense expenditures and foreign policy behavior.

Dale Smith (1987a, 1987b) developed a scenario allowing him to analyze the effects of such a policy change. The scenario simulates a U.S. policy intended to improve the military balance of the United States in comparison to the Soviet Union by spending more for defense. It also assumes a tougher position of the United States towards its opponent, the Soviet Union.

Not one but two scenarios were implemented: the first postulates this policy change to begin 1981 and remain effective until 1988, when Reagan leaves office. The second postulates that the policy change will remain effective until the end of the simulation run, that is the year 2010. The difference is therefore the time frame of such a policy shift.

The change of the defense spending policy has been implemented in the budgetary submodel by increasing the bargaining power of the defense bureaucracy and therefore decreasing the leverage of the other bureaucracies in their "fight" for their share of the governmental expenditures. Such a strategy seems more meaningful than simply setting the defense expenditures level at a fixed rate. "The results of such parameter changes should produce shifts in spending patterns which are similar to what has been observed under the Reagan administration: increased defense spending, decreased civilian expenditures, and reduced control over the total level of spending" (Smith 1987b, 13).[16]

Simulating ideologically based foreign policy processes with computer models is not easy. In GLOBUS, that part of the scenario, the hard-line position of the United States towards the Soviet Union, can be implemented without too many difficulties, if one accepts the level of generality with which the foreign policy interactions are represented. Hostile interactions between nation-states as well as cooperative actions are included in the model too. The empirical foundation for both is provided by the data bank on conflict and cooperation between nations, COPDAB (*C*onflict and *P*eace *D*ata *B*ank), collected by Azar (Smith 1987a, 572–74).

Without going into a detailed description of this part of the model, the "hard line" policy of the United States towards the Soviet Union has been implemented by changing the base levels of desired cooperation and conflict sent by the United States to the Soviet Union. The focus on these base levels of the desired actions, which determines in part the actual interaction flows, takes into account the ideological character of this part of the policy shift. The respective parameter for hostile reactivity to the Soviet Union by the United States was increased by one standard deviation computed from the historical COPDAB data series. The desired cooperative base level was decreased by one standard deviation. In contrast to the defense expenditures side, no data were available for validating this part of the scenario for the first years of the Reagan presidency.

In order to investigate the effects of such policy changes implemented with the scenarios, we need a reference point. This reference point is the standard run of the model. That GLOBUS run is itself to be considered as a scenario, but the one that serves as the benchmark against which any changes resulting from specific scenarios are assessed. The reference run itself is worthy of a study. But that cannot be done here. Some information has been published in Bremer (1987b). In sum, we have three scenarios: the base run, the temporary scenario (1981–88), and the permanent scenario (1981–2010).

I will not give a detailed analysis of the scenario results. These are reported by Smith (1987a, 1987b) at great length. The point I want to make is what international interdependence can possibly mean. For that purpose, several figures are provided.

Figure 5–6 represents the East–West climate as measured by the ratio of conflict to cooperation. The U.S. policy shift obviously does not just affect the two superpowers but has also effects for their respective allies. The change in behavior results in a dramatic worsening of the international climate. Interesting to note is the fact that the temporary policy shift has long-term implications: The increased level of hostility relative to cooperation remains at a higher level in comparison to the base run. These results are as one would expect. The East–West climate, given in the temporary scenario, might be unexpected.

Defense expenditures (figure 5–7) do increase dramatically in the United States. But that policy does not continue forever. After the year 2000 a negative trend

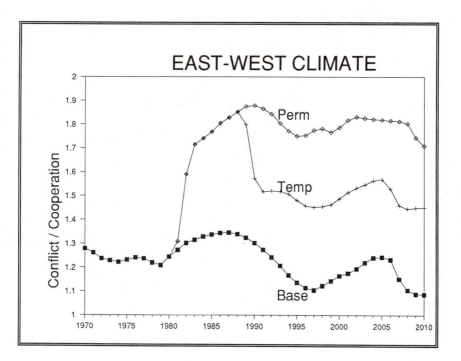

Base = base run; temp = temporary policy shift; and perm = permanent policy shift

Figure 5–6. The East–West Climate: Scenario Results (Hostility Relative to Cooperation)

takes place. In the temporary scenario the negative trend is systematic but the level of defense expenditures remains higher than in the base run. For the Soviet Union the effects are completely different in terms of the actual percentage changes resulting from the scenarios in comparison to the base run. The dynamic pattern over time, however, is basically comparable to that of the United States. In the Soviet Union the permanent scenario leads to increases, as expected, but a negative trend occurs beginning around the year 1995. The temporary scenario, in contrast, leads the defense expenditure levels to drop below the base-run level beginning in the year 2001. These results are not surprising and are fundamentally in tune with what one would expect.

The same cannot be said for the two German states. The Federal Republic of Germany (FRG) shows a pattern that indicates a "free rider" type of behavior with some differences between both scenarios. But most of the time defense expenditures in the FRG remain below the base level, which is true only for the

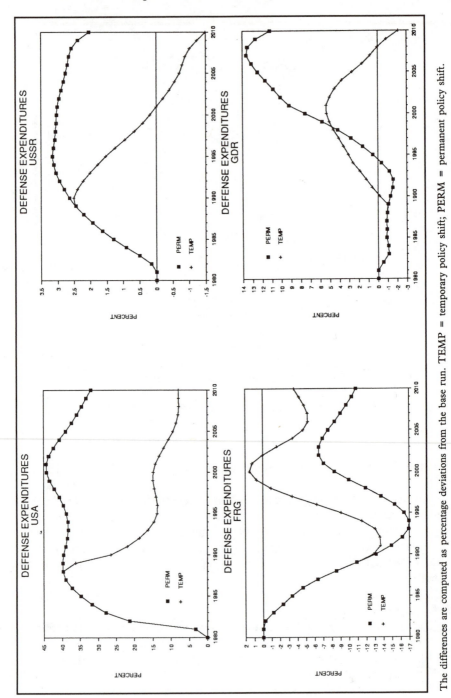

The differences are computed as percentage deviations from the base run. TEMP = temporary policy shift; PERM = permanent policy shift.

Figure 5-7. Defense Expenditures: Scenario Results

temporary scenario. A greater degree of compensation is found in the German Democratic Republic (GDR). Though almost parallel to the relative decline in defense expenditures in the Soviet Union (resulting from the permanent policy shift), this does trigger a relatively important boost in that expenditure category. In the temporary case a time delay of a decade or so occurs in the GDR before the defense expenditures follow the negative trend in the Soviet Union and also drop below the base-run level. In this case we find patterns over time not necessarily expected.

Intuitively one would expect civilian expenditures to decline as a result of the increased defense expenditures. But as figure 5–8 shows, this is not true as a general rule nor is a more or less unique pattern identifiable for all the four nations shown. In the United States the policy shift leads to a systematic negative trend in the expenditures for all other purposes than defense in both scenarios. That pattern is comparable to that found in the GDR. In the Soviet Union, in contrast, a negative trend is followed by a positive upward trend in both cases, but at different points in time. The reference run levels, however, are never reached again, with the temporary scenario run leading to slightly higher levels for just eight years.

The exception to that rule is the FRG, where the U.S. policy shift leads to higher levels of civilian expenditures with a considerable delay. In addition that process is systematic and leads to higher levels beginning in the year 2002 (temporary scenario) and 2007 (permanent scenario). These results are by no means intuitively plausible or to be expected. What they show, however, is that these four nations must be highly interdependent.

Turning to the economic growth, the patterns found are to some extent comparable with those for the civilian expenditures (figure 5–9). The differences are primarily found in the time path of gross domestic product resulting from the temporary scenario run.

The final and certainly most important question to answer is to what extent postulated U.S. policy has achieved the goal it has been designed for: an improvement of the balance of power of the United States towards the Soviet Union. Figure 5–10 shows that the United States does not fundamentally improve the balance of power.[17] The net result is deceiving. The permanent scenario only improves the situation temporarily, with the United States being probably even worse off by the year 2010. The temporary policy shift, in contrast, seems to pay moderately. But the price the United States and some others have to pay is certainly much higher than the gains.

This result, in conjunction with the others illustratively reported, does show that the goals a nation (in this case the United States) pursues unilaterally against the rest of the world, so to speak, cannot be achieved in a highly interdependent environment. It even seems that the price paid for such a policy shift is highest in the case of the United States. The results also show that others may profit from the policy pursued by another nation. This is definitely the case for the FRG.

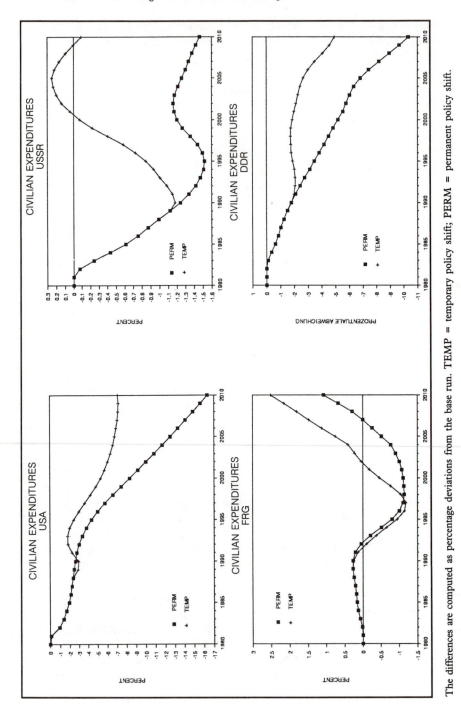

The differences are computed as percentage deviations from the base run. TEMP = temporary policy shift; PERM = permanent policy shift.

Figure 5–8. Civilian Expenditures: Scenario Results

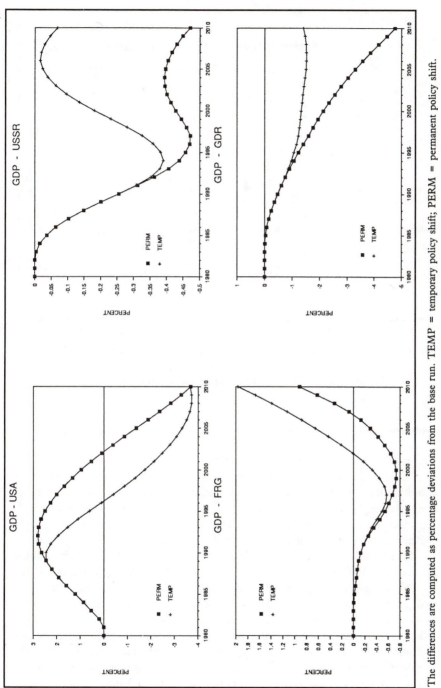

The differences are computed as percentage deviations from the base run. TEMP = temporary policy shift; PERM = permanent policy shift.

Figure 5-9. Gross Domestic Product: Scenario Results

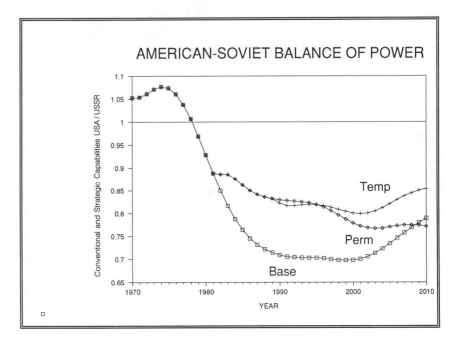

Base = base run; temp = temporary policy shift; and perm = permanent policy shift.

Figure 5-10. The Balance of Power: Scenario Results

Conclusions

The main thrust of the arguments developed are briefly summarized.

In order to understand what international interdependence means, there is no substitute for theory. There are different options for conceptualizing the international system. My own preference is to conceptualize the international system with the nation-state as the dominant actor. This does not exclude alternative concepts that take into account the nongovernmental actors and lower levels of aggregation.

Whichever conceptualization is chosen, none of the theoretical formulations allow us to draw inferences about the resulting international interdependence and the loss of control it might entail for the individual governmental actors. Interdependence results from the dynamic processes charcterizing the direct and indirect relationships specified in the theoretical statements and linking directly and indirectly the various nation-states composing the international system. Interdependence is considered as a property resulting from the specification of the relationships existing between the actors in the global environment on the one hand, and the dynamics these relationships entail on the other hand.

The dynamics of these relationships cannot be understood intellectually. Modeling these relationships and simulating them is the only way to analyze their implicit dynamics. For studying the phenomenon of international interdependence global models are in principle ideal instruments to use.

As the results reported for illustrative purposes have shown, a specific policy pursued by a specific national govenment does not, first of all, necessarily lead to the goal it was designed for. This illustrates what loss of control can imply in a dynamic structural framework of analysis. Secondly, the results have shown that a price has to be paid for such a unilateral course of action. Given the level of international interdependence, some nations have to pay a higher price than others. But the results also show that some nations profit more than others. But in sum, the results reported indicate that it is very unlikely that any nation is able to shield itself against the effects of policies others pursue.

Loss of control is inevitable given the level of international interdependence. Maybe greater cooperation among nations might compensate that effect. We cannot yet draw any general conclusions in substantive terms on the basis of the results presented. But they do certainly strongly support the position that I have outlined: To understand the fundamental process of structural changes in international politics, international interdependence, and the loss of control of the individual nation state, we need to analyze explicitly the dynamics implied in our theoretical statements. Using global models such as GLOBUS is therefore necessary.

Notes

1. It is a different question whether or not the practitioners of politics are really interested in the long-term consequences of political developments.

2. This model has been developed at the Science Center for Social Research in Berlin. It has been fully described in the book edited by S.A. Bremer (1987b). The Science Center, Berlin (today the Social Science Research Center, Berlin (Wissenschaftszentrum Berlin für Sozialforschung) was founded in 1969. That institution is funded by the government of the Federal Republic of Germany and by the Berlin Senate. The work on GLOBUS initially began under the directorship of Professor Karl W. Deutsch in the International Institute for Comparative Social Research. Since 1985 the work has been conducted by the GLOBUS Research Group under the leadership of Dr. Stuart A. Bremer. For a historical overview of the development of GLOBUS see Bremer (1985).

3. I rely on a number of the core arguments developed by Rosenau (1987). In fact, this paper greatly contributed to the clarification of my own ideas.

4. This is the reduced form of his argument in the introductory part of the analytical index, p. 10.

5. A multi level conceptualization of international politics, for example, is certainly required, but thus far I have not seen any approach that comes close to that methodological norm.

6. I do not understand why a vast interactive system of feedback loops is considered to be chaotic. The results may be chaos, true, but from the logical point of view the specification

of feedback loops is equivalent to the operational definition of the relationships of a theoretically defined system that will determine its dynamic behavior.

7. Donella Meadows (1980) has convincingly shown why econometric techniques cannot really capture a system's dynamic structure.

8. I am not concerned with the empirical validation at this point and will exclude it from consideration even though I consider this part of theory building as important.

9. A detailed overview of global modeling and the specific properties of that research can be found in Siegmann (1987), and Eberwein and Siegmann (1987).

10. For more information contact Bohniclo, edition Sigma, Grossbeerenstrasse 13a, D-1000 Berlin 61.

11. The Micro-GLOBUS version includes a subroutine that will allow users themselves to cross-check the output of the model for the first decade against data that the package provides on real-world developments.

12. This selection reflects one of the specific biases of the model, which takes only into account those few nations that seem to dominate the globe and that are assumed to play a decisive role in shaping the future of the world. The notion of bias is important. Every global model, and in particular, any scientific model or theory in general, cannot avoid it. The problem is to make that bias explicit and to justify it on normative and theoretical grounds.

13. In the international political sector there are 25*24 such dyadic linkages for international conflict, and 25*24 such dyadic linkages for international cooperation, which gives a total of 1,020 dyadic linkages. In the international economic sector, there are 26*25 such dyadic trade linkages for six different commodities, a total of 3,900 bilateral linkages in international economics. In this case the twenty-sixth actor is the residual category "Rest of the World."

14. This can be exemplified with respect to the unemployment targets of the western nations. These targets fluctuate as a function of the actual levels. No government would posit zero unemployment as its goal if the actual level is in the order of 8 percent or more.

15. Such a reference base could only be obtained by conducting experiments, which is impossible to do in the real world of politics.

16. Comparing the results from the scenario runs with the historical growth rates of the defense budget for the 1981–86 period, Smith found similar patterns between reality and the GLOBUS run. This provides a strong argument for the validity of the scenario.

17. A precise definition of capabilities is found in Cusack (1987). The capability index has been derived from indices on manpower and major weapon systems such as tanks, ships, and aircraft.

References

Brecke, Peter (1985). *Who Wins and Who Loses from Protectionism*. West Berlin: Wissenschaftszentrum Berlin, IIVG/dp 85-103.

Bremer, Stuart A. (1985). "The GLOBUS Model: History, Structure, and Illustrative Results." In Michael D. Ward, ed., *Theories, Models, and Simulations in International Relations*. Pp. 39–78. Boulder, Colo.: Westview.

—— (1987a). "Demographic Processes."In Stuart A. Bremer, ed., *The GLOBUS Model: Computer Simulation of Worldwide Political and Economic Developments*. Frankfurt a. M.: Campus; Boulder, Colo.: Westview.

Bremer, Stuart A., ed. (1987b). *The GLOBUS Model: Computer Simulation of Worldwide Political and Economic Developments*. Frankfurt a. M.: Campus; Boulder, Colo.: Westview.

Bremer, Stuart A., and Barry B. Hughes (1987). *Reducing East-West Tension and the North-South Gap*. West Berlin: Wissenschaftszentrum Berlin, FGG/87-3.

Cusack, Thomas R. (1984). *One Problem, Three Solutions: A Simulation Analysis of Alternative Western Defense Policy Options*. West Berlin: Wissenschaftszentrum Berlin, IIVG/dp 84-109.

―― (1987). "Government Budget Processes." In Stuart A. Bremer, ed., *The GLOBUS Model: Computer Simulation of Worldwide Political and Economic Developments*. Pp. 415-34. Frankfurt a. M.: Campus; Boulder, Colo.: Westview.

Cusack, Thomas R., and Barry B. Hughes (1986). "Using GLOBUS to Explore Alternative Taxation and Security Policies in the West." In Margaret P. Karns, ed., *Persistent Patterns and Emergent Structures in a Waning Century*. Pp. 237-72. New York: Praeger.

Eberwein, Wolf-Dieter (1987). "The Domestic Political Model." In Stuart A. Bremer, ed., *The GLOBUS Model: Computer Simulation of Worldwide Political and Economic Developments*. Pp. 176-200. Frankfurt a. M.: Campus; Boulder, Colo.: Westview.

Eberwein, Wolf-Dieter, and Wil Groenen (1988). "Domestic Political Stability: A Scenario Analysis." Paper prepared for presentation to the IPSA Round Table Conference on Global Modeling, Moscow, March.

Eberwein, Wolf-Dieter, and Heinrich Siegmann (1987). *Evaluating Long-term Developments by Using Global Models*. Paris: Studies and Documents, Bureau of Studies and Programming (BEP), UNESCO, BEP/GPI/4.

Feyerabend, Paul (1975). *Against Method*. London: Verso Ed.

Hughes, Barry (1987). "Domestic Economic Processes." In Stuart A. Bremer, ed., *The GLOBUS Model: Computer Simulation of Worldwide Political and Economic Developments*. Pp. 121-38. Frankfurt a. M.: Campus; Boulder, Colo.: Westview.

Meadows, Donella (1980). "The Unavoidable A Priori." In J. Randers, ed., *Elements of the System Dynamics Method*. Pp. 23-57. Cambridge: MIT Press.

Meadows, Donella, Dennis L. Meadows, Jørgen Randers, and William W. Behrens III (1972). *The Limits to Growth*. New York: Universe Books.

Pollins, Brian (1986). *Assessing the Political and Economic Effects of Protection against Third World Exports*. West Berlin: Wissenschaftszentrum Berlin, FGG/dp 86-1.

―― (1987). "International Power and Unequal Exchange." Informal papers. Columbus: Mershon Center, Ohio State University.

Pollins, Brian, and Peter Brecke (1987). "International Economic Processes." In Stuart A. Bremer, ed., *The GLOBUS Model: Computer Simulation of Worldwide Political and Economic Developments*. Pp. 515-33. Frankfurt a. M.: Campus; Boulder, Colo.: Westview.

Rosenau, James N. (1987). "Patterned Chaos in Global Life: Structure and Process in Two Worlds of World Politics." 2d draft. Mimeo, Institute for Transnational Studies, University of Southern California, Los Angeles, April.

Siegmann, Heinrich (1987). *World Modeling*. Paris: Studies and Documents, Bureau of Studies and Programming (BEP), UNESCO, BEP/GPI/2.

Smith, Dale L. (1987a). "International Political Processes." In Stuart A. Bremer, ed., *The GLOBUS Model: Computer Simulation of Worldwide Political and Economic Developments*. Pp. 639-65. Frankfurt a. M.: Campus; Boulder, Colo.: Westview.

―― (1987b). *Reagan in Machina. Model-based Analyses of Recent Changes in American National Security Policy*. West Berlin: Wissenschaftszentrum Berlin, FGG/dp 87-4.

Appendix 5A

Below is a list of the problems investigated thus far with GLOBUS. It shows the variety of issues that the model allows the user to address:

- What are the possible national and international long-term consequences of alternative Western defense postures (Cusack 1984)?
- Who is likely to gain and who is likely to lose from the imposition of protectionist measures by nations of the West (Brecke 1985)?
- How beneficial would it be for the West to adopt a policy of giving special preference to imports from the South (Pollins 1986)?
- What could be the impact of different long-range patterns of taxation and defense spending in major Western industrialized nations (Cusack and Hughes 1986)?
- What are the socioeconomic implications of alternative assumptions about long-term population growth (Bremer 1987a)?
- Under what conditions can foreign aid accelerate development in the Third World (Hughes 1987)?
- What might be the political effects of "fiscal responsibility" in Western nations (Eberwein 1987)?
- What might be the effects of a policy shift in the United States towards the Soviet Union for domestic political stability in Western Nations (Eberwein and Groenen 1988)?
- Would the granting of special trade concessions by nations of the West to nations of the South facilitate development, and who would bear the cost of these (Pollins and Brecke 1987)?
- How might efforts on the part of Western governments to balance their budgets affect the long-term growth of government in those nations (Cusack 1987)?
- What might be the implications of the adoption of a "hard-line" foreign policy by the United States towards the Soviet Union in the long run (Smith 1987b)?

- Can a combination of arms-reduction measures in the North and increased aid flows to the South reduce both East–West tension and the North–South gap (Bremer and Hughes 1987)?
- Does the global market economy operate in such a way that the terms of trade for developing nations almost inevitably decline over time (Pollins 1987)?

6

Reflections on Paradigmatic Complementarity in the Study of International Relations

Werner Link

When talking about different "worlds in world politics" (Rosenau 1987), the distinction between ontological and paradigmatic/methodological propositions should not be neglected. In the reality of "global life" we have only one world—not two. The intriguing theoretical question is whether the phenomena existing in the real world can be described, analyzed, and explained by using one paradigm or whether we need two or more paradigms. And if we need more than one, then it has to be asked whether one paradigm excludes the other(s) or whether mere *parallelism* or rather *complementarity* should be assumed. Taking into consideration the complexities of the real world, especially the complex interconnections between "state" and "society," the last alternative seems to be appropriate.[1]

Before elaborating this thesis, a short look at the competing paradigms is in order. They can be distinguished as follows:

(1) the paradigm of the decentralized anarchic system of states;
(2) the paradigm of the quasi-institutionalized society of states; and
(3) the paradigm of the transnational relations system.

As these three paradigms are well known in the community of political scientists, further descriptions are not necessary. In passing, I want only to mention that the concept of international regimes can be partially subsumed under paradigm 2, and that Rosenau's "multicentric world" is to a certain degree a variant of paradigm 3. Deutsch's concept (1966, 12) of linkage groups also belongs to this paradigm 3 because these social groups "with links to the domestic system and with some particular links to the international or foreign input" can be regarded as particularly suited to the creation of transnational relations and can serve as either consignee or interacting partner in the activities of foreign governments or foreign social groups. More important for the subsequent discussion is the observation that as to the main actors, the crucial difference is between paradigms 1 and 2 on the one hand and paradigm 3 on the other. That is, in paradigms 1 and 2 the states-as-actors assumption and in paradigm 3 the assumption that in addition to states, societal, nongovernmental groups or organizations carry on actions and transactions across national borders; such actors interact with their counterparts and other social groups in foreign countries and with governments at home and abroad; they perform specific functions (as, for instance the transmission of information, capital, and commodities) and contribute to the distribution of capabilities in the international system.

The usefulness of these assumptions has to be tested by empirical analyses. Is the transnational "world" (the "multicentric world," to use Rosenau's term) to be considered as an emergent new world order in international politics or, from the very beginning of the modern states system, are transnational relations complementary to inter-state relations? I shall try to give a tentative answer by putting the questions in a broader historical perspective (in the next section)[2] and by then reporting on the findings of two empirical studies.

Transnational Relations in Social-Historical Perspective

The External Aspect

Seen in a social-historical context, the phenomenon of relatively autonomous foreign relations conducted by social groups, which are linked in various ways to their home governments, is the result of European national and social development. During the course of this development, the medieval transterritoriality (which was related to another type of foreign affairs by social groups) was replaced by the novel form of transnationality. At that time, and under specific social-political conditions, the "state" (that is, the territorial nation-state) as a sovereign entity became the major actor in international politics; it broke up the *old* transterritorial pattern of relations and, because of its specific structure, enabled *new* transnational relations to emerge.

In its origins, the modern state is a "product of the decomposition of medieval ecumenicity" (Weber 1925, 15). It developed as a countermovement to the transterritorial universality that was represented by the Catholic church and the Holy Roman Empire and whose legal standardization resulted from Roman law (dispensed through the transnational legal schools of Bologna and Ravenna). The transition phase occupied a historical period of the two centuries roughly bounded by the Council of Constance (1414–18) and the Peace of Westphalia (1648) (Bozeman 1960).

The Council of Constance—although itself still a product of the old transterritoriality—introduced the transition period to the extent that it employed voting procedures organized according to nations, in imitation of the principles of national administration developed by the University of Paris (Bozeman 1960, 504; Maier 1954, 1 ff). In the struggle between the old and the new principles of organization (a conflict that characterized the decades to follow) there were various attempts made by the forces of universality to mount religious rearguard actions against national-territorial forces pressing their claims of sovereignty. Bellarmine's teachings on the *potestas indirecta*, for example, were intended to appropriately justify the all-encompassing authority of the Catholic church, both on religious and legal grounds, in terms of the new situation (Schmitt 1938). With the advent of the Reformation, however, the transterrritorial basis for a uniform religion was already vanishing; the Protestant sovereign, by way of designation, was simultaneously the *summus episcopus*. In retreat, transterritorial universality could still conduct a running fight. But after the long chaos of religious and civil wars, the Peace of Westphalia finally recognized a general principle of European organization based on the territorially determined sovereignty of nation-states; this represented an unmistakable demarcation of both imperial and papal universality (the Anti-Protest Clause) (Dickmann 1972; Mansbach et al. 1976, 7 ff).

This development corresponded to changes in the area of commercial relations; even there, transterritorial organizational structures had existed until they were dissolved by the sovereign nation-state and until that connection between sovereign state and national bourgeoisie arose that outlasted even the period of mercantilism. The most important example of commercial, pre-nation-state transterritoriality was the Hanse, which rose to prominence in the twelfth and thirteenth centuries, and which in the fourteenth century took on its most effective form as the Hanseatic League (whose predecessor, by way of designation, had been called the *universitas communium mercatorium*) (summarized in Bozeman 1960, 505 ff).

The Hanseatic League arose, as did the other Hanse groups, in response to a common interest of the merchants of the large trade towns of northern Europe. They wanted to defend themselves against piracy and areas of legal uncertainty, and they also sought a common representation of their claims in foreign countries. Free access to places of trade and legal protection were the main goals of the Hanse. It was originally a commercial association and not a political-military alliance; it had no territorial boundaries, but rather spread out over wide areas on both land and sea. Its identity grew out of the commercial foreign relations of its members. Even before the discovery of America or the finding of a sea route to India created new policies of trade, however, the Hanse had lost some of its importance. The rise of the sovereign nation-state led to the previously mentioned connection between powerful governments and an indigenous mercantile bourgeoisie (in the Netherlands, England, Denmark, and Russia), and as consequence the Hanseatic privileges were increasingly taken away. The new territorial nations provided *their* merchants with new privileges—a development typified by the British East India Company (1600). These new, nongovernmental, commercial foreign relations were rooted in the nation-state and connected to its interest.

The nation-state based on territoriality achieved its fullest development with the emergence and expansion of industrial capitalism. "The modern state and modern, North-Alpine capitalism are in fact correlative historical phenomena" (Weber 1925, 14). On an internal level (and with many variations in the respective

European countries), there arose the power structure that Schumpeter (1972, 221) has termed an "active symbiosis" between the feudal and the bourgeois layers; the feudal layer gives political support to the bourgeoisie and in turn receives from them economic support. And this internal symbiosis and division of labor had its counterpart in foreign activities.

Aside from occasional mercantilist reversions, the preferential structure of the civil state opened up to its industrial and commercial citizenry an extensive freedom of operations. This structure offered the further possibility—within the established framework of the state—that business could be actively and independently conducted in the following areas: economic exchange across national boundaries; the development of markets for raw materials and finished goods; and the expansion of industrial production. Nongovernmental social-economic actors could thus enter into commercial and productive activities in other countries; the economic results of these activities at least partially benefited their own country. In such a manner, they established a new form of transnationality, namely those relations that transcend national boundaries and are relatively independent of the national governments, but that in many other ways remain connected to the state. This combination still holds true for the modern transnational actors, the "multinational concerns" (although one must differentiate according to the various positions of home and host governments) (Fayerweather 1973; Wilkins 1974).

The new forms of transnational activities are as a rule not directed towards political control, but rather towards the acquisition and security of free access to foreign territory and towards the guarantee of free economic or ideological operations (Huntington 1973, 344; Moran 1973). Because of the fragmentation of the international system into sovereign nations, this security can be peacefully attained only through a free agreement, arrived at through political negotiations with and between these states. Such an agreement is constantly threatened by the anarchic conditions of international competition. The nations find themselves in a security dilemma. That is, the sovereign nations, which live alongside each other without being organized into a higher unity must, "as a result of their mutual distrust of the intentions of the others," always fear for their own security; they therefore "are driven to acquire more and more power in order to escape the impact of the power of others" (Herz 1974, 39 ff). Transnational activities take place under the conditions of such international constellations, and they simultaneously have their own shaping effect on those conditions.

The two tendencies, one towards a maximization of external national power, and the other towards economic expansion or, as the case may be, towards protection against economic intervention, have in the past come together in the well-known manner of producing imperialist wars and creating colonial empires. This took place as long as there were still territories that had not yet been completely organized into nation-states. In the period of classic imperialism, the economic expansion by nongovernmental actors was partially secured, and partially first made possible or first stimulated by, the governmental, colonial policy (itself by no means always motivated by economic reasons). In the postcolonial period, informal penetration has replaced direct conquest. Even in this form, the national government, on the one hand, can attempt to take advantage of the transnational activities of social groups for its own purposes; those social groups, on the other hand, may themselves exploit the governmental policy of penetration. Despite these possible combinations of governmental and social-economic expansion, such examples as the racist social imperialism of the Third Reich and the socialist imperialism of the Soviet Union demonstrate that the thesis about the economically (that is, capitalistically) determined basis for imperialism is not tenable. The fragmentation of the international system into competing and unequal nations may rather be the decisive structural factor (Cohen 1973).

To the extent that industrial-technological development in our century has enormously increased the foreign activities of social groups and thereby generated, at the level of a "transnational stock of useful knowledge," expanding global interlacings within the international community (Morse 1973, 46), and to the extent that the principles of national organization have simultaneously prevailed worldwide, the connection between governmental foreign relations and transnational relations has come to be a central political phenomenon.

The Internal Aspect

The fact that foreign activities by social groups (transnational relations) have relevant consequences for both the domestic and foreign policies of a country is a result, not only of the increasing structural contrast between global social interlacings and fragmentation into nation-states, but also of the *internal* relationship between the state (the government) and the society in highly industrialized countries. "Fundamental democratization" (Mannheim), which accompanied the integration of the working class into the nation-state, and the related expansion of national welfare policies, have qualitatively and quantitatively changed the relations between government and society. The government takes on the regulatory function in regard to the economy and the society. Social interests become politicized, because every social group must endeavor to translate its interests into rights protected by law and to gain in its own interest an influence on the regulatory means of the government. The classic civil state has in this way been transformed into an intervention state in which the rigid separation of government and society has been succeeded by a close interaction of the two (Fijalkowski 1958, 96 ff; Mannheim 1967, 1970).

These internal changes of structure are an essential precondition for transnational relations to become politically effective, something that Karl Kaiser (1969, 95) has already recognized and aptly formulated:

> Unless there is a minimum of vertical interaction, there can be no intensive horizontal communication leading to transnational policies. Stated more concretely, this means that as long as the government of a laissez faire state fails to appropriately

regard as part of its field of interest the changes or disturbances created within its own society by the transnational society, then no transnational policies can develop in this area. . . . The likelihood that a nation-state system will participate in forms of transnational policies becomes greater—assuming that there is a transnational society—according to how strongly marked the interventionist functions are of the governmental institutions.

To carry this thought further, one could ask to what extent the forms of social organization have changed along with the intensification of relations between government and society. The national government does not "communicate" with "the society," but it communicates with large social associations that have grown up in various areas out of the process of industrialization and mass mobilization. Fundamental democratization and the emergence of large, oligarchic social organizations are two sides to the same coin. The large social associations standardize the various separate social interests within the different social subareas. In the interactions between the social groups, as well as in their relations to the government, these associations are important actors (as shown by the "concerted Action" and by the advisory boards in the Federal Republic of Germany and the advisory committees in the United States) (in general, Galbraith 1967; Shonfield 1968; Behrman 1971; Foreign Affairs Division 1975).

In contrast to the state monopoly of socialist countries, the *relative* autonomy of social groups is thus not infringed on. The intensive cooperation between government and large social organizations (employers' association, trade unions, and so on) rather depends on the condition that the social groups remain autonomous and can operate relatively independently on the intra- and transnational level.

The empirical data support the hypothesis of social theory that, despite the shift from a liberal society based on competition to an organized mass society (Mannheim 1967), the economic area of production and trade can still be distinguished from the political-administrative area. The mechanism of the market is certainly not the sole determining regulatory element any longer. But although the development towards economic oligopolies and the diverse political mechanisms of intervention have changed the relationship between the economic and the political-administrative areas, this has not resulted in an amalgamation of the two. As before, there exists the "separation of the political and economic headquarters" (Heller 1934, 137); economic power does not completely coincide with political power; social-economic elites are not identical to national-political ones. Economic elites attempt to stimulate national-political activities to the benefit of their own economic ends, just as national-political elites attempt to employ economic interactions for their own political-economy and/or noneconomic ends. In fact, even independently from the respective intentions, equivalent results can be seen (see, among others, Rose 1967).

Just as the relative independence of the social sphere led to relative freedom of operations for the social groups or their respective elites, so did, on the other hand, the convergence of government and society (a convergence that came about through the circumstances discussed) become the material basis for the close relations between national-political groups and social groups or their respective operational elites (including even the exchanges of personnel that often take place between the two groups) (Mann and Doig 1965; Kolko 1971).[3] In this sense, "pluralism of elites" (Baratz 1956), brought about by the competition of large political and social-economic associations, is based on both intra- *and* transnational structures. Autonomy *and* interdependence are constituent aspects of the position held by social groups or their directing elites respectively in relation to the national-political actors.

Thus, the internal (domestic) structure is reflected and reproduced in the international system; that is, states (governments) and societal groups—and the interactions between them—form the structures of the international system. Bear in mind that the autonomy of states (called "sovereignty") as well as the autonomy of social groups or organizations is only a *relative* one. It is limited by structural interdependences that interactions generate, internally and externally. The autonomy of states ("sovereignty") is limited by other states; by foreign-based societal groups (insofar as they have external impact); and by societal groups in their own domestic realm. Similarly, the autonomy of social groups or organizations is limited by the home government; by foreign governments; and by other social groups, domestic and foreign. But there is a crucial difference between both with respect to the ordering principle: The ordering principle between modern states (as well as between societal groups) was and is still "coordination." Between states and governments and foreign-based societal groups it is "coordination" *and* "superordination/subordination." That is to say, understandings and contracts between societal actors based in country A and the government of country B are concluded through free negotiations and, eventually, free agreements. Both sides have to find a consensus on specific arrangements, actions, and transactions. Thus far the ordering principle is "coordination." But the subsequent operations *within* the host country are in principle subordinated to the legal order of that country and to its political decisions ("the authoritative allocation of values") (Easton 1965). To which degree these ordering principles can materialize depends primarily upon the power relations, which differ according to issue areas, context, and power structures.

Under the conditions of the intervention state the subordinating tendency increases rather than diminishes. This also holds true with respect to the multinational firms. They have not yet developed a real "transnational" organization, as Peter Drucker (1987) has recently stated. Therefore, the home government can control the internal and external activities of the multinational firms via its jurisdiction over the multinational's national headquarters and the host government can do this via its jurisdiction over the multinational's affiliate. Even James Rosenau (1987) conceded that because the actors of his "multicentric world" have their headquarters within the jurisdictions of states, "virtually all of them have to conduct their affairs in conjunction with, if not accommodative to, the activities of states."

The Findings of Empirical Case Studies

In the end, the assumptions about the relationship between inter-states and transnational politics and the thesis of the complementarity of both paradigms have to be tested by detailed empirical research—which until now has been rather meager, thus allowing only tentative conclusions.

The pioneering studies of Keohane and Nye brought to the fore that one must differentiate between international effects according to the structure of the overall context of relations, especially according to symmetrical and asymmetrical relations. This thesis was confirmed by a detailed examination of the role of transnational actors in the relations between the U.S. and Canada, the results of which were published in 1974 (Nye 1974). Studies that point in the same direction have been carried out by Dowty (1971) on the creation of close supporting connections between a foreign government and an internal political faction of another country. According to Dowty's work, the strategic situation in the relationship between the countries in question is *one* of the important dimensions to the conditions for such connections ("foreign-linked factionalism"). A further dimension beyond that is the internal structure of the particular society made up of its various factions. Deutsch has pointed to similar connections using his concept of the linkage group (see the beginning of this chapter). He hypothesized that the effects of the foreign-policy linkage groups depend on their internal organization, on the internal positions of power held by the respective actors (governmental as well as social), and on the international context.

State and Societal Actors in German-American
Relations, 1920–33

As an extension of these considerations, I have analyzed the relevance of societal actors within the framework of a comprehensive empirical study of German-American relations in the 1920s. That is, I have investigated the relations between the United States and the Weimar Republic in the context of the international system of the twenties and the contributions that businessmen made to the development of these relations. The results of this study have partly confirmed and partly modified the previously stated theses about the effects of transnational relations (under the conditions of asymmetry and the internal structural similarities of the interacting societies) (Link 1970, esp. 556 ff).

Those businessmen concerned with the export of goods and capital transmitted as intermediaries (alongside of, and often to a more intensive degree than, the diplomatic agencies) the respective foreign influence between the United States and Germany—in fact in both directions. They were important transmitters of information about foreign economic and political development, and they created independent information channels between the two societies. Related to that was the transmission of goods, capital, and technology, by which Germany was materially integrated into the community of western nations.

Contrary to the hypotheses of Karl W. Deutsch, the German and U.S. linkage groups were, for all of that, not increasingly susceptible to foreign influence as their ties to their respective domestic systems became weaker. There was the case of an intimate liaison in both countries between the foreign-policy linkage groups of industry and banking representatives and the internal, policy-making system. The constitutive characteristic was, however, that the linkage groups, in comparison to the governmental actors of Germany or the United States, were capable of a greater sensitivity, receptivity, and responsiveness towards foreign influence; and they created an area of unofficial transnational interactions that were not subject to direct parliamentary controls. It was precisely their intensive participation in domestic operations that was an important precondition for the ability of the U.S. and German linkage groups to quickly augment reciprocal responsiveness, to feed foreign information and influences into the communications and operations systems domestically and in the foreign country, and to speed up the feedback process.

The information from Germany was gathered by the representatives of the U.S. linkage group in Germany, or it was transmitted through the German linkage group into the U.S. political system. The orientation of members of the U.S. linkage groups towards the German and European markets had the effect that they could react to disturbances more quickly and intensively than the overall economy or society. They initiated U.S. stabilization measures for Germany and Europe and actively participated in the implementation of these measures. They took over those monitoring and advisory functions related to U.S. involvement in Germany and were for a time directly involved in the German decision-making process. The U.S. government could in this way afford to stay aloof and follow more flexible policies. From the German point of view, this form of transnational penetration was more acceptable than interference by U.S. governmental officials.

The U.S. and German businessmen who were interested in mutual economic relations on a cooperative basis moved closer together through the formation of a community of interests by mutual investments of capital and by the exchange of shares; they formed partial transnational coalitions that had an associative effect and that were correspondingly used by the governments. In other branches, meanwhile, representatives of the foreign-oriented groups in question directly clashed as competitors. The German government, against the internal opposition of directly concerned interests, pushed for a harmonization of the conflicts between the competitors and promoted the tendencies towards cooperation; the strategy for such a position was that the economical asymmetrical dependence existing in favor of the United States could be politically exploited in favor of Germany. The German political and export-economy leadership recognized that the seemingly one-sided commitment to the United States in reality represented a reciprocal commitment, and they anticipated that this German-American intersocietal interdependence, in crucial issue areas, would have favorable consequences for Germany at the level of global politics.

The transnational relations established a basis for the associative policies and politics of the German and U.S. governments, just as on the other hand the German-American policies administered by the governments promoted the associative consequences of transnational relations. As a whole, the economic ties transmitted by social groups between the United States and Germany (similar to the social-cultural transnational relations) worked in the direction of a close, friendly relationship between governments and societies; increasingly broader layers in the societies, for both material and nonmaterial reasons, had an interest in this relationship, through which a reciprocal understanding arose that further stimulated the attempts at harmonization by the governmental and social actors. It was not until the political transformation of Germany into a national-socialist dictatorship that any of the essential and fundamental conditions for this structure changed—namely the similarities between the internal structures of both countries. And with that transformation, there also came a change in the possibilities for transnational operations between the two social groups.

This outline of the empirical results of this study demonstrates (just as did the previously reported hypotheses) that in analyzing the effect of transnational relations, it is necessary to identify the respective social actors—differentiated according to the various types of actors—within their structural context. The question as to what *effects* transnational relations could have *within* societies or countries and in the context of relations *between* societies or countries likewise raises the questions as to what *functions* the social actors exercise, through their transnational relations, in the respective domestic or international context of operations (the structural context) and how they in this way help shape this context. The result of the discussion thus far further suggests that the hypothesis of the Mertonian theory is empirically substantiated, namely that "structure affects function and function affects structure (Merton 1968). This means that the functions exercised by the social actors in their transnational activities contribute to the formation of domestic and international/intersocietal structures, just as these structures make possible, impede, or prevent the exercise of certain functions.

State and Societal Actors in German-American Relations, 1945–75

The second study to which I want to refer is an empirical analysis of German-American trade-union and business relations after World War II (Link 1978)—again (as in the first study) in the systemic context. This study also has revealed a variety of transnational activities and contexts of effects. Trade unions and businessmen (or groupings and organizations of businessmen), as societal, nongovernmental actors, have established direct relations with their particular societal counterparts and to the particular governments in West Germany or the United States; they have autonomously transmitted information, ideas, goods, and capital, thus putting together a tightly woven net of relations as well as partially institutionalizing the transnational contacts. In this process, they have diversely helped to shape the inner-societal as well as the intersocietal or inter-state relations. Without these transnational activities, internal development and the development of German-American relations as a whole would have proceeded differently and would have been structured in a fundamentally different fashion.

The relations between U.S. and German societal groups, in connection with the previous close transnational relations of the 1920s and 1930s, were developed and then intensified after World War II and *before* the creation of the Federal Republic of Germany as a state or the establishment of its diplomatic representation. To that extent, we are dealing with a special case in which the influence of various environmental constellations during a period of time can be especially well identified. At the same time, the basic pattern of transnational relations between the United States and European countries during the postwar period (a pattern often obscured by the pattern of sovereignty) came clearly into focus in this special case. That means that during the phase of U.S. hegemony, transnational relations between the United States and West Germany were an especially pronounced expression of a pattern of relations also existing between the United States and other Western European countries.

These circumstances have already been surmised by astute contemporaries such as Jean-Jacques Servan-Schreiber (1950a, 1950b), and have been confirmed by the present research results in comparison with other historical/political-science studies. Relations between German-American trade unions and business groups exhibit as a consistent characteristic the feature that, within a government-established framework, societal groups with a corresponding external orientation and a basis of resources are the main carriers in an exchange of persons, information, ideas, goods, and capital that transcends national boundaries; that these groups function as foreign-policy linkage groups through such transmissions; and that their views and conceptions are in turn taken into consideration by the governments in the establishment of frameworks. Conditions and effects, structures and functions are related (as was hypothesized above in the theoretical inferences).

The *conditions* for the realization and development of transnational German-American relations, and for the exercise of the transmission and linkage functions described, were, and still are, found in the internal structure of the particular society on the one hand, and in the external structure on the other. When these structures, not in the least because of the activities of German and U.S. societal groups, changed over time, the conditions also changed within which transnational activities unfolded.

One basic internal condition hypothesized in the section on theory was consistently met and remained relatively constant, namely, the autonomy on principle of the two societal groups, an autonomy anchored in the two systems. The internal structures were and are homologous insofar as the trade unions and businessmen of one socio-political system have in each case a corresponding counterpart, an analogous discussion and interaction partner, in the other system. In other words, the

United States and the Federal Republic have a preferential structure excluding a state monopoly on external information and activity and opening up to societal actors a broad area in which to act.

So that the built-in structural opportunity of developing transnational relations is actually exploited by societal actors, however, special conditions—as the analysis has shown in detail—must be added to the general condition. Externally oriented U.S. businessmen were interested in the stabilization of the international economic system through West German reintegration as well as in commercial- and investment-oriented activities in West Germany; in the first decade after the war, this interest corresponded to an equivalent one held by all relevant West German groups, an interest then intensified during the reconstruction and consolidation phase by the demand for U.S. capital. Among U.S. and German trade unions, the interest of both sides in reintegration came together with the West German unions' need for external support from the U.S. unions for their internal rebuilding and power struggles. Shortage of capital and need for assistance were the preconditions in West Germany for the fact that, in the orientation towards the views and conceptions of U.S. business and labor, those measures were adopted that allowed the transmission of ideas, goods, and capital to West Germany. Political and societal directions most closely approximating U.S. business and labor views were thus supported by the transnational activities of U.S. societal groups. Transnational coalitions thereby emerged that in part reproduced the inner-societal factional structure at the level of transnational relations.

During the reconstruction and consolidation phase, the external (that is, international) structural conditions were meaningful insofar as West Germany's geographical and political situation in the Cold War convinced both sides that support by U.S. societal groups was absolutely necessary to achieve a socio-economic stabilization in West Germany (without which a military stabilization would have been ineffective), and to establish and develop societal interconnections as a foundation for political cooperation. An increasing internal consolidation took place in the late 1950s and even more so in the 1960s; and on the basis of transnational transactions, asymmetries in the bilateral relationship were broken down and initial approaches to lessening the tension in the international system were gradually adopted. Because of these changing circumstances, transnational relations between the Federal Republic and the United States were no longer determined by internal scarcities or (except for the military dimension) by need for assistance, but rather by a new set of conditions. This was seen above all in interconnections established in the meantime, by common interests growing out of those interconnections, and by the need to harmonize interests and competition. Symmetries in the bilateral relations and a letup in the common perception of communism as a threat fundamentally changed the conditions for transnational relations, as German-American trade-union relations have most clearly shown.

The exercise of the transmission and mediation functions by trade unions and business groups had certain *effects* on internal development in West Germany and (to a lesser degree because of long-term asymmetries) in the United States on the one hand, and on the development of German-American relations on the other. These effects varied according to the nature of the issues and the issues areas. The direct interactions of the two societal groups created specific transnational contexts of issues primarily located in the socio-economic sector, but which indirectly, and in a mediated fashion, also extended into the political sector. These contexts arose in part out of originally inner-societal constellations of issues (such as the questions of socialization and codetermination) and in part out of originally international issue situations (such as reorganization of the international economic and political system after World War II or development of the relationship between the United States and the EEC).

Without going in further details, it should be mentioned that even in the sector of security policy, traditionally assigned exclusively to the level of intergovernmental activity, transnational politics had an impact. For instance, *rearmament* (and later the disengagement policy and *Ostpolitik*) became a transnational issue in the 1950s because full integration of the Federal Republic into the western defense alliance was regarded by U.S. businessmen as a precondition for the security of direct investments, and because the U.S. trade unions, on the basis of the principles of militant democracy, felt that a corresponding policy was required. German-American business activities subsequently concentrated on integrating the West German economy into the U.S. arms program. U.S. trade unions had already at an early stage (namely, in the fall of 1945) cautiously raised the question of German rearmament; after 1950, in open and internal discussions, they supported those Deutscher Gewerkschaftsbund (DGB; Federation of German Trade Unions) groupings assuming a positive attitude towards this question—to the point of attempting in 1955 to form a Grand Coalition (a plan developed by the AFL and taken up by DGB Chairman Christian Fette). Through this support, the intergovernmental policy of rearmament and defense received a transnational basis.

Seen as a whole, transnational cooperation between U.S. and West German businessmen (or their organizations) has shown itself to be more stable than cooperation between West German and U.S. trade unions. In a similar manner, the regulation of conflicts and competition, in accommodating new internal and external conditions, succeeded better on the whole with the businessmen than with the trade unions; the associative or dissociative effects of transnational activities also assume correspondingly different shapes for the respective relations of the groups. With reference to the overall development of relations between the United States and the Federal Republic, the associative effects of intersocietal contacts carried the most weight. At the intergovernmental level they generated only a slight potential for conflict. The relatively successful regulation of competition, dealt with in an autonomous and transnational manner between West German and U.S. business, unburdened the governmental actors. The governments could use the associative effects of transnational relations for the friendly organization of official relations. For security-policy reasons, the two governments were also interested in an associative policy independent of the development of transnational relations; it is to that extent difficult to determine the relative weight of the intersocietal interactions. Nevertheless, de Gaulle's attempt to pursue with the West German government a policy directed against the United States shows that the close German-American business and labor relations placed narrow limits on such a dissociative policy. In other words, this miscarried attempt still demonstrates that associative transnational policies between the Federal Republic and the United States have the power to impede, if not to prevent, a dissociative governmental policy. In this sense, transnational relations between West German and U.S. societal groups have postulated and established the direction of official intergovernmental relations (and conversely, transnational relations have been promoted by intergovernmental relations).

In contrast to the relationship between the United States and Canada, in which rapidly expanding transnational relations under asymmetrical conditions have promoted Canadian nationalism and have not produced associative effects, in German-American relations the societal connections have done much more to strengthen the alliance. That may primarily depend on the fact that the importance of the political-military alliance still ranks very high, even under changed world-policy conditions, because of the exposed position of the Federal Republic and Berlin; and that the alliance in West Germany (in contrast to Canada) was therefore not subjected to any aggravating erosion. In other words, West Germany's strategic situation was and is favorable for a transnational relation of an associative nature. As our analysis has shown, however, this is only one aspect (although a very important one). Transnational interconnections in the socio-economic area between the United States and the Federal Republic are created by a more far-reaching interconnection of interests, one that was effective in the past and that, with the increasing importance of economic questions, is perceived by the actors themselves as highly significant in the present. Out of transnational relations of the past come the common interests of the United States and the Federal Republic in the reorganization of the world economic and monetary system. Even aside from and in addition to military-policy interdependencies, transnational relations point the way for the coordinated, associative policy presently followed by the West German and U.S. governments.

The empirical findings prove that societal and governmental actors do *not* occupy the same level of importance. The qualitative difference lies in the basic fact that only governmental actors are in a position to make binding decisions for all citizens. Connections and decisions made at the intersocietal level, however, do carry weight in the process of arriving at and implementing policy decisions, especially when political decisions can only be realized through the voluntary activity of the societal groups in question (which holds true within and between countries with a pluralistic liberal-democratic order, at least in the economic area). In this sense, German-American intersocietal relations have contributed to shaping the development of overall relations. The case study has shown that transnational relations condition international relations (but do not definitely determine them). The importance of transnational interactions for overall relations between two states thus tends to resemble that of inner-societal relations for a state's overall policy when (as in the case of German-American labor or business) "transnational coalitions" are formed in regard to individual problems.

And finally, transnational relations between the United States and West Germany show that, even under asymmetrical conditions, an associative policy can promote an international peace order to the extent such a policy is affirmed by the relevant societal groups. West German and U.S. union members and businessmen together with their governments pursued the reintegration of the democratic part of Germany into the democratic community of nations and into the capitalist world market under extremely asymmetrical conditions. The associative-reintegrative policy has not consolidated or deepened those asymmetries to West Germany's disadvantage, however, but has rather removed them step by step and has tended to promote the development of symmetries in areas where the asymmetries were not of a geopolitical or military-policy nature. Transnational relations between West German and U.S. societal groups with correspondingly interconnecting and interdependent effects created a potential that the governments could, and in the past consequently did, use in an associative way. Whether or not this potential will serve in present and future political tensions (which may be greater than in the past) as the foundation for friendly relations, as "accident insurance," or to limit damaging effects, is an open question.

Concluding Remarks

To be sure, these empirical studies have not explicitly been done on the systemic level. They concentrated upon the analysis of dyadic relations. However, the dyadics were put into the systemic contexts; the positioning of both states in the international system was a central analytical aspect. In other words, the dyadic interactions were dealt with not in isolation from, but as parts of the system.

Therefore, notwithstanding all caveats due to the mentioned restrictions, some systemic conclusions seem to be in order. Empirical research has confirmed the fruitfulness of using the transnational paradigm complementarily to the states-as-actors paradigm. That is, the transnational paradigm is not substituting the paradigm of the decentralized system of states but it is to be used in a complementary way. Consequently, the realist concept of international system (with the components of structure and interacting units) should be modified.

As to the three criteria of structure (see Waltz 1979, 88 ff) the following assumptions seem to be pertinent:

1. The predominant *ordering principle* of the international system is coordination. This is clearly so with respect to the positional relationship between states. As to such societal groups that enjoy relative autonomy in the respective states

and conduct transnational activities, there is a mixture of coordination and subordination. They are positioned vis-à-vis foreign states and their counterparts in foreign countries according to the principle of coordination. However, *within* the respective states societal actors from foreign countries do *not* enjoy extraterritorial rights (as diplomats do); that is, operating *in* host countries, they are subordinated to the state authorities of these host countries. The degree to which both principles materialize depends on the correlation of powers.

2. *Units* of the international system are states and, additionally, such societal actors who relatively autonomously conduct transnational activities. It can be assumed that both actors, states, and societal groups, seek to preserve their relative autonomy/sovereignty (that is, self-preservation and self-development). But as to systemic functions, differences prevail. By their transnational activities societal groups perform specific functions (foremost the transmission of informations, capital, goods, and so on) and they have associative or dissociative effects on the grouping of states. Exerting these functions, they contribute to task/function performance of states as well as to arrangements between states.[4]

3. The *distribution of capabilities* between states in the international system is codetermined by power and transactions that societal actors represent and conduct. This is especially so in the economic area.[5] Thereby, societal groups contribute to the formations and configurations of the international system.

In sum, as in internal/domestic systems, differential units can be discerned and should be assumed in the international system, too. There are two different types of actors exerting different functions. It is by the interactions between states; between societal groups of different countries; and between societal groups and foreign states or governments that international structures are generated. Obviously, these conclusions are similar to those that Ruggie (1983) has drawn modifying Waltz's theory. Pradigmatic complementary enables us to better cope with the real world of the modern international system and to recognize its partial internal changes as well as its "*possible* future transformation."

Notes

1. It should be noted that complementarity is not unusual in the theoretical field, even not in the natural sciences; see, for instance the complementarity between wave theory and quantum theory in physics.

2. This section represents a slightly revised translation of pages 10–18 from my study *Deutsche und amerikanische Gewerkschaften und Geschäftsleute 1945–75: Eine Studie über transnationale Beziehungen* (Düsseldorf: Drosste, 1978).

3. The occasional inclusion of nongovernmental experts or representatives of societal groups in government bodies or bureaucracies under certain conditions gives rise to an intermediate type of "external bureaucrat"; see Alger 1962.

4. For a recent example see the role played by foreign firms in the realization of the SDI program (where foreign firms are contractual partners of SDI).

5. It goes without saying that the distribution of power in the economic area also has an impact on the power distribution in the military-security area.

References

Alger, Chadwick F. (June 1962). "The External Bureaucracy in United States Foreign Affairs." *Administrative Science Quarterly* 7:50 ff.

Baratz, Morton S. (1956). "Corporate Giants and the Power Structure." *Western Political Quarterly* 9:406 ff.

Behrman, Jack N. (1971). *U.S. International Business and Governments*. New York: McGraw-Hill.

Bozeman, Adda B. (1960). *Politics and Culture in International History*. Princeton: Princeton University Press.

Cohen, Benjamin J. (1973). *The Question of Imperialism*. New York: Basic Books.

Deutsch, Karl W. (1966). "External Influences on the Internal Behavior of States." In R.B. Farrell, ed., *Approaches to Comparative and International Politics*. Evanston, Ill.: Northwestern University Press.

Dickmann, Fritz (1972). *Der Westfälische Friede*. 3d ed. Münster: Aschendorff.

Dowty, Alan (1971). "Foreign Linked Factionalism." *Journal of Conflict Resolution* 15:229 ff.

Drucker, Peter (1987). Quoted in Hugo Müller-Vogg. "Nur wenige deutsche Vorstandsmitglieder leben in Amerika." *Frankfurter Allgemeine Zeitung*, 4 March, p. 14.

Easton, David (1965). *A Framework for Political Analysis*. Englewood Cliffs, N.J.: Prentice-Hall.

Fayerweather, John, ed. (1973). *International Business: Government Affairs*. Cambridge: Harvard University Press.

Fijalkowski, Jürgen (1958). *Die Wendung zum Führerstaat*. Cologne and Opladen: Westdeutscher Verlag.

—— (1967). "Methodologische Grundorientierung soziologischer Forschung." In *Enzyklopädie der geisteswissenschaftlichen Arbeitsmethoden*. Pp. 556 ff. Munich and Vienna: Oldenbourg.

Foreign Affairs Division (1975). *The Role of Advisory Committees in U.S. Foreign Policy*. Washington, D.C.: Library of Congress, Congressional Research Service.

Galbraith, John Kenneth (1967). *The New Industrial State*. Boston: Deutsch. In German (1968). *Die moderne Industriegesellschaft*. Munich and Zurich: Droemer, Knaur.

Heller, Hermann (1934). *Staatslehre*. Leiden: Sijthoff.

Herz, John H. (1974). *Staatenwelt und Weltpolitik*. Hamburg: Hoffmann und Campe.

Huntington, Samuel P. (April 1973). "Transnational Organizations in World Politics." *World Politics* 25:333 ff.

Kaiser, Karl (1969). "Transnationale Politik." In E.O. Czempiel, ed., *Die anachronistische Souveränität*. Pp. 80 ff. Cologne and Opladen: Westdeutscher Verlag.

Kolko, Gabriel (1971). *Hintergründe der U.S.-Außenpolitik*. Frankfurt a. M.: Europäische Verlagsanstalt.

Link, Werner (1970). *Die amerikanische Stabilisierungspolitik in Deutschland, 1921–32*. Düsseldorf: Droste.

—— (1978). *Deutsche und amerikanische Gewerkschaften und Geschäftsleute 1945–75: Eine Studie über transnationale Beziehungen*. Düsseldorf: Droste.

Maier, Anneliese (1954). "Internationale Beziehungen an spätmittelalterlichen Universitäten." In *Festschrift für Carl Bilfinger.* Cologne and Berlin: Heymann.

Mann, Dean E., and Jameson W. Doig (1965). *The Assistant Secretaries.* Washington, D.C.: Brookings Institution.

Mannheim, Karl (1967). *Mensche und Gesellschaft im Zeitalter des Umbruchs.* 2d ed. Bad Homburg: Gehlen.

—— (1970). *Freiheit und geplante Demokratie.* Cologne and Opladen: Westdeutscher Verlag.

Mansbach, Richard W., Yale H. Ferguson, and Donald E. Lampert (1976). *The West of World Politics.* Englewood Cliffs, N.J.: Prentice-Hall.

Merton, Robert K. (1968). *Social Theory and Social Structure.* New York: Free Press.

Moran, Theodore H. (April 1973). "'Foreign Expansion' as an 'Institutional Necessity' for U.S. Corporate Capitalism." *World Politics* 25:369 ff.

Morse, Edward L. (1973). "Transnational Economic Processes." In Robert O. Keohane and Joseph S. Nye, eds., *Transnational Relations and World Politics.* Cambridge: Harvard University Press.

Nye, Joseph. S., Jr. (Autumn 1974). "Transnational Relations and Interstate Conflicts: An Empirical Analysis. Canada and the United States: Transnational and Transgovernmental Relations." *International Organizations* 28:961 ff.

Rose, Arnold M. (1967). *The Power Structure.* New York: Oxford University Press.

Rosenau, James N. (1987). "Patterned Chaos in Global Life: Structure and Process in the Two Worlds of World Politics." 2d draft. Mimeo, Institute for Transnational Studies, University of Southern California, Los Angeles, April.

Ruggie, John Gerard (January 1983). 'Continuity and Transformation in the World Polity: Toward a Neorealist Synthesis." *World Politics* 35:278 ff.

Servan-Schreiber, Jean-Jacques (1950a). "Durch die Lupe gesehen." *Frankfurter Allgemeine Zeitung,* 14 March.

Jean-Jacques (1950b). "Die Amerikaner in Deutschland." *Frankfurter Allgemeine Zeitung,* 15 March. Published at the same time in *Le Monde.*

Schmitt, Carl (1938). "Völkerrechtliche Neutralität und völkische Totalität." *Auswärtige Politik* 5:613 ff.

Schumpeter, Joseph A. (1972). *Kapitalismus, Sozialismus, und Demokratie.* 3d ed. Munich: A. Francke Verlag.

Shonfield, Andrew (1968). "Business in the Twenty-first Century." *Daedalus* 98:191 ff.

Waltz, Kenneth N. (1979). *Theory of International Politics.* Reading, Mass.: Addison-Wesley.

Weber, Alfred (1925). *Die Krise des modernen Staatsgedankens in Europa.* Stuttgart: Deutsche Verlags-Anstalt.

Wilkins, Mira (1974). *The Maturing of Multinational Enterprise.* Cambridge: Harvard University Press.

7

Internationalizing Politics: Some Answers to the Question of Who Does What to Whom

Ernst-Otto Czempiel

When T.S. Kuhn argued that paradigms cannot be changed, they can only die, he certainly did not have international relations in mind. In our discipline paradigms abound and correctly so. Only by trial and error, Karl Popper reminds us, is science able to move forward. It invents paradigms, tries them, and tries to find the best able to explain our world. And this world is changing rapidly. Change is speedy. No wonder that our discipline is often out of breath in sorting out different and divergent concepts in order to find the best. Is our world still a world of states, as the realist paradigm will have it? Is it a world of states and of nonstate actors, as the neorealist concepts suppose? Is it already a world society, as John Burton argued in the sixties? Or are we living within two worlds, one composed of states and the other populated by states and societal actors, as James Rosenau submits in his contribution to this book? These are important and difficult concepts. They all touch upon the role the state plays in contemporary international politics.

This is as it should be. If conventional and political language has its way, we still live in a world of states. Only Marxists argue that, to the contrary, our world is a market dominated by capital and capitalists. Interestingly enough, some non-Marxist economists share this view without, of course, the philosophical implications. In many economic theories states appear, if at all, at the periphery of the market. Political science knows, of course, that states do play an important role in international politics. The question is only: what role. Here, often enough, prescientific attitudes with their ideological and political preferences give the answer. A conservative emphasizes the power of the state because he or she likes the order–obedience relationship in general. The liberal points towards the power of nonstate actors, for example, transnational corporations, because he or she prefers bargains and profits to wars and victories. The difference between the realist and the neorealist paradigms very often is a difference between preferences of strategies.

The controversy between different and divergent theories is unavoidable and is acceptable as long as these prescientific attitudes and political preferences are transferred into scientific hypotheses that can be tested against empirical reality. The crucial problem of our discipline does not lie in the fact that we have different conceptual approaches but in the tendency to eliminate the competition between these concepts by isolating the preferred one, highlighting its selection of actors and processes and blacking out all the other factors. We use models that have been constructed to fit our predilections. If the model shows only states or corporations as actors it certainly will confirm the realist or the Marxist interpretation; if it shows both it will sustain the neorealist paradigm, which keeps the state as actor but adds societal actors (mainly of the economic kind). Nobody doubts that all these models, in spite of their shortcomings, have been useful and helpful. The argument here is in favor of a larger model that by showing all possible actors will be neutral against the theories it should permit to test. Such a comprehensive model of international politics would not per se eliminate certain hypotheses or preconfirm others. It would be open to all kinds of competitive theories and it would remind all theorists that their concepts have to take into account all visible actors—not only those preferred by a particular theorist.

The Model of the World as an Asymmetric Broken Grid of Interactions

By necessity such a model must be formal and avoid all metaphors. Our world is neither a marketplace nor a concert of nations, nor a society. It comprehends so many different societies living under different cultural, economic, and political conditions that any kind of metaphoric unification is impossible. Elsewhere (Czempiel 1981) I have portrayed our world as an "asymmetric broken grid of interactions." Such a model may not stimulate the imagination, but it permits a rather comprehensive modeling of all existing relations between all active actors. It accepts that not everything is related to everything, that our world is not a unity, and that there are no "global" relationships in the true sense of the word. The model reflects that there are niches of isolation and clusters of interactions.

The model uses submodels for the analysis of different parts of the world. The Second and the Third Worlds are drastically different from the First World. The phenomena that have eroded the realist paradigm and fostered the neorealist one are confined to the world of western industrialized states. They cannot be found within the socialist or the developing countries. In those parts of the world governments still play a dominant role and subdue all societal actors. There, the model of the world as a world of states, the realist paradigm, still applies. It has become obsolete in the world of industrial democracies, the world of the OECD. It is here that modern theory building has been put to task. Here all the old questions have to be answered anew. Who acts in addition to governments? What is the state? What distinguishes foreign and domestic politics? What distinguishes politics from economics? It is an OECD world that demands the search for, and the test of, new paradigms. The model of the world as an asymmetric broken grid of interactions tries to serve the understanding of the OECD world, and I confine myself to this world.

In order to do so the model shows all interactions that are of political relevance. It must, therefore, answer one question that is seldom asked: What is politics? International relations theory mostly evades this question or treats it as already answered. This theory deals with power (Morgenthau 1948), or its balance (Claude 1962), with hegemony (Keohane 1984), or interdependence (Keohane and Nye 1977), and with war and peace (Lebow 1981). This terminology treats international relations and foreign policy as something separate and unique, not belonging to politics in general. Even Waltz (1979) takes the title of his book for granted.

With this terminology the old model of the world as a world of states returns, if only implicitly. The old model submits that there is a world of relations between states, called international politics or international relations, which is different from politics in general, and is at least characterized by a separate special form of politics with particular contents, rules, and patterns. Even the neorealist paradigm keeps this understanding and widens it only by adding societal actors to the international scene made up of states.

If, by contrast, we assume that politics is the basic process taking place at all levels, local to international, we might find the common denominator, the common property of all relevant events. This radical solution has two important advantages. It ends the splended isolation within which international relations and foreign policy have been kept so far, and it eliminates the aura of "high politics" coronating our subject and demanding a special discipline for its treatment. Nobody denies that international politics has its specialties, with war as the most important one. But even understanding war as (a particular form of) politics might help us to understand its origins better than we do now. Von Clausewitz gave us the hint. We quote him but we do not take him seriously.

More important, by using politics as the basic process taking place at the local, the regional, and the national levels and characterizing interactions within cities as well as within and between states, we shall be able to abandon the notion of the state as actor. Nobody refers to the state when analyzing domestic policies. We recognize the president, the Congress, the parties, and interest groups as actors. When discussing international politics, however, the state as actor returns. It still dominates our language and influences our thinking and our models. It reanimates the time-honored distinction between domestic and foreign policy, between economics and politics, between governmental and nongovernmental actors. Defining politics as the basic process would get rid of these traditional but outmoded concepts. It would not, of course, neglect such phenomena; rather, it permits us to treat them as processes along a continuum of levels rather than as separate, distinct events. Each process has its peculiar properties and orders, its actors working within a special context describing and constraining their possibilities. These contexts make for the differences. But what is going on within these different contexts is politics, directed inward and outward. Thus, the most important task before us is to define politics. A definition might offer a clue not only to the better understanding of all these processes but also of the actors and units that are active within the different contexts.

To define politics is not easy. On the other hand, we do not have to do it ourselves; we can borrow from the shelves of political science. This, again, is not easy because there are many controversial definitions, none of them completely convincing. In my view, the best solution stems from structural-functional theory as developed by David Easton (1965). He defines politics as the authoritative allocation of values within a societal environment by its political system. This definition has survived criticism and is, in spite of many problems and shortcomings, widely accepted, if sometimes only implicitly. It certainly needs refinements, above all for our analytical purposes. However, it points correctly to the core of politics: the authoritative allocation of values. This is the unique and common characteristic of politics—domestic, foreign, or international.

As indicated, this definition needs two clarifications. For Easton "authoritative" means that these allocations are legally binding. It is the unique property of a government to make those authoritative decisions, the implementation of which can, if necessary, be enforced upon members of the society. This definition is very close to Max Weber's definition of *Herrschaft*. Both definitions are sound. Only governments have this capability. It distinguishes them from all other actors in the field and distinguishes value allocation within a society from all other cases. When we speak about the "state," we mean predominantly this particular mode of value distribution: by the government and legally binding.

However, this definition is incomplete in two ways. First, governments acting within the international environment lack the capacity to allocate values authoritatively. Within the international context they have to rely on other means, mainly on power. With or without violence, power is an effective means for the distribution of values. Its consequences (not its legitimacy) are as binding functionally as those stemming from the authoritative allocations of governments. If this is true, the term "authoritative" is too narrow for the purpose of definition. It should be reserved for the particular mode of value distribution by governments within their societal environments. For a general definition of politics "authoritative" can usefully be replaced by the term "cogent." The application of power can be as cogent as the application of law.

Second, what governments do in the international environment—namely, use power for the allocation of values—cannot be distinguished (with the exception of the use of organized violence, that is, the military) from what societal actors are doing within the societal and the international environments. These actors use power—economical, societal, ideological—to raise and to distribute values in both environments. This distribution is not "authoritative" in the Eastonian/Weberian sense, but it is equally effective, equally cogent. Politics can be defined, accordingly, as the distribution of values that is cogent by way of authority and/or power.

This definition covers the actions of governments and societal actors within their societies and the world. It integrates all relevant actions and actors; it bridges "domestic" and "foreign" policy, "politics" and "economics" because what is meant by these terms can now be expressed as the cogent distribution of values by different means in different contexts.

Because interdependence has intensified the international interaction of governmental and societal actors, politics as value distribution has trespassed more and more upon the territorial boundaries of society. The authoritative value allocation by governments at all levels of their societies has become intertwined with the generation of values in the international environment. The fact of such overlaps is well-known. Manning (1977) proposes naming them "intermestic affairs." But the time has come to integrate them into a more encompassing context. This growing integration of formerly separated contexts is what I call "internationalizing politics." There are more actors in the western world now than formerly. All actors, including political systems, move frequently and freely between the different contexts, integrate them and use the different modes of value allocation for the maximizing of benefits. It is probably true that the majority of value allocations still remain in the national-regional-local context, above all within a superpower. But also in the United States, and primarily within the small Western European countries, the overlap and mingling of contexts is growing and is being exploited by the actors who know how to use it.

Figure 7–1 outlines this realm of "internationalizing politics," showing two "states," a democratic and an autocratic one, and the interactions between the different group actors. The wide arrows describe the authoritative distribution of values between the political systems and their societal environments; the narrow arrows represent the actions of, or the interactions between, the political systems, societal actors, and between these two groups. The broken circle shows the realm of internationalizing politics by invading the political systems and the societal environments and even the processes whereby values are authoritatively allocated between the political system and the societal environment.

Defining politics as the authoritative or otherwise cogent distribution of values solves the problem posed by the different contexts. However, it produces another problem. Cogent distribution of values obviously takes place also in nonpolitical segments of the society. Parents, clergy, schoolteachers, university professors— they all distribute values cogently. Politics, therefore, cannot be defined only by the mode of distribution. Easton evaded this problem because he confined himself to the relationship between the society and its political system. The enlarged definition of politics, however, is confronted by the necessity of also defining the issue areas within which the cogent distribution of values constitute politics.

This is an old problem that has resisted solution. Because an extended discussion is impossible (and unnecessary) here, I shall limit the analysis to three issue areas within which the allocation of values constitutes politics: security, economic well-being, and rule (*Herrschaft*). Politics, then, comprehends the authoritative or

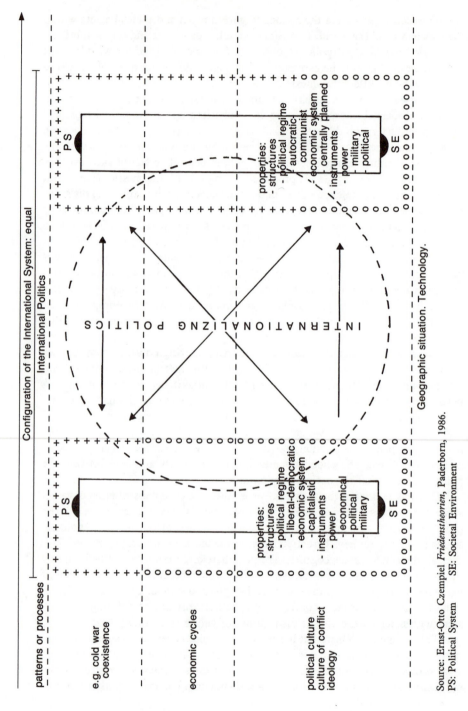

Figure 7-1. The Realm of "Internationalizing Politics"

Source: Ernst-Otto Czempiel *Friedenstheorien*, Paderborn, 1986.
PS: Political System   SE: Societal Environment

otherwise cogent processes of value allocation in the fields of security, economic well-being, and rule (Czempiel 1986, 27 ff.). The term "internationalizing politics," then, includes what political systems and societal actors are doing to generate and distribute values within the international system and in their societal environments. It includes also the pertinent societal demands and the demand-conversion processes between the political system and its societal environment as long as these processes are used for, or affected by, the generation and allocation of values in the international environment.

It is fairly obvious that the value distribution in the issue area of security is monopolized by the political systems. To guarantee the physical security of the individual and society is the supreme task of the political system—the reason it has been created and accepted. Usually societies grant whatever means the political system demands, including armies and armaments, in order to establish security. Providing for security, therefore, has become the major road for governments to expand their domestic power position. President Nixon's "imperial presidency" is a case in point.

Although in liberal theory the state is created by an act of society, the issue area of rule and the degree of political codetermination and participation of the citizens is regulated by the political systems. Here, however, they do not have the monopoly. Political parties cooperate; interest groups intervene. Neocorporatism has been treated so far as a "domestic" phenomenon but it is certainly one major factor of internationalizing politics. Political parties do not restrict their activities to the societal environment. In the United States the "National Endowment for Democracy," charged with spreading the American way of democracy into the Third World, is implemented by political parties and societal groups while being financed mainly by the U.S. government. U.S media cooperate when it comes to spreading the American way of life throughout the world.

The issue area of economic well-being in Western democracies is the domain of societal actors with the political system cooperating. The state plays only a minor role in this issue area; it sets the conditions and regulations within which societal actors pursue their economic interests.

What is interesting is that in two of the three issue areas, political systems and societal actors interact in the allocation of values. Security is the exception. Here the political systems have the monopoly with regard to the international and the societal environments. They can use military power, if necessary, and they can impose the financial and human burden upon the societal environment. In the issue area of rule and, above all, of economic well-being, political systems are only coplayers. Within the international environment they give help to their respective societal actors by concluding agreements for tariffs and trade. Within the societal environments they regulate the possibilities for businesses to make profits and for consumers to buy as cheaply as possible. They impose taxes and distribute chances of economic development.

The model of an asymmetric broken grid of interactions shows that the OECD world is not divided into two different worlds but exists of three different contexts of political behavior. There is the context of authoritative value allocation, maintained exclusively by the political system in its demand-conversion relationship with its societal environment. This environment presents the second context, where societal actors distribute values cogently by the use of power. There is the third context, the international environment, where political systems and societal actors use power to generate and to distribute values. The integration of these three contexts of value allocation by political systems and societal actors produces "internationalizing politics." Governments use authority in the domestic contexts and power in the international one; societal actors use power in both environments and interact with their own political systems and with those in other societies.

This complex process produces the impression of anarchy, but it is a complexity stemming only from interdependence and augmented interactions. It reflects properly the existing degree of interdependence in the western world where political systems are still important actors but societal actors are gaining relevance and are, as transnational corporations, already integrating interactions in the field of economic well-being.

With this in mind, we can now reformulate what formerly was meant by the term "state." It becomes simply a special context for the distribution of politically relevant values. In former times it used to be a unit integrated by the force of the monarch and defined by his sovereignty. With the advent of democracy and technology this integration has been dissolved, reduced to the particular demand-conversion relationship between the society and its political system. This is what we are finding when we open up the black box called the "state." It is this particular relationship between the political system and its societal environment that takes place on the local, regional, and national levels. Given technology and democracy, this subsystem is only one of several others that distribute values. It is still the most important one, the only one that is able to distribute values authoritatively. Whether it is the most effective one, whether the authoritative allocation of values is the most relevant one, remains to be seen.

Redefining the "state" as the particular political system for distributing political values in a society clarifies our language and our understanding. We can leave behind not only the realist but also the neorealist paradigm, which only adds societal actors to the "states." We are now able to open up this black box and trace the distribution of political values in three different contexts: by political systems, societal actors, and their interactions.

The model of the western world as an asymmetric broken grid of interactions facilitates description of this complexity and locates the actors and these interactions. By being comprehensive the model eliminates the possibility of excluding certain processes and isolating others. Showing all actors the model facilitates the formulation of discriminate hypotheses. Being neutral it permits the test of all, even contradictory, hypotheses. But it does not permit the prescientific selection of certain actors and the processes predicting an outcome.

Actors, Actions, and Interactions

It is not enough to locate the actors and to describe the interaction, although this alone would produce a very interesting but somewhat formal list of interactions. We are interested in outcomes and in their causes. Our discipline should be able to analyze them on the third—and last—level described by Waltz (1979): on the level of the system. We should be able to analyze interactions. Because today we lack the methodology to do so, we are bound to confine ourselves to the analysis of actions undertaken by actors. This limitation is not without danger. Actions as such are not discernible because they are always part of interactions. As we are unable to analyze them we have to accept the disadvantages stemming from the reductionism. On the other hand, the analysis of action is difficult enough. As the discussion of war-proneness and regime type (Garnham 1986) demonstrates, the causes of actions still are not being understood properly. There are three different types of causes: the interests of the actor; the structures of the system; and interactions. I confine my discussion to the level of actions and to interests. My intention is to demonstrate how the model and the pertinent approach would facilitate the understanding of actors and actions ("foreign policy" in the old language) within the Western world and the resulting flow of events from the micro to the macro level.

Political Systems

By accepting and converting societal demands, political systems act within their societal and the international environments in order to

- guarantee the security of the society and produce the necessary means for defense;
- stabilize the system of rule and possibly spread it into the world;
- organize/influence the international environment in such a way that societal actors can pursue their economic/societal interests; and
- produce and augment the domestic consensus in order to stabilize the political system and to conserve the distribution of power and influence.

For all those goals political systems use authority in the societal environment and power in the international environment. To provide the necessary defense, for example, political systems raise armies, impose taxes, and buy arms. From the local to the national level burdens are thus allocated. So are benefits in terms of investments, dividends, governmental positions, and influence. The structure of the society is affected and the political system gains power. The United States of the 1980s is completely different from what it used to be before 1939.

The more the security function of the political system grows, the more societal actors try to benefit from it. Analyses of the military-industrial complex may exaggerate their case, but they demonstrate how economic actors participate in the value allocation by the political systems. This takes place in the international system as well. U.S. corporations, for instance, have benefited from the political hegemony the United States exerted until the mid-1970s. The political systems, in their terms, use the military power not only for defense but also for the acquisition of values in the international environment and their distribution there as well as in the domestic environment. U.S. access to the oil in the Middle East and deregulation within the United States are illustrative in this regard.

The assessment of an "external threat" depends not only on the threat itself (which seldom can be analyzed objectively), but also on the domestic goals it can serve. President Reagan used conflict with the Soviet Union in order to diminish the welfare state at home. President Carter managed to cut the defense budget; because he did not cut the defense establishment accordingly, it was ready for new demands after President Reagan and the Republican majority decided to confront the Soviet Union. In the Federal Republic of Germany the Soviet threat has justified the reestablishment of the system of conscription. It can possibly become a major roadblock to West Germany's adaptation to a new wave of détente, because so many positional and individual interests are vested in the system.

In the history of political thought it is well known that by allocating values simultaneously in the societal and the international environments, governments connect and even integrate these two environments with each other. Tocqueville (1840, 1959) has pointed out that the defense organization of a society, without being inherently aggressive, is dangerous for democratic societies because its interest as an organization can benefit only from war. Before him, Jean-Jacques Rousseau (1756, 1953) has alluded to the possibility that ministers and government officials might even induce a war if necessary for keeping and improving their governing positions. These are early cases of "internationalizing politics" and they no longer exist in this form. But the relationship between "foreign" and "domestic" has become much more intensive. Henry Kissinger did not dare to present the Vladivostok agreement with Brezhnev to the U.S. public because he feared conservative criticism. President Reagan, on the other hand, pushed the INF treaty partly to compensate for his weakness in the Iran-contra affair.

In the United States foreign lobbies are the most active link between the allocations of the political system and its international environment. The security of Israel has been made part and parcel of the decision-making process in the United States, affecting public opinion, chances of reelection, and the relation between the president and Congress generally. The Greek lobby tries to equal the American-Israeli Political Affairs Committee (AIPAC). In the 1940s and 1950s the "China lobby" was no less effective in steering the U.S. political system.

Security leads the political system of the United States to overextending its legal reach, as Reagan's pipeline sanctions against the Europeans demonstrate. The president did not only treat U.S. Majority-Owned-Foreign Affiliates (MOFAs) in Europe as if they were U.S. corporations, he tried to do something similar with original European firms.

How far politics have become internationalized can also be demonstrated in the issue area of economic well-being. Usually in Western democracies business is the matter of business. But business benefits, or suffers, from actions of the political system that are bound to affect business interests. In the GATT rounds political systems try to harmonize the international with their national market. In the European Community, which is on its way to further integration, governments decide upon agricultural prices. The U.S. trade act of 1988 will decide upon export chances worldwide and consumer prices domestically. In monetary affairs, if the U.S. political system does not cooperate, interest rates in Europe are affected— with consequences for investments there and for exchange rates. Thus, it is not only the superpower that experiences internationalizing politics, it is the smaller powers as well. Interdependence is not a one-way street.

The issue area of rule is seldom addressed in discussions of foreign policy. It is nevertheless a very important one, beginning with the French Revolution and the conflict between monarchy and democracy. Since 1917 it is the conflict between democracy and communism that still lies at the center of the East–West conflict. It will remain even if the disarmament process successfully diminishes the arms race. In this ideological conflict all governments try to preserve their system of rule and to spread it worldwide. It is not only the Soviet Union that is eager to export communism; the Western democratic states are very active in trying to protect their liberal system of government and at the same time to persuade other states, above all in the Third World, to accept it. That is as it should be. As Brzezinski (1983, 127) observed, a wave of interest in human rights is mounting all over the world and the Western democracies feel obliged to contribute to its success. President Carter's campaign for human rights worldwide is a case in point.

Seen from the inside, identical or similar regimes in the international environment are an important precondition for the conservation of the system of rule at home, for the spreading of influence, power, and economic opportunities in all environments. Because it was doubtful whether the United States could survive in a noncapitalistic world, President Truman started the Marshall Plan. The Voice of America and its Western counterparts spend several hundreds of hours a week broadcasting to the world. So does the Soviet Union, which with the Communist Party is (or at least tries to be) able to present herself and her views within the Western and the Third Worlds. Under the Reagan Doctrine U.S. government officials went so far as to violate the Constitution in order to fight communism in Nicaragua. The congressional testimony of Lieutenant Colonel North has demonstrated clearly this intertwinement of the international and the national environment in the issue area of rule.

In sum, governments are important factors for the internationalizing of politics. Because they command authority and power for the allocation of values they are in a unique position. Whether this position can be conserved against the competition of societal actors or whether it will be weakened remains to be seen.

Societal Actors

Societal actors have at their disposal the means of power only. At the same time their interests are much more one-dimensional. They are interested in benefits for themselves and for their clientele. For economic actors the benefit is profit and the domination of markets. For trade unions the benefit is jobs and shares of well-being for their members. For the churches the goal is to spread religion and to influence the systems of education and culture.

Societal actors use power in two different ways. first, they influence the political system. This is an old story. Jeremy Bentham (1953) and James Mill (1944) have criticized the negative consequences for the whole society if governments act on behalf of the "few." The politics of imperialism that dominated European foreign policy in the late nineteenth and early twentieth centuries offers much proof for this criticism. Today, the situation has changed considerably. The foreign economic policies of governments consider not only the interest of the "few" but of the "many." The outcome of value allocations in the international and the domestic environments is now of a different character. The connection, however, has become much closer. Several parts of the U.S. Trade Act of 1974 had been formulated by the U.S. Chamber of Commerce and the National Association of Manufacturers. The AFL-CIO, on the other hand, has written the so-called Gephardt Amendment, which the House of Representatives incorporated into its trade bill in early 1987. The trade act of 1988 contains many special favors for the U.S. import business to be gained in the international environment.

European agribusinesses are still successful in making the European political systems stick to the Common Agricultural Policy, which leads to high consumer prices in Western Europe and highly subsidized export offensives into the international environment, thus damaging the U.S.-European relations. A West German corporation, Siemens, uses government regulations to keep its monopoly in supplying telephone equipment to the Deutsche Bundespost. The Catholic church, a relevant actor in the issue area of rule and economic well-being since the Middle Ages, trades cooperation with the political systems against their signing of concordats.

In general terms it is the "linkage group" (Link 1978) made up of societal actors with at least one political system cooperating that characterizes this kind of internationalizing politics. Societal actors and corporations use the authoritative property of political systems within the societal environment and their power position within the international environment to maximize their own generation and allocation of values in both contexts.

The second way societal actors use power is even more important. They use their own power to dominate their clients and their markets. Some economic actors have grown to such a size that they can also use this power in the international environment. They, above all others, have created what Rosenau called the "multicentric world."

The most important societal actors are, of course, the transnational corporations (TNCs). There are some twenty thousand of them now with more than a hundred thousand affiliates worldwide. Several of them have net sales much larger than the GNP of most developed countries (United Nations Centre on Transnational Corporations 1988). TNCs monopolize international investment and dominate the reserve assets of the western world. It is no exaggeration to say that the TNCs have reprivatized the world economy and that the stability of the western currency system depends to a large extent on the behavior of transnational banks and corporations. They also push forward in the services sector. The big media corporations and the news agencies homogenize the information available to the world. They influence political understanding and cultural behavior. They shape images and alter perceptions. In other words they distribute important political values (Somavia 1976).

One-fifth to one-fourth of value added in the production of goods within the western world is accounted for by the six hundred largest companies. International trade has become to a significant degree an intrafirm trade. Thirty percent of U.S. exports and around 40 percent of U.S. imports are already of this kind, indicating the degree to which markets have been integrated. Under these circumstances the term "American-European trade" loses its meaning.

The international labor movement also has become an important societal actor but only by cooperation, not by integration. The same is true for political parties. In Western Europe there are European parties—conservative, liberal, and socialist— but they do not act as such. They cooperate in the European Parliament but they are far from integration. Belonging to different political systems, they maintain their distance. The Catholic church is still an active actor but is obviously losing power. By contrast the anonymous, nonpersonal forces of cultural assimilation are effective in the western world; they amalgamate modes of behavior and choice.

There is one more international actor that cannot be forgotten: international terrorism. Its proper assessment is difficult, but it would seem that this actor, by locating its bases in the Third World and starting its action from there, internationalizes other societal environments and political systems.

It is the growing interaction of societal actors that mainly produces the phenomenon of internationalizing politics. The cooperation between these actors has linked, and sometimes already combined, the societal environments that political systems must take into consideration when allocating values in their own environment.

It is open to speculation where this situation in the Western world will lead. There are several possibilities. One is the closer cooperation and later integration of the political systems, which in this case would follow the path of societal actors. This outcome is probable within Western Europe, which would then constitute a new entity (but not a new "state") and a new configuration of problems. The second possibility is a renaissance of the political system that would probably result from the aftermath of an international holocaust destroying interdependence. The third—and most probable—outcome will be the strengthening of the link between societal actors and political systems. If such a development occurs, the function of political systems might be reduced to the administration of interdependence.

Internationalizing Politics and Change

Without stating it explicitly, I have already dealt at some length with the problem of change in international relations. The development leading to the "internationalizing of politics" originated at the micro level of the society, changing the societal and the international environments within which political systems must act. These systems were forced, at least induced, to adapt accordingly. Political systems must now give more consideration to societal demands, must permit a higher degree of social participation, and must accept societal actors as equals. International politics these days looks completely different than it used to look when the world was a world of states. Societal actors have taken over much of what formerly was the exclusive domain of political systems. Societal actors have come to see political systems more as a means than a master. The technological-economic process has neither destroyed the nation-state nor abandoned the political systems, but it has weakened these systems and blurred territorial boundaries. These boundaries still are meaningful but they have ceased to confine the processes of value allocation.

Nevertheless, political systems have played a decisive role in societal change. The more democratic these systems are, the more easily change occurs and transmits its consequences into the system. If the system is of the autocratic type it not only keeps these changes from entering the political system, but it sometimes inhibits social change.

The most striking examples are the United States and the Soviet Union. In the United States, one of the most democratic and participatory political systems in the world, two developments occurred during the 1970s. The TNCs emancipated themselves and expanded autonomously in the world market. A wave of democratization swept over the United States, weakened the political system, and enforced upon it a certain noninterventionist behavior. Even President Reagan, who tried very hard to reestablish the prerogative of the political system by fanning the flames of the East–West conflict, lost this battle after three years. Societal preferences and demands command the behavior of the political system. Societal groups, interest groups, and corporations successfully influence the distribution of values.

France and West Germany with their more conservative democratic organization of the political system display more moderate change. The two countries are similar in many political and societal aspects. They are somewhat different, however, with regard to the stability and tradition of liberal democracy. Both these are strong in France and relatively weak in West Germany. This explains why societal changes have entered the political system of France so slowly, modifying its behavior only slightly. In the Federal Republic, with its comparatively young democratic tradition (and its tendency towards the extremes), the political system has been—and still is—oscillating heavily between conservative and liberal answers to societal changes. This is why the Federal Republic sometimes prefers compromise and arms control, sometimes sticks to the politics of strength. More than is the case in the United States, the political systems of France and West Germany have been in the position to decide what amount of societal change could enter—and alter—the political system. What these systems could not hamper was, of course, the emancipation of societal actors as autonomous actors within the international environment. West German and French TNCs are as active as their U.S. counterparts.

Japan offers another variety. In this country societal, above all economic, actors virtually have become unleashed and exerted tremendous power in the societal and international environments. Nevertheless, the political system of Japan has managed to remain free of any changes. The Japanese society enjoys all the benefits of modern technology, of the electronic revolution, of rapid communication. But the political system has kept its informal autocratic character with only a low degree of participation. Japan certainly is the most industrialized country in the world; at the same time it remains a rather underdeveloped democracy.

Leaving the nuances aside, within the OECD countries the democratic organization of the political systems facilitated societal change, permitted its consequences to unfold, and produced what I call "internationalizing politics." The rapid adaptation of the political systems permitted the production and distribution of a formerly unimaginable wealth and well-being.

The opposite happened in the Soviet Union and Eastern Europe. As industrialized countries, they share in the technological and economical progress. They could have produced the same amount of societal change. But the autocratic rigidity of the communist system of rule kept this from occurring. The political system with the predominant position of the communist parties simply did not permit these changes to happen. The technological progress was confined to heavy industry and the production of arms, but it could not spill over into the production of consumer goods. Communication remains severed; societal actors by no means have received the permission to act on their own. With those measures the political systems managed to keep the changes outside the communist bloc and to keep their power and control intact. There was no "internationalizing politics." On the contrary, even within the CMEA, the political systems kept their dominant roles by controlling all other actors.

It is ironic that the communist countries, by their behavior, have falsified the Marxist theory that the state of production determines the state of mind. Perhaps the appearance of Gorbachev is the historical factor that will bring the Soviet Union into harmony with its theory. Until he appeared communist countries stemmed the tide against technological progress although their countries suffered. The regimes were strong enough to deny the possibility—even the necessity—of societal change.

If proof for the crucial role of regimes is needed, Gorbachev offers it. He uses the political system to induce changes within his society. Perhaps this is the only possibility for autocratic systems to adapt to change without changing the autocratic system itself. It is open to question (and contrary to Marxist theory) whether this experiment will be successful. For the time being the Soviet Union—and the GDR—demonstrate to the extreme how the regime type and the respective structures of the political systems influence the political consequences flowing from societal change—if not the change itself. Political philosophy must consider whether this blockade of change is a historical contradiction or not. For political science and its short- and middle-range theories the role of regimes and of political systems remains crucial. They decide, positively or negatively, to what degree societal changes alter the system of value allocation within the societal and the international environments.

In the Western world—to which I return now—the rapid adaptation of the political systems to changing circumstances have led to the "internationalizing politics" that we are witnessing today. The challenge before international theory is how to cope with this development; how to define the processes; how to name them; and how to predict (if only very cautiously) their future. All this cannot be answered here; it should be the focus of further research.

What can be stated right now is that we have to give up the notion and the concept of the state as well as the terminology that is traditionally connected to it. It is no longer possible to speak of the "relative decline of the United States" (Kennedy 1987, 514f) if the world economy is dominated by U.S.-based TNCs. Keohane's assumption (1984, 246) that institutions and regime will fill the "period of potential transition" is interesting and, in my view, correct, though its analytical wealth would be greater if it were not cast in realist terminology. There are no "states" acting in the transitional world; there is no use preserving in terminology what can no longer be found in reality.

What we are finding empirically in our world are political systems interacting with their societal environments and acting in the international environment. We are finding societal actors in both contexts. Thus what could formerly be called the state still exists but in a different form. It should not be shielded from analysis by using black-box terminology. It should be named properly as a demand-conversion relationship between a society and its political system. Only then can we demonstrate how this process is embedded in, and used by, the interactions of other actors. What we need, therefore, is a "realistic paradigm" that permits the Western world to be portrayed as this asymmetric broken grid of different but interconnected systems of interaction. With such an approach and an adequate terminology, it should be possible to assess properly who is doing what to whom in internationalizing politics.

References

Bentham, J. (1953). "Grundsätze für Völkerrecht und Frieden." In Kurt von Raumer, ed., *Friedensrufe und Friedenspläne seit der Renaissance.* Pp. 372–73. Frieburg: Alber.

Brzezinski, Z. (1983). *Power and Principle: Memoirs of the National Security Adviser 1977-81.* New York: Farrar, Straus, Giroux.

Claude, I.L., Jr. (1962). *Power and International Relations.* New York: Random House.

Czempiel, E.-O. (1981). *Internationale Politik: Ein Konfliktmodell.* Paderborn: Ferdinand Schöningh Verlag.

—— (1986). *Friedensstrategien: Systemwandel durch internationale Organisationen, Demokratisierung und Wirtschaft.* Paderborn: Ferdinand Schöningh Verlag.

Easton, D. (1965). *A Framework for Political Analysis.* Englewood Cliffs, N.J.: Prentice-Hall.

Garnham, D. (1986). "War-Proneness, War-Weariness, and Regime Type: 1816-1980." *Journal of Peace Research* 23, no. 3:279-89.

Kennedy, P. (1987). *The Rise and Fall of the Great Powers: Economic Change and Military Conflict from 1500 to 2000.* New York: Random House.

Keohane, R.O. (1984). *After Hegemony: Cooperation and Discord in the World Political Economy.* Princeton: Princeton University Press.

Keohane, R.O., and J.S. Nye, Jr. (1977). *Power and Interdependence: World Politics in Transition.* Boston: Little, Brown.

Lebow, R.N. (1981). *Between Peace and War: The Nature of International Crises.* Baltimore: Johns Hopkins University Press.

Link, W. (1978). *Deutsche und amerikanische Gewerkschaften und Geschäftsleute 1945-75: Eine Studie über transnationale Beziehungen.* Düsseldorf: Droste.

Manning, B. (1977). "The Congress, the Executive, and Intermestic Affairs: Three Proposals." *Foreign Affairs* 55, no. 2:309.

Mill, J. (1944). "Essays." Reprints from the *Supplement* to the *Encyclopedia Britannica.* In K.E. Knorr, ed., *British Colonial Theories 1570-1850.* Toronto: University of Toronto Press.

Morgenthau, H. (1948). *Politics among Nations.* New York: Knopf.

Rousseau, J.-J. (1756, 1953). "Urteil über den ewigen Frieden 1750-82." In Kurt von Raumer, ed., *Ewiger Friede.* Freiburg: Alber.

Somavia, J. (1976). *The Transnational Power Structure and International Information.* Mexico.

Tocqueville, A. de (1840, 1959). *Über die Demokratie in Amerika.* Vol. 2. Stuttgart: Deutsche Verlags-Anstalt.

United Nations Centre on Transnational Corporations (1988). *Transnational Corporations in World Development: Trends and Prospects.* New York: United Nations.

Waltz, K.N. (1979). *Theory of International Politics.* Reading, Mass.: Addison-Wesley.

8

Microeconomics and International Political Economy: The Neoclassical Approach to Institutions

James A. Caporaso

O n the one hand we operate in a daily environment where goals, incentives, purpose, and conscious ends-oriented activity are central. On the other hand, we understand the importance of external limits, structural constraints, and social forces, to put it generally, of the limit-setting environment within which we act. The former set of terms defines human agency, that is, the capacity of individuals to form their own preferences, to at least weakly order states of the environment, and to act in such a way as to achieve these preferences, given constraints. The second set of terms refers to the external environment of action. It includes the limitations imposed by resource scarcities, the state of technology, the conflicting wants of others, prevailing patterns of norms, and extant social and political structures. Both agency and structure seem important, indeed crucial. Agency provides an account of meaningful human action. Structure describes the context within which that action takes place.

There is a direct link between the agent-structure problem as articulated by Wendt (1987) and Giddens (1979) and the micro–macro problem, one of the organizing themes of the conference that resulted in this book. It is not a new theme but rather one that is part of the classical tradition in international relations theory. Indeed, much of the discussion since the 1950s has been carried out as a level-of-analysis debate. The systemic level of analysis, central to realist and neorealist theory, downplays individual, group, and societal factors in favor of whole system properties such as the distribution of capabilities, polarity, and alliance structure. Individual analysts black-box the systemic level and try to understand international politics as the playing out of individual orientations, attitudes, and perceptions. Wherever one starts, one must take the other levels into account. The individual must internalize information about the environment as part of the "definition of the situation." The systemic approach must assume a set of behavioral agents (rational or not) to execute systemic imperatives.

The author gratefully acknowledges the support of the Center for International Affairs, Harvard University, under whose auspices this chapter was written. He also acknowledges the comments of Hayward R. Alker Jr., Raymond Duvall, and Robert O. Keohane, all of whom read an earlier draft of this chapter.

Thus, the levels-of-analysis debate connects to a more general problem—the micro–macro problem. Perhaps the simplest statement of this problem is as follows: We live in a world of individuals along with their motives, purposes, actions, and consequences, both intended and unintended; at the same time, we are all aware of and speak (at least for convenience) of phenomena that suggest the importance of organized social wholes. If we assume that the latter domain is not just a series of shorthand expressions for discussing bundles of individuals, then a pointed question suggests itself: What connective tissue exists, if any, between the micro and macro levels?

Though most scholars recognize the importance of linking micro and macro levels, few make the effort to develop these links as a rigorous component of their research and theory. Much social theory takes place at the level of analyzed social wholes. Sometimes this holism is explicitly defended: "social facts are real and autonomous"; at other times holistic language is used more for its metaphoric than explicitly theoretical value. Similarly, individual-level theory is pursued without regard either for the context within which it takes place or the structured consequences it may have. As Carling (1987) put it, it sometimes seems ". . . as if there is one box, marked 'agentless structure,' in which one peers to find modes of production, grand historical designs, . . . , sociological analysis, determinism and constraint, while one looks to another, marked 'structureless agency,' to find the individual volition and choice . . . ."

Discussion about the ontological priority of social wholes or atomic individuals can be illuminating (indeed it is hard to see how theory can be well grounded without it) but such discussion often takes the form of assertion rather than argument. It is as if the priority of different levels were an object of metaphysical decision rather than rational argument or evidence.[1] As a result, how we should think about levels has become nonproblematic, except for the empirical assessment of the importance of different levels whose fundamental conception is itself not taken as controversial.

Fortunately, there are a few approaches to social theory that do take the micro–macro problem seriously, that is, there are approaches that actually make problematic to some extent the connections among levels.

Three such approaches are recognized here. First, there is a methodological approach that is closely associated with the cross-levels fallacy literature. This approach to bridging the micro–macro gap started out as a methodological puzzle, then gradually became transformed into a way of looking at substantive-theoretical issues. In 1950 William Robinson published his "Ecological Correlations and the Behavior of Individuals" in the *American Sociological Review*. In it he identified a puzzle that was to influence strongly the course of cross-level research for the next three decades. At the aggregate (ecological) level, a strong relationship (+.95) existed between the proportion of blacks in an area and illiteracy. But at the individual level, this relationship was negligible (+.20). What accounted for this discrepancy? Scholars who inferred from the group relationship that race and literacy were strongly correlated were clearly making a mistake.

Robinson's article stimulated three decades of research on cross-level relationships. Some of it was technical (Goodman 1959) but the general thrust of the research during the 1950s and 1960s transformed the methodological issue into a theoretical one. By 1969 Hayward Alker was speaking of the transition "from ecological fallacies to cross-level hypotheses" (Alker 1969, 83) and five years later Adam Przeworski was writing about "Contextual Models of Political Behavior" (Przeworski 1974). No longer was cross-level thinking *automatically* a fallacy. It simply had to be done carefully, with full specification of the model on which cross-level relationships rested, and exhaustive identification of the variables and interactions that might operate at different levels.

How do we characterize this approach as a way of understanding the relations between micro and macro levels? First, it starts with the assumption that society is composed of individuals enclosed by spatial boundaries. The boundaries could be those of cities, counties, provinces, census tracts, or even nonpolitically identified regions. The crucial thing is that the group or macro level is not underwritten by social structure but by spatial context. Thus counties and states rather than class and power structure. Second, the relationships among levels are conceived as either part–whole questions or questions concerning the effect of properties at one level on properties at other levels. Does the level of urbanization, proportion of Swedes, or type of political structure affect individual behavior (political participation, work patterns)? If individual behavior is unaffected by variations in macro conditions, no structural (ecological, contextual) effects exist. If the slopes and means of individual relations change, structural effects are present.

What is limiting about the ecological approach is that it has no conception of society except that of a spatial unit with a number of properties associated with it. By default, society must be a list of variables tied up with the unit: its size, level of urbanization, percentage of women in the work force, structure of political parties, and so on. Very little independent theoretical work is done on the structure of society as a whole or, for that matter, on how the separate properties characterizing the unit fit together. As a result, research tends to be a bit mechanical and perhaps overly concerned with the ways in which parts and wholes interrelate within wholes that themselves have not been theoretically investigated. Why spatial units rather than some other aggregation criterion? Why "these" spatial units rather than others? These are questions that are rarely asked.

Finally, one should ask the following question: What if there are theoretically important properties that are not congruent with the unit in question? The ecological approach works best when theoretically important variables lie precisely at the group or the individual level or when they can be composed and decomposed by some direct means (for example, adding together individuals to form proportions, or separating group categories into subcategories). If the properties in question are not so easily manageable, difficulties arise. What does one do if these properties spill over the units in question, if they crisscross in complicated ways, or if they cannot be neatly assigned to one unit or another? It is difficult to see how the idea of a transnational class, a vertical division of labor, a power structure, or a dependency framework can be dealt with inside this part–whole approach.

The next two approaches are termed macro social theory and micro economic. Each approach starts from a pole opposite the other and tries to expand from its initial premises to encompass the other. The macro approach takes the existence of organized social wholes as axiomatic. The theory (populated by terms such as social groupings, social networks, and systemic functions) attempts to locate the individual within a structure of social relations. The micro approach attempts to do the opposite, that is, it starts from isolated individuals and tries to express macro structures as extensions of individually calculated action.

The macro approach has a long intellectual history. It dominated the model of classical political economy and it has provided the foundation of much modern social theory, from Durkheim through Parsons, Levy, and Skocpol. In Marxian political economy, individuals are of course present but they are members of social categories: landlords, workers, and capitalists. Behavior is not free forming; it does not arise from psychological dispositions. Rather, it is, as Adam Przeworski put it, an "execution of class position" (Przeworski 1985, 379). Individuals are not represented as bundles of utilities facing a featureless environment. Instead, they have definite locations, and make their decisions under heavy constraint and cultural guidance.

The above view may not seem to go very far toward bridging the micro–macro gap. It is fair to say that classical political economy did not take human agency very seriously. Individual decision making was represented in only the most stylized ways. What counted was the reproduction of laborpower, a quantity sufficient to drive the capital of society as a whole. However, there is a branch of social theory that does take agency seriously. One starts from macro premises, from a "logic of society" that is more than the projection of individual actions. But one does not stop here, nor simply dismiss individual actions as compliant with abstract systemic needs.

This particular approach tries to embed a theory of individual action within a social setting, that is, to articulate a theory of personality and society. The work of Talcott Parsons is representative of this line of thought. Despite the identification of Parsons with unanchored, abstract causes, he spent considerable effort at integrating a conception of personality and human agency with a general logic of social relations. The Parsons who talked of "systemic needs" and "functional imperatives" is also the Parsons who concerned himself with the insights of Freud as well as Durkheim, and of Hobbes as well as Weber and Marx (1949, 1960).

To summarize, the macro social approach starts out from the macro level and provides a conception of society as a set of determinate relations. It then tries to deduce a theory of human agency from macro premises. Of course, if individual behavior is completely determined by macro conditions, the idea of agency is restricted, if not impoverished. If individual action conforms to a script written at another level, then people are playing bit parts in exchange for economic rewards.

They execute but do not write the story. But at least a part of social theory allows room for human agency, however constrained by social structure.

The third approach to the micro–macro problem is the neoclassical microeconomic alternative. Because it is the framework pursued in this chapter, I will say little about it here. It starts from assumptions about the individual and tries to build upward toward the macro level. The core idea is that the self-interested individual is central and that, given information about his or her needs and goals, one should be able to derive information about macro characteristics (institutions, social norms, social structure) from the interactions of contracting individuals.

The third approach is individualistic in the sense that the individual is the starting point of analysis as well as the fundamental unit to which all complex social interaction must ultimately refer. Complex social structure, institutions, and norms ultimately represent combinations of actions that can be "factored down" and reexpressed as a series of individual-level propositions. The very idea of a "social" or "structural" level, existing as an independent domain of analysis, is held suspect, except as a loose, metaphorical way of expressing aggregates of individual properties.

The Neoclassical Model: A Brief Sketch

In historical terms, modern neoclassical economics is that branch of economic theory that formed out of the marginalist reaction to classical political economy in the 1870s. The emerging neoclassical school differed from the classical tradition over the correct theory of value, the centrality of the price mechanism, the autonomy of the accumulation process, and the degree to which institutions (including social relations of production) were determinants of income distribution and relative prices. Even this brief list of intellectual focal points suggests a complex body of thought. This summary statement is therefore highly simplified.

Without entering too deeply into the specific ideas of the neoclassical model, let me suggest that a quick grasp of the basic structure is possible by focusing on three things: the basic units of action, the structure of the institutional environment, and the predominant behavioral maxim guiding actions of the basic units.

The Actors

The basic units of action in neoclassical economics are individuals. This is so because it is within individuals that the basic terms of neoclassical theory are invested with meaning (for example, consumer demand, costs, marginal utility, efficiency, and so on). Individuals are the fundamental particles of the economic system, occupying a role somewhat similar to that of various elementary particles in physical theory. Individuals provide the irreducible units of analysis as well as the units to which more aggregate references (for example, firms and national economies) should be reduced. The shift to individuals was part of a general reorientation of economics away from the classical focus on structural aggregates and cost-based theories of value to the more micro concerns necessitated by theories of value grounded in subjective utility and final demand (Dobb 1973, 167–68). Thus, the term methodological individualism aptly describes the basic methodological underpinnings of the neoclassical model (Lachmann 1984).

Institutional Environment

The world of neoclassical economics is not composed of free-floating individuals. Instead, the basic behavioral units are joined to a particular institutional environment. That environment is the market. The market is a large, usually impersonal arena integrating large numbers of producers and consumers, buyers and sellers. It is an arena designed to allow expression of man's self-seeking faculties, his propensity to "truck, barter, and exchange." Indeed, within a market environment, it is possible for large numbers of people to engage voluntarily in coordinated (but not collusive) acts of exchange, of goods, services, productive factors, and so on. The market is a mechanism for harnessing individual self-interest to the social good. If the conditions for existence of markets are in place, resources will be efficiently allocated, production techniques will respond flexibly toward new optima, and individuals will consume at the highest possible level.

Behavioral Function

Neoclassical theory's basic unit is the individual and the individual's stylized environment is the market. But what kind of individual is it that occupies center stage in the theory? What is this person made of? What are its basic values, sentiments, emotions, purposes, and preferences? The neoclassical model says very little about most of these categories. What it does say is that individuals have goals, can at least weakly order them, and engage in maximizing behavior. Without stating anything about the content of preferences, except to say that they are stable (Becker 1976, 5), the model postulates individuals who strive to get the most of what it is they want, always subject to constraints, aware of trade-offs, and sensitive to costs and benefits at the margins.

These are the three elements of neoclassical theory: a unit of observation and analysis, an environmental field, and a characteristic behavioral function. Put together, the approach can be described as a micro-level theory grounded in a logic of choice, a theory of rational decisionmaking under constraints. This system of individuals, with well-defined preferences, maximizing within institutional environments, fosters certain kinds of activities and discourages others. It encourages self-seeking behavior, efficiency in the allocation of resources, the underproduction of public goods, and the overproduction of "goods" with nonpriced negative externalities for others.

Finally, the neoclassical model embodies a conception of the fundamental nature of economic transactions. Because the theory rests on individual, goal-oriented action, it provides an understanding of society as a collection of voluntaristic, non-coerced exchange relations. It is easy to get from here to the idea that all transactions occur at their value. If this is so, transactions must represent two-way flows, and these flows must leave all parties to the transactions better off compared to the baseline of no transaction. As Hollis and Nell (1975) argue, this two-way flow can be generalized to the circular flow of all goods and services, "the stream in one direction in each market for goods or factors being matched by a corresponding traffic in the other" (Hollis and Nell 1975, 208). The neoclassical model is thus closed, each transaction representing payment for productive services, everyone benefiting *ex ante*, all incomes in direct proportion to their marginal contribution to the product. Price determination and income distribution are expressed within the same theoretical system, making an internal critique of distribution difficult and further distancing distribution from institutional issues.

In the following section I will present the emerging neoclassical program attempting to account for institutional change. Because this research program is very new, and may not be familiar to many people in political science and international relations theory, I will spend some time on a description of what this effort entails. I will try to develop the associated ideas of institutions and property rights and to show how economists attempt to endogenize them in the basic analytic structure of neoclassical theory. From here I will move on to a critique of the theory and an assessment of the prospects of this theoretical departure.

Neoclassical Economics and the Promise of a Theory of Endogenous Institutional Change

The idea of institutions represents a classic concern of political science. Indeed, for a period of time, the very identity of political science as a discipline was closely associated with the study of political institutions, especially constitutions, which represented the overarching rules of a country. Institutions can be defined as political structure, or rules describing and prescribing permissible behavior. In a sense then, at the broadest level, institutions define the patterns of interaction in which people may participate.

Why are institutions important in economic terms? Isn't the only institution of economic relevance the market, and doesn't the market inherently provide its own determination of choice and constraint? The market does indeed represent choice and constraint by representing goods and productive factors at different costs. However, institutions bear on the market economy in ways that may not be readily visible. Institutions can affect what legally is in the choice set and can determine associated costs for violations of these prohibitions. To take some extreme though not implausible examples, the average person is not normally allowed to print his own money, even if he possesses all the required raw materials, skills, and technology. Nor may he use his own office to conduct his own foreign policy, or to sell votes that others have placed at his disposal. He may not sell his labor before a certain age nor below a certain price, though this last condition is often violated in practice. Certainly he will not be allowed to appropriate his neighbor's assets for his own productive purposes, nor to use public assets (for example, public office) directly for private gain.

All of the above is not to suggest that these activities have never occurred. Some scholars spend their lives studying the deviations from the above norms. But the point is that there are institutional provisions against these deviations. Violation of these rules comes with a risk of paying a high cost. As a result, these choices and many others, may be placed outside the scope of individual utility functions. In a completely anomic society, the "prohibitions" would not exclude choices from utility functions but would simply amount to the added costs of these alternatives.

An extension of this basic line of thought shows that some specification of rules is needed to make the neoclassical model work. Without some determination of entitlements to and control over economic resources (labor, natural resources, various forms of capital) and technology, including which assets can be exploited and transferred and who has claim to the output, very little rational economic behavior can occur. As Libecap recently put it, "property rights are the basis for individual rational choice, which is the core of the neoclassical economic theory employed in much of the recent research in economic history" (Libecap 1986, 228).

Can a theory of the emergence, development, and decline of institutions be produced as part of a process of elaboration and refinement of the basic premises of neoclassical economics? That is the central question taken up by the "new economic history" (NEH), sometimes called the "new institutional history" (NIH). Institutions, and the associated idea of property rights, occupy central positions in this literature as independent and dependent variables. Important contributions have been provided by North (1978, 1981), Alchian and Demsetz (1972, 1973), Demsetz (1967), Furubotn and Pejovich (1972), Field (1981), and Libecap (1986).

To see why the project of the NIH is so important and a significant new direction for neoclassical economic theory, we need to recall the fundamentals of the neoclassical model. This model takes preferences, the distribution of endowments, technology, and institutions as given and proceeds to examine rational, maximizing behavior within these givens. Thus, institutions and property rights are treated as parametric givens; they do not vary within the time span of most economic models (most of which are atemporal); and they are not themselves explainable within the standard neoclassical model. Yet, the neoclassical economist will readily admit that "rules are not natural constants" (Basu et al. 1987, 3) and "property rights are the basis for individual rational choice" (Libecap 1986, 228).

Perhaps the broad historical scope of economic history, its attempt to understand a subject matter that traverses important institutional rifts, and the important changes in structures and rules even in the post–World War II era have encouraged the movement from constants to variables. In any case, the NIH has created the project of developing an endogenous theory of institutions.

Before proceeding to a more detailed discussion of property rights, a brief word on the arenas within which institutions and property rights evolve may be helpful. The predominant context for analysis of changing property rights is of course domestic society. Indeed, law and authoritative institutions are often taken as the very defining properties of domestic society, with legislatures and courts playing key roles in formulating and interpreting law. By extension, the absence of both a codified legal framework and authoritative institutions identifies the international system as an anarchy.

General critical perspectives of this hard-and-fast distinction are available (Alker 1986; Ashley 1986; Nardin 1983) so that ground will not be covered here. But it should be pointed out that the ideas of institutions and property rights are sufficiently flexible to span different arenas. Though no one would deny the centrality of laws and institutions domestically, they are also important at the international level. The substantial body of law that has accumulated around entitlements to and use of the ocean and its resources, outer space, international trade, and the employment of capital in foreign countries are cases in point.

In addition, there is a strong family resemblance between the idea of institutions and the concept of regime as used for a long time by international legal scholars and more recently by general international relations scholars. Keohane and Nye define regimes as "sets of governing arrangements that affect relationships of interdependence" (1977, 19). They clearly include rules and procedures in their definition. In addition, the special issue of *International Organization* (Krasner 1982) had much to say on this topic and Krasner's definition of regimes as "principles, norms, rules, and decision-making procedures around which actors' expectations converge" (1982, 186) shows the key underlying similarities.

Property Rights

In what follows I will use property rights and institutions interchangeably, recognizing some differences with respect to inclusiveness. Property rights refer to rules, laws, even customs (for example, customary entitlements), governing ownership of, use of, rights of access to, and rights of appropriation of resouces, productive factors, and output. As Ekelund and Tollison (1986, 50) point out, property includes physical goods, productive factors, and intangible property such as knowledge, music, and specialized technique.

In capitalist society, the property rights system at a minimum must specify rights of private ownership of wealth-producing property (that is, capital), of labor, and the product that flows from the productive process. Though neoclassical economics may not place it at the center, capitalism in one sense is a system of economic organization where owners of capital have a right to dispose of the surplus privately.

One conceptual advantage of focusing on property rights is that, unlike societies' macro institutions (provided in part by their constitutional structures), property rights are more divisible and open to constant change. Formal institutions are often very rigid and change very slowly. In this sense the idea of property rights points us toward a concept with more continuous properties than macro institutions per se. Property rights are not only of interest in that original condition where rights must be put in place in order for exchange to occur at all. Rather, the content of these rights evolves with changing patterns of production and resource utilization. A rights structure in which individuals do not gain from risk-taking and wealth-producing activities may lead to low levels of innovation, the substitution of leisure for work, and replacement of wealth-production energies with rent-seeking and redistributional claims. The concern in the United States today about the "litigious society," "paper entrepreneurialism" (Reich 1983), and rent-seeking (Krueger 1974; Bhagwati and Srinivasan 1980) attests to the significance of property rights in our contemporary setting.

The idea of property rights is a fundamental one and is not a mere embellishment of economic theory. It speaks to nothing less than what is sometimes vaguely referred to as "the framework of economic activity." As one scholar put it: "Property rights institutions underlie the performance and income distribution of all economies. By defining the parameters for the use of scarce resources and assigning the associated rewards and costs, the prevailing system of property rights establishes incentives and the time horizons for investment, production, and exchange." (Libecap 1986, 227).

Dimensions of Property Rights

Property rights are not of one cloth. There are huge differences between competing conceptions of property rights, such as private versus communal rights, matriarchial versus patriarchial, growth-oriented versus redistributive, and so on. Some of the grand debates in political economy have turned on these choices. Smith's *Wealth of Nations* (1776, 1976) is a critique of the rent-seeking properties of mercantilism. Marx's *Capital* (1867, 1906) is in part a critique of the distributional laws of capitalism. Olson's *Rise and Decline of Nations* (1982b) and Aharoni's *The No-Risk Society* (1981) draw attention to the ways in which distributive property rights (for example, minimum income) and risk-reduction rights affect, among other things, economic growth rates. Engel's *Origin of the Family, Private Property, and the State* (1884, 1985) attempted to link the emergence of private property rights to patriarchy and new forms of state power. Plainly, the idea of property rights is broad.

The focus of neoclassical property rights theorists is usually not quite so general, though the writings of Douglass North have quite a broad historical and theoretical sweep. However, for the most part, modern property rights theorists set their sights at closer range and examine the evolution of property rights from the standpoint of things like capturability of "external" profits, reduction of transaction costs, shirking, and uncertainty. Because these terms may not be familiar, let me say a few words about them.

Douglass North, in *Structure and Change in Economic History* (1981) and Davis and North in *Institutional Change and American Economic Growth* (1971) attach great importance to the capturability of profits. North has argued that throughout history, a huge share (perhaps 50 percent of gross national product) of all wealth created has not been appropriated by those creating it (North 1984, 7). Thus, neoclassical economics, focusing mostly on market (that is, price-governed) interdependencies, misses much of what happens that is recognizably economic in substance. Forms of economic organization (for example, the firm) and law (for example, patent law) can be assessed as devices allowing private internalization of wealth-creating activities. The creation of rights structures to internalize external costs would also be relevant.

Transaction costs identify another important area of property rights research. This idea refers to the total costs of information, measurement, negotiation, uncertainty, implementation, and monitoring of transactions. They are, in short, "the costs of specifying and enforcing the contracts that underlie exchange" and though of obvious importance for understanding efficient allocation, these costs "are nowhere integrated into a general framework that allows us to analyze the changing structure of economies over time" (North 1984, 7).

Countless numbers of transactions occur daily, most of them so routine that they are almost effortless. Those carried out on a limited scale, within a framework of shared values and based on a common set of laws, fall into this category. However, there are also numerous transactions that are carried out over long distances, and between different legal and value systems. More to the point, the contract may be imperfectly specified and lend itself to competing interpretations. Furthermore, there may be all kinds of obstacles to free exchange. Heilbroner's traveling merchant, who is stopped once every six miles to pay a customs toll, and is subjected to "112 different measures of length, 92 different square measures, 65 day measures" (1980, 20) is merely an extreme instance of high transaction costs. And this is clearly not a case where things are getting better all the time; for example, that through improvements in transportation, communications, codification of law, the costs of transactions are being progressively reduced. The increasing specialization of labor, intensified occupational and factor mobility, and the fragmentation (perhaps even collapse) of common value systems all raise the costs of "doing business."

A third dimension of property rights involves shirking, or the defection of an individual involved in group production. This defection is possible, perhaps even attractive because the consequences of team production are public goods, at least from the standpoint of the producing unit. Though team production and the development of the social division of labor encouraged huge economies of scale, they probably also increased shirking, or at least the opportunity for such (North

1984, 14). As the production process became more socially interdependent, it became more and more impractical to calculate individual output, or even more difficult, the "individual's marginal contribution to the product."

Responses to shirking go along a number of different lines, some of them more difficult to accommodate within a property rights paradigm than others. Moral suasion and group pressure may be important and seem to have been influential in Mao's China and postwar Japan. As the People's Republic of China increasingly produces for markets, as the division of labor and scale of production grow, will more attention to the control of shirking occur? And within advanced capitalist societies, what alternative to the close monitoring of output will emerge?

A Theory of Institutional Change

How does the neoclassical model account for institutional change? This is the central question and by asking it we open a large number of other questions. How does the legal structure of society emerge and change? A similar question can be asked about the major institutions of capitalism—the corporation, the stock market, or insurance. Political institutions are also important, especially insofar as they establish incentive structures for wealth creation, rent-seeking, welfare entitlements, and so on. Clearly these questions are of fundamental importance and the neoclassical approach attempts to answer them frontally within the model, rather than by importing a different theory of institutions.

First, what is the basic structure of the standard neoclassical model and second, how is this changed in the model offered by the NIH? The neoclassical model starts with variation in certain variables as given (exogenous) and tries to explain change in other variables (endogenous) as results. That is, the model simply assumes a system of variables asymmetrically interacting in such a way that some are results of others whereas the reverse is not the case. This is a standard social science approach involving a priori specification of independent and dependent variables. It roughly provides an ex post facto equivalent (without full controls) to the experimental approach, in which exogenous variation (in the strong sense of non-reciprocal causation) is assured by physical manipulation of the independent variables by the experimenter.

But what is independent and what dependent? The distribution of endowments of land, labor, and capital as well as tastes (preferences), technology, and rules are generally taken as given. Then the economist goes on to explain the effect these variables have on the distribution of outputs and their prices. How much can be produced and at what prices are the dependent variables. Resources, technology, and preferences are the independent variables.

The neoclassical institutional model is not fundamentally different. The major alteration is that rules are shifted from the right-hand side of the equation to the left, that is, they become dependent variables to be explained in the model. Thus, the basic model now says that variations in the form and content of institutions are explicable by appealing to exogenous changes in endowments, preferences, and technology. For example, a hypothesis might be as follows: Given an exogenous increase in the labor-to-land ratio, property rights assignments should shift in favor of holders of the scarce resource, that is, they should become more favorable to landowners, less favorable to workers.

At one level, the changes involved in the NIH seem extraordinarily modest. A single variable has moved from one side of the equal sign to the other. Why all the fuss? It is important to recognize what this apparently small shift entails. Previously, economic analysis was thought to rest on a firm bedrock of what one innocently used to call "noneconomic claims." Ultimately, these were claims about the nonreducibility of at least some political, social, and cultural variables: institutions, social structure, beliefs, and norms. Institutions have enjoyed a perhaps unanalyzed privileged status. "Rule structures have served as the bedrock of that 'non-economic bottom' " as Field put it (1981, 176).

If rules, as population and preferences, functioned as fundamental givens, that is, as data inexplicable within the theoretical system, the project that the NIH sets for itself would alter this fact. Thus, an important question can be asked: "Is neoclassical economics a theory resting ultimately on noneconomic primitives or a comprehensively closed system where everything is explained in terms of everything else?" Simply asking the question is suggestive of the spread of economic theory outside an arena one might think of as "an economy." The spread of economic method (for example, in public choice theory) is paralleled by the spread of the scope of substantive phenomena that can purportedly be explained by reference to economic factors.

The preceding explanatory sketch concerned institutional change, a topic previously thought to be resistant to analysis within the neoclassical paradigm, though a long-standing Marxist tradition of explaining large-scale institutional change exists. But though Marxism has something to say about long-run institutional equilibrium, it says very little about shorter-range institutional variations. Given the Marxian interest in the institutional supports accompanying qualitatively different productive modes, this within-epoch astigmatism is understandable, as is the between-epoch silence of the neoclassical model.

At least for the short run, neoclassical economics provides an alternative. Forces of production, capitalists, proletarians, and landlords are reexpressed as holders of productive factors, with greater or lesser ability to use them efficiently in factor markets. This attempt should be welcomed as an effort to explain an important set of phenomena, but we should be skeptical too, and subject this research program to the same scrutiny as any other paradigm.

I have four sets of criticisms regarding the NIH. These concern the analytic structure and empirical preconditions of the model; reliance on the efficiency criterion to assess change; the absence of power considerations from the model; and the systematic omission of moral-ethical standards as having any independent significance in shaping institutions.

Analytic Structure and Empirical Prerequisites
of the Neoclassical Institutional Model

There are three logically separate though theoretically interrelated issues involved here. They concern the utility functions of institutional maximizers; the meaning of rationality in an institutional setting; and the assumption of a market structure for institutions.

First, we can ask about the status of the claim that individuals choose from a menu of alternative institutional arrangements. This claim rests on a number of assumptions, including that a variety of institutions exists, that they can be at least weakly ordered in terms of desirability, and that individuals can calculate the costs and benefits (including opportunity costs) of these alternative arrangements. In short, this amounts to saying that institutional arrangements are represented in the utility functions of individuals, just the same as grades of oranges, automobiles, and so on. This assumption seems inherently implausible to me and given the absence of some micro-level evidence of a nonbehavioral sort, I would argue that the burden of proof rests on those urging the opposite.

A second point concerning rationality is a continuation of the first. If institutions are in utility functions, then individuals can rationally choose. In a sense, this proposition is already logically entailed in the first. To rank outcomes and calculate trade-offs is to provide the conditions for choice. But here the economic approach is highly misleading because it does not examine the process of choice per se but only the outcomes of a choice process. Simon (1978) is quite right in arguing that the neoclassical model focuses on substantive rationality, not procedural rationality. The problem raised is that, because rationality is an inference drawn from adaptive outcomes, this interpretation cannot be distinguished from others that are capable of explaining a fit between individual and institutional environment (for example, models based on selection pressure rather than conscious motives). In the neoclassical model, the operational weight of the analysis rests on a type of functional analysis. The existence of adaptive (efficient) institutions is used to implicate a choice process that is never observed.

A third point relating to the analytic structure of the model has to do with the environment of our rationally choosing individuals. This environment approximates a market in that there is a sufficiently wide range of options available. Again, this condition is really presupposed by the whole idea of choosing. Market structure simply represents the objective side of subjective choices in individual utility functions. However, upon closer examination, the idea of a market for institutions is likely to raise some eyebrows, both as an empirical claim and a conceptual category. Can insitutions be thought of as grades of beef, types of cars, or varying masses of productive factors? The idea of an institution is something about which it is inherently difficult to think in the small, and still more difficult to imagine as the exclusive object of choice. Can I choose my institutions and you yours?

This last question must be answered in the negative. There is something intrinsically more general about institutions compared to the normal objects of production and consumption. Indeed, institutions are characterized by system-wide indivisibilities (Olson 1987). An institution is an institution by virtue of the fact that it goes beyond purely private consumption. It provides a common framework of rules for people bound together in some way (territory, productive enterprise). Macro-level institutions represent system-wide indivisibilities and as such lead to the collective action problem. Thus, the choice of institutions, assuming the process is conscious and rational, forces rational actors into an intensely political situation.

The notion that indivisibilities associated with institutions present collective action dilemmas is not new, and it is certainly not fatal to neoclassical economic theory. However, the NIH literature rarely deals with the nature of institutional goods in such a way as to activate the analysis of collective action. And, finally, this literature provides no account of the extant institutional structure that might or might not facilitate collective action. In other words, if the microeconomic analysis of institutional change leads to collective action problems, it is incumbent on the approach to offer an institutional description of the rules that govern and constrain individuals. Absent such a description, the neoclassical project runs aground.

History's Direction: The Efficiency Claim

The idea of efficiency provides the central mechanism by which economic history acquires its telos, its direction. Without it, history would amount to a series of hapless founderings, with no resultant goal or directional drift. Field cites Posner's *Economic Analysis of Law* (1973) as arguing that "judge-made law in the United States has tended to evolve in a manner that facilitates the movement of resources to their most highly valued use or, in other words, the efficient allocation of resources." (Field 1987, 4) To the extent that production and capturability of wealth are responsible for motivating economic decision makers, and to the extent such decision makers choose among a collection of at least weakly ordered institutional outcomes, efficiency and choice are directly linked. To the extent that such foresight and conscious choosing are not present, but differential reinforcements for particular institutions are, a nonconscious drift toward more efficient institutional outcomes could still result. Whatever the specific mechanism, efficiency is seen as the basic force (either the "end" or the "end in view") providing history with its direction. Hegel's world spirit is replaced by neoclassical institutional optimizers equating political costs and benefits at the margin.

At its simplest, efficiency simply means getting the most out of a constant set of resources. Given a certain distribution of endowments, preferences, technology, and rules, a society is efficient when the outcomes are Pareto-optimal, that is, when they are such that no reshuffling of them can take place so as to make someone better off without harming someone else.

The problems are several. If a diversified and fluid market for institutions does not exist, there is little reason to expect that outcomes will approach Pareto-optimality. Surely the simple lack of information will work against coordination of interests even when they are in harmony. Beyond this, a variety of low-level equilibrium traps are likely to exist, that is, stable outcomes for which Pareto-superior exchanges exist. An example would be privileged groups, who by throwing their weight behind progressive institutions could benefit society as a whole, but don't do so. The number of cases where alternative rules could yield a net benefit to society, yet were not adopted, even though the losers could have been compensated, is probably very large. On normative, analytic, and empirical grounds the idea that institutions are chosen for their efficiency is highly suspect.

Power and the NIH

The establishment of institutions will put in place a property rights structure with system-wide indivisibilities (that is, excludability from benefits and costs will be very difficult). This rights structure will set the rules within which economic activity takes place. In addition, the initial assignment of property rights will make for large distributional differences in economic outcomes. What holdings are "one's own," how one may or may not dispose of them, and with what claims to income generated, are all at issue. These are weighty matters, involve large redistributional as well as wealth effects, and are inherently political. Yet power, mobilization, and conflict do not so much as surface in the model of institutional change. Why not?

My argument is that power is absent from the neoclassical account of institutional change, and that this absence, far from being a casual omission, reflects a fundamental silence of the model. This is because economic behavior refers to contractual behavior within markets. Markets are large, dispersed structures of choice that the individual actor confronts as an external fact. The individual consumers or producers are so small in relation to the rest of the market that their micro choices cannot affect aggregate properties, or the behavior of others. Strategic behavior, bargaining, and power are impossible within well-defined market settings. Power is ruled out on deductive grounds.

Proponents of the NIH may object that not all neoclassical economics takes place within perfectly competitive Walrasian markets. There is also a game-theoretic version of neoclassical theory and this version presents an opening for power. And because the provision of institutions has elements of problems of public goods production, the question of how institutions emerge and develop looks similar to a prisoners' dilemma game. This argument has a large component of truth. However, relations among actors may be strategic, but power is still not involved. Actors in a prisoners' dilemma game are searching for the best individual outcome over either one or repeated plays, given what the other is expected to do. The game is still voluntary (though being in it is not) and oriented toward the search for Pareto-superior moves.[2]

Ultimately, a prisoners' dilemma game does not rest on power, bargaining, or relative capabilities. Pure dominance, or using one's power to enforce one's preferred position at the expense of others, is not entertained. Actors generally come to the game under symmetric conditions with respect to capabilities, choices, and payoffs, the relevant quantity for each player simply being the mirror image of the opponent's. Nonsymmetric games can of course be constructed. There is no technical barrier to doing so. But the crux of game theory is strategy and the analysis of equilibrium and disequilibrium outcomes—not the deployment of superior capabilities to influence outcomes.

The NIH and Morality

Morality, ethics, and norms are generally absent from the NIH's attempt to explain the emergence and development of institutions. Although norms may be chosen by self-interested individuals, normative standards are not employed in the act of choice. As with institutions and rules, the task here is the same, to ground norms on a firm economic bottom, that is, to demonstrate how norms themselves can be produced through a process of rational, self-interested choice.

The question, Should norms be included in any account of institutional change? is not itself a normative question, despite the "should." The question addresses the explanatory adequacy of the theory. Can the introduction of norms and moral standards improve our explanations and understanding? Evidence (ranging from casual empiricism of everyday observation to disciplined psychological experiments) strongly suggests the importance of norms (see North 1981, 47; Frolich and Oppenheimer 1984, 3–5; Kahneman et al. 1986, 101–4).

Despite the prevalence of evidence in favor of the descriptive importance of norms, economists have tended to downplay them. They have either denied their existence (assume that humans are egoistic and without normative standards), grudgingly accepted their existence but treated them as anomalous, incorporated them as special cases of interdependent utility functions, or argued that they represent only disguised self-interest and maximizing behavior. One recent article asked "If Homo Economicus Could Choose His Own Utility Function, Would He Choose One with a Conscience?" (Frank, 1987). Through their scientific practice, economists demonstrate a revealed preference for the nonimportance of norms.

The debate in international relations theory, especially its realist and neorealist components, similarly discounts norms. In a paper critical of the entire project of deriving cooperation from anarchy, Hayward Alker (1986, 18) pointedly observes:

> although not *formally* forbidden from doing so, no non-cooperative game theorist specializing in international relations has included—to my knowledge— "international injustice norms" in the extensive or normal form representations (and payoff vectors) which are supposed to embody all the "rules of a non-cooperative game."

The theorization of norms within the NIH approach encounters some difficulties. As mentioned, norms are either presented as congruent with self-interest or antagonistic to interest. In the former case, norms are redundant data (hence not information) and can be looked upon as the verbal paraphernalia accompanying the hard, underlying, self-interested behavior. In the latter case, norms and interests are antagonistic, pitted against one another in a perpetual tug-of-war. Social cooperation and individual selfishness are formally represented as dilemmas in the prisoners' dilemma game. Of course, parties may learn to cooperate but it is hard to see how such learning is endogenous to the game, especially when at any particular play, the incentive to defect exists.

Despite these difficulties, advocates of the NIH argue that norms can be explained by an egoistic, rational choice model. This approach either explicitly draws on or is broadly consistent with Axelrod's research on the "emergence of cooperation and norms among egoists" (1981, 1984) and the neorealist project of explaining cooperation under anarchy (Oye 1985).

Has the program enjoyed much success? It is still early to tell. As Campbell has argued, Axelrod has shown that cooperation can result among egoists under conditions of "sustained two-person interactions with near-perfect memory, near-perfect ability to reidentify a particular individual, a valuation of future payoffs nearly as highly as present ones, and . . . no option to withdraw from the interaction" (1986, 795). On the other hand, laboratory results on the prevalence of rationality have proved surprisingly unstable (Frolich and Oppenheimer 1984, 4). I would suspect the self-interest axiom, which is conceptually distinct though often conflated with rationality, to be even less robust. But there is no way of resolving these issues in the abstract—except by assumption—and the fragmentary results so far do not present a solid case either way. Whether these results will expand into a broad research program or dissipate once the restrictive assumptions are relaxed is hard to say.

Though we cannot be definitive about the research program one way or the other, we can offer a few words of caution.

First, the NIH starts with a definite idea of a person as an asocial egoist. He is asocial because his preferences are purely personal by default. He is primed only to truck, barter, and exchange in pursuit of self-interest. This view is not unproblematic. It identifies one place to start, perhaps a reasonable one, but it is not the only starting point. The idea of a socialized person, concerned with fairness, equity, and the welfare of others is equally plausible as a starting point. Polanyi's message in *The Great Transformation* (1944) is that economic man is a historical product. He is not born but made.

A second caution is due to the important work of Alexander Field (1981, 1984). Field argues that the neoclassical project of deriving norms from a norm-free world, or institutions from an institution-less environment, is doomed to failure. It is not that norms are inherently inexplicable but that any successful explanation of normative change must appeal to a prior normative and institutional base.

But it is precisely this necessity of appeal to prior states that is denied by the NIH. Game theorists attempting to provide a norm-free explanation of norms have defined their task as one of demonstrating how cooperative games can result from noncooperative games.[3] Field counters this approach by two means. First, he points out that even noncooperative games rest on certain cooperative understandings, which are assumed to be part of the very definition of the game. In a prisoners' dilemma game, insurrection, mutiny, and escape are not part of the strategy space (Field 1984, 703). Why not? Second, it is a common device of game theory to bootleg in cooperative assumptions under the guise of the boundary conditions of the game. The ideas of repeated play, symmetric payoffs, and enforcement of the payoffs are part of the stipulative structure of the game. These points, which are rather important in determining the outcomes of different strategic situations, are treated as defining properties of games rather than as falsifiable hypotheses.

A third caution concerns the relations between norms and preferences. The two are of course separate. Preferences identify what people "like" in colloquial terms, in particular how they order various outcomes in terms of likes and dislikes. Norms are the arguments and abstract standards used to defend positions. The problem, as Charles Plott insightfully points out, is that the two are conflated in economic theory. Plott does not seem to be overly concerned about this conflation, "since preference theory requires no theory about the source of preferences, no overriding need for a separate theory of moral behavior has been solidly demonstrated" (Plott 1986, 140).

Plott seems to be committing the same error as he has just identified. If morals are preferences, they are just another element in individual utility functions. The problem is that they should not be so conceived. Morals and norms are not simply data within utility functions. They are rules about how utilities should be pursued, even which objects are permissible to include in utility functions. There is a large range of things for which there are bans on exchange. Rights, obligations, and many moral norms are of this type. One is not legally permitted to sell his vote just as moral doctrine urges us not "to covet our neighbor's spouse." In the former case, the object of the prohibition is an activity: in the latter, it is the want itself. If properties such as integrity, rectitude, and obligation can enter utility functions, the idea of preferences becomes confused with much that is normally thought separate. If such properties are left out, it must be conceded that there are some things that lie beyond economic understanding.

Conclusion

The question posed at the beginning of the chapter was, Can there be a microeconomics of political economy? The research program of the NIH makes a positive answer to this question its central plank. It attempts to explain how institutions and norms emerge out of accretions of self-interested, rational, maximizing behavior.

Though this chapter is only an exploratory probe, making no pretense to definitive answers, it did try to identify the blind allies and suggest avenues to pursue with caution. To summarize these basic reservations, the NIH attributes too much information and problem-solving capacity to the actor, suggests far more foresight about the environment than reasonably exists, and too much rationality in achieving institutional outcomes.

The NIH approach tries to reduce norms and institutions to an economic calculus of consciously chosen outcomes of utility-maximizers. This is radically different from the standard economic practice of analyzing maximizing behavior within a context of norms and institutions. As Field argued (1981, 1984), this program must degenerate because any choice structure presupposes prior rules and institutions. Present norms and institutions can be derived from past norms and institutions (plus information on endowments) but it is difficult to see how they can be derived from an institutional void and a normless world.

Having said all this, it may still be the case that the long-term drift of institutions is in a more efficient direction. Recognizing this possibility, the NIH sometimes flirts with an evolutionary alternative, usually without explicitly adopting its language and conceptual tools. At a minimum, this alternative would introduce three concepts: some source of variation (in institutions); stable environmental selectors; and a method for reproducing the selected institutions. If this alternative were to be taken seriously, it would involve a language shift from efficiency to adaptation, from utilities to selectors, and from conscious choice to blind (unforesightful) probes.

The result, in terms of the existing patterns of institutions and norms, could (or could not) be pretty much the same. The institutions that exist might be the ones that would have been chosen by rational actors in a market. But viewing these outcomes in the "as if" mode runs the risk of seriously misunderstanding the underlying causal mechanism. In the evolutionary paradigm, extant institutions would be viewed as the results of haphazardly produced but systematically selected institutional and normative alternatives. Economically efficient institutions, to the extent that they are efficient at all, are the residues, rather than the anticipated products, of rational choice.

To posit the evolutionary alternative is merely to whet the appetite, not to provide answers. Nevertheless, let me suggest a few of the attractive features of this paradigm. First, evolutionary theory is open on the question of human "sociality." Norms and institutions exist as descriptive facts. Are they due to selective factors operating at the individual or group level? There is a research program in evolutionary biology that is dealing with the possible genetic basis of cooperation, either as an extension of kin selection theory or as part of the "efforts" to achieve social optima (Trivers 1971; Campbell 1983). Some argue against an individual selective basis for such norms among people, because here, unlike the social insects, genetic competition among cooperators exists (Campbell 1972, 21). Group selection, with consequences for individual survival, is not ruled out. To put it differently, evolutionary theory would not support a sustained selection of traits good for group survival but harmful to the reproductive opportunities of individuals.

Second, evolutionary theory provides an account of adaptive outcomes that does not rest on positing unrealistic assumptions about environmental information contained by the decision maker or the extreme foresight and computational faculties necessary to possess to make rational choice a plausible story. The pioneering work of Herbert Simon has shown that rational economic man falls short on the economic model's requirements, even in the much less complicated, more certain areas of consumer choice (Simon 1978, 1982, 1986). In this regard, the advantage of the evolutionary model is that it purports to combine floundering and blind trial and error learning at the individual behavioral level with a directional drift at the level of institutional development. Such institutional development is not a deductive certainty, not a tautological restatement of model premises, but rather a hypothesis to be explored with evidence.

Third, evolutionary theory does not need to assume a "market for institutions," an assumption that at the level of macro institutions seems particularly unrealistic, because of both scale economies and mutual interference. Evolutionary theory does have to assume some institutional variety in order for the selective process to work, but the difficult questions of costs of establishment of alternative institutions, as well as future rates of return, are left to a process of winnowing that is at best only partly *ex ante* rational, and is quite possibly governed by accident and difficult-to-reverse path dependencies.

To say that people, along with their norms and institutions, are "irrreducibly social" is too strong, and in any case not very helpful unless the reduction rules are specified. What can be said with greater confidence is that a good part of human sociality escapes the microeconomic paradigm, at least during the short period it has been applied to norms and rules. One can say this without conjuring up images of "group minds," "social organisms," and a host of supraindividual properties. But whereas the individual remains the elementary unit of account in society, this does not necessarily mean that society is only understood as a collection of individuals, nor that piecing together unit properties will produce a coherent understanding of social wholes. Even less does it mean that macro qualities—structures, institutions, and norms—can be derived by a self-powered, individual, interest-governed process of exchange in which norms, structures, and institutions are not also treated as exogenous.

Man's complex social interdependence, the reality of his group life, the social dimensions of production, distribution, and consumption, not to mention his explicitly public life, surely say something about the limits to which he can be "pared down" and represented even for analytical purposes as an unmodified, asocial, utility-maximizer. Whether this sociality is hard-wired in our genetic equipment or transmitted as part of our collective socio-cultural evolution, is at least for present purposes, beside the point. I close with a quote from Donald Campbell's "On the Genetics of Altruism and the Counter-Hedonic Components in Human Culture" (1972, 31–32):

Man and the social insects demonstrate the great survival value of extreme social interdependence . . . [M]an can have achieved his social-insect-like degree of complex social interdependence only through his social and cultural evolution, through the historical selection and cumulation of educational systems, intragroup sanctions, supernatural (superpersonal, superfamial) purposes, etc.

Notes

1. This is not to say that the status of entities can ever be free from metaphysics. Rather, my point is that such entities can also be the object of substantive theory, as in Campbell (1972), Parsons (1949), and Waltz (1959).

2. This is true, I think, even though a prisoners' dilemma game has a dominant strategy, that is, even though there is a preferred move no matter what the other actor has done. At least in the repeated form of the game, if one actor can convince the other that the first's choice depends on what the second does, a mutually beneficial outcome is possible.

3. To some extent, this general approach characterizes the work of Keohane (1984), Axelrod (1981), as well as the neoclassical institutional economists discussed in this chapter.

References

Aharoni, Yair (1981). *The No-Risk Society*. Chatham, N.J.: Chatham House.

Akerlof, George (1975). "The Economics of Caste and of the Rat Race and Other Woeful Tales." *Quarterly Journal of Economics* 90:599–617.

Alchian, Armen A., and Harold Demsetz (1972). "Production, Information Costs, and Economic Organization," *American Economic Review* 62:777-795.

——— (1973). "Property Rights Paradigm." *Journal of Economic History* 33, no. 1:16–27.

Alker, Hayward R., Jr. (1969). "A Typology of Ecological Fallacies." In Matei Dogan and Stein Rokkan, eds., *Quantitative Ecological Analysis in the Social Sciences*. Pp. 69–86. Cambridge: MIT Press.

——— (forthcoming). "The Presumption of Anarchy in World Politics." Hayward R. Alker, Jr., and Richard Ashley, eds., *Anarchy, Power, and Community: Understanding International Collaboration*. Pp. 1–62.

Ashley, Richard K. (forthcoming). "Social Will and International Anarchy: Beyond the Domestic Analogy in the Study of Global Collaboration." In Hayward R. Alker, Jr., and Richard K. Ashley, eds., *Anarchy, Power, and Community: Understanding International Collaboration*. Pp. 1–118.

Axelrod, Robert (1981). "The Emergence of Cooperation among Egoists." *American Political Science Review* 75, no. 2:306–18.

——— (1984). *The Evolution of Cooperation*. New York: Basic Books.

Basu, Kaushik, Eric Jones, and Ekkehart Schlicht (1987). "The Growth and Decay of Custom: The Role of the New Institutional Economics in Economic History." *Explorations in Economic History* 25:1–21.

Becker, Gary S. (1976). *The Economic Approach to Human Behavior*. Chicago: University of Chicago Press.

Bhagwati, Jagdish N., and T.N. Srinivasan (1980). "Revenue-Seeking: A Generalization of the Theory of Tariffs." *Journal of Political Economy* 88:1069–87.

Bornschier, Volker (1987). "The Business of Violence and Legitimacy." Paper prepared for the twenty-eighth annual convention of the International Studies Association, 15–18 April, Washington, D.C.

Brodbeck, May (1968). "Methodological Individualism: Definition and Reduction." In M. Brodbeck, ed., *Readings in the Philosophy of Social Science*. Pp. 280–303. New York: Macmillan.

Campbell, Donald T. (n.d.). "Natural Selection as an Epistemological Model." In R. Naroll and R. Cohen, eds., *A Handbook on Method in Cross-Cultural Anthropology*. New York: American Museum of Natural History.

—— (1959). "Methodological Suggestions from a Comparative Psychology of Knowledge Processes." *Inquiry*, no. 2:152–82.

—— (1972). "On the Genetics of Altruism and the Counter-Hedonic Components in Human Culture." *Journal of Social Issues* 28, no. 3:21–37.

—— (1983). "Two Distinct Routes beyond Kin Selection to Ultra-sociality: Implications for the Humanities and Social Sciences." In Diane Bridgeman, ed., *The Nature of Prosocial Development: Theories and Strategies*. Pp. 11–41. New York: Academic Press.

—— (1986). "The Agenda beyond Axelrod's *The Evolution of Cooperation*." *Political Psychology* 7, no. 4:793–96.

Carling, Alan (1987). "Rational Choice Marxism." *New Left Review*, no. 160:24–62.

Carnoy, Martin (1984). *The State and Political Theory*. Princeton: Princeton University Press.

Davis, Lance E., and Douglass C. North (1971). *Institutional Change and American Economic Growth*. Cambridge: Cambridge University Press.

Demsetz, Harold (1967). "Toward a Theory of Property Rights." *American Economic Review* 57, no. 2:347–59.

Dobb, Maurice (1973). *Theories of Value and Distribution since Adam Smith*. Cambridge: Cambridge University Press.

Dogan, Mattei, and Stein Rokkan, eds. (1969). *Quantitative Ecological Analysis in the Social Sciences*. Cambridge: MIT Press.

Durkheim, Emile (1895, 1938). *The Rules of Sociological Method*. New York: Free Press.

Dussenberry, James (1960). "Comment." In Universities-National Bureau Committee for Economic Research, *Demographic and Economic Change in Developed Countries*. Pp. 231–34. Princeton: Princeton University Press.

Ekelund, Robert B., Jr., and R.D. Tollison (1986). *Micro Economics*. Boston: Little, Brown.

Engels, Friedrich (1884, 1985). *The Origin of the Family, Private Property, and the State*. New York: Penguin Books.

Enthoven, Alan C., and K.W. Smith (1971). *How Much Is Enough?* New York: Harper and Row.

Field, Alexander J. (1981). "The Problem with Neoclassical Institutional Economics: A Critique with Special Reference to the North/Thomas Model of pre-1500 Europe." *Explorations in Economic History* 18:174–98.

—— (1984). "Microeconomics, Norms, and Rationality." *Economic Development and Cultural Change* 32:683–711.

—— (1987). "Do Legal Systems Matter? The Impact of Law on U.S. Economic Development." Mimeo. Pp. 1–46. Santa Clara, Calif.

Frank, Robert H. (1987). "If Homo Economicus Could Choose His Own Utility Function, Would He Want One with a Conscience?" *American Economic Review* 77, no. 4:593–604.

Frolich, Norman, and Joe Oppenheimer (1984). "Beyond Economic Man: Altruism, Egalitarianism, and Difference Maximizing." *Journal of Conflict Resolution* 28, no. 1:3–24.

Furubotn, E.G., and S. Pejovich (1972). "Property Rights and Economic Theory: A Survey of Recent Literature." *Journal of Economic Literature* 10, no. 4:1137–62.

Giddens, Anthony (1979). "Agency, Structure." In Anthony Giddens, *Central Problems in Social Theory*. Pp. 49–95. Berkeley and Los Angeles: University of California Press.

Goodman, Leo (1959). "Some Alternatives to Ecological Correlation." *American Journal of Sociology* 64:610–25.

Heilbroner, Robert L. (1980). *The Worldly Philosophers*. New York: Simon and Schuster.

Hollis, Martin, and Edward J. Nell (1975). *Rational Economic Man*. London: Cambridge University Press.

Jacobs, R.C., and Donald T. Campbell (1961). "The Perpetuation of an Arbitrary Tradition through Several Generations of a Laboratory Microculture." *Journal of Abnormal and Social Psychology* 62:649–58.

Kahneman, Daniel, Jack L. Knetsch, and Richard H. Thaler (1986). "Fairness and the Assumptions of Economics." In Robin M. Hogarth and Melvin W. Reder, eds., *Rational Choice: The Contrast between Economics and Psychology*. Chicago: University of Chicago Press.

Keohane, Robert O., and Joseph S. Nye (1977). *Power and Interdependence*. Boston: Little, Brown.

Krasner, Stephen D., ed. (1982). "International Regimes." *International Organization* 36, no. 2. (Special issue.)

Krueger, Anne O. (1974). "The Political Economy of the Rent-Seeking Society." *American Economic Review* 64:291–303.

Lachmann, Ludwig M. (1984). "Methodological Individualism and the Market Economy." In Daniel M. Hausmann, ed., *The Philosophy of Economics*. Pp. 303–11. Cambridge: Cambridge University Press.

Lane, Frederic C. (1979). *Profits from Power*. Albany: State University of New York Press.

Libecap, Gary D. (1986). "Property Rights in Economic History: Implications for Research." *Explorations in Economic History* 23:227–52.

Marx, Karl (1867, 1906). *Capital: A Critique of Political Economy*. New York: Modern Library.

Nagel, Ernest (1955). "On the Statement 'The Whole Is Greater Than the Sum of its Parts'." In P.E. Lazarsfeld and M. Rosenberg, eds., *The Language of Social Research*. New York: Free Press.

Nardin, Terry (1983). *Law, Morality, and the Relations of States*. Princeton: Princeton University Press.

North, Douglass C. (1978). "Structure and Performance: The Task of Economic History." *Journal of Economic Literature* 16, no. 3:963–78.

—— (1981). *Structure and Change in Economic History*. New York: Norton.

—— (1984). "Transaction Costs, Institutions, and Economic History." *Journal of Institutional and Theoretical Economics*, no. 140:7–17.

North, Douglass C., and Robert P. Thomas (1973). *The Rise of the Western World*. Cambridge: Cambridge University Press.

Olson, Mancur (1982a). "On the Priority of Public Problems." In R. Maris, ed., *The Corporate Society*. Pp. 294–336. London: Macmillan.

—— (1982b). *The Rise and Decline of Nations*. New Haven: Yale University Press.

—— (1987). "Toward a Unified View of Economics and the Other Social Sciences." Pp. 1–38. Paper presented at Harvard Seminar on Political Economy, 1 December, Cambridge.

Olson, Mancur, and Richard Zeckhauser (1966). "An Economic Theory of Alliances." *The Review of Economics and Statistics* 48, no. 3:266–79.

Oye, Kenneth A. (1985). "Explaining Cooperation under Anarchy: Hypotheses and Strategies." *World Politics* 38, no. 1:3–24.

Parsons, Talcott (1949). *The Structure of Social Action*. Glencoe, Ill.: Free Press.

—— (1960). "Durkheim's Contribution to the Theory of Integration of Social Systems." In Kurt H. Wolff, ed., *Emile Durkheim*. Pp. 118–53. Columbus: Ohio State University Press.

Plott, Charles R. (1986). "Rational Choice in Experimental Markets." In Robin M. Hogarth and Melvin W. Reder, eds., *Rational Choice: The Contrast between Economics and Psychology*. Pp. 117–43. Chicago: University of Chicago Press.

Polanyi, Karl (1944). *The Great Transformation*. Boston: Beacon Press.

Posner, Richard A. (1973). *Economic Analysis of Law*. 2d ed. Boston: Little, Brown.

Przeworski, Adam (1974). "Contextual Models of Political Behavior." *Political Methodology* (Winter).

—— (1985). "Marxism and Rational Choice." *Politics and Society* 14, no. 4:379–409.

Reich, Robert (1983). *The Next American Frontier*. New York: Penguin Books.

Robinson, William S. (1950). "The Ecological Correlations and the Behavior of Individuals." *American Sociological Review* 15:351–57.

Russett, Bruce (1970). *What Price Vigilance?* New Haven: Yale University Press.

Simon, Herbert A. (1978). "Rationality as Process and as Product of Thought." *American Economic Review* 68:1–16.

—— (1982). *Models of Bounded Rationality*. 2 vols. Cambridge: MIT Press.

—— (1986). "Rationality in Psychology and Economics." In Robin M. Hogarth and Melvin W. Reder, eds., *Rational Choice*. Pp. 25–40. Chicago: University of Chicago Press.

Smith, Adam (1776, 1976). *An Inquiry into the Nature and Causes of the Wealth of Nations*. Oxford: Clarendon Press.

Tilly, Charles, ed. (1975). *The Formation of National States in Western Europe*. Princeton: Princeton University Press.

—— (1985). "War-Making and State-Making as Organized Crime." In Peter B. Evans, Dietrich Rueschemeyer, and Theda Skocpol, eds., *Bringing the State Back In*. New York: Cambridge University Press.

Trivers, Robert L. (1971). "The Evolution of Reciprocal Altruism." *The Quarterly Review of Biology* 46, no. 4:35–57.

Waltz, Kenneth (1959). *Man, the State, and War*. New York: Columbia University Press.

Wendt, Alexander E. (1987). "The Agent-Structure Problem in International Relations Theory." *International Organization* 41, no. 3:335–70.

9

Toward a Theory of Transnational Empire

Susan Strange

> The American Empire is one of the most successful inventions in history, and all the more remarkable because no one knows it's there.
>
> —Gore Vidal

In any discussion among academics about the theory, or theories, underpinning their field of study, it is important that each participant should make explicit his or her assumptions about the nature of theory; about how these assumptions are justified. He or she should also give some general indication of his or her general opinions about past theorizing and about desirable directions for future theorizing. Without such preliminary clarification, discussion can easily become confused and incomprehensible to the outsider. I shall start therefore by making my own position on each of these four points as explicit as I can.

There is a great deal of confusion about the nature of theory concerning the working of the international system, political and economic. This has resulted in a lot of "theoretical" work that is not really theory at all, in the sense in which that word should be used and is defined in dictionaries (for example, "a supposition explaining something, especially one based on principles independent of the phenomenon to be explained"—*Concise Oxford Dictionary*).

Because of this we cannot proceed to discuss future directions for theoretical work nor can we assess recent contributions to it, whether real or imagined, until we have made some judgment about what is real theory and what is phoney theory.

I make four negative assumptions about what is *not* theory and three positive assumptions about what *is* theory. Both are necessary to explain my general pessimism about the current state of theory in international studies, and my own rather tentative explanatory supposition with regard to the current state of the international political economy (which will constitute the second part of this chapter).

Negative Assumptions Concerning Theory in Social Science

First, a great deal of social theory is really no more than description, often using new terms and words to describe known phenomena, or to narrate old stories without attempting theoretical explanations. Putting one event after another without explaining the causal connection, if any, cannot count as theory. Sometimes, though, there are indeed implicit theories underlying the narrative that are so taken for granted that they are not even mentioned.

Second, some so-called theory in international studies merely rearranges and describes known facts or well-chronicled events in new taxonomies. This is not to say that a fresh taxonomy may not be necessary to the elaboration of a new theory. But the taxonomy by itself does not constitute an explanation and therefore does not qualify per se as a theory. The same is true of using new terms or words to describe known phenomena.

Third, simplifying devices or concepts borrowed from other social sciences or fields of knowledge often have their pedagogic uses in teaching; they can help get across to students or readers a certain aspect of individual social behavior. Examples are the story of the prisoners' dilemma, or a demand curve, or the graphic presentation of the concept of marginal utility. But none of these by themselves explains the paradoxes or puzzles of the international system. Their current appeal to some teachers, I suspect, is that they offer a politically and morally neutral explanation (indeed, an exculpation) for the recent failures and inadequacies of the international organizations dominated by the United States in which postwar America put so much faith. Their appeal to students lies in their simplicity; it confirms what their common sense already tells them that individuals are apt to act selfishly. But these are simplifying devices, not theories of social behavior. They do not help to explain the actions of corporations, of political parties, or of states in a global political economy. They do not even constitute evidence that would be relevant to a theory—in the way in which a map of the world might be relevant evidence for, say, a theory of continental drift and the existence of Old Gondwanaland. Moreover, those in the other disciplines who have developed such pedagogic devices are usually under no illusion as to their usefulness to policymakers or the possibilities of their practical application to real-life situations.

Fourth, the development of quantitative techniques applied to international studies has not advanced theory. The choice of what is to be counted is too arbitrary and the determination of what is causal and what is coincidental is too subjective to provide a basis for explanation. For the most part such methods have been used only to substantiate platitudes and to reinforce conventional wisdom concerning historical patterns of state behavior in relation to other states.

Positive Assumptions Concerning Theory in Social Science

First, theory must seek to explain some aspect of the international system that is not easily explained by common sense. It must serve to explain a puzzle or a paradox where there is some aspect of the behavior of individuals, groups, or social institutions for which a simple explanation is not apparent. It is not necessary to look for a theory to explain why people try and leave a burning building. It *is* necessary to find a theory to explain why they patronize shops on one side of the street more than another. International relations started with the puzzling question why did nation-states continue to go to war when it was already clear that the economic gains made in war would never exceed the economic costs of doing so (Miller 1986; Aron 1958, 1978). Theories resulted. International political economy today addresses another puzzling question: Why do states fail to act to regulate and stabilize an international financial system which is known to be vitally necessary to the "real economy" but which all the experts in and out of government now agree is in dangerous need of more regulation for its own safety? Theories result. By contrast, the common use of the term "information revolution" does not usually reflect good theory. Although it notes rapid technological change, it does not postulate a clear causal connection, supported by logic or evidence, between that technological change and social change—change in political or economic relationships so great as to result in a redistribution of power and/or wealth. It does not, therefore, advance our understanding or add anything to our capacity to make causal connections and to see the consequential effects of certain phenomena.

Second, the theory need not necessarily aspire to predict or to prescribe. This is where social science differs from natural science. Natural science can aspire to predict—though it does not always nor necessarily does so. Much science, from astronomy to microbiology, enlarges understanding of *what* happens without being able to offer conclusive explanations of *why* it happens. Social science can never confidently predict because the irrational factors involved in human relations are too numerous, and the permutations and combinations of them are probably countless. The one social science that has most notably aspired to predict is economics. But its record of success is so abysmal that it should make all those that seek to emulate the economists and to borrow from them try something else. (I think I can explain why their record of success in prediction is so bad but that it is not necessary to my argument.) They are particularly bad at prediction when it comes to the world economy because many of the basic theories regarding international trade and exchange rates are based on assumptions that no longer hold good in the present state of the integrated world market economy.

As to prescription, that is a matter of choice. Whether the theorist chooses to proceed from explanatory theory to policy prescription is up to him or her. He or she need not necessarily apply theory to policy-making, because policy-making necessarily involves value judgments and risk assessments that are exogenous to theory and that are better made by practical policymakers than by irresponsible academic theorists.

And third, theory should be scientific only in the sense that the theorist respects the scientific virtues of rationality and impartiality and aspires to the systematic formulation of explanatory propositions. The title of "social science" is only justifiably used to remind us that, although our subject lies closer to our emotions than the origin of rocks or the composition of molecules, and although it has to do with subjectively important questions concerning power and wealth, we must nevertheless still try to preserve a "scientific" attitude in our studies. Indeed, many of the problems regarding theory and social science stem ultimately from the inferiority complex of social scientists towards natural scientists and, more specifically for us, the inferiority complex of political economists towards the apparent rigor of economic "science."

A Basic Proposition

This is that structural power is more important to an understanding of the international system than relational power; and consequently, that because the United States has more actual and potential structural power than any other political authority in the international system, its power in the system is undiminished.

This runs against hegemonic stability theory and the many theoretical (and often conflicting) conclusions about the functioning of the international political economy and of international economic organizations that derive from it. I have explained elsewhere why I think these are wrong and also why they have been so popular in recent years (Strange 1987; 1988).

The important point here is—as I shall argue more extensively later—that the failure to understand and appreciate the extent of U.S. structural power has led too many writers and teachers to compose premature epitaphs on the American Century and American hegemony (cf. Russett, 1985). This conventional—but in my view quite unwarranted—conclusion has foreclosed any debate on how an American empire (which is very different from the empires of the past because it is based on structural power in the world economy and world society) might be improved, maintained, and prolonged. My concluding proposal for further thought and research is that we should reopen such a debate, more particularly because the alternatives to prolonging American hegemony are either demonstrably impracticable, or unattractive, or both.

But first I have to explain why I think the assumption of hegemonic decline is wrong and why we have to look for a new point of departure for theory concerning the international system and the management of the world economy. In short, I am like the man in the story the English like to tell about yokels from parts of the country other than their own. "Can you tell me the way to get to Norwich (or Dorchester, Wigan, Maidstone or wherever)?" asks the bewildered stranger, lost in a maze of country lanes. "Ah well," replies the local, "if I were you, I wouldn't start from here!"

My starting point in this discussion is that although there is disorder in the world economy and some disintegration of "regimes" so-called, the reason for this is not to be found in the decline of U.S. power. Rather, the explanation lies in the misuse of American hegemonic power in a unilateralist manner and in pursuit of national interests far too narrowly and shortsightedly conceived. Asymmetric structural power has allowed the United States to break the rules with impunity and to pass the consequent risks and pains of adjustment on to others. This has damaged the stability and prosperity of the whole world economy and has not been in the long-term best interests of the United States itself. But to persuade the reader to get to that alternative starting point, or even to consider it as a possibility, I must first elaborate a little the outline of a structural analysis that leads me to it. I propose to show that, in the four structures basic to an integrated world economy in an international society with diffuse political authorities, the underlying assumptions of much contemporary theorizing are false. False points of departure have therefore led to false theory.

Structural Power

The concept of relational power is clear and consists in the ability of A to get B by coercion or persuasion to do what B would not otherwise do. The concept of structural power is less clear and requires some definition. It consists in the ability of A to determine the way in which certain basic social needs are provided. One is a lever; the other is a framework. The target of relational power, B, if it should decide not to do what is required of it by A, has to suffer the consequences determined by the other. For the target or object of *structural* power, the price of resistance is determined more by the system than by any other political authority. Structural power comes closest to the outside (that is, broadest) definition of "regimes" in the debate that proceeded the Krasner collection of essays on the subject (Krasner 1983). In short, it embraces customs, usages, and modes of operation rather than the more narrow definition that stays closer to state-state agreements and state-centered institutions.

There are, in my view, four basic structures of the international political economy and each is interrelated with, and inseparable from, the other three. Although they can be described separately, it is hardly practical to disassociate any one from the other three, or to treat it in isolation from them. Power in one will tend to reinforce (though it does not always exactly coincide with) power in the others.

The four societal needs for a modern world economy are security, knowledge, production, and credit. Who or what provides for these needs in a society enjoys structural power through the capacity to determine the terms on which those needs are satisfied and to whom they are made available.

Production is the basis of life and therefore the fundamental essential. But production (or wealth) cannot be enjoyed, or even produced, without order; and order requires the provision of security. Credit supplied by the financial structure is a necessary condition for all but the most basic production structures. In the highly developed, highly capitalized production structure of any industrialized economy, a decisive role is played by the provision of credit through the financial structure. But the choice of social goals and the means of reaching them is determined by the knowledge structure. The power exercised over the nature of the knowledge to be acquired, and over the means used for its storage and communication, is a necessary complement to power exercised through the other three structures. Only by considering all four can the study of economic power and political power be treated together; and only by considering all four can power exercised by the primarily economic entities be seen in the context of power exercised by the primarily political authorities. Only by structural analysis is it possible to develop theoretical propositions regarding the impact of political authority (for example, states) on economic transactions in markets, and conversely of the impact of transactions in markets upon states (Strange 1988).

The concept of a production structure is the most familiar because it is central to a marxist analysis of the capitalist system. Marx pointed out long ago that power in society is exercised through the relations of production. That is to say, whoever determines what shall be produced by what means and modes, and who shall work at producing on what terms, exercises structural power irrespective of the political system. It follows that a production structure can, conceptually and actually, be market-based; or it can be market-managed by monopolies, oligopolies, or vertically integrated enterprises that "internalize" a market; or it can be command-based, in which case some political authority "plans" the market and determines what shall be produced by what means and modes, and who shall work at producing what and on what terms.

If we analyze the world system as a production structure, we find the following features.

First, that part of the world economy responding directly to political command (which might be described as socialist if that word were not so badly abused) is the smaller part and is shrinking. Even in the avowedly socialist countries more and more production of goods and services is designed for and sold on a world market, over which the political authorities of the socialist states have little influence, even if they wished to exert it. (Gold and shipping are two exceptions.)

Second, that part of the world economy that responds entirely to market signals, and obeys the laws of supply and demand with the absolute minimum of interference by governments and other authorities, is also shrinking. Trade in primary products—food and unprocessed raw materials—is more often conducted in markets over which individual buyers and sellers have little or no capacity to determine price than is trade in manufactures and services where more prices are "administered" in Galbraith's words. But trade in primary products constitutes a shrinking proportion of total world trade.

Third, that part of the production structure geared to purely national markets over which national authorities may if they wish exercise a choice of policies to influence the preferred combination of factors of production, the price and terms for the employment of labor, land, and capital, and the rules incumbent on employers, banks, landlords, buyers, sellers, brokers, and other intermediaries, is also shrinking. The technological imperative to sell on a world market reduces the area common to all states over which national governments are able to exercise exclusive regulatory power.

Fourth, the largest part of the global production structure in raw materials, in manufacturing, and in service industries is dominated by large transnational corporations (TNCs). The TNCs account for an ever-growing proportion of world trade. This is intrafirm trade that is not subject either to the market and not necessarily affected by the trade barriers imposed by states. In this largest and fastest-growing section of the world production structure, TNCs based in the United States, plus TNCs based elsewhere but having a large part of their profit-making operations in the United States, play a dominant role. Any TNC, whatever its nationality, that hopes to keep a substantial share of the world market now finds it indispensable to operate in the territorial United States. The political authority, therefore, that most TNC executives are likely to heed and most anxious to avoid offending is that based in Washington. Some Japanese executives will still respond more readily and out of habit to Japanese political authority, but if they wish to operate on a global market, even they will find it increasingly necessary in the future to pay close attention to what goes on in Washington.

The combined effect of the above dynamic features of the contemporary production structure is to increase the asymmetric influence of some governments compared with others over what is produced, where, by whom, and on what terms. All the decisions about the regulation of market operators and intermediaries that used predominantly to be the prerogative of each national government are now shared unevenly between a few governments of the largest and richest countries— of which the government of the United States is by far the most important.

It follows that the structural power of the United States is not to be measured by the value of the goods and services produced within the territorial United States (that is, the U.S. GNP). Nor yet is it to be measured by the value of such goods sold on (exported to) the world market. If it can be estimated at all, it is the total value of goods and services produced by large companies responsive to policy decisions taken by the U.S. government. A good example of this is the power of the United States to restrict trade between the world market economy and the Soviet bloc. This is not exercised primarily, as recent experience shows, by bludgeoning the governments of NATO allies to conform to the COCOM list. It is exercised by the implicit (and occasionally explicit) threat of the U.S. government to make life hard for any non-U.S. corporation that flouts its will. Another example is the influence of U.S. policy on the corporate strategies of major oil companies, including those like Shell or BP that are not themselves U.S.-based.

The dominance of the U.S. government over the financial structure of the world economy—what Peter Drucker has called the "flywheel" of the real economy—and the enormous leverage that is exercised through this particular form of structural power is even more evident (Drucker 1986). How much credit is provided by governments, by international organizations, and by banks, and to whom, and on what terms is more important than what they produce or sell on the world markets. Whether the U.S. decides to let loose the hounds of inflation or to bang the door of deflation is something over which the rest of the world has little control. Yet it is the world economy that is the anvil and the United States the hammer, in Lenin's apposite metaphor. The story of deregulation of banking and financial services is too long and complex to go into here but there is absolutely no disagreement today among the experts who have researched its progress over the last decade that the initial steps were every time first taken in Washington. And because of the worldwide integration of financial and money markets, because of the competition of banks in an integrated global financial system, and because of the competition of governments as hosts for financial and capital markets, it has proved impossible for any country involved in this financial structure to resist the magnetic pull of U.S. policy. Whether its good effects (opening new opportunities for borrowing and hedging for instance) are worth the bad effects and the risks involved is beside the point. The point is that policy-making power has rested—as it has done throughout the postwar period—with the United States. The perception that the United States has lost power to the banks or to the foreign exchange markets is only correct in the short term. As the experience of the Roosevelt administration in the 1930s showed clearly, bankers like everyone else (even insider traders) are subject to the law, and the law can be changed to bring them back under the control of the states.

The knowledge structure is the least familiar concept to scholars in international relations, even though all are familiar with the adage that "knowledge is power." In this short chapter there is hardly space to explain the concept in full. But just as the power to determine what shall be produced by whom and on what terms constitutes structural power in production, so the power to determine what knowledge shall be sought; how it shall be accumulated and applied; how and where knowledge once accumulated shall be stored; and to whom it shall be communicated and on what terms, constitutes another kind of structural power in world society and in the world economy (Strange 1988).

Some of the illustrations of American dominance in the global knowledge structure that may be cited are the continued dominance of U.S. corporations in most of the high-technology industries; the dominance of U.S. banks in transborder data flows; the dominance of U.S. media organizations in news and entertainment; the outward spread from the United States to the rest of the world of management, marketing, and advertising techniques; the dominance of U.S. banks and consultancy enterprises in debt management; the dominant position of U.S. government and U.S. corporations in satellite communications; and the ability of U.S. universities to attract and use scientists and academics from the rest of the world, drawing them not simply by better salaries but by better opportunities for research and exchange of information and ideas with their peers. Above all, perhaps, it is evident in the use of the American version of the English language as the world's lingua franca even for the French, the Russians, and the Chinese.

Finally, there is the structural power exercised in matters of security. It is the United States, in response only to the Soviet Union, that has determined the world's dependence for its security on the balance of nuclear deterrence conveyed by an armory of intercontinental, intermediate, and short-range missiles. This is the only global structure of them all where the United States shares power with the Soviet Union. In all the other three, Soviet structural power extends only as far as the reach of the Red Army; U.S. structural power reaches deeply into the developing continents of Africa and South America, into Asia and the Middle East, and relentlessly even into Eastern Europe and China. This structural power over who is assured security and by what means, at what costs, and at what risk is, however, reinforced by the United States' structural power over the world's productive system, over its financial structure and the credit institutions and markets that function in it, and over the producers and communicators of knowledge in the knowledge structure.

The conclusion to be drawn from this structural analysis is that the decline of U.S. hegemony is a myth—powerful, no doubt, but still a myth. In every important respect the United States still has the predominant power to shape frameworks and thus to influence outcomes. This implies that it can draw the limits within which others can choose from a restricted list of options, the restrictions being in large part a result of U.S. decisions. As Wallerstein emphasizes, hegemony does not mean total power to command. It means predominance; and predominance conveys the ability to change the range within which it is reasonably possible for others to choose among various courses of action.

All that happened in the late 1970s in the aftermath of Vietnam, of Watergate, of the fall of the Shah and of the partly self-inflicted humiliation over the Tehran hostages, is that American self-confidence faltered under the leadership of a weak, tired, and shallow-minded president. The academics of the 1980s have been living in the past and figuring out theories of hegemonic stability to account for the public mood of the late 1970s. This is not, however, the first time that social scientists have behaved like generals who, overtaken by events, make elaborate preparations to fight the last war.

The other thing that has happened, and not only to the United States, is that structural change has at last severed the connection between the power of the state and its control over territory. The territorial frontiers of the state are now important only inasmuch as there is a consensus among existing, mutually recognized political authorities that regulatory power over the *consumers* living within its frontiers rests with the authorities of the territorial state. The power over the producers, and over the security, credit, and ideas available to both producers and consumers may be exercised by other authorities beyond the territory. This structural change has perforated the borders that define national societies, national defensive systems, national monetary and economic systems, and to a large extent national cultures. But the perforations operate unevenly, and certainly asymmetrically, so that the borders of the United States are far less perforated by structural change than those of others, and the United States has had more influence than others over the nature and direction of the structural change.

What is emerging therefore is a nonterritorial empire with its imperial capital in Washington, D.C. Where imperial capitals used once to draw courtiers from outlying provinces, Washington draws lobbyists from outlying enterprises, outlying minorities, and globally organized pressure groups. Authority in this nonterritorial empire is exercised directly on people—not on land. It is exercised on bankers and corporate executives, on savers and investors, on journalists and teachers. It is also of course exercised on the heads of allied and associated governments, as successive summit conferences have clearly shown. Moreover, all the major policy trends of the 1980s that have commonly afflicted most of the developed and semideveloped countries and that have appeared to be of a national and internal character—deregulation, deflation, privatization, and so on—have been set off in the United States and have been followed by others who felt unable to resist. In all these policy areas, frontiers have been no defense against pressures emanating from the United States.

This is the major difference between the American and Soviet empires. The Soviet empire is more old-fashioned. It remains much more firmly territorial, much more dependent, like the empires of old, on a clearly defended perimeter frontier all around it, marking off those inside the empire from those outside.

The American nonterritorial empire is different.

To start with, the perimeter fence around those American client states corresponding to the Soviet client states of Eastern Europe is not a rigid containing wall, preventing movement outside and enforcing conformity inside. Canada and Mexico both live in the shadow of the United States but their degree of freedom to choose is very substantially greater than that of Poland or even Hungary. Moreover, beyond the U.S. "backyard" of North and Central America and the Pacific and Caribbean islands, there is another American empire that really *is* nonterritorial and in some respects is more like the Roman empire than the French or British empires. As in Rome, citizenship is not limited to a master race and the empire contains a mix of citizens with full legal and political rights, semicitizens and noncitizens like Rome's slave population. Many of the semicitizens walk the streets of Rio or of Bonn, of London or Madrid, shoulder to shoulder with the noncitizens; no one can necessarily tell them apart by color or race or even dress. The semicitizens of the empire are many and widespread. They live for the most part in the great cities of the noncommunist world. They include many people employed by the large transnational corporations operating in the transnational production structure and serving, as they are all very well aware, a global market. They include the people employed in transnational banks. They often include members of "national" armed forces, those that are trained, armed by, and dependent on the armed forces of the United States. They include many academics in medicine, natural sciences, and social studies like management and economics who look to U.S. professional associations and to U.S. universities as the peer group in whose eyes they wish to shine and to excel. They include people in the press and media for whom U.S. technology and U.S. examples have shown the way, changing established organizations and institutions.

Because the Americans once fought a war of independence to be free of British domination, they have ever since counted themselves as among the world's anti-imperialists. They think of empire building as a peculiarly European foible in which they themselves do not indulge. They think of empires as if they were all like European empires. For this reason they find it particularly hard to abandon their embedded image of themselves as inveterate liberals and anti-imperialists, or to recognize U.S. foreign and economic policies as in any sense the policies of an imperial power (Strange 1986; Dale 1986; Nunnenkamp 1986).

Americans are not, of course, the only ones to nurture a delusion about themselves or to suffer the myopic inability, as Robert Burns put it, "to see oursels as ithers see us!" But in their particular case the myopia has had the side effect that it has shut scholarly inquiry off from a whole range of questions that could be of great significance for the future of the world. It has made most U.S. scholars temperamentally rather indifferent to theoretical analysis of all aspects of the phenomenon of empire. Recent exceptions are Doyle (1986), Olson (1982) and Kennedy (1987). But even these studies have addressed the question of what it is that makes some empires decline, rather than what it is that makes other empires last.

Interest in imperialism as a phenomenon of world society already has a bias toward the negative aspects rather than the positive aspects of the subject, for which Hobson and Lenin and much subsequent marxist writing are chiefly responsible. This has emphasized the negative causes—reasons such as the falling rate of profit on capital—for the acquisition of empires, and the negative consequences of imperialism for the inhabitants of empires and for international relations generally. The major divergence of interpretation was that between Lenin and Kautsky as to whether competition between capitalist states for imperial possessions was apt to increase the chances of war between them or, alternatively, whether their shared interest in the exploitation of human and natural resources of less economically developed parts of the world would lead them to form an implicit cooperative structure that would make it more difficult for dependent peoples to throw off their inferior, disadvantaged role in the world economy. The presumption of most writers on imperialism has been that imperialism was undesirable, so that the main policy-related issue was how to get rid of it.

Standing back a little from the literature on imperialism, it is at once apparent that it has been very narrowly based upon European experience. Certain characteristics of imperial power have been taken for granted that in fact need not apply universally, but that were characteristic of the European empires of the sixteenth to twentieth centuries. For example, it is often assumed that empires are *overseas* empires, and that they are not usually contiguous to the territory of the metropolitan power—even though it is clear that in the Russian case (under the tsars and under the soviets), and in the case of China, this is not so.

Prevailing theories also assume that the imperial power is more advanced in its economic development and in its command of technology than the areas it dominates. Again, Soviet domination of Eastern Europe, and especially of East Germany, Czechoslovakia, and Hungary contests this assumption. Soviet technology is more advanced in defense-related industry, but not in other sectors. This suggests that some U.S. writers may be wrong who assume that the United States must lead the world in *every* sector of economic life or else resign itself to total loss of hegemonial power.

Prevailing theory also assumes that the advanced country surrounds its territorial empire with protective barriers in order to give itself a market sheltered from foreign competition. As a consequence, the prices of many goods sold to the local inhabitants are higher than they would otherwise be. Furthermore, it extracts minerals and other raw materials at low prices, thus doubly exploiting the inhabitants. By focusing exclusively on this exploitative character of territorial empires, a theory of imperialism has naturally been inclined to ask only a limited range of questions.

It seems to me that what is needed now is some fundamental reconsideration of the nature of empires; about the benefits they may confer, the risks they may modify, and the opportunities they may open up as well as the costs they may impose—on which so much attention in past theories of imperialism has concentrated. Secondly, we need some serious reexamination of the policy options open to imperial powers. (You may call them "hegemonic powers" or "states exercising leadership in an alliance" if labels bother you.)

The justification for pushing theoretical work in these directions is twofold. One is that imperial decline is a common source of instability and conflict in international systems. The other is that if the alternative to a power vacuum in the wake of an American empire is either a Soviet, a Japanese, or even a Chinese—or (less likely) a collective European empire—or else a collective, multipolar system, none of these would be as acceptable to the constituents as is the present American empire.

On the first point, it is a fact that the major destabilizing developments in the international system of the last hundred years have all been associated with the decline and breakup of old territorial empires. The fall of the tsarist Russian empire, of the Turkish Ottoman empire, of the Manchu Chinese empire, of the British Raj, of the French empire and even of the Belgian and Dutch empires have all been followed by quite serious conflict between the successor states or would-be states. As Denis Brogan once wrote in a book titled *The Price of Revolution* (1948), revolutionaries always overestimate the fruits of revolution and grossly underestimate the costs. There is therefore much to be said in politics and in political economy for gradualist solutions, and for gentle and gradual rather than violent change. Systematic study devoted to the development of a theory of nonterritorial empires would seem to serve just this purpose.

On the second point, that an American nonterritorial empire is much to be preferred to either a Soviet or a Japanese one, it seems obvious that most Europeans, Asians, and Latin Americans associate an unacceptable restriction of both political freedom and of economic freedom and enterprise with what they know of the present Soviet empire and are not keen to see it extended. Similarly, the corresponding suspicion of and resistance to a second Japanese empire in East Asia is not just a matter of bitter memories from the early 1940s.

The big difference between the Japanese and the Americans is that it is very easy to become an American and very hard to become a Japanese. Koreans who were born in Japan and have lived there all their lives are still not accepted by the native Japanese—not even as much as Turks who have lived far less long in West Germany are accepted by the native West Germans. Such is the cultural obsession with national purity that Japanese companies in Latin America do not even trust second-generation Brazilian Japanese to take managerial responsibility in running their Brazilian subsidiaries. As the British would have put it in the days of the Raj, they are considered to have "gone native," to have lost their pure Japanese cultural status. By contrast, as American semicitizens are aware, it is not difficult for foreigners to merge into the American melting pot. And once in it, the American free enterprise culture emphasizes the opportunities of upward mobility, economically, and afterward socially. It is much easier in the United States for foreign students to work their way through college or for foreigners to buy property and establish rights of residence in the United States than in most other countries of the world. As European and especially British imperial experience showed, racial discrimination is a major handicap in running and maintaining a stable and successful empire. The Americans have less of it than most.

The absence of an alternative that is both stable and acceptable is therefore the rationale for pushing theory building in international studies toward some reexamination of those policies for governing an empire that are essential and ineluctable and those that are less essential or even counterproductive. There is no lack of historical material here to draw on. For example, it suggests that direct rule is not necessary for stable imperial government. Direct British rule in India coexisted with indirect control over the Indian princely states. They were only taken over or interfered with—as in Oudh—in cases of grossest incompetence or the most extreme strategic necessity. Even in Africa, the British managed a dual system, governing indirectly through tribal chiefs and directly through district commissioners who were sometimes almost beardless former public schoolboys given authority over hundreds of square miles of territory. Experience suggests that one of the recurrent problems for imperial powers—and one of the most difficult—has always been how much support and in what form to give to the local rulers and how much to interfere in their decision making. The United States currently faces precisely this problem both in South Korea and in the Philippines.

The evidence of history also suggests that among the policy areas requiring close imperial control are defense and communications. How the imperial armed forces protecting the empire are to be recruited, equipped, commanded, and paid for has always been a major policy question—as it is now for the United States and its NATO allies (Calleo 1987). In communications—so vital to the cohesion and control of any empire from Rome and ancient China to the U.S.-dominated financial system of today—the question who shall have access to the means of communication, how these shall be paid for, and what they may be used for in addition to the messages of state remains a crucial one.

Students of international organizations familiar with the history of INTELSAT and MARISAT will readily appreciate the similarities of U.S. policies to those of the Roman and Chinese empires, with their roads and pony express systems, and the British and French empires with their steamship routes, their air routes, and telegraph and telephone cable links.

Not every state is well suited to an imperial role nor to act as leader of an affluent alliance of protected states taking collective responsibility for managing the world's monetary, financial, and other economic affairs. It would seem from historical experience that two variables will make for good imperial government. One is a political philosophy that has some universal appeal to fundamental ethical principles, and which will therefore find an echo in the hearts and minds of affluent associates and less affluent "subjects." The other is a political system, whether formally run according to a written constitution or not, that allows the coordination of policy directed at the imperial state with other policies directed at the government of the empire. (The semi-independent status of the India Office in nineteenth-century Britain is one good example of this.)

The United States is more fortunate on the first count than on the second. It was a state inaugurated with a formal Declaration of Independence that embodied universal principles of liberty, equality, and democratic control. It does still pay lip service to these ideals though there is a persistent conflict between those who believe that the principles apply primarily within the United States (and that therefore the United States is an exceptional country), and those that see the principles broadly described as political human rights as having universal validity—or at least as ultimate goals. In recent years there have been signs of growing awareness in Washington of the long-term U.S. interest in a more stable and growing world economy and of the need to adapt U.S. policies (for example, on development finance to the Third World) to this imperative. There are therefore some grounds here for optimism.

The outlook for change in the U.S. political system is less favorable. The Constitution (whose bicentenary was recently celebrated with such piety and devotion) was obviously admirably adapted to prevent tyranny and ensure freedom for a developing country on the periphery of the world system. A matter for serious consideration now is how it could be adapted and improved for the future in such a way as to enable the United States to avoid the blind unilateralism, the violent changes of foreign and financial policy, and the short-sighted selfishness of its commercial policies that have marked recent years.

Even more difficult are the central political questions of legitimacy and hegemonial power as understood by Gramsci. A common weakness of most territorial empires is the risk of allowing rivalry to develop between military and civil authority.

Dependence on the military for the defense of the territorial frontier has always threatened the political stability of constitutional empires—as the example of Julius Caesar in the early Roman empire showed. It seems that concentrated military power corrupts more quickly to the detriment of civil society within an empire. The American nonterritorial empire certainly has the strength of an efficient communications system. The very fact that it *is* nonterritorial ought to make it possible to curb the power of the military within it because, although power in the security structure is one source of strength for the United States, it is not by any means the only one. The military interest is balanced by industrial and financial interests, as in Britain's nineteenth-century empire, and this may well be a source of strength.

A reasonable hypothesis for such a theory might be that a nonterritorial empire will remain strong and stable as long as there are shared interests between the dominant center and important sections of society in the peripheral parts of the empire. These shared interests would maintain a sort of internal balance of power preventing disintegration. This at least seems to be a conclusion that could be drawn from the history of federal states in recent times. In all of these there is a latent danger of secession, jeopardizing the cohesion of the state. Think of Bavaria in the Federal Republic of Germany, of Québec in Canada, or the deep South in the United States. Earlier on, there were other examples, like Bohemia in the Hapsburg empire. In each case, coercive power was more effective when it was tempered with placatory concessions. But equally, coercive power has sometimes to be used to prevent secession or unilateralist revolt. An instance was when the Australian Commonwealth government had to act forcefully in the 1930s to prevent New South Wales—the largest and richest of the states of the Australian federation—from defaulting on its foreign debt. Or when the Indian government more recently has had to use force to prevent secession by the Sikhs. The result of a lack of such coercive authority can be seen in the failed East African federation—and possibly in the future—in Yugoslavia after Tito.

A theory of nonterritorial empire would seek to ask the political questions of which problems were the same as in territorial empires, and which are likely to be different. And it would ask—though from a totally different point of departure—some of the same economic questions as those posed by students of "interdependence." How, for instance, can an international banking system be effectively managed without the risk of panic or collapse? Or, how can a Keynesian policy of demand management be effectively developed to stabilize a flagging world economy? These are questions that will find no answers so long as they are approached from a state-centric point of view. Only by assuming the existence of a nonterritorial empire may we be able to find the way in which policy could be moved.

It would seem to me that the recognition by U.S. scholars of the full implications of the structural power of the United States would lead in many interesting new directions and would produce many more constructive and creative ideas for policymakers than the present obsolete, state-centric, territory-bound debates that ignore some of the fundamental changes that have taken place in the world political economy in the last twenty-five years.

References

Aron, R. (1958). "War and Industrial Society." Stevenson Lecture, London School of Economics and Political Science.

Calleo, D. (1987). *Beyond American Hegemony: The Future of the Atlantic Alliance.* New York: Basic Books.

Dale, R. (1986). *The Regulation of International Banking.* London: Macmillan.

Doyle, M. (1986). *Empires.* Ithaca: Cornell University Press.

Drucker, P. (1986). "The Changing World Economy." *Foreign Affairs* 64 (Summer):768–91.

Kennedy, P. (1987). *The Rise and Fall of the Great Powers: Economic Change and Military Conflict, from 1500 to 2000.* New York: Random House.

Krasner, S., ed. (1983). *International Regimes.* Ithaca: Cornell University Press.

Miller, J.D.B. (1986). *Norman Angell and the Futility of War.* London: Macmillan.

Nunnenkamp, P. (1986). *The International Debt Crisis of the Third World.* Brighton: Wheatsleaf.

Olson, M. (1982). *The Rise and Decline of Nations.* New Haven: Yale University Press.

Russett, B. (1985). "The Mysterious Case of Vanishing Hegemony; or, Is Mark Twain Really Dead?" *International Organization* 39, no. 2 (Spring):207–32.

Strange, S. (1986). *Casino Capitalism.* Oxford: Basil Blackwell.

—— (1987). "The Persistent Myth of Lost Hegemony." *International Organization* 41 (Fall):551–74.

—— (1988). *States and Markets.* New York: Blackwell.

Wolfe, A. (1977). *The Limit of Legitimacy: Political Contradictions of Contemporary Capitalism.* New York: Free Press.

10
The Real Decline in Nuclear Hegemony

Bruce Russett

S ome time ago I wrote a piece (Russett 1985) arguing that the decline in U.S. hegemony of the international system had been greatly exaggerated. I contended that the U.S. ability to influence outcomes, as derived from its economic strength, military capabilities, and global cultural and ideological penetration, remained at least as high as that of previous "hegemons" and not substantially below that which the United States itself wielded in the preceding decades. I still believe that characterization is essentially correct.[1] But the discussion of military instruments of power, especially the role of nuclear weapons, needs to be very carefully nuanced. Observers have been too quick to proclaim the decline of economic hegemony by the United States, and too slow to recognize the decline in nuclear hegemony generally.

In this chapter I will contend that the primary purpose of superpower nuclear weapons—extended deterrence—has always been of somewhat doubtful utility, and that the doubts have grown substantially, and with good reason, over the past two decades. Concurrent with the military situation, international norms have evolved to reinforce the unusability of nuclear weapons. Their unusability has meant that the role of nuclear weapons in reinforcing hierarchies of centralized power (hegemony), whether globally, within alliances, or within states, has declined, with uncertain consequences for the world system.

What Are Nuclear Weapons Good For?

Nuclear weapons remain extremely effective instruments to achieve some military and political purposes; they have little utility—less than previously—for others. They are not necessarily very important for those purposes for which they seem useful.

Nuclear weapons remain most useful for the purpose for which they are least needed, and have always been least needed: deterrence of nuclear or conventional

---

I am grateful to William Foltz, Joshua Goldstein, Paul Huth, Peter Katzenstein, Robert Keohane, Joel Rosenthal, and Dieter Senghaas for comments on an earlier draft.

attack on the home territory of a superpower. Whatever Soviet leaders may have feared following World War II, it is clear that they did not need to fear a deliberate, unprovoked attack by the United States on their home territory, either in the form of conventional invasion or nuclear strike. Despite some talk on the fringes, "preventive war" never remotely approached acceptance as U.S. policy; moral restraints, the vast challenge of subduing and occupying the Soviet Union, and the inability to prevent Soviet conventional devastation of Western Europe in the meantime were, in some mix, fully sufficient deterrents long before the Soviet military actually received operational nuclear weapons in 1952. Similarly, the United States deployed its nuclear weapons long before the Soviet Union had its, and has always been fully as immune from invasion.[2]

Now that both sides have vast numbers of nuclear weapons it is plausible that if either one undertook total nuclear disarmament while the other did not the side retaining nuclear weapons might be tempted to strike with them. That would present an opportunity to end the troublesome rivalry, and to eliminate the risk of subsequent nuclear rearmament by the adversary. But unilateral nuclear disarmament by either side is not very likely. So long as both sides maintain sophisticated, diverse systems of nuclear deterrence, the chance of deliberate, unprovoked nuclear attack is close to nil. This principle is well recognized by even the most cautious strategic analysts. Even the strongest proponents of the idea of a "window of vulnerability" worried about the risk of attack during the escalation of a severe crisis, not about an adventurous strike "out of the blue."

The fact is that nuclear weapons were originally built and deployed not to deter direct attack but for the purpose of extended deterrence or compellence; that is, to protect the security of allies and client states. As such, they were to be a pillar of American post–World War II hegemony. The first implicit threat to use nuclear weapons was by the United States to defend West Berlin and West Germany in 1948; subsequent ones were to try to roll back nascent Chinese entry into the Korean War, to coerce China to accept U.S. terms to end that war, and to deter Chinese attack on the offshore islands of Quemoy and Ma-tsu. In each case the target of the threat was a nonnuclear power. After the Korean War the U.S. principle of "massive retaliation" with nuclear weapons in response to conventional attack by a Soviet "satellite" was made explicit policy. During the 1950s the British developed their own "independent" nuclear deterrent not because they feared being the object of a direct attack, but to cover threats to remaining imperial interests that might be too peripheral to engage U.S. commitment. And the first Soviet nuclear threat was a rather transparent bluff to try to halt the British and French advance at Suez; Britain's nuclear weapons at that time posed little threat to the Soviet Union, and the French still had none. Extended deterrence and compellence formed the game.

The Soviet Union's achievement of an assured retaliatory capability sharply limited any use for U.S. nuclear weapons in making compellent or extended deterrent threats. If one side's assured retaliatory capability were really in serious doubt, then it might be subject to compellent or deterrent threats. But the doubts would have to be very substantial, more than seems plausible with anything like current technology and the numbers of weapons on either side. Otherwise the risks of catastrophe would seem too high for any remotely rational decision maker actually to carry out the threat.

Paradoxically, with a deliberate nuclear strike in full peacetime virtually out of the question, nuclear weapons as deterrents become the problem rather than the solution. A direct nuclear attack on a superpower's homeland would happen, if at all, only during an extended deterrence crisis. To the degree either power's retaliatory capability is in any doubt, the danger of preemption in the face of threat raises its head. (A few such threats have been made, but to no apparent effect, as we shall see below.) Perhaps if, and only if, a nuclear power were faced either with the imminent loss of a truly vital national interest, or with the perception that the other nuclear power was about to attack it in desperation, a nuclear strike might appear to be the least unattractive option available. In an interacting high-level alert, where *they* might preempt because they think *I* might preempt, and so on, the risks of *not* striking might be high. To wait might mean losing the capacity for any effective "damage limitation" or even retaliation. If it is no longer possible to win a nuclear war, it is possible to lose one, with degrees of losing on an absolute scale (rather than one merely relative to the condition of the adversary) ranging from very bad to dreadful. Under those conditions, and given vulnerability and counterforce capabilities, nuclear weapons create a very real problem of crisis stability. Thus nuclear weapons prevent what they are little needed to prevent (a direct attack "out of the blue") but become a lightning rod to draw fire during the storm of an extended deterrence crisis.

A Brief History of Nuclear Threats

A review of the full history of nuclear threats will show their decreasing frequency and utility. Table 10–1 lists these threats, with the following characterizations: For their purpose, I distinguish between general deterrence, immediate deterrence, and compellence. General deterrence applies to an adversarial relationship with no particular overt challenge; immediate deterrence, by contrast, is "where at least one side is considering an attack while the other is mounting a threat of retaliation in order to prevent it" (Morgan 1983 ch. 1). Whereas a deterrent threat says "don't do it," a compellent threat says "stop doing it," or "do something else." Threats may be conveyed explicitly by verbal communication, overtly by the manipulation of military forces, or only implicitly and ambiguously by words. Finally, a threat may succeed or fail in its purpose, or be irrelevant. If the adversary defies the threat, it has failed. If the adversary does as directed, it may be because the threat succeeded, or because action was taken for some reason other than the nuclear threat— because of some other influence, or because the act was intended anyway. If the latter, the nuclear threat is simply irrelevant.

Table 10–1
Nuclear Threats since 1945

Year	Threatener	Recipient	Interest	General Immediate Coercive	Explicit Overt Implicit	Succeeded Failed Irrelevant
1948	U.S.	USSR	W. Berlin	I	O?	S?
1950	U.S.	China	Korea	C	E	F
1953	U.S.	China	Korea	C	I	S?
1955	U.S.	China	Quemoy & Ma-tsu	I	E	S?
1956	USSR	UK & France	Suez	C	E	I
1958	U.S.	USSR	Lebanon	G	O	I?
1958	U.S.	China	Quemoy & Ma-tsu	I?	E	I?
1958	USSR	U.S.	W. Berlin	C	I	F
1959	U.S.	USSR	W. Berlin	I?	I	I?
1961	U.S.	USSR	W. Berlin	I?	I	I?
1962	U.S.	USSR	Cuba	C	O & E	S
1969	USSR	China	Border	I?	I	I?
1969	U.S.	N. Vietnam	S. Vietnam	C	E?	F
1973	U.S.	USSR	Israel	I	O	I?
1975	U.S.	N. Korea	S. Korea	G	E	I?
1980	U.S.	USSR	Persian Gulf	G	I	I

Sources: Principally Betts (1987); also Bundy (1984), Ellsberg (1981), Halperin (1987).

There are often doubts and ambiguities attached to any of these judgments, and it is not possible to clear them all up or document all the judgments here. I indicate the more serious cases of doubt with question marks, and I do not believe that a contrary judgment would severely compromise the conclusions to be drawn. Before trying to draw any conclusions from table 10–1 it will be helpful to explain very briefly some of the question marks.

In the 1948 Berlin crisis the U.S. threat constituted movement of B-29 bombers to bases in Britain. Whereas the B-29 was then the primary delivery instrument for U.S. atomic bombs, those B-29s were not equipped to carry nuclear weapons and Soviet intelligence may well have known that. Hence the nature of the threat and its efficacy are questionable.

Coincident with its three threats to China between 1953 and 1958 the United States achieved its goals, but it is questionable what role the nuclear threats played in that achievement. Evidence that the Chinese intended to invade Quemoy and Ma-tsu is weaker for 1958 than for 1955.

There is no indication that the Soviet Union had any intention of opposing the 1958 U.S. landing in Lebanon or taking other military action.

Soviet intentions in the later Berlin crises are also in doubt. Arguably the Soviet Union achieved its primary goal by erecting the Berlin Wall.

Chinese intentions in 1969 are likewise unknown.

Halperin (1987, 41) declares that Nixon and Kissinger conveyed several explicit nuclear warnings in demanding that North Vietnam accept a negotiated settlement. Documentary evidence to support Halperin is not publicly available. If the threats were made they certainly failed.

Betts (1987, 129) says of the 1973 alert, "More than in most cases, the circumstantial evidence for inferring efficacy in the U.S. nuclear threat is weak, and much points in the direction of concluding that it was beside the point."

Halperin (1987, 44) includes Defense Secretary James Schlesinger's warning to North Korea, delivered in 1975 soon after the fall of South Vietnam, but there is no evidence that North Korea was seriously considering military action. The "threat" was directed more toward a South Vietnamese audience as part of American post-Vietnam reassurance.

Truman said that he made a nuclear threat when in 1946 he demanded that the Soviet Union leave northern Iran. The consensus of historians, however (see Bundy 1984, 45), is that all relevant documents are available and none show a nuclear threat; hence it is not listed in the table. The widespread belief that such a threat was made, and succeeded, may nevertheless have contributed to policymakers' faith in the efficacy of nuclear threats.

Table 10–1 shows why Bundy can characterize the record of nuclear diplomacy as "unimpressive." The only unambiguous success was in the Cuban missile crisis of 1962. Weaker and less plausible, but not refutable, arguments can be made for two of the U.S. threats to China in the 1950s and, still more weakly, for what was only an ambiguous threat in the first Berlin crisis. Other cases range from very weak indeed to clear evidence of the failure of nuclear threats. This corresponds to the results of several studies that have been made of the role of the *existence* of nuclear weapons (not necessarily a threat to use them) in extended deterrence crises. Systematic comparative analysis, including multivariate statistical examination of a fairly large number of cases of extended deterrence crises, concludes that nuclear weapons in the hands of the defender have not increased the probability that deterrence will succeed, at least since the 1950s. Rather, other elements of the balance of power—especially local military forces in the immediate region at stake—and interests, plus the bargaining behavior and reputation of the principals, make the difference. This conclusion is put forth with some tentativeness, but when stated carefully—there is little evidence that nuclear weapons systematically make a difference—it is important (see Huth, 1988a; Huth and Russett 1988; Blechman and Kaplan 1978; Kugler 1984; with a contrary conclusion by Weede 1983).

Save for the Cuban missile crisis, all the plausibly successful threats were made in the first decade of the nuclear era and against adversaries who did not themselves possess nuclear weapons. Even allowing for Soviet nuclear weaponry in the 1953 and 1955 threats to China, this was undeniably a period of very great U.S. nuclear superiority. Ten of the nuclear threats were made in the first sixteen years of the nuclear era, before the Cuban missile crisis. Only five have been made in the subsequent twenty-six years, even counting the doubtful 1969 Nixon threat to North Vietnam.

Reference to the Cuban missile crisis inevitably raises the question of how important strategic nuclear superiority has been in determining both whether nuclear threats were made and whether they would succeed. Participants and analysts disagree vehemently about whether U.S. strategic nuclear superiority or U.S. local conventional superiority in the Caribbean made the greater difference in persuading the Soviet Union to pull out its weapons. But the facts of U.S. nuclear superiority, the threat to use nuclear weapons, and Soviet acquiescence are not in doubt.

Some participants in decision making during the crisis emphasize their hesitancy, even given superiority, in light of Soviet retaliatory capabilities: "They were finally forced out, but it was not through the threat of use of nuclear weapons. We never conceived of using nuclear weapons under those circumstances. It was our tremendous conventional power in the region which forced the Soviets to take those missiles out" (Robert S. McNamara, quoted in Charlton 1987, 23). The crisis showed "not the significance but the insignificance of nuclear superiority in the face of survivable thermonuclear forces" (Bundy 1984, 55). Henry Kissinger, who was not there, says a bit differently, "Khrushchev withdrew from Cuba because we had local superiority. On top if it, what made it easy was that we also had strategic superiority" (quoted in Charlton 1987, 55). Revelations at a 1987 "reunion" of Cuban missile crisis participants made it clear how much of the received wisdom on that event (for example, Allison 1971) is misleading, and how difficult it is to reconstruct motives and decisions in national security crises.

Nuclear threats were more common in the years up through the Cuban missile crisis than afterward. If made by the United States, with its nuclear superiority, they were more likely then to have at least some semblance of success. Is this because U.S. leaders believed that their nuclear superiority gave them near-immunity from Soviet retaliation? The most thorough review of the historical documentation concludes that was not the case. U.S. leaders usually believed that a Soviet retaliatory strike would impose severe costs on the United States; they did not feel immune and perhaps felt more vulnerable than now-available information about the nuclear balance suggests they need have been. "There may, conceivably, have been a golden age when U.S. leaders could be confident in their ability to limit damage from Soviet nuclear retaliation to a remotely acceptable level—say, total blast and fallout fatalities under 10 percent of the population. But it was an age that comprised, at best, only two brief periods: the years before the mid-1950s and a few years in the early 1960s" (Betts 1987, 174). Even in the possible "golden age," this is a very weak statement about immunity.

Betts's conclusion is carefully balanced: U.S. escalation dominance perhaps "made nuclear superiority if not a rational comfort, a visceral one" (p. 178). U.S. decision makers were not prepared deliberately to make nuclear war, but were willing to take some risks that matters might escalate to nuclear war. One may or may not judge that willingness to have been adventurism, but the circumstances that made it possible passed with the advent of nuclear parity and "essential equivalence."[3]

The five cases since the Cuban missile crisis deserve some attention. The Soviet nuclear threat to China was verbally somewhat ambiguous, but we know the Soviet leadership seriously considered using nuclear weapons—if with the assent of the United States. When the United States failed to reply favorably, the Soviets then did nothing. The Chinese moved to reduce military tensions in the border conflict, for reasons we cannot fully know. Relieved of the immediate danger and devoid of any U.S. support for relief from their longer-run worries about China as a nuclear power, the Soviets stood down despite their overwhelming nuclear superiority over the Chinese. The alleged U.S. threat to North Vietnam in 1969 may never have been made; if it was, it is clear the Nixon administration had no intention whatever of carrying it out. The 1973 nuclear alert and signaling was a pale shadow of the Cuban missile crisis. Neither Schlesinger's 1975 threat nor Carter's in 1980 was made at a time of international crisis or immediate threat of communist attack. Delivered under conditions of general deterrence, the threats were not very provocative, and did not create problems of crisis alert and signaling; Schlesinger and Carter were not at immediate risk of having to put up or shut up. None demonstrated the credible willingness to initiate nuclear war that might have been inferred in some previous crises. There have been no nuclear threats since 1980. Whereas Betts points out that U.S. leaders have been willing to make nuclear threats without possessing nuclear superiority, those few threats simply do not carry the same weight (note that Betts does not even include the 1969 and 1975 U.S. threats in his list).

Crises without Nuclear Threats

Further clues to the infrequency and ineffectiveness of nuclear threats emerge when we look at the instances when nuclear threats might have been made and were not. Elsewhere a colleague and I have examined the universe of extended immediate deterrence crises over the past century (Huth 1988b; Huth and Russett 1988). Omitting several crises that were included in table 10–1 as nuclear threats, these fourteen involved nuclear powers as defenders. Table 10–2 presents them somewhat in the format of table 10–1. The labels "defender" and "attacker" replace "threatener" and "recipient," however, precisely because no nuclear threat was made. For that same reason the second column for characterization of the threat is omitted, and the first such column is not needed because these are by definition all cases of immediate deterrence.

Several observations can be made. First, of these fourteen cases, three were instances when deterrence did not succeed, despite the fact in two of them only the defender, not the attacker, had nuclear weapons. The mere existence of those weapons in a one-sided relationship was no guarantee of success. Nor in the third instance (1979) was clear Soviet nuclear superiority over China very helpful. Second, all of the failures occurred since 1964. Third, in one instance (China in 1964) deterrence succeeded against a thermonuclear superpower even though the defender's nuclear capability was but nominal (tested but not operational). Fourth, in many of the successes, especially recent ones, it is impossible to believe that the defender's possession of nuclear weapons played any role in the attacker's decision not to press forward. It is absurd to think of the United Kingdom "nuking"

Table 10-2
Extended Immediate Deterrence Crises with Nuclear-Armed Defenders

Year	Defender	Attacker	Interest	Deterrence Succeeded or Failed
1946	U.S.	USSR	Iran	S
1946	U.S.	USSR	Turkey	S
1950	U.S.	China	Taiwan	S
1957	USSR	Turkey	Syria	S
1961	U.K.	Iraq	Kuwait	S
1961	U.S.	N. Vietnam	Laos	S
1964	U.K.	Indonesia	Malaysia	F
1964	China	U.S.	N. Vietnam	S
1964	U.S.	N. Vietnam	S. Vietnam	F
1971	China	India	Pakistani Kashmir	S
1975	U.K.	Guatemala	Belize	S
1977	U.K.	Guatemala	Belize	S
1979	USSR	China	Vietnam	F
1983	France	Libya	Chad	S

Source (with definitions and qualifications): Huth and Russett 1988.

Guatemala, and whatever Khadafi's provocations, it is not much more plausible to postulate a French nuclear strike against Libya. Full multivariate examination of the conditions for success or failure of deterrence is properly left elsewhere. But it is hard to see here any evidence that nuclear weapons have made much difference and, if they once did, that they have done so in the last fifteen years or so.[4]

The essential irrelevance of nuclear weapons even against nonnuclear adversaries emerges even more clearly in a case that did not make either of the above tables: the Falklands/Malvinas war between Britain and Argentina in 1983. It did not appear in the tables because the British never made any deterrent threat at all; they avoided doing so before the Argentine invasion in order not to be provocative. Some British ships in the South Atlantic had nuclear weapons aboard and the Vulcan aircraft used to bomb the occupied airstrips were originally built for carrying nuclear weapons. Nevertheless, even during the course of the war the British made no threat, explicit or implicit, to use those weapons. (Recall that the United States was quite ready to make such threats against China over an equally piddling set of islands in the 1950s). At no time did the Argentine government, though powerless to retaliate in kind and not under the U.S. nuclear umbrella, ever seriously fear that it would be hit by British nuclear weapons.

The Evolution of Norms

Nuclear weapons were understood to. be normatively disproportionate in the Falklands/Malvinas war; perhaps licit in the defense of a homeland or some truly vital national interest, but not of a peripheral one even though British soldiers and sailors were dying in defense of that "peripheral" interest. There has emerged in the global community a recognition that nuclear weapons are unusable across much of the range of traditional military and political interests; that recognition has been strengthened by actions as diverse as the Reagan administration's repeated statements that it does not target Soviet population centers per se, the U.S. Catholic Bishops' Pastoral Letter, and Soviet pledges—however reliable—to take a no-first-use posture.

First use, as a doctrine of deliberate action in a policy of extended deterrence, is in disrepute around the world. In 1982, McGeorge Bundy, George Kennan, Robert McNamara, and Gerard Smith became the first members of the national security establishment to issue a public call for a no-first-use policy. McNamara (1983, 79, his emphasis) subsequently declared, *"Nuclear weapons serve no military purpose whatsoever. They are totally useless—except only to deter one's opponent from using them,"* and said that at least the leaders he served seemed quietly to agree: "In long private conversations with successive Presidents—Kennedy and Johnson—I recommended, without qualification, that they never initiate, under any circumstances, the use of nuclear weapons. I believe they accepted my recommendation." A survey of generals and admirals in 1984 found 61 percent saying they could not justify a nuclear first strike against the Soviet Union (Kohut and Horrock 1984). (Technically, of course, abjuring a first strike does not necessarily mean abjuring first *use* in the face of conventional attack.)

The people of Western Europe (as distinct from their governments) have for three decades expressed themselves in favor of a no-first-use policy. By 1981 fewer than 20 percent of the population in any of the big Western European countries (Britain, France, West Germany, and Italy) thought that NATO should use nuclear weapons to defend itself even "if a Soviet attack by conventional forces threatened to overwhelm NATO forces," and sentiment has not changed significantly since then (Russett and DeLuca 1983; Adler 1986). Americans were somewhat slower to reach this conclusion, but by the late 1960s a majority were opposed to using nuclear weapons to defend their European allies, and by 1982 it was a two-thirds majority. In 1984, three-quarters said they favored a policy of no-first-use in general (Yankelovich and Doble 1984; Kramer et al. 1983; Graham 1987). In this respect popular sentiment has run ahead of elite attitudes.

The disillusionment with first use is of course not just a result of normative developments, and certainly norms themselves are hardly fully independent variables. The numbers and destructive power of the weapons, plus the achievement of a secure second strike capability by the superpowers and probably the secondary nuclear powers (Britain, France, and China) are almost surely the major factors. But fear of retaliation does not account for many of the instances when nuclear weapons were useless to deter nonnuclear states, especially those states like Argentina, which lacked any plausible nuclear defender. No one wants to be the first since 1945 to use a nuclear weapon in war. "Self-deterrence" of the use of nuclear weapons began in the Truman administration (Gaddis 1987, ch. 5); the experience of forty-two years has more firmly established a de facto norm of nonuse.[5]

Betts is inclined not to credit U.S. post-1962 restraint too much to the Soviet achievement of nuclear parity. He rightly points out that U.S. leaders have made nuclear threats on two subsequent occasions (1973 and 1980), and Halperin somewhat tenuously adds two more (1969 and 1975). Nuclear superiority is not a necessary condition to making such threats, and lack of it did not prevent the Soviets from making nuclear threats (ineffective ones) in 1956 and 1958. Some decision makers may be sufficiently risk-prone, or see such vital interests engaged, that they will do so from positions of parity or even inferiority. But they are less likely to do so, especially in real crises where the escalation dynamic of alert and counteralert might become engaged. General deterrence threats, as against North Korea in 1975 or regarding the Persian Gulf in 1980, are much safer—and therefore less impressive.

Reasons for Restraint

Betts also rightly points out that superpower conflicts since 1962 have occurred exclusively at the periphery of superpower interests (that is, not in Europe). Two explanations come to mind. One is that the superpowers have grown more cautious in Europe, with its vital interests to both, and have perhaps done so because of their mutual fears of nuclear weapons use. That is almost surely true. But it is not because the deliberate use of nuclear weapons in Europe is more credible. The deliberate use of those weapons has rather become less credible; that threat has been replaced with what Schelling (1966, 99) called "the threat that leaves something to chance." The threat is that nuclear weapons may be used without the intention or authorization of the central command authorities. In normal peacetime the weapons are under tight control; in a high-level crisis they would likely be widely dispersed, with the capabilities to fire them delegated to low-level military commanders. In wartime those commanders could readily find themselves in situations of "use them or lose them," and of losing their troops, if they hesitated to fire their nuclear weapons. Moreover, commanders of the opposing forces would be aware of those pressures, and consequently be under great temptation to preempt (Bracken 1983; Charles 1987). All these pressures are made worse by the use of dual-capable aircraft and missiles and by the close integration of nuclear and conventional weapons in the field.

These are not the threats of the archetypal rational nuclear deterrent theorist, but threats of losing "rational" centralized control. They illustrate a certain continued utility for nuclear weapons, ironically a perhaps greater utility than against a nonnuclear state. But it is hardly what was envisaged for a dominant nuclear power. The risk is that the political events that give rise to crises may be no more controllable than are military events in the "fog of war." The reluctance of the superpowers to challenge each other in Europe is therefore hardly an indication of their confidence in nuclear weapons as deliberate, manageable instruments of deterrence or war. Such a potentially unstable equilibrium in crisis is hardly what most of the classical nuclear theorists thought they were buying. In the best-informed study of these problems with strategic weapons, Blair (1985) considers the risks of crisis instability to be so serious that he recommends adopting a posture of no immediate *second* strike, allowing time for an informed decision and reducing the pressures on an adversary to preempt. Doing so would, by eliminating the threat that leaves something to chance, mark the end of extended nuclear deterrence as a viable strategy.

A second reason for the credibility of deterrence in Europe has everything to do with the network of economic and political interests, cultural and institutional ties, and past commitments that exist between each superpower and its group of European allies. The superpowers stand ready to fight in Europe not because they think they would benefit by some tilt in the nuclear balance, but because they cannot afford to lose their varied investments (Quester 1987). That fear makes them willing to accept the risks inherent in the threat that leaves something to chance. To counter any possible adventurism on either side there is also, and perhaps as important, the fear of conventional war. Europeans (including Russians) have lived with the experience of full-scale conventional war in their homelands. Nuclear war is an extra and still more horrible threat, but the prospective levels of casualties and property damage from conventional war alone provide an enormously powerful deterrent.

Conventional war among rich industrial states is particularly horror-inducing. They are rich and industrial and could sustain the production of great quantities of war materiel; they could be self-sufficient enough to fight long and hard enough to level the continent. Being rich already, they have all the more to lose by the large-scale devastation of war, and virtually nothing worth gaining. If the deterrent effect of memories of World War II has faded slightly, the entrenchment of interest in preserving postwar prosperity can balance it. Prosperity also is embedded nontrivially in East–West ties of economic interdependence.[6] Even without taking nuclear weapons into account, Europeans in effect are operating at points on the marginal cost and benefit curves where those curves become very flat, and the pattern of incentives is already heavily against war. As Mueller (1988) nicely put it, "A jump from a 50th floor window is probably a bit more horrible to think about than a jump from a 5th floor one, but anyone who finds life even minimally satisfying is extremely unlikely to do either."

A more general reason for the recent infrequency of nuclear threats worldwide is the irrelevance of the dangers they are best designed to deter: loss of territory or the extinction of national sovereignty. By historical standards, national borders have been extraordinarily stable since the end of World War II. Boundaries have been unchanged in Europe. Even in Africa, with so many ethnically arbitrary colonial boundaries, there have been almost no postindependence changes.[7] Cases of loss of sovereignty have been even rarer: only the peaceful union of Tanganyika and Zanzibar into Tanzania, and the hardly peaceful reunification of North and South Vietnam. The essence of nuclear threats is, "Don't cross the boundaries."

Nuclear weapons may have made a contribution to the stability of borders and statehood in Europe. Many observers think so, and think that the effect has on balance been desirable.[8] But it is hard to maintain that they have much to do with the experience in, for example, Africa. Furthermore, whereas nuclear weapons help to deter change in the formal boundaries in Europe, they can do little to deter the kinds of changes that are much more probable—for example, the shift toward market economies in Eastern Europe, or maybe toward greater political pluralism there. These, not boundaries, are what matters for the quality of life in that part of the world. Outside of Europe, U.S. nuclear superiority could not prevent the Soviet Union from aiding armed insurgencies against pro-Western government; now Soviet nuclear parity does nothing to keep the United States from aiding guerrillas in Afghanistan, Angola, Ethiopia, Kampuchea, or Nicaragua.

The nonusability of nuclear weapons has little to do with the fine points of the strategic nuclear balance. Henry Kissinger's exclamation, "What in the name of God is strategic superiority? . . . What do you do with it?" is well known. True, he later stepped back, saying, "If we opt out of the race unilaterally, we will probably be faced eventually with a younger group of Soviet leaders who will figure out what can be done with strategic superiority" (Betts 1987, 212). Yet even the later qualification means only that we must not, by opting out of the race, permit our adversary to achieve superiority; it does not mean that either side can achieve a politically or militarily significant imbalance so long as the other follows the rules of normal prudence.

It may not even be extreme to say that a no-first-use of nuclear weapons regime has grown up, de facto, despite efforts of the nuclear powers (especially the United States) to prevent it. Certainly there are major common norms, expectations, and decision-making procedures for crisis behavior and hence crisis stabilization. The hotline, crisis management centers, and a series of arms control agreements such as for managing contacts between warships at sea and monitoring troop movements in Europe all are intended to stabilize crises. That in turn must mean an ability to assure the other side that one is not intending to use nuclear weapons, or if a few are used inadvertently to establish the inadvertence.

Arenas of Nuclear Hegemony

Nuclear hegemony has operated in two senses. First is the hegemony of the nuclear powers in the international system. Initially it was U.S. hegemony, and then the bipolar nuclear hegemony of both the United States and the Soviet Union within their own blocs. The superpowers talked about nuclear disarmament, but studiously avoided doing it. The late Alva Myrdal characterized their activities as "the game of disarmament." "Behind their outwardly often fierce disagreements . . . there has always been a secret and undeclared collusion between the superpowers. Neither of them has wanted to be restrained by effective disarmament measures." For her the reason was rooted in international politics: "Military competition results in an ever-increasing superiority—militarily and technologically—of the already overstrong superpowers, thus sharpening the discrimination against all lesser powers" (Myrdal 1976). They kept an enormous lead over the other nuclear powers (about ten thousand warheads apiece for the United States and the Soviet Union as compared with only a few hundred for any of the others), and sponsored the Nonproliferation Treaty to prevent the rise of any other nuclear powers.

Indeed, the nonproliferation arena has consistently marked the high point of Soviet-U.S. cooperation on arms control. The form of that cooperation has become a matter of bitterness among many of the nonnuclear states. The bargain for "horizontal" nonproliferation was supposed to be that the superpowers would reduce their "vertical" nuclear proliferation, which they have not done. A major hurdle to any truly substantial reduction of the U.S. and Soviet nuclear armories remains their worry about significantly reducing the gap between themselves and secondary nuclear powers. A European nuclear deterrent—perhaps of substantial capability—is a real possibility in the long run.

Nevertheless, whether or not they fully realize it their position of dominance is beginning to erode. Britain, France, and China all are engaged in programs to expand and modernize their nuclear retaliatory forces. When these programs are completed, each will then have something like a secure second-strike capability—not enough remotely to permit them to engage in extended nuclear deterrence of conventional attack on their own allies, but enough pretty reliably to deter direct attack on themselves. Many knowledgeable observers fear that the nonproliferation regime is about to break down. Even allowing for frequent cries of wolf in the past, the situation is worrisome. Israel has an unannounced but significant de facto nuclear capability; South Africa may well also have joined the club, and efforts to control the situation in South Asia (India and Pakistan) are clearly faltering. It is worth noting that all of these new or candidate nuclear powers are among the minority of states with serious problems about where their boundaries should lie.

The Strategic Defense Initiative (SDI) can be seen as a desperate effort by the United States to restore either its own unilateral nuclear hegemony, as the Soviets apparently fear, or to reestablish on a firm basis the conditions of Soviet-U.S. nuclear cohegemony. Modernization of the British, French, and Chinese forces will give them an assured retaliatory capability only so long as the superpowers do not have a decent SDI. A good SDI for either superpower—however unlikely it may seem—would give that superpower nuclear hegemony. A good or even pretty good SDI for both superpowers would give them joint hegemony against ICBMs in their game of duopoly, because that SDI would be much more effective against the smaller retaliatory force of a secondary or nth nuclear power than against the other superpower. Notice the terms of the Reagan administration's characterization of SDI: something that would include America's allies as contractors and protégés and something for which—if one believes in the tooth fairy—the technology could be shared with the *Russians.*

The other last-gasp means of restoring U.S. nuclear hegemony or cohegemony is represented by the effort to create feasible and credible "limited nuclear options." An ability to fight limited nuclear war, and to keep it limited, would revitalize the principle of extended deterrence as a rational act for a superpower. The effort has proceeded at both the strategic and tactical levels. Kissinger, looking back at his 1956 advocacy of tactical nuclear weapons for the European theater, said, "Sooner or later (I thought it would come sooner than it did) strategic nuclear weapons would tend towards a kind of parity that would make absolute war impossible, and I called for alternatives" (Charlton 1987, 33). Some Americans may like the idea because it implies a "limited" nuclear war could be kept limited to, say, Europe. For the same reason, neither European governments nor their people like the idea.

Ironically, a variety of small accurate weapons, theoretically usable, now exist. More lacking than ever is a sane scenario for limited nuclear war. I have already indicated some of the reasons why the effort to make the deliberate initiation of limited nuclear war credible is unlikely to succeed. The matter cannot be settled to everyone's satisfaction, but there is an impressive array of opinion, from academics to national security professionals to senior military officers that the effort must fail (Ball 1981; Bracken 1983; Steinbruner 1981–82; Bundy et al. 1982; Collins 1982). To these, as well as to most members of the mass public, limited nuclear war is an oxymoron advocated by morons. (Limited nuclear options are essential if the goal is quick war termination, and I agree that such planning for very limited "countercombatant" use is, with great caution, appropriate [most recently in Russett 1988]. Plans for protracted war-fighting, escalation dominance, and war-winning are not.)

If nuclear weapons represent an instrument of centralizing power in the hands of a hegemon or alliance leader, they must secondly be recognized as an instrument for retaining societal hegemony by the leadership of the central government. Governments are regarded as the "legitimate wielders of the instruments of violence." "Terrorists" often are defined as nongovernmental wielders of collective violence, ignoring what others would characterize as state terrorism. Nuclear weapons are the instruments of violence par excellence—the instruments of state terrorism if you will. Only a large modern central government can gather the resources to build, deploy, and control nuclear weapons. Even it can do so only under perceptions of great national danger. The need to limit access to nuclear weapons, and the knowledge of how to build them, becomes the basis for legitimizing state control over a wide range of information. Local governments are not permitted to play with those instruments; small national governments and private individuals can afford to do so with only the greatest of difficulty. States around the world would applaud the extermination of any nonstate actors who tried to use nuclear weapons. Nuclear proliferation into the hands of nonstate actors would erode the basis for state hegemony over national societies.

In his chapter and in his forthcoming book, John Ruggie maintains that the global system of rule is becoming transformed, that the assumptions of territoriality and differentiation among states are becoming ever more invalid. One can argue about whether that is true, and if true whether it will be a "good thing" for humanity. One can also argue about whether the ability of nuclear weapons to reinforce hegemony and territoriality is in fact declining, and whether, if so, that is a good thing. I have no doubts that nuclear weapons have served that function, and am at least inclined to believe that their utility in that function is diminishing. That diminution carries great dangers as well as opportunities. The result may be decentralization of power and reduction of hegemonies in the global system into a form of "patterned chaos," the chaos of war of each against all, or the imposition of a new hegemony in the form of a global state. Whether any of those would prove to be a good thing must be the subject for another occasion.

Notes

1. One exception: the emergence since then of the enormous U.S. trade deficit and net foreign indebtedness, which endangers the economic foundations of hegemony.

2. A stimulating and unorthodox argument for the existence of mutual superpower security without nuclear weapons is Shepherd (1986).

3. Halperin (1987, ch. 2) dismisses the efficacy of nuclear threats virtually throughout the era, and so underplays the significance of this trend.

4. The situation is reminiscent of that in the sixteenth century, when the weapons and tactics of war among the great powers proved of little use in the periphery. See Braudel (1984, 58). Remember also that the context here is immediate deterrence—whether nuclear weapons make a difference once a crisis has arisen—not general deterrence preventing a crisis even from occurring.

5. This argument has been elaborated, in a formulation that to be sure is not legally binding, by a group of international lawyers in the statement by Lawyers' Committee on Nuclear Policy (1981, 1984).

6. West Europeans are of course richer than Russians and other East Europeans, but the easterners still are far better off than in their past and hardly about to jeopardize those hard-won gains. On Soviet motivations, see MccGwire (1987). The argument that modern war (not merely nuclear war) rarely has any utility for rational purpose has a long tradition, from Sir Norman Angell before World War I, to a provocative statement by Deutsch and Senghaas (1971).

7. The important exception would be the border between Chad and Libya. There have been only two others: negotiated minor adjustments between Mali and Mauritania and between Mali and Burkina Faso. South Africa has wanted to make several changes in its area, but despite its status as regional hegemon has been unable to do so.

8. Weede (1983, and in chapter 12 here) is one who holds that they have helped the hegemons to keep the peace within their alliance systems as well as between them. He sees the Falklands/Malvinas war and the Soviet failure to deter China in 1979 as dangerous portents of decline in this ability. In my opinion (for example, Russett and Starr 1989, ch. 14) there are other, much more persuasive, explanations for the achievement of peace, at least among the Western industrialized states.

References

Adler, Kenneth P. (1986). "West European and American Public Opinion on Peace, Defence, and Arms Control in a Cross-national Perspective." *International Social Science Journal* 110:589–600.

Allison, Graham T. (1971). *Essence of Decision: Explaining the Cuban Missile Crisis.* Boston: Little, Brown.

Ball, Desmond (1981). "Can Nuclear War Be Controlled?" *Adlephi Paper*, no. 161.

Betts, Richard K. (1987). *Nuclear Blackmail and Nuclear Balance.* Washington, D.C.: Brookings Institution.

Blair, Bruce G. (1985). *Strategic Command and Control: Redefining the Nuclear Threat.* Washington, D.C.: Brookings Institution.

Blechman, Barry, and Stephen S. Kaplan (1978). *Force without War.* Washington, D.C.: Brookings Institution.

Bracken, Paul (1983). *The Command and Control of Nuclear Forces.* New Haven: Yale University Press.

Braudel, Fernand (1984). *The Perspective of the World.* New York: Harper and Row.

Bundy, McGeorge (1984). "The Unimpressive Record of Nuclear Diplomacy." In Gwyn Prins, ed., *The Nuclear Crisis Reader.* New York: Vantage.

Bundy, McGeorge, George Kennan, Robert McNamara, and Gerard Smith (1982). "Nuclear Weapons and the Atlantic Alliance." *Foreign Affairs* 60, no. 4:753–68.

Charles, Daniel (1987). *Nuclear Planning in NATO.* Cambridge, Mass.: Ballinger.

Charlton, Michael (1987). *From Deterrence to Defense: The Inside Story of Strategic Policy.* Cambridge: Harvard University Press.

Collins, General Arthur S., Jr. (1982). "Theatre Nuclear Warfare: The Battlefield." In John F. Reichart and Steven R. Sturm, eds., *American Defense Policy.* 5th ed. Baltimore. Johns Hopkins University Press.

Deutsch, Karl W., and Dieter Senghaas (1971). "A Framework for a Theory of War and Peace." In Albert Lepawsky, Edward Buehrig, and Harold Lasswell, eds., *The Search for World Order.* New York: Appleton-Century-Crofts.

Ellsberg, Daniel (1981). "Introduction: Call to Mutiny." In E.P. Thompson and Dan Smith, eds., *Protest and Survive.* New York: Monthly Review Press.

Gaddis, John Lewis (1987). *The Long Peace: Inquiries into the History of the Cold War.* New York: Oxford University Press.

Graham, Thomas W. (1987). *Future Fission: Extended Deterrence and American Public Opinion.* Occasional Paper. Cambridge: Harvard University, Center for Science and International Affairs.

Halperin, Morton H. (1987). *Nuclear Fallacy: Dispelling the Myth of Nuclear Strategy.* Cambridge, Mass.: Ballinger.

Huth, Paul (1988a). *Research Note: The Extended Deterrent Value of Nuclear Weapons.* Occasional paper. Ann Arbor: University of Michigan, Institute for Social Research.

—— (1988b). *Extended Deterrence and the Prevention of War.* New Haven: Yale University Press.

Huth, Paul, and Bruce Russett (1988). "Deterrence Failure and Crisis Escalation." *International Studies Quarterly* 32, no. 1:29–45.

Kohut, Andrew, and Nicholas Horrock (1984). "Generally Speaking: Surveying the Military's Top Brass," *Public Opinion* 7, no. 5:42–45.

Kramer, Bernard, Michael Kalick, and Michael Milburn (1983). "Attitudes toward Nuclear Weapons and Nuclear War, 1945–82." *Public Opinion Quarterly* 39, no. 1:7–24.

Kugler, Jacek (1984). "Terror without Deterrence." *Journal of Conflict Resolution* 28, no. 3:470–506.

Lawyers' Committee on Nuclear Policy (1981, 1984). "Statement on the Illegality of Nuclear Weapons." Reprinted in Burns H. Weston, ed., *Toward Nuclear Disarmament and Global Security: A Search for Alternatives.* Boulder, Colo.: Westview.

MccGwire, Michael (1987). *Military Objectives in Soviet Foreign Policy.* Washington, D.C.: Brookings Institution.

McNamara, Robert S. (1983). "The Military Role of Nuclear Weapons." *Foreign Affairs* 62, no. 1:59–80.

Morgan, Patrick M. (1983). *Deterrence: A Conceptual Analysis.* Beverly Hills, Calif.: Sage.

Mueller, John (1988). "The Essential Irrelevance of Nuclear Weapons: Stability in the Postwar World." *International Security* 13, no. 2:55–90.

Myrdal, Alva (1976). *The Game of Disarmament: How the United States and the Soviet Union Run the Arms Race.* New York: Pantheon.

Quester, George (1987). *The Future of Nuclear Deterrence.* Lexington, Mass.: Lexington Books.

Russett, Bruce (1985). "The Mysterious Case of Vanishing Hegemony; or, Is Mark Twain Really Dead?" *International Organization* 39, no. 2:207–32.

Russett, Bruce (1988). "Extended Deterrence with Nuclear Weapons: How Necessary, How Acceptable?" *Review of Politics* 50 (Spring):282–302.

Russett, Bruce, and Donald R. DeLuca (1983). "Theater Nuclear Forces: Public Opinion in Western Europe." *Political Science Quarterly* 99, no. 2:179–96.

Russett, Bruce, and Harvey Starr (1989). *World Politics: The Menu for Choice.* 3d ed. New York: Freeman.

Schelling, Thomas C. (1966). *Arms and Influence.* New Haven: Yale University Press.

Shepherd, William G. (1986). *The Ultimate Deterrent: Foundations of US–USSR Security under Stable Competition.* New York: Praeger.

Steinbruner, John (1981–82). "Nuclear Decapitation." *Foreign Policy* 45 (Winter):16–28.

Weede, Erich (1983). "Extended Deterrence by Superpower Alliance." *Journal of Conflict Resolution* 27, no. 2:231–53.

Yankelovich, Daniel, and John Doble (1984). "The Public Mood." *Foreign Affairs* 63, no. 1:33–46.

11
Global Transactions and the Consolidation of Sovereignty

Janice E. Thomson
Stephen D. Krasner

Challenges to state-centric paradigms are nothing new in the study of international affairs. Before World War I some analysts maintained that the level of economic interdependence in Europe was so high that war was basically unthinkable. After World War II functionalists argued that specific functions could be assumed by political entities that would eventually supersede individual states. Advocates of the concept of transnational relations saw a world not only of interaction among national-states but also a transnational world involving interactions among nonstate actors or between nonstate actors and states (Keohane and Nye 1972). Some analysts saw multinational corporations escaping from the jurisdiction of any one state or any set of states. Hence the concern with the relationship between micro–macro interactions expressed in James Rosenau's micro formulation (Rosenau 1988), and especially the impact of greater individual competence on macroprocesses, has a lengthy intellectual pedigree.

One thread that runs through most of these arguments is that technological innovation is the most important factor explaining changes in the international system. Technological change is itself an exogenous variable; it is left unexplained, at least in relation to the political system. Technological change has reduced transactions costs. Transportation and communication are much cheaper than they have been in the past. The importance of geographic propinquity, of the territoriality that is at the core of the modern state system, has declined. Japan could become the world's most efficient steel producer even though both its coal and iron are thousands of miles away, a feat that would have been impossible in the nineteenth and early twentieth centuries before the development of bulk shipping. Billions of dollars can be transferred from one end of the world to the other in a matter of seconds—a far cry from the Rothschilds' use of carrier pigeons to secure information on the outcome of the Battle of Waterloo so that they could decide whether to buy or sell British sovereigns. Technological change may increase the competence of specific actors, whether individuals or organizations, by providing them with a vastly improved knowledge base.

The argument that interdependence has undermined the effective sovereignty of the state (the ability of the state to control activities that are nominally or juridically subject to authoritative decisions) has been most fully elaborated for economic transactions. International flows have made it more difficult for national governments to independently manage their own economies. Policies could be nullified by new international transactions over which national decision makers had no control. For instance, the effort by a small state to dampen domestic economic activity by raising interest rates could be frustrated by international capital inflows attracted by these same higher interest rates, which would increase the state's money supply and lead to lower interest rates (Cooper 1968). Formal sovereignty remains but actual control diminishes or even disappears. The basic causal sequence is as follows: technological change leads to increased economic flows, which erodes state control.

Realists have been extremely skeptical of all variants of the interdependence position. Realism has attempted to incorporate, to swallow up, the kinds of empirical evidence pointed to by interdependence formulations and to endogenize their theoretical variables. Realists argued first that growing interdependence has been a function of political power and political choice, not of exogenous technological change. The international rules of the game that are necessary for an open international economic system (the precondition for growing interdependence) precede, rather than follow, technological change. These rules had to be created by political choice and political power. In the postwar world only the United States could play an effective leadership role and even then only for those political entities that were not part of the Soviet bloc. U.S. desire for global liberalism has been explained in a variety of ways, including domestic preferences: a desire to internationalize the market-oriented economy that characterized the domestic U.S. economy; lessons drawn from the past: the conclusion accepted by U.S. leaders that the protectionism of the 1930s, especially the Smoot–Hawley Tariff Act, had contributed to economic breakdown, economic breakdown to authoritarian regimes, and authoritarian regimes to war; and finally to the realpolitik and national interest preferences that would be natural for any dominant state (Goldstein 1986; Krasner 1976; Maier 1977; Gilpin 1975). All of these arguments presuppose a hegemonic position for the United States, a level of dominance that would allow it to propagate its domestic preferences, act on the lessons its leaders drew from the past, and attain its realpolitik goals. The fact that technology has not led to an integration of the communist and noncommunist worlds strongly suggests that technology alone is not an adequate explanation for the pattern of international economic transactions.

Some realists, notably Kenneth Waltz, took a somewhat different tack. They argued that interdependence and global power were being confused. Transactions in and of themselves did not have any political significance. What counted was the ability of a state to adjust to change or to use its economic position for political leverage. A state that is heavily involved in the international economy, but could easily shift to relative autarky, is not vulnerable. Such a state may even be in a strong position to exercise political leverage over its economic partners because the relative opportunity costs of change weigh heavily in its favor (Waltz 1970; Hirschman 1945).

This chapter points to three other problems with arguments that see the macro structure of the international system (national-states) being undermined by micro processes driven by changes in individual competencies. First, such arguments lack historical perspective, often tacitly assuming that states have, in some golden age in the past, been able to effortlessly control transborder movements, or taking recent changes as indicative of long-term trends. In comparison with the past, contemporary changes in the level of international transactions do not appear particularly spectacular. The kinds of technological changes that have reduced international transaction costs have also reduced domestic transaction costs. Although some ratios of international to domestic transactions have increased, others have gone down. To the extent that historical data can be obtained they do not suggest any powerful long-term trends.

Second, interdependence arguments have ignored different trajectories of state consolidation that have occurred in different issue areas. They have focused on economic transactions and ignored military and security concerns. Indeed, the analysis of international security issues has, with a few exceptions such as discussions of terrorism, hardly dealt with any of the concerns raised by the interdependence literature. In the past, however, the ability of states to control the international use of force was not at all clear. Mercenaries were an important component of European militaries into the nineteenth, and in some cases even the twentieth, centuries. States would charter private, that is, nonstate actors to conduct military as well as commercial activities. Mercantile companies acted like quasi-states, maintaining their own courts and armed forces. Privateers were authorized to attack foreign shipping. Private citizens did engage in military intervention. (The fact that the activities of private citizens associated with Irangate are considered illegitimate is an indication of how much attitudes and legal stipulations have changed since the early nineteenth century.) One of the achievements of the state over the last two centuries has been to curtail the number, activities, and kinds of nonstate actors in the security issue area. Thus, though some aspects of international economic relations might suggest that micro processes have become more important, others, such as the private use of coercion, indicate that they have declined.

Third, and most important, interdependence arguments ignore the relationship between the growing level of some transactions, both domestic and international, and the consolidation of sovereignty; that is, of the control of a defined territory by a stable government that exercises final authority. High levels of exchange and market-rational outcomes (outcomes that reach the Pareto-optimal frontier given existing preferences and distributions of income) require stable property rights which, in a capitalist economic system, internalize costs and benefits. The only actors currently able to provide such rights are national-states. National-states may not always establish such property rights: socialist states will not routinely vest the right to freely alienate property in private entities; many states have arbitrarily altered the distribution of property rights. Nevertheless, in the modern world consolidated national states are the necessary if not sufficient condition for stable property rights that internalize costs and benefits. Other things being equal, the more stable the pattern of property rights the higher the level of economic transactions. Hence the commonplace notion that there is an inherent conflict between sovereignty and economic transactions is fundamentally misplaced. The consolidation of sovereignty—that is, the establishment of a set of institutions exercising final authority over a defined territory—was a necessary condition for more international economic transactions.

Challenges to State Control

At least some of the literature on economic interdependence regards recent challenges to state control as qualitatively different from challenges that have arisen in the past. There has not, however, been any golden age of state control. States, conceived of as central administrative apparatuses, have never been able to free themselves from concerns about external and internal challenges. The Peace of Westphalia went some way toward domesticating and routinizing the international and civil conflicts generated by religious differences. The eighteenth century saw persistent conflict between the major European powers, culminating in Napoléon's attempt to establish complete dominance over the continent of Europe, an effort that was also a threat to the existing domestic orders of the major European states. High levels of war placed persistent strains on the financial resources of states, compelling them to alter their relationships with their own civil societies.[1]

Compared to earlier periods the nineteenth century was relatively peaceful. The number of international challenges to state boundaries, or even the existence of states, declined. In the center of Europe, however, internal challenges increased. The enervation of the Ottoman and Hapsburg empires precipitated a series of nationalist challenges that led to the creation of new states in the Balkans. In Germany and Italy fragmented political entities were consolidated into nation-states. There has been no past golden age in which Machiavelli's Prince could take a nap secure in the knowledge that external and internal challenges had disappeared.

The kinds of international economic flows that have attracted the attention of analysts who see micro phenomena altering macro structures in the international system are not unprecedented. Technological change has reduced transaction costs domestically as well as internationally. The direction of the long-term trend in the relative importance of international as opposed to domestic flows has not always been clear.

State control over the movement of capital and goods in the international system is the primary focus of interdependence arguments. Huge increases in the absolute volume of world trade, international capital movements, and multinational manufacturing are taken as indicators of declining state control. If these observations are put in the context of domestic activities, it is not clear that international flows are relatively more important today than they were a century or more ago.

Table 11-1 presents a measure of the volume of international flows of goods, corrected for changes in world GNP. With some exceptions (1900 and 1910), world trade progressively increased, and grew more rapidly than GNP, until World War I. From 1830 to 1913 the volume of world trade increased more than twice as fast as world GNP. In the post–World War II period, trade has also outstripped the growth in world GNP. However, the ratio of trade to GNP did not reach its pre–World War I high of 11 percent until the early 1970s. During the thirty years immediately following World War II, the trade-to-GNP ratio was at a level comparable to that of the 1850–70 period. One interpretation of these data is that between 1950 and 1975, world trade was simply recovering from the disruptions caused by two world wars.

It is true that world trade increased much more rapidly than GNP in the 1970s, but the differential slowed markedly during the recession of the early 1980s. Whether the increased level of trade to GNP will persist remains to be seen.

Disaggregated figures for world output and exports in agricultural products, minerals, and manufactures are presented in table 11-2. Between 1950 and 1970, exports increased more rapidly than production in all three categories. Agricultural production grew by 70 percent as exports more than doubled. Although the output of minerals nearly tripled during the twenty-year period, exports in 1970 were

Table 11-1
World Trade

Year	World Exports/World GNP
1830	0.046
1840	0.057
1850	0.068
1860	0.093
1870	0.098
1880	0.114
1890	0.111
1900	0.104
1910	0.104
1913	0.114
1950	0.081
1960	0.092
1965	0.090
1970	0.100
1975	0.139
1980	0.169

Sources: Paul Bairoch, *Commerce Extérieur et Développement Économique de l'Europe au XIXᵉ Siècle* (Paris: École des Hautes Études en Sciences Sociales, 1976): 78; *UN Statistical Yearbook*, various years; UNCTAD, *1983 Handbook of International Trade and Development Statistics;* and B.R. Mitchell, *International Historical Statistics: The Americas and Australasia* (Detroit: Gale Research): 886–89.

Note: Data for 1830–1913 only include the United States and Europe (including European and Asian Russia, but not Turkey). The gap in the data (1913–1950) is due to the paucity of reliable figures in the war and interwar years.

Table 11-2
Indices of World Output and Trade of Commodities[a]

Year	Agricultural Products		Minerals[b]		Manufactures	
	Output	Exports	Output	Exports	Output	Exports
1950	58	42	38	23	26	16
1955	66	50	49	35	38	25
1960	78	68	59	50	49	37
1965	88	82	79	64	72	58
1970	100	100	100	100	100	100
1975	114	106	109	103	122	143
1980	124	141	131	118	152	199
1985	141	150	115	98	177	252

Source: GATT, *International Trade 1985–86*. Geneva: 1986, 139.
[a]Based on volume.
[b]Includes fuels and nonferrous metals.

four times their 1950 level. In manufacturing, output quadrupled, while exports grew by a factor of six.

After 1970, however, the picture is decidedly mixed. Though the export of manufactures more than doubled between 1970 and 1985, and production increased by nearly 80 percent, increases in the other commodity categories were more modest. No real trend is evident in agricultural commodities, though it appears that exports and output have increased at about the same rate. As of 1985, production was up about 41 percent over the 1970 level; exports were up 50 percent. More striking are the post-1970 trends in the minerals category. Here exports have consistently grown less rapidly than output. In 1985, mineral production was only 15 percent greater than in 1970; the volume of exports was actually less than the 1970 level.

Both output and trade in manufactures have increased dramatically over the past thirty-five years, but this does not necessarily imply an increase in interdependence—if growing interdependence is meant to imply increasing vulnerability to external forces. Rather, the agricultural and mineral commodities production and export statistics suggest that dependence on items that are basic to the reproduction of labor and the production of manufactures has stabilized or even declined. This implies that vulnerability to disruptions in the flow of basic raw materials, and therefore at least one measure of interdependence, has diminished. Moreover, one of the striking characteristics of trade in manufactures is the growth of intrasectoral trade. This is especially true for the United States and Western Europe. Trade has increased most in commodities where countries are most able to adjust to external changes.

In the area of trade, institutional structures (as opposed to actual patterns of behavior) have deteriorated. There are more departures from the General Agreement on Tariffs and Trade (GATT) principles of nondiscrimination and reductions in trade barriers. Efforts to expand the GATT regime to nontariff barriers (NTBs) have met with mixed results. Only relatively few countries have signed the NTB codes negotiated during the Tokyo Round, and the provisions of these codes are limited to the signatories. The Department of Commerce has estimated that barter trade rose from 2 to 3 percent of world trade in 1976 to 25 to 30 percent in 1983. The percentage of automobile trade among advanced industrialized countries affected by NTBs increased from 1 percent in 1973 to 50 percent in 1983 (Gilpin 1987, 195, 207).

Another indicator of the volume of international economic transactions is capital flows, including direct foreign investment, loans, and bonds. Table 11–3 presents the ratio of foreign investment to GNP for Western industrialized countries. Here again, the pre–World War I period was one in which foreign investment increased much faster than GNP. Unlike world trade, however, foreign investment has yet to reattain the level it reached in 1913. Foreign investment in the 1950s and 1960s stabilized at 12 percent of GNP, well below the 19 percent it reached in 1840.

The Western industrialized countries have been investing relatively decreasing amounts of capital abroad since 1965. From 0.25 percent of GNP in 1965, to 0.22 percent in 1970, the amount of new foreign investment declined to 0.17 percent in 1981 (United Nations Conference on Trade and Development, 1983, 446; Organisation for Economic Co-operation and Development 1981, 39, 52).

Bank loans and bonds emanating from Eurocurrency markets are other forms of international capital movements that have attracted a great deal of attention. This involves lending in currencies other than that of the country in which the venture is taking place, such as dollar transactions in London, or yen transactions in Frankfurt. Eurocurrency markets first developed in the 1950s when the Soviet Union and China deposited dollars in European banks because they were afraid that holdings in the United States might be seized. U.S. corporations began making Eurodollar deposits in the 1960s to secure higher interest rates, and they greatly

Table 11–3
Total Foreign Investment

Year	Foreign Investment/GNP
1840	0.19
1870	0.57
1900	1.02
1913	1.08
1929	0.24
1938	0.27
1960	0.12
1970	0.12

Source: Bairoch (1976), 99.

Note: Data for 1840–1913 include only Germany, Belgium, France, Sweden, Switzerland, the United Kingdom, and Holland. All Western developed countries are included for 1929 and later.

increased their borrowing in Eurodollar markets when capital controls were imposed in the United States in the mid-1960s. The influx of petrodollars during the 1970s further enlarged Euromarkets, although activity decelerated sharply with the onset of the Third World debt crisis in the 1980s. In aggregate Eurocurrency markets in the European reporting area grew from $12 billion in 1964 to $920 billion in 1984. This was a rate of growth far higher than for any other major international economic activity (Frieden 1987, 81–84; Cohen 1986, 21–25).

The increase in size of international capital markets has been accompanied by what appears to be a dramatic change in institutional structures. National capital markets have become integrated. Staggering sums of money can be transferred across international boundaries almost instantaneously by modern communication links. Bankers can respond instantaneously to developments in any part of the globe (Frieden 1987, 80). There is always a major financial market open in some part of the world.

Both the size and institutional character of Eurocurrency markets have led many observers to regard them as a quintessential example of the impact of micro developments on macro structures. Eurocurrency markets have not been subject to much supervision by national regulatory authorities. The size of the international currency pool has made it extremely difficult for central banks to intervene effectively to manage exchange rates. Walter Wriston, president of Citibank during the 1970s, has argued that there is a new world information standard that "is exerting discipline on the countries of the world, which they all hate. For the first time in history, the politicians can't stop it. It's beyond the political control of the world, and that's good news" (quoted in Frieden 1987, 115).

As in the area of trade, however, this viewpoint is woefully lacking in historical perspective. International banking has been important since the Renaissance. Lending rose dramatically during the nineteenth century, with Britain at the core of the system. Almost half of all British savings were lent overseas. The United States replaced Britain as the world's leading creditor after World War I, and lending grew considerably during the 1920s. The amount owed to U.S. banks by foreign borrowers was, as a percentage of GNP, about the same in 1929 as in the mid 1980s—in both cases around 12 percent (Frieden 1987, 89; Cohen 1986, 84–90). The Depression and the aftermath of World War II were the aberrant periods. In the 1970s, as in the case of trade, international lending approximated levels that had been reached in the nineteenth century and the 1920s.

Nor is it obvious that new institutional structures and the ability to rapidly deploy capital around the world indicate that state control is more tenuous than it has been in the past. At least some Renaissance sovereigns were more dependent on international capital markets than contemporary rulers. International capital movements were seen as a threat to domestic financial stability by the end of the nineteenth century. When a major British banking house, Baring Brothers, was threatened with bankruptcy in the early 1890s by Argentine defaults, an international rescue operation was put together by the Bank of England which included not only the Bank but also the British Treasury, the Bank of France, other London banks, and J.P. Morgan (Cohen 1986, 94–95; Frieden 1987, 117–18).

In general national governments, especially Britain, took a more laissez-faire attitude toward international lending in the nineteenth century than is presently the case. Most lending was in the form of bonds rather than bank loans, making it easier for states to argue that responsibility lay with private bondholders, rather than with the national regulatory authorities that were, in any event, much less well developed. Despite the increase in international banking operations in New York during the 1920s, the U.S. government was extremely reluctant to become involved, an attitude that contributed to the onset of the Great Depression (Cohen 1986, 110–11). There were private bondholder committees in the nineteenth century that tried to deal with default, and as gunboat diplomacy (which was often prompted by defaults) indicates, governments did become involved. But the institutional structure for state or at least official involvement in international lending is much more elaborated now, including Paris Clubs and the IMF as well as private arrangements.

Jeffrey Frieden, who is in many ways quite sympathetic to the autonomy of international capital markets, sums up the present situation in the following terms:

> Nevertheless, the Euromarkets are not stateless; they rest on the implicit, and sometimes explicit support of major western governments. The offshore markets arose, after all, in response to actions by national governments, and they grew because national governments tolerated or encouraged them. At any point in the last thirty years, the U.S. government could have put a stop to much Euromarket activity by prohibiting American banks from participating and by blocking the use of the U.S. dollar offshore [1987, 116].

We do not mean to imply that states cannot be affected by international capital markets that they cannot directly control, but it is critical to recognize that this is not a new development and that these markets have only been able to develop within a broader institutional structure delineated by the power and policies of states.

International travel is another area in which microprocesses have been seen as challenging or altering macrostructures. Technological developments in transportation have facilitated world travel, making it economically feasible for millions of people. Yet the increase in the international flows of people is not so striking if we look at the ratio of foreign to domestic travel. Table 11–4 presents data on air travel for the world and for the United States. Since 1950, the number of foreign travelers has fluctuated between 20 and 30 percent of the number of domestic travelers. The data for U.S. air travel shows similar fluctuations, but between 7 and 11 percent of the domestic volume. Although the number of international travelers leaving the United States in 1980 was almost six hundred times what it was in 1930, the number of domestic air travelers has increased even more rapidly.

Table 11-4
Air Travel

Year	International/Domestic (World)	International/Domestic (U.S.)
1930		0.114
1940		0.075
1950	0.29	0.097
1955	0.21	
1960	0.27	0.105
1965	0.29	
1970	0.31	0.110
1980		0.088

Sources: ICAO, *Digest of Statistics: Traffic 1961–71;* Air Transport Association of America, *Air Transport Facts and Figures,* various years; and FAA, *Airport Activity Statistics,* various years.

In fact, the postwar high for the United States, 11 percent in 1970, was still less—albeit marginally—than it was in 1930. Neither U.S. nor world air traffic demonstrates any trend in the ratio of international to domestic travel.

James Rosenau and others have placed considerable emphasis on the communications revolution as a source of micro changes that may alter macro structures. Telecommunications and computer technology make possible dramatic increases in the flow of information across state borders. They make, so the argument goes, state control of information problematic. Though it is premature to gauge the impact these developments will have on state control of international communications, it is instructive to examine what happened with an earlier communication technology. Table 11-5 presents data on the ratio of international to domestic mail flows for the world, Europe, and the United States. Europe and the world as a whole reattained their pre–World War II highs only in the late 1960s and 1970s; the United States has yet to reach the level it saw in 1928–29. By the late 1970s, the ratio of foreign to domestic mail had reached new highs both worldwide and in Europe, though not in the United States.

Table 11-5
Mail Flows

Year	Foreign Mail Sent/Total Domestic Mail		
	World	United States	Europe
1928–29	0.072	0.018	0.067
1936–38	0.058	0.014	0.051
1948–49	0.058	0.009	0.054
1958–59	0.069	0.009	0.065
1967–68	0.068	0.008	0.071
1975–77	0.093	0.010	0.083

Source: *U.N. Statistical Yearbook,* various years.

The ratio of international to domestic telephone calls for selected countries is presented in table 11–6. Data on telephone traffic are more difficult to obtain and—at best—available for only the last twenty years.[2] However, the figures in table 11–6 do suggest a general trend toward the internationalization of this mode of communication. With only four exceptions, the number of international calls has increased more rapidly than that of domestic calls. The four exceptions (Mozambique, Rwanda, Pakistan, and Burma) are all LDCs whose flat or declining ratios are due not so much to a reduction in their international telephone calls as to rapid growth in the amount of domestic traffic. Though these data must be interpreted with a great deal of caution, they do suggest that in the realm of telephone communications, international flows are growing more rapidly than domestic ones.

These data on the flows of goods, money, people, and information do not definitively answer the question of whether state control has eroded. All of the data presented here are in the form of ratios between international and domestic flows. The worldwide flow of goods has reached new highs since the 1970s, but it took ninety years to attain the previous historic high achieved in the 1880s. Capital flows, in the form of foreign investment, increased dramatically until World War I, but consistently declined after 1938. Lending in the 1970s was at a level comparable to that of the nineteenth century. International air travel in comparison

Table 11–6
Telephone Traffic

Country	International/Domestic Traffic (%)				
	1966	1970	1975	1980	1984
Bahamas	0.48	0.91	0.78	1.78	—
Burma	0.008	0.006	0.005	0.008[a]	—
Canada	0.15	0.18	0.25	0.35	0.38[b]
Chile	0.014	0.028	0.024	0.042[a]	—
Costa Rica	—	0.26	0.24	0.30	0.33
Czechoslovakia	0.04	0.05	0.05	0.12	0.13
Gambia	0.29	0.51	0.63	1.36[a]	—
Mexico	—	0.14[d]	0.17	0.23	0.26
Mozambique	0.62	1.05	0.56	0.33[a]	0.36[b]
Pakistan	1.06	1.05	0.36	0.98	0.90[b]
Philippines	—	11.2	12.5	18.8	25.0
Poland	0.18	0.16	0.24	0.07	0.25
Rwanda	0.43	0.58	0.57	0.39	0.27[c]
United Kingdom	0.12	0.16	0.23	0.54	0.81[b]
West Germany	0.43	0.60	0.85	1.18	1.42

Source: International Telecommunication Union, *Yearbook of Common Carrier Telecommunication Statistics*. Geneva: various years.

[a]Data are for 1979.

[b]Data are for 1983.

[c]Data are for 1981.

[d]Data are for 1971.

with domestic has been relatively stable for the past thirty years. Mail flows in the late 1960s were about the same as they were in the 1920s, though they increased slightly in the 1970s. Among the indicators we have considered here, it is only the pattern of telephone communications that is consistent with growing interdependence.

International flows of all kinds have increased dramatically during the last century. But domestic transactions have increased as well. The relative importance of domestic and international flows has not followed any clear trend. Perhaps states have lost control over all kinds of economic and noneconomic activities in domestic society, and interdependence analyses of the loss of control at the international level could be married with similar arguments about domestic activities. But given the growing scope of state activities, and the steady increase in the ability of states to extract resources from their own societies, arguments about the domestic loss of state control are problematic at best. At the very least the effectiveness of state control domestically, coupled with the absence of any clear increase in the relative importance of international transactions, suggest that there is no prima facie case for the assertion that international flows are more of a challenge to state control now than they have been in the past.

The Consolidation of Sovereignty

A second problem with interdependence arguments is that they ignore the consolidation of final authority within a defined territory. Historically, the overarching problem for statesmen has been the survival of their state. Although Kant was right to argue that the state of nature of the international system was less malignant than the state of nature for individuals, the existence of states, or at least their geographic boundaries, has often been threatened (Kant 1963). The minimalist goals of preserving territorial and political integrity could not be taken for granted in the past.

Annihilation Rates

The contemporary international system is not nirvana, but the situation for individual states has become more secure. The number of official actors in the international system declined until the Napoleonic Wars; it began to increase in the nineteenth century. After World War II the number of states in the international system exploded. At the same time the number of states that have disappeared has continued at a low level. Figures for the last two centuries are shown in table 11–7.

The low annihilation rate of states since World War II can be explained in several ways. Nuclear weapons have made force less usable. The weapons themselves are most credible when they are associated with maintaining the central balance between the Soviet Union and the United States, although even here their utility has been challenged.[3] Nuclear weapons may also, however, play some role in deterring conventional conflicts because of the fear of escalation.[4]

Table 11-7
Creation and Disappearance of States

Decade	Number Created	Number Destroyed	Total
			34
1816–25	7	0	41
1826–35	5	0	46
1836–45	6	0	52
1846–55	1	0	53
1856–65	2	6[a]	49
1866–75	3	9[b]	43
1876–85	3	0	46
1886–95	1	0	47
1896–1905	5	1[c]	51
1906–15	3	0	54
1916–25	14	3[d]	65
1926–35	1	0	66
1936–45	1	4[e]	63
1946–55	21	0	84
1956–65	43	1[f]	126
1966–73	17	0	143

Source: Arthur S. Banks, *Cross-National Time Series Data Archive User's Manual.* Binghamton: SUNY, 1975.

[a]These were Modena, the Papal States, Parma, Sardinia, Tuscany, and Two Sicilies in 1862.

[b]The nine were Hanover, Hesse (Electorate), Hesse (Grand Duchy), Mecklenburg, Prussia, and Saxony in 1867, and Württemburg, Baden, and Bavaria in 1870.

[c]In 1905 Russia recognized Japan's "paramount interest" in Korea, though Japan did not formally annex Korea until 1910.

[d]These were Austria-Hungary (1918), Montenegro (1919) and Serbia (1919).

[e]These were Estonia, Latvia, and Lithuania (1940) and Germany (1945).

[f]This was Zanzibar, which joined Tanganyika in 1964 to form Tanzania.

The survival rate of states may also be enhanced by the growing significance of juridical sovereignty. Jackson and Rosberg (1982) have pointed out that many of the states created since the conclusion of World War II do not have the attributes that have been traditionally associated with the recognition of sovereignty. Some have not been able to effectively control activities within their own territory. Most lack the material resources that would be needed to resist an external attack by more powerful states in the system. Despite this they have survived. Jackson and Rosberg argue that the most efficacious resource that these states have is juridical sovereignty: the fact that they are recognized as sovereign by other states in the international system. This gives them access to international resources and discourages depredations by other states.

Finally, the high survival rate of states since World War II may reflect the bipolar balance of power. The interests of the two superpowers in Europe are well defined. Any change, particularly a change as dramatic as the elimination of a state, would be very threatening to either the Soviet Union or the United States, a development that neither would welcome. In the Third World the superpowers have cautiously tracked each other's initiatives. There is no playing field where the superpowers are indifferent to outcomes. The most recent disappearance of an arguably sovereign entity, South Vietnam, occurred only after an extended and bloody conflict in which one of the superpowers committed its own forces. Hence, the bipolar distribution of power, which engenders balancing by the poles, may also contribute to the security of states in the postwar world.

Regardless of whether the consolidation of the state system (as indicated by the low annihilation rate for states in the postwar period) is attributable to nuclear weapons, juridical sovereignty, or bipolarity, the pattern of development here does not suggest that basic macro structures are being undermined by micro processes or anything else.

The Control of Military Activity

State control over the use of violence in the international system today is substantially greater than it was as recently as the mid-nineteenth century. In the eighteenth century, most European armies depended on large contingents of foreign mercenaries. Privateers played an important role in sea warfare. The great mercantile companies of Britain, France, and the Netherlands fought wars with each other, governments, and pirates. Piracy was rampant everywhere. Filibustering—"private" military expeditions into neighboring states launched by adventurers, politicians, and renegade military officers, often in collusion with local government officials— flourished in the Americas until the 1860s.

These activities suggest that as recently as the mid-nineteenth century, state control over the exercise of coercion beyond its borders was far from complete. Control was incomplete because state authority claims on coercion were minimal, conflictual, or unsettled. States did not claim the exclusive authority to raise an army within their own borders. They did not claim the exclusive right to employ the military services of individuals residing in their jurisdiction. Individuals were quite free to exercise violence in the international system for their own ends.

The story of how the state gained a monopoly over the coercive forces domestically is well known (Tilly 1975). Less familiar is the process through which the state achieved the exclusive right to deploy violence beyond its borders. This process involved the assertion of new authority claims and the development of appropriate enforcement capabilities. It began in the fourteenth and fifteenth centuries when the Hundred Years' War (1337–1453) marked the demise of the feudal methods of warfare (Preston and Wise 1970, 85) and culminated in the late eighteenth and early nineteenth centuries.

One way to view the process is in terms of the allocation of military capabilities. Valued goods, including coercive forces, can be allocated by the market or an authoritative body.[5] The feudal levy was an authoritative allocation of military capabilities. Nobles and knights had a duty to provide military force in behalf of the king in exchange for the privilege of landholding. Men served, not for pay, but because they were obligated to serve. By the time of the Hundred Years' War, however, the market had already begun to erode this system, with many knights fighting for pay. In Europe, the fifteenth and sixteenth centuries were the age of the mercenaries (Mockler 1969, 25–27). Market forces were even more evident in sea warfare where "until the end of the fifteenth century maritime warfare was largely in the hands of privateers" (Jessup and Deak 1935, 12). Mercenaries, mercantile companies, privateers, pirates, and filibusters appeared as authoritative allocations gave way to more market-oriented allocations.

Yet by the end of the nineteenth century, all of these nonstate actors had virtually disappeared. Market forces had been supplanted by state authority. State claims to a monopoly on the use of violence in the international system had replaced market allocation of military forces. State control, which for centuries had been problematic, was virtually uncontested in 1900.

Mercenaries. As table 11–8 indicates, about one-half of the world's armies today are based on conscription. Only one state, the United Arab Emirates, relies on an almost exclusively mercenary army. France's conscript army is supplemented with the mercenaries of the French Foreign Legion. The rest have volunteer armies, though many of these employ some mercenaries as well.

In the eighteenth century, European armies were based on voluntarism. Mass conscription was not introduced until the French Revolution (Preston and Wise 1970, 181). Because peasants and the urban unemployed rarely volunteered in sufficient numbers, troop quotas could be met only by impressment or hiring foreigners. In practice, the typical army was highly dependent on foreign mercenaries.

All the major European armies relied heavily on foreign mercenaries for troops. Half the Prussian army was comprised of mercenaries (Gooch 1980, 22). Foreigners constituted one-third of the French army (Preston and Wise 1970, 139). Britain used eighteen thousand mercenaries in the American War for Independence and

Table 11–8
Modern Armies

Recruiting Method	Number of States	Proportion of Total
Conscription	75	49%
Volunteer	59	39%
Conscription/mercenary	6	4%
Volunteer/mercenary	10	7%
Unknown/mercenary	2	1%
Total	152	100%

Sources: John Keegan, *World Armies*. 2d ed. London: Macmillan, 1983; International Institute for Strategic Studies, *The Military Balance 1986–87*. London: IISS, 1987; R. Sellers, *Armed Forces of the World*. 4th ed. New York: Praeger, 1977.

thirty-three thousand mercenaries in its 1793 war with France (Bayley 1977, 6–7). The presence of large numbers of mercenaries in eighteenth-century armies implies that at least some states allowed their subjects to sell their military-related services to other states.

Until the eighteenth century, it was common practice for a state to negotiate bilateral treaties in which it granted its treaty partner the right to enlist its subjects in time of war (Jessup and Deak 1935, 26–30). It was only in the eighteenth century that states began to claim the exclusive authority to raise an army in their own territory. On several occasions, beginning in 1561, the British crown issued proclamations forbidding its subjects from serving in foreign armies. However, this proscription was not made permanent until the mid-eighteenth century when legislation to that effect was passed by Parliament (Burchett and Roebuck 1977, 179). In the late eighteenth century Holland also enacted laws against foreign enlistment; the Two Sicilies, Venice, and the Papal States issued edicts forbidding enlistment with a foreign belligerent (Hall 1924, 703).

So although the state generally retained the right to supply troops to its treaty partners, some states had begun to impose permanent and universal prohibitions on their subjects' foreign enlistment. In other words, the state could still choose to supply troops to an ally, but it would no longer allow an ally to recruit its subjects in its own territory, nor its subjects to freely alienate their military services.

Privateers. Privateers played an important role in eighteenth-century naval warfare. British and U.S. privateers captured more than two thousand prizes during the War of the Spanish Succession (Sherry 1986, 202). French privateers nearly put an end to slave trade between Africa and British colonies in the Americas. In its war for independence, the United States commissioned more than twenty-five hundred privateers who captured twenty-three hundred prizes from the British. French privateers seized twenty-one hundred English vessels between 1793 and 1796. In the War of 1812, one U.S. privateer captured or destroyed $5 million worth of English property (Sherry 1986, 359–60).

Privateering was the naval counterpart to the mercenary army. Privateers were "privately owned vessels that governments commissioned in time of war, by special 'letters of marque,' to attack and capture the shipping of enemy nations" (Sherry 1986, 23). The practice of privateering was legalized piracy during wartime. A state granted a commission or issued a letter of marque to the individual owner of an armed vessel. This authorized him to commit acts of violence against the vessels of countries designated by the state employing him. A privateer differed from a pirate only in that the former acted with the authority of the state; the latter did not (Hall 1924, 312–13). Both committed acts of violence for private gain. States did not pay privateers; they simply allowed them to keep whatever they seized from the designated targets.

Eighteenth-century privateering grew out of the practice of private reprisals that flourished until the end of the sixteenth century. Under the system of private reprisals, "private individuals were granted permission to recover damages suffered on the sea" by seizing or libeling property belonging to the perpetrators (Jessup and Deak 1935, 12–14). Prize courts provided the mechanism through which such cases were resolved (Jessup and Deak 1935, 203–4).

"The activities of the privateer and the use of private reprisals . . . illustrate that the line between war and peace was for centuries 'as thin as gossamer' " (Jessup and Deak 1935, 12). So long as states authorized individuals to use violence, it was difficult to tell when a state was at war or at peace with another. If a privately owned ship was used in the commission of some depredation against the ship of another country, it was not immediately obvious whether the perpetrator was acting on his own behalf or a state's. In the former case, the deed was an act of piracy, which came under the auspices of criminal law. However, if the perpetrator were acting under state authority, the deed was potentially an act of war.

Like the early, privately raised mercenary army, privateers could prove troublesome once the state no longer required their services. Piracy was lucrative, and the incentive to engage in it did not disappear when state authorization ceased. So long as individuals owned armed vessels there was the possibility that they would use coercion in their own interests. Moreover, the ordinary seaman had few alternatives to employment in commercial shipping (Ritchie 1986, 234). He could find another kind of work, serve in the regular navy, or join the crew of a pirate ship. In a great many cases, the last was the most attractive because life for the ordinary sailor in the navy was extremely harsh (Phillips and Reede 1936, 20–21).

Piracy flourished because there was a market for the booty. Where state restrictions on commerce were imposed, pirates were welcomed as suppliers of scarce goods. For example, the British Navigation Acts produced a thriving U.S. black market for pirate and privateer plunder (Sherry 1986, 24). Pirates performed a vital service to states that lacked the naval power to keep their trade routes open. Moreover, colonial merchants profited greatly by provisioning pirate ships in both home and foreign ports (Ritchie 1986, 36–37).

Some states were largely financed by piracy. The pirates of the Barbary Coast provided much of the revenue for the states of Tripoli, Algiers, and Morocco by preying on Mediterranean commerce. Interestingly, when U.S. shipping came under attack by these pirates in the late eighteenth century, the United States attempted to end the practice by paying protection money. It negotiated treaties in which the governments of Tripoli, Algiers, and Morocco agreed to prevent pirate attacks on U.S. shipping in exchange for cash or commodities (Malloy 1910, 1786).

So the eighteenth century navy resembled the army in that a major component of both was mercenary. It was assuredly *not* the case that pirates, mercenary armies, and privateers flourished simply because states lacked the means to control them. In fact, rather than claim exclusive authority to engage in violence in the international system, states exploited privately owned military forces to their own advantage. It was only in the nineteenth century that the state asserted the claims that were crucial to achieving its monopoly on the use of violence in the international system. But "the development from private warfare to warfare conducted by the naval forces of the state is marked by an intermediary stage, namely, by the fleets of the overseas commercial companies" (Jessup and Deak 1935, 14).

Mercantile Companies. Mercantile companies were based on a state-granted monopoly on trade between the home country and regions outside of Europe. Though they were financed largely with "private" capital, they were not private organizations in the modern sense. They possessed military, judicial, and diplomatic power. For example, the charter of United East India Company of the Netherlands granted it the power "to make war, conclude treaties, acquire territories and build fortresses" (Mukherjee 1974, 59). These companies made treaties with each other and with foreign governments, governed subjects of their home states, raised armies (Mukherjee 1974), and even coined their own money (Sherry 1986, 105). Initially, their "trading" activities were nothing more than acts of piracy (Mukherjee 1974, 71; Ritchie 1986, 17–18). Increased trade between Europe and the East sparked a dramatic rise in piracy. Although the British East India Company did get some assistance from the Royal Navy, the latter was frequently occupied with European wars so the company had to provide military protection for its own shipping (Sherry 1986, 109).

The confusion between public and private interests inherent in the mercantile company became apparent when English-speaking pirates began to attack shipping in the region. In response to an attack by an English pirate on his ships, the Mughal of India held the British company responsible, seizing some of its property and jailing fifty of its officials. In essence, the Mughal treated the company like a state. He held it responsible for the actions of British subjects in the region and for guaranteeing the safety of his vessels on the high seas (Sherry 1986, 107–9; Ritchie 1986, 14, 131). By the end of the eighteenth century, the British state had revoked the company's political powers and assumed for itself the task of governing (Mukherjee 1974, 354).

The importance of mercenaries, pirates, privateers, and mercantile companies had declined substantially by 1900. After the French Revolution, European states relied on mass conscription to form citizen armies. Britain's last attempt to raise a large mercenary army was for the Crimean War, though the sixteen thousand troops it enlisted never saw action (Bayley 1977, 138). Commissions for privateers were not issued by European states after 1815, and the practice was officially abolished by the 1856 Declaration of Paris (Baumgart 1981, 165). Privateers were employed in the U.S. Civil War, but the United States, as well as Spain, refrained from using them in the Spanish-American War of 1898 (Hall 1924, 621–22). Britain's mercantile companies were obsolescent by the early nineteenth century and defunct by 1860 (Mukherjee 1974, 431). The last major source of piracy—the Barbary Coast—was suppressed by the establishment of European sovereignty in North Africa during the nineteenth century.

It is no coincidence that all of these actors, which had existed for centuries, virtually vanished so quickly and at the same time. States eliminated them. Though the ease with which they were suppressed should not be overestimated, it is the case that once the state made certain authority claims and acted to enforce them, these actors quickly disappeared.

Filibusters. The nineteenth century was filled with U.S. presidential proclamations warning individuals not to participate in military expeditions against neighboring states (see table 11–9). Motivations for these expeditions included personal honor and glory or enrichment, bringing new territories into the United States as slave states, and "liberating" European colonies. Numerous so-called filibustering projects were launched by ambitious Americans—individuals, politicians, and military officers—and foreign nationals. Local officials were often actively involved, and members of the state executive may even have been involved in a few cases.[6] Nevertheless, filibustering declined sharply after the 1850s.

There were many reasons for the demise of filibustering. Repeated failure, severe reprisals by target states, and the abolition of slavery in the United States reduced the incentives and raised the costs associated with the practice. However, market forces alone were not responsible for the elimination of filibustering. The state altered the incentive structure by making it a criminal offense.

Thus, state control over the use of coercive force in the international system has increased, even if it is not perfect.[7] Micro processes are not undermining the

Table 11–9
Proclamations against Filibustering

Date	Target of Expedition
November 1806	Dominions of Spain
September 1815	Dominions of Spain
January 1838	Canada
November 1838	Canada
September 1841	Canada
August 1849	Cuba and Mexico
April 1851	Cuba and Mexico
October 1851	Mexico
January 1854	Mexico
May 1854	Cuba
December 1855	Nicaragua
October 1858	Nicaragua
June 1866	Canada
May 1870	Canada
October 1870	Canada and Cuba
June 1895	Cuba
July 1896	Cuba
March 1912	Mexico

Sources: Charles G. Fenwick, *The Neutrality Laws of the United States*. Washington, D.C.: Carnegie Endowment for International Peace, 1913, 33–58; James M. Seavey, "Neutrality Legislation in the United States." S.J.D. thesis, Georgetown University, 1939, 122–23.

macro structure. Indeed, the macro structure, the national state, has enhanced its control over time.

Property Rights and the Consolidation of Sovereignty

Let us accept for the moment the proposition that the relative importance of international economic transactions has increased and that effective state control has been eroded. This is a position that supports the contention that major changes may be afoot in the international system. At the same time, however, state control has been consolidated in other areas, especially core areas related to survival and the use of force; this is a development that supports the contention that the existing macro structure (that is, a world of national states) will persist. In fact, these apparently contradictory trends may be causally related.

Optimal market resource allocation, and the high levels of economic exchange with which such allocation is likely to be associated, requires secure property rights. Property rights can be thought of as a set of economic and social relations among individuals that defines "the position of each individual with respect to the utilization of scarce resources" (Furubotn and Pejovich 1972, 1139). Without secure property rights market activities would be constrained because of uncertainty about the possessor's right to sell the commodity and the threat to achieve transfers through force and coercion rather than voluntary exchange.[8] Individuals would place a high discount rate on the future. Capital allocation would be aimed at maximizing short-term gain—getting out before the rules of the game were changed. International trade would concentrate on luxury goods that offered the possibility of very high payoffs if a transaction were successfully completed.

In the present environment the state is the only actor capable of establishing stable property rights. The transaction costs of allocating such rights privately could be prohibitive, especially in cases involving externalities and collective goods (Calabresi and Melamed 1972). The state also has the most developed legal apparatus for enforcing property rights including contractual arrangements.

Stability alone, however, is not a guarantee of an optimal market allocation of economic resources. To achieve this end, property rights must also internalize costs and benefits. States are more than capable of establishing stable property rights that encourage suboptimal economic behavior. Douglass North (1981) has argued that states are torn between securing revenue by seizing a larger slice of the existing pie (which discourages market rational economic behavior), and limiting revenues to encourage a more productive allocation of resources. Robert Bates (1981) has elegantly delineated how the policies pursued by many African states have discouraged agricultural production. Hence the extent to which a particular pattern of exchange approaches market rationality is a function of both the stability of property rights and their specific substance. These two dimensions are depicted in figure 11–1.

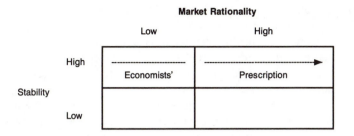

Figure 11-1. Property Rights

The highest level of exchange activity will occur in the upper right quadrant, where property rights are both stable and market rational. (We assume here that all other things being equal, optimal allocation will be associated with higher levels of exchange at least up to the point where transaction costs outweigh further market activity.) Industrialized market economy states fall somewhere in this quadrant. Market activity will be least in the lower left quadrant. Perhaps Afghanistan is now an example. Centrally planned economies fall in the upper left quadrant. Neoclassical economists have also generally argued that many Third World states also belong in this quadrant by having established stable property rights that encourage misallocation. To some extent economists have tended to view entitlements through property rules as a natural state of affairs and restrictions on such entitlements as a product of misinformed or pernicious government policies.[9] The economist's prescription calls for moving from the upper-left-hand quadrant to the upper-right-hand quadrant of figure 11-1.

The history of property rights is, however, much richer than this economist's prescription suggests. Property rights, as Hobbes, Locke, and Smith recognized, were not endowed by nature. Rights are not always stable. Political authority can disappear. New revolutionary regimes may, or may not, honor the international commitments of their predecessors. Private actors caught in the midst of boundary changes may have their property rights radically altered.[10] The movement from feudalism to capitalism was not always functionally optimal; that is, it did not always represent a shift from the upper-left quadrant to the upper-right quadrant of figure 11-1. Japan did, in fact, make such a move after the Meiji Restoration. In Europe, however, some areas moved from the upper-left to the lower-right quadrant only later shifting to the upper-right quadrant. Depending on how colonial property rights are assessed some might argue that recently independent states have moved from the upper-right to the upper-left quadrant or even from the upper-right to the lower-left.

The increase in international economic transactions (absolute if not relative) to which the adherents of interdependence arguments so frequently point has occurred primarily in countries that fall in the upper-right-hand quadrant. But almost all areas of the world have, to some extent, participated in the absolute growth of international transactions. At least in part this must be attributed to the consolidation of sovereignty at the global level. Property rights are, in the contemporary world, only rarely threatened by external invasion or boundary changes. Disorder has emanated primarily from internal sources.[11] The consolidation of the state system has facilitated, indeed made possible, increased levels of exchange, both domestic and international.

At the international level, as suggested earlier in this chapter, the hegemonic distribution of power in the noncommunist world did facilitate the creation of a set of international property rights that encouraged international exchange. The trading regime embodied in GATT gave some assurance that the international flow of goods would not be arbitrarily changed by states.[12] Bilateral treaties helped to secure stable treatment for direct foreign investment. The Bretton Woods agreements, which reflected U.S. initiatives, power, and values, contributed to stability in international capital markets. National laws were, however, the base on which these international arrangements were erected. Without stable property rights enforced by national governments, international regimes would have been meaningless. In a world of national states, transactions take place within national jurisdictions.

Conclusion

Arguments that contend that changes in micro processes driven by exogenous technological innovations are fundamentally altering macro structures are vulnerable to several objections. First, they have exaggerated the growth in international transactions relative to domestic ones and have ignored the difficulties that states have always encountered in trying to control at least some transborder movements. Second, such conceptualizations have not taken sufficient account of the importance of hegemonic powers in at least initially creating stable international regimes. Third, they have not confronted the fact that in some issues areas, especially those related to security and the international use of coercion, states have become more consolidated: they have successfully eliminated almost all nonstate actors; and their existence and borders have become more secure. Finally, interdependence arguments have paid little attention to the way in which the consolidation of sovereignty has facilitated the creation of stable property rights that are a necessary if not sufficient condition for a market-rational allocation of resources.

If macro structures crumbled micro processes would almost certainly collapse as well. The transition from the present macro structure to some alternative will not be accomplished by the burrowing from below of micro processes, a fact that students of functionalism and neofunctionalism recognized more than a decade ago (Haas 1975). If such a transition is accomplished at all, more subtle and symbiotic changes will have to take place, and the new institutional forms that emerge will be different from any that exist now, and different than those the more mundane among us could even imagine.

Notes

1. Skocpol (1979) argues that in one case, France, the financial pressures were so great that the king was compelled to enter into negotiations with civil society (through the Estates General) which ultimately precipitated the French Revolution. For a discussion of the relationship between war and taxation see Tilly (1975) and Ardant (1975). For a discussion of the benefits of an efficient domestic tax system for international military power see Rasler and Thompson (1983).

2. Problems with the ITU series are numerous. Many countries did not provide any statistics before the 1970s; others use different means for measuring international and domestic telephone traffic (for example, pulses versus number of calls), or change the method of measurement in the middle of the series. Of the countries for which twenty years of consistently reported data exist, we have selected countries from as many geographical regions, levels of development, and political systems as possible.

3. Jonathan Schell (1982), for instance, has argued that once a first strike has been launched, the original rationale for retaliation (which was to prevent that strike) has disappeared. But if the rationale is undermined by a preemptive strike then the logic of deterrence unravels. The standard response to this line of argument is the threat that leaves something to chance.

4. For a discussion of the declining utility of force see Keohane and Nye (1977) and Rosecrance (1986). For the ability of nuclear weapons to deter nonnuclear conflict see Robert Jervis (1984).

5. McNeill (1982) argues that the history of modern European warfare reflects the transition from the feudal command (that is, authoritative) allocation of military capabilities to a market-based system, and back to a command system.

6. For filibuster literature, see Brown (1980), Murdoch (1951), Wallace (1957), Stout (1973), and Roche (1891).

7. Terrorism is the obvious possible exception. The effort by the United States to give terrorism an address is either a claim that terrorism is in fact instigated by states or an effort to get states to control terrorist activities.

8. Calabresi and Melamed (1972, 1092) have argued that an entitlement may be protected by property rules, liability rules, or it may be inalienable. If an entitlement is protected by property rules then its ownership or use can only be changed through the voluntary agreement of the current owner by, for instance, sale in a market. An entitlement protected by liability rules may be destroyed by another party so long as that party is willing to pay an objectively determined value. A right is inalienable if it cannot be transferred, even if there are willing buyers and willing sellers.

9. For example see Furubotn and Pejovich (1972, 1140).

10. The movie *The Mission* gives a graphic example of such a change when the shift from Spanish to Portuguese rule transformed some South American Indians from recognized Christian individuals into slaves.

11. As U.S. assistance to the Nicaraguan contras illustrates, however, external intervention has hardly come to an end.

12. It is not clear whether the recent U.S. imposition of tariffs on $300 million worth of Japanese goods, given a bilateral trade deficit of tens of billions of dollars, should be taken as an indication of the strength of existing rules or of their malleability.

218 • *Global Changes and Theoretical Challenges*

References

Ardant, Gabriel (1975). "Financial Policy and Economic Infrastructure of Modern States and Nations." In C. Tilly, ed., *The Formation of National States in Western Europe.* Princeton: Princeton University Press.

Bairoch, Paul (1976). *Commerce extérieur et développement économique de l'Europe au XIXe siécle.* Paris: École des Hautes Études en Sciences Sociales.

Bates, Robert (1981). *Markets and States in Tropical Africa: The Political Basis of Agricultural Policies.* Berkeley: University of California Press.

Baumgart, Winfried (1981). *The Peace of Paris 1856.* Santa Barbara, Calif.: ABC-Clio.

Bayley, C.C. (1977). *Mercenaries for the Crimea.* London: McGill-Queen's University Press.

Brown, Charles H. (1980). *Agents of Manifest Destiny.* Chapel Hill: University of North Carolina Press.

Burchett, Wilfred, and Derek Roebuck (1977). *The Whores of War.* New York: Penguin Books.

Calabresi, Guido, and A. Douglas Melamed (1972). "Property Rules, Liability Rules, and Inalienability: One View of the Cathedral." *Harvard Law Review* 85 (April).

Cohen, Benjamin J. (1986). *In Whose Interest? International Banking and American Foreign Policy.* New Haven: Yale University Press.

Cooper, Richard (1968). *The Economics of Interdependence.* New York: McGraw-Hill.

Frieden, Jeffrey (1987). *Banking on the World: The Politics of American International Finance.* New York: Random House.

Furubotn, Eirik G., and Svetozar Pejovich (1972). "Property Rights and Economic Theory: A Survey of Recent Literature." *Journal of Economic Literature* 10 (December).

Gilpin, Robert (1975). *U.S. Power and the Multinational Corporation.* New York: Basic Books.

—— (1987). *The Political Economy of International Relations.* Princeton: Princeton University Press.

Goldstein, Judith (1986). "The Political Economy of Trade: Institutions of Protection." *American Political Science Review* 80, no. 1 (March).

Gooch, John (1980). *Armies in Europe.* London: Routledge & Kegan Paul.

Haas, Ernst (1975). *The Obsolescence of Regional Integration Theory.* Berkeley, Calif.: Institute for International Studies.

Hall, William E. (1924). *A Treatise on International Law.* Oxford: Clarendon Press.

Hirschman, Albert (1945). *National Power and the Structure of Foreign Trade.* Berkeley: University of California Press.

Jackson, Robert H., and Carl G. Rosberg (1982). "Why Africa's Weak States Persist: The Empirical and Juridical in Statehood." *World Politics* 35 (October).

Jervis, Robert (1984). *The Illogic of American Nuclear Strategy.* Ithaca: Cornell University Press.

Jessup, Philip, and Francis Deak (1935). *Neutrality: Its History, Economics, and Law.* Vol. 1. New York: Columbia University Press.

Kant, Immanuel (1963). *On History.* New York: Bobbs–Merrill.

Keohane, Robert, and Joseph Nye (1972). *Transnational Relations and World Politics.* Cambridge: Harvard University Press.

—— (1977). *Power and Interdependence.* Boston: Little, Brown.

Krasner, Stephen (1976). "State Power and the Structure of International Trade." *World Politics* 28 (April).

McNeill, William H. (1982). *The Pursuit of Power*. Chicago: University of Chicago Press.

Maier, Charles (1977). "The Politics of Productivity." In Peter J. Katzenstein, ed., *Between Power and Plenty*. Madison: University of Wisconsin Press.

Malloy, William M. (1910). *Treaties, Conventions, International Acts, Protocols, and Agreements between the United States of America and Other Powers, 1776–1909*. Washington, D.C.: G.P.O.

Mitchell, B.R. (1983). *International Historical Statistics: The Americas and Australasia*. Detroit: Gale Research.

Mockler, Anthony (1969). *The Mercenaries*. New York: Macmillan.

Mukherjee, Ramkrishna (1974). *The Rise and Fall of the East India Company*. New York: Monthly Review Press.

Murdoch, Richard K. (1951). *The Georgia–Florida Frontier 1793–96: Spanish Reaction to French Intrigue and American Designs*. University of California Publications in History, J.W. Caughey, D.K. Bjork, and R.H. Fisher, eds., Vol. 40. Berkeley: University of California Press.

North, Douglass (1981). *Structure and Change in Economic History*. New York: Norton.

Organisation for Economic Co-operation and Development (OECD) (1981). *International Investment and Multinational Enterprises*. Paris: OECD.

Phillips, W.A., and Arthur H. Reede (1936). *Neutrality: Its History, Economics, and Law*. New York: Columbia University Press.

Preston, Richard A., and Sydney F. Wise (1970). *Men in Arms*. New York: Praeger.

Rasler, Karen, and William Thompson (1983). "Global Wars, Public Debts, and the Long Cycle." *World Politics* 35.

Ritchie, Robert C. (1986). *Captain Kidd and the War against the Pirates*. Cambridge: Harvard University Press.

Roche, James J. (1891). *The Story of the Filibusters*. New York: Macmillan.

Rosecrance, Richard (1986). *The Rise of the Trading State*. New York: Basic Books.

Rosenau, James N. (1988). "Post-International Politics: The Micro Dimension." Paper presented at the fourteenth World Congress of the International Political Science Association. Washington, D.C., 28 August–1 September.

Schell, Jonathan (1982). *The Fate of the Earth*. New York: Knopf.

Sherry, Frank (1986). *Raiders and Rebels*. New York: Hearst Marine Books.

Skocpol, Theda (1979). *States and Social Revolutions*. New York: Cambridge University Press.

Stout, Joseph A. (1973). *The Liberators*. Los Angeles: Westernlore Press.

Tilly, Charles (1975). *The Formation of National States in Western Europe*. Princeton: Princeton University Press.

United Nations Conference on Trade and Development (UNCTAD) (1983). *1983 Handbook of International Trade and Development Statistics*. Geneva: UNCTAD.

United Nations (various years). *U.N. Statistical Yearbook*. New York: United Nations.

Wallace, Edward S. (1957). *Destiny and Glory*. New York: Coward-McCann.

Waltz, Kenneth (1970). "The Myth of National Interdependence." In Charles P. Kindleberger, ed., *The International Corporation*. Cambridge: MIT Press.

—— (1979). *Theory of International Relations*. Reading, Mass.: Addison-Wesley.

12

Collective Goods in an Interdependent World: Authority and Order as Determinants of Peace and Prosperity?

Erich Weede

Some scholars are impressed by the rapid changes that we can observe everywhere. Some changes are indeed obvious and of supreme importance for world politics. With the advent of nuclear weapons and contemporary delivery systems we can kill each other much faster and more effectively than ever before. Possibly, this very capability to effect previously inconceivable damage has reduced the risk of war, at least in some places of the globe. Both our capability to press the button on the doomsday machine and the incentive not to do it have profoundly transformed world politics. On the other hand, it is equally easy not to see any fundamental change in other important aspects of human affairs. From man-eating headhunters in the stone age to the century of Hitler and Stalin, of Idi Amin and Pol Pot, is there any unambiguous trend toward moral improvement—in particular where it matters most, with the ruling classes?

By and large, I perceive a trend towards ever more powerful technologies of a productive and destructive variety, and a related trend towards larger political units, but almost no other changes that transform the political problems we face.[1] War has become less likely among the leading military powers. Nevertheless, our physical survival has become more precarious. Human actions have much more impact than ever before and may start to transform the natural environment. But the nature of the political problems of authority and order, of peace and prosperity, have not changed much. As ever, the solution of one problem seems to be related to the generation of another one.

I am very grateful to Raymond Duvall and Bruce M. Russett for their critiques of this chapter. They are not to be blamed for the remaining shortcomings of my chapter.

Authority and Order within Societies as Public Goods

I want to start my analysis with what I perceive to be the *permanent* features of politics because (like Gilpin [1981], Krasner [1985], Russett [1983b], and Waltz [1979]) I do not perceive many changes of fundamental importance. First, there is the need for property rights, authority, and order. This point may be clarified by following Tullock's (1974) lead: Let us imagine an anarchical society where everyone takes what he or she needs because property rights do not exist. An observer from a capitalist society might say that theft is legal under anarchy. Obviously, the absence of property rights affects incentives. It is rather unlikely that you benefit from the fruits of your labor. Somebody else will pick them before you do. It is much easier to roam through the country and look for something that others have produced in order to take it rather than to work for it. Because almost everybody stops working, and because almost everybody tries to take advantage of the labor of others, an anarchical society without property rights must be and remain poor, unless property rights can somehow be established.

Conceivably, there are two ways to establish property rights and incentives to work. Either the would-be producers agree to some set of property rights and generate some sort of government and police to enforce the agreement, or a gang of robbers gets together and enforces a monopoly of theft. Although we might prefer the former development, the latter one is *much* more likely. For the producers, government and property rights are collective goods. If some set of property rights is enforced, if (say) everyone has title to the fruits of his or her labor, if stealing is punished, then everyone becomes better off. The establishment of property rights is in everyone's interest, but there are incentives to free ride in a large group: Let others pay taxes and serve in the police and government, but save your inputs for what benefits you rather than the entire group. It is difficult to overcome this dilemma in a large group of selfish people. According to Olson (1965) selective incentives and coercion might help to procure public goods even in large groups. But coercion and, to a lesser degree, selective incentives presuppose that the problem is already solved (Hardin 1982, 34)—that somebody gets the rest of the group to do what is in their common interest. Under the assumption of selfishness, the freeriding tendency should prevent even moderately large groups from establishing property rights, authority, and order.

A gang of would-be robbers faces much better incentives. Their idea is that a *small* group of robbers forces a *larger* group of producers into submission, enforces a monopoly of theft for their nascent organization, and provides the producers with protection against rival criminals. It is easier for a small group to organize itself for collective action than it is for larger groups (Olson 1965). Moreover, the criminals want to become an exploiting ruling class, which is an excellent selective incentive. Add the plausible idea that they are more inclined to use violence, and because of their inclination more practiced in it, and thus the establishment of order and some type of property rights by "organized criminals" looks rather likely. Those readers who dislike ahistorical theorizing and the term "organized criminals" may instead turn to Tilly's (1985) treatment of European history or think of nomadic tribes who have again and again conquered, plundered, enslaved, and ruled more civilized and more productive peoples than themselves (Ruestow 1950; McNeill 1982; Hall 1985). Often a ruling class or tribe could prevail because of political decay approaching anarchy under the previous regime.

It is important to recognize that the "organized criminals" do provide a true public service or good[2] by repressing anarchical theft, by providing incentives to work rather than to look around for opportunities to steal. The closer the "organized criminals" come to an intuitive understanding of the Laffer curve, the better it is for the society as a whole.

Raw power is not yet authority. But a tradition of obedience, an interest in the preservation of some type of order (almost any type of order), and in the long run certainly the aid of gods or priests will turn power into authority. My point is that authority and order are requisites for peace and prosperity within societies; that the collective good of authority and order is likely to be provided at the expense of making society less equal than it was before, because the positional good of becoming or being a member of an exploitative ruling class is an important selective incentive for contributing to the establishment or maintenance of order.[3] Inequality within groups speeds the establishment of some kind of order.[4] More importantly, inequality necessarily results from the establishment of order. Coercion is an essential part in establishing and maintaining order.

In my view, the concentration of power in the hands of some "organized criminals" or ruling class is a necessary first step in the establishment of order and authority. Most of mankind never experienced a better kind of rule. But some of us do, particularly in contemporary Western societies. There are two analytically distinct improvements over despotic and "kleptocratic" (Andreski 1968a, 92) rule. First, whimsical and arbitrary power must be limited. Second, subjects become citizens where rights of political participation are established and later expanded. Although both types of improvement seem to be correlated, the first improvement occurred earlier in European history than the other one. Moreover, without severe limitations of political power, in particular without a rather autonomous economy, there never has been substantial popular participation in choosing governors and policies. The whimsical and arbitrary power of "organized criminals" or ruling classes was overcome, and political power became "domesticated" (Albert 1986), because European ruling classes never succeeded in empire building, but had to live under the constraints of a competitive international system. The discussion of this topic, however, shall be postponed.

Rivalry between States as a Collective Bad

Historically, order and authority have been produced locally rather than globally; that is, there has always been a multiplicity of territorial units with independent governments. Where the need to establish authority and order as prerequisites for peace and prosperity finds multiple solutions, where at least some political units are contiguous to others, where they know how to apply violence and coercion against each other, and where no superior authority is capable of guaranteeing peace, these units face a security dilemma (Herz 1950; Waltz 1979).[5] In itself, the local character and the multitude of solutions to the problems of order and authority had to produce new problems and actually did so. Within independent political units, hierarchical arrangements kept order and maintained peace. Between or above independent political units such an element was lacking. War being possible, it had to be prepared for, deterred, and—sooner or later—to be fought. In addition to the security dilemma itself, territorial conflicts (that is, incompatible claims to rule the same piece of territory) have been a primary cause of war, even in the twentieth century (Luard 1968; Weede 1975).

The problem of order within societies has two conceivable solutions, as discussed above: a contractarian solution and an imposed solution, with the former being more desirable and the latter being more likely. The same is true for the problem of order among strategically interdependent political units. It is conceivable that decision makers from all political units might get together and decide to outlaw violence, to disarm, and to agree on some nonviolent modes of settlement of issues—possibly even to create some kind of world authority. But effectively outlawing self-help and war in the international system is a collective good. Given a large number of independent actors, there will be a freerider problem.[6] Concretely, decision makers from diverse political units dislike to renounce violence first and to disarm first. Processes that never start don't go far. Thus the security dilemma and the territorial delimitation dilemma have persisted through the millennia.[7] And mankind has suffered from wars again and again. One should add the observation that contractarian solutions to the security and territorial dilemmas were not even regularly considered for many centuries. For the major part of the twentieth century, contractarian solutions to the security dilemma mainly served propaganda purposes. Given the ultimately coercive nature of rule at home almost everywhere, even the idea of a different type of international order could stand little chance.

Conceivably, the international "order" based on coercion, threats of war, and war itself might be overcome if all major states could overcome repressive rule at home first. For inter-state relations between democracies are remarkable for their absence of war (Small and Singer 1976; Rummel 1983; Doyle 1986) although not necessarily for their avoidance of lesser types of conflict (see Vincent 1987 against Rummel 1987). But this (conceivable) prerequisite for a better international order is not yet met and unlikely to be met in the foreseeable future. Moreover, there is little reason to believe that more democratic or less repressive regimes avoid war involvement more successfully than other types of regime as long as there is an abundance of nondemocratic states (Chan 1984; Weede 1984b). The security dilemma is here to stay.

One may still object to my analysis of international relations by pointing to the contemporary industrialized democracies that together constitute a zone of peace. Here at least peace does not seem to be underwritten by force or deterrent threats of force. Conceivably, "stable peace, economic rights of equality, decent living conditions, and political liberties all may be bound together in an inseparable package" (Russett and Starr 1981, 443). In this optimistic view, economic cooperation among equals (that benefits all participants) and democracy have contributed to the generation of a noncoercive zone of peace, although it remains restricted to industrialized democracies. Though one certainly would wish to believe in the stability of this zone of peace and in its noncoercive foundations, there is some room for doubt. A single industrialized democracy, the United States, has always had more military power than all of her democratic allies. The United States deploys military forces in some of the most important industrialized democracies: in Britain, in West Germany, in Italy, and in Japan. In my view, national security decision making in some other democracies (most notably, in West Germany) is actually penetrated by the United States. Moreover, the zone of peace encompassing Japan, North America and Western Europe has to be perceived in connection with its origins of the end of World War II and in connection with its relationship with the East–West rivalry.

You may overcome a security dilemma by general disarmament—or by imposing your rule on everybody else. The former route suffers from a difficulty of attracting resources for the procurement of the public good, but the latter one easily overcomes this problem. The prospect of hegemony is a positional good (Hirsch 1976; Weede 1985) and a very strong selective incentive to overcome the security dilemma by imposing an imperial peace. Just as the coercive solution to the domestic problems of property rights and order is more likely than the contractarian one, so the coercive solution to the international problem of security is more likely than a conceivable contractarian one. There *may be* islands of a contractarian solution—by tacit agreement—but the coercive attempt at a solution has typically defined the nature of world politics despite its often self-defeating character.

Wherever an empire overcomes the security and territorial delimitation dilemmas (or, more precisely, a set of local dilemmas) and forcefully pacifies a major part of the globe, it does provide a true public service. War is ruled out, although insurrections may now and then provoke warlike campaigns of "pacification." In our nuclear missile age there are local and therefore imperfect solutions to the problems of order at the international level. There is Pax Sovietica in the East and there has been Pax Americana in the West—at least in the 1950s and 1960s (Weede 1975, 1983a). In my view, the greater effectiveness of the Soviet kind of peace compared to the U.S. brand is related to the greater coerciveness of the Soviet regime.[8] To this day, order and peace remain rooted in coercion—at the international level even more so than in the national level, where power has been domesticated at least in *some* states.[9]

Rivalry between States as a Collective Good

It is obvious that authority, order, and peace within and between nations contribute to prosperity. Therefore, international rivalry and related threats to peace should be an unambiguous collective bad. This is, however, an unjustified simplification of the relationship between international rivalry and prosperity. According to Chirot (1986), Hall (1985), Jones (1981), Wallerstein (1974), and Weber (1981, 288–89), competition, rivalry, and nearly permanent threats of war in the European state system are related to "the Rise of the West" or "the European Miracle." Western Europe developed faster and became more prosperous than the Islamic, Indian, and Chinese civilizations because Western Europe was never unified into a single empire, like China, Moghul India or the Ottoman Empire. European states always had to compete with other European states of roughly equal levels of economic development and technological and military competence. Historically, national security has always been precarious for European states. Why should European disunity and quasi-permanent threats of war have contributed to European development and prosperity? My basic proposition is: The European state system produced something like limited government—even in an age of absolutism (see Andreski 1964, 312, about Louis XIV).[10]

First, competition between European rulers and princes limited the degree of damage each one of them could do. Superstition and inefficiency were as widespread in European ruling circles as elsewhere in the world, but they never could harm the entire European civilization. By contrast, in united China unwise policies could and did damage the development prospects of the entire civilization. In the fifteenth century Chinese ships explored the vast area between the East African coast and Kamchatka, but then the emperor and his bureaucracy prohibited overseas exploration and trade. After a while, the Chinese even forgot how to build ocean-going vessels. Small and comparatively backward European nations could rule the waves. Rivalry and hostility between European rulers, the sometimes rather tiny patches of land where princes ruled, and the often fairly close political borders made it impossible to repress innovation in Europe.

Religious disunity and fragmentation were about as helpful in Europe as political disunity (Albert 1986). Since the Reformation no church enjoyed continental power. Damage by political and ecclesiastical rulers had to be limited. Nobody could repress innovation, the development of science, and the application of technology to economic problems. The Catholic church might have liked to try, but it could not succeed. Political rulers did encourage monopolies, guilds, and other restrictive practices. The more successful local rulers were at imposing economic regulation, the easier it became for their rivals to overtake them—as the comparison of British and French economic development illustrates (Ekelund and Tollison 1981).

Second, the existence of an international system in Europe contributed to the safeguarding of property rights. If merchants transport relatively cheap products for mass consumption and do so repeatedly within rather short intervals of time—as has been true in Europe since the Middle Ages—and if the ruling prince controls a small piece of territory, he rationally should not rob the merchant and confiscate his goods.[11] By confiscation the small prince achieves some immediate, but modest gain at the expense of generating a steady stream of protection rents that he might collect from merchants. The robber prince simply forces trade routes to bypass his territory to the benefit of more farsighted rulers nearby. In a huge empire, merchants can find no way around exploitative rulers and their agents. The competitive nature of European politics and the international system in Europe made irregular confiscation less attractive to European rulers, but made them concede comparatively safe property rights to traders. In an international system self-interest in future gains forces ruling classes to concede property rights to merchants and producers. Moreover, rulers who are too shortsighted to grant property rights damage their economic base and ultimately the survival prospects of their rule. Where shortsighted rulers suffer the fate of maladapted species, relatively safe property rights spread. The safety of property rights is perhaps the most important background condition of economic development and prosperity.

The relationship between governmental or state strength and property rights is always a delicate matter. To overcome the insecurity inherent in anarchy, we need government to protect property rights. But who protects people from their protectors and the latter's predatory appetites? In European history, the competitive international system or European disunity contributed to doing the job. From an economic perspective, the *main* question is not political participation, but how much government to have. There should be some government strong enough to safeguard property rights, but weak enough not to overwhelm society. Limited, but effective, government is desirable. Unlimited or whimsical government, even by merchants or capitalists, is bad for economic development. As Andreski (1984, 142) has aptly put it, "new forms of production and trade (i.e. industrially oriented capitalism) develop only where the business class is too strong to be fettered and exploited but not strong enough to accumulate wealth by extracting it from others, and where, in consequence, production and trade offer to the members of this class the most promising road to satisfactory livelihood and enrichment."[12]

Although the European wars did cause a lot of suffering and destruction, simultaneously the permanent threats to ruling-class ambitions and security did affect the balance of power within societies for the benefit of the lower classes. European rulers had to become interested in economic development because of its relationship to the tax base and their ability to pay for ever more expensive armed forces. European rulers had to become interested in the loyalty of their subjects. At least since the early nineteenth century, a loyal population became an asset at times of war. Because European rulers had to entrust many of their citizens with weapons, the scope for whimsical action and mistreatment of subjects by ruling classes had to be narrowed. Moreover, rulers even became interested in well-fed conscripts. By contrast, ruling classes can concentrate on the exploitation of their subjects wherever the risk of war is close to zero. Even in the contemporary world, threats to national security still seem to contribute to economic growth and income equalization (Andreski 1968b; Dixon and Moon 1986; Garnier and Hazelrigg 1977; Kahn 1979, 334, 457; Kriesberg 1979, 379; Weede and Jagodzinski 1981, 1987; Weede 1983b, 1986b).

The positive effect of international rivalry on economic development does *not* depend *only* on relatively safe property rights and the corresponding limitation of governmental power in a competitive international system and on the balance of power between rulers and ruled within societies. Conscription and military life itself may have some direct modernizing impact even where they undermine limited government, as has been suggested by Dahrendorf (1965, p. 68, my translation): "Military training on the Prussian pattern might be much more successful as a preparation for industrialization than Calvinist creeds might be even under optimal circumstances." Almost everywhere the military teaches young men the habit of obeying orders. In industry, particularly in the early phases of industrialization, many workers face routine assignments. There, a habit to do what one is told to do and to accept lowly jobs constitutes a useful kind of human capital. Therefore, the European armed forces may have served as schools of modernization.

In this section of the chapter I have argued the benefits to be derived from an international system of competing states. Because too much authority is a collective bad for everybody who is not a member of the ruling class, the limitation of governmental power by the very existence of competing states is welcome. Exit is the ultimate protection against misrule. And exit depends upon the existence of competing states. Though many refugees may go to countries that are friendly to the government of their home state, some competition and even hostility between governments is useful in order to prevent the foundation of a "holy alliance" or "trade union" of governments against peoples. In the section before this I made the more obvious point that security dilemmas within an anarchical system of states pose a quasi-permanent threat to peace that is a collective bad for almost everyone. In international politics, authority and order seem to be good and bad at the same time. India did not develop autonomously because there was too little authority and order (Hall 1985). China, by contrast, suffered from too much order and authority through long periods of her history (Hall 1985; Jones 1981). Europe, however, struck a lucky balance.

In my view, the rise of Europe between the Middle Ages and the late twentieth century cannot be adequately explained without giving much causal weight to inter-state rivalries, security threats, and even frequent wars in modern European history. Writers who disagree on almost everything else seem to share this evaluation of the macroscopic relationship between security threats or limited government and economic dynamism (Chirot 1986; Collins 1980; Hall 1985; Jones 1981; Wallerstein 1974; Weber 1981). If we narrow our perspective from half a millenium to the twentieth century only, from a comparison of the great Asian civilizations with Europe to an analysis of what happened in Europe, then it is obvious that inter-state rivalry may generate garrison states (Lasswell 1941) rather than limited government.

In modern wars young men are conscripted. They lose the property right in themselves and are effectively "nationalized." Moreover, the observation of centralized decision making in European war economies provoked one of the staunchest defenders of capitalism and liberty to write his *Road to Serfdom* (Hayek 1944). Preparations for war, war-making, and war debts have raised taxes and government expenditures as a share of GDP and, conceivably, even contributed to the generation and expansion of the welfare state.[13] Finally, it is sometimes quipped that the Pentagon runs the largest centrally planned economy outside of the Soviet Union. In the twentieth century, only unconditional surrender after total defeat has *sometimes* contributed to some limitation of government.[14] By and large, threats to national security seem to limit liberties and to reinforce political and economic centralization in our times.

I see no reason why the economically beneficial effects of political fragmentation should not persist. Competition between sovereign states and—unfortunately too restricted—opportunities for international migration of talent and capital still do limit governmental inclinations towards expropriatory or predatory taxation. But it seems plausible to maintain that the beneficial effects of inter-state competition among modern states depend not only on the avoidance of war in the nuclear age, but also on the avoidance of serious preparations for large-scale conventional warfare, as we have witnessed in the previous world wars.[15]

Authority, Order, and Stability within Societies as Public Bads

Within societies, there has to be some minimum of authority and order to safeguard property rights and to provide incentives for productive purposes. Obviously, all kinds of rule or rulers are not equally desirable. Exploitative rule by "organized criminals" or robber princes should contribute much less to development and prosperity than some type of authority that is limited and where producers cannot easily be overruled. Setting some obvious questions of the quality of rule aside, one may even argue that authority, order, and the safety of property rights are not necessarily good things.

According to Ekelund and Tollison (1981), Britain could overcome restrictive practices (like monopolies, guilds, or cartels) and the mercantilist "rent-seeking society" earlier than France or other continental European states because authority was more fragmented in Britain than elsewhere.[16] In seventeenth-century Britain, there was competition for supremacy between king and Parliament and between the royal courts and common law courts. If, say, the king granted special privileges to certain producers, the royal courts were likely to uphold the corresponding rights, but the common law courts were not. By and large, the fragmentation of the political and judicial system tended to devalue special privileges that could not consistently be enforced. Therefore, the incentive to engage in distributional struggle or rent-seeking behavior was minimized. Because rent-seeking diverts effort from more productive purposes, its curtailment has to improve economic performance. According to this account of British development, the very fragmentation of the British political and judicial system—or one might even say, its rather disorderly character and the weakness of certain (discriminatory) property rights—actually promoted development and prosperity.

On the one hand, authority and order are essential background conditions of economic development (Huntington and Dominguez 1975). On the other hand, authority and order seem to be equally essential background conditions to the generation of institutional sclerosis and social rigidities (Olson 1982). The phenomenon is not restricted to Western democracies, but democracies are certainly not immune to sclerosis and rigidities (Bernholz 1986; Choi 1983; Lane and Errson 1986; Olson 1982; Olson and Colander 1984; Vedder and Gallaway 1986; Weede 1984a, 1986d). Olson (1982, 77) suggested that "countries that have had democratic freedom of organization without upheaval or invasion the longest will suffer the most from growth-repressing organizations and combinations." Or, to repeat the same message in other terms: The older a democracy becomes, the slower its economy will grow. Stability and order may be the background conditions of an economic decline, even in a democracy.

Olson's (1965, 1982) argument may be crudely summarized like this. In every society there are latent groups that could gain from forming a distributional coalition and from distorting prices. Take a small number of oligopolistic producers of some final consumption good as an example. They might become better off if they form a cartel and fix a higher price than the one they could obtain in competitive markets. In order to maintain the higher-than-necessary or distorted cartel price, the oligopolistic producers have to cut production and to share the market in an orderly manner, say by quotas. The formation of a successful cartel has a number of effects: The producers sell smaller quantities of more expensive products at better profits to themselves. There is a generally regressive transfer of income from consumers to producers. There is some deadweight loss. Those would-be consumers who would buy the goods at lower competitive prices, but no longer do so at cartel prices, suffer a welfare loss. Nobody, not even the cartel producers, enjoys a gain corresponding to this loss. Worst of all, cartelization is likely to be contagious. If some economic actors perceive that others succeed in rigging prices and capturing contrived transfers, they will try harder to follow the bad example.

According to Olson (1965, 1982), oligopolistic producers enjoy a head start in the formation of distributional coalitions and in enforcing restrictive practices. In his view, small groups find it easier to overcome the freeriding problem. Because cartel prices constitute a collective good, either all producers can charge them or none can do it. So every producer would like to sell as much as possible at high cartel prices and make other producers suffer the limitation of production that is essential if high cartel prices are to be maintained. Every producer would like a cartel best where he himself could cheat and enjoy a free ride, but where everybody else carries the burdens. The smaller the group, the more visible cheating is, the more likely cheating is to run down the cartel price to the detriment even of the offender, and the more likely cheating is to be detected and somehow penalized by others. In a large group, however, everyone knows that success depends mainly on the actions of others, and that one's action has close to invisible effects. Therefore, incentives to freeriding are much greater in a large than in a small group. More generally, large groups find it more difficult than small groups to provide themselves with public goods.

But some large groups have made it. Basically, trade unions are little different from other cartels. Because workers in some sectors of the economy are very large groups, it is not easy to understand how they could ever overcome the freeriding problem. Olson (1965) explains this by reference to selective incentives and coercion. One might add political entrepreneurship and even governmental support as additional explanatory factors. In the context of this section it may suffice to focus only on the effects of cartels, trade unions, and other distributional coalitions. They always aim at the provision of public goods for their membership. The major effect of freeriding tendencies and of the head start of small compared with large groups is that a society should not hope to achieve a just or balanced distribution of income through the efforts of interest groups or distributional coalitions (Olson 1982; Tullock 1983). Although the equity effect of distributional struggles and income transfers resulting therefrom may be either negative or negligible, the growth effect is certainly negative.

Distributional coalitions must aim at favorable price distortions. They must protect their "achievements" (that is, distorted prices) by the elimination or reduction of competition, by restrictive practices, and by erecting barriers to entry into protected markets for goods and labor. Such restrictive practices and distortions interfere with allocative efficiency, impede innovation, and divert energy from productive purposes to negative-sum struggles for political power and transfers. Ultimately, restrictive practices drive economic growth rates down and, perhaps, unemployment up (Olson 1982; Bernholz 1986; Choi 1983; Lane and Errson 1986; Olson and Colander 1984; Vedder and Gallaway 1986; Weede 1984a, 1986d).

By granting the liberty to form business, farm, and professional associations or trade unions to their citizens, democracies permit interest groups to play their selfish, shortsighted, and ultimately destructive game. If there is a contemporary crisis of authority in Western societies, it derives largely from our inability to control distributional struggles and to prevent the reestablishment of the rent-seeking society. It is little consolation that the predicament of much of the Third World can be traced back to the fact that most of it never overcame the rent-seeking society in the first place (Economist 1987; Lipton 1977; Weede 1986c; World Bank 1983, 57–63). Nor does it help that centrally planned economies are capable of their own kinds of sclerosis and rigidities. Possibly, limited governments and autonomous economies turn out to be a mere transition phase from the earlier and oligarchical rent-seeking society to the more modern and egalitarian version of the rent-seeking society.

Our problem is that the effects of authority, order, and stability are inherently ambiguous. On the one hand, authority, order, and stability are essential if property rights are to be safeguarded and incentives for productive activities are to be provided. On the other hand, order and stability permit those with access to ruling circles to exploit government in order to enforce transfers. Democratic government does not necessarily limit distributional struggles and rent-seeking. Elected governments certainly wish to promote their reelection chances by growth and prosperity for all, but they more urgently have to acquiesce in restrictive practices, price distortions, and rent-seeking by interest groups (Bernholz 1977)—sometimes merely to win their confidence and votes, sometimes even for the sake of political stability. Governments may buy political stability or election victories in the short run by concessions to distributional coalitions. But they end up with sclerosis and stagnation in the long run. The *core* problem of a social order is whether the scope of government can be limited to the provision of public goods for entire societies, such as domestic order, safe property rights, and defense or external peace. Participation in government may be less important than limitation of the scope of government. Compared to anarchy, almost any kind of government is a public good. Compared to overgovernment, the restriction of governmental activities is a public good.

Permanent and Emergent Features of World Politics

There are some permanent problems of politics, that is, the necessities to establish and to maintain domestic order, to settle disputes between individuals and groups, and to safeguard property rights and incentives to work. So far the solution to this set of problems has created new problems. Local solutions to the problems of government have created security dilemmas and dilemmas of territorial delimitation. The differentiation of the population into rulers and ruled has generated the problem of how to make rulers responsive to the needs and desires of the ruled—or to put the same point somewhat differently, how to make rulers provide public goods instead of private and positional goods for themselves only. In European history one set of problems has contributed to a partial solution of the other set of problems. Rivalry and nearly permanent threats of war in the international system made a primary contribution to the limitation of arbitrary and whimsical government, to the protection of property rights for producers and traders from kleptocrats. As admitted above, this relationship does no longer hold in the twentieth century. Limited government made Europe more prosperous than the Asian civilizations.[17]

Where they exist government and order are likely to be abused. International competition has been a rather imperfect cure. Even expanding political participation and democracy have done little to contain the abuse of public power for private purposes. Stable democracies seem to accumulate distributional coalitions and the price distortions for which these interest groups fight. Crudely put, democracy substitutes rent-seeking by all strata (although with unequal success and the outcome still definitely favoring the privileged classes) for kleptocracy from above. At the national as well as at the international level the problem of order remains largely unsolved. Predation and war occur again and again.

Because the readers of this chapter are likely to be most skeptical about my focus on the benefits of an international system with its inherent threats of war, I want to stress again that the ultimate and penultimate defenses of ordinary people against their rulers depend upon the existence of unfriendly neighbors—insurgency being the ultimate defense and exit being the penultimate defense. For insurgents the prospects of success or even survival are greatly improved by external assistance (Gurr 1968; Gurr and Duvall 1973).[18] Without sovereign and unfriendly neighbors, refugees might find nowhere to go to. Constitutional limitation of power looks like an attractive and low-cost alternative to international hostility. But constitutional limitations of power look to me to be modeled on much older international balances of power.[19] Conceivably, constitutional limitations of power could not persist for long without governments being limited by international competition and hostility.

But I do not want to argue that human history is an endless reoccurence of coercive impositions of order, of kleptocracy and rent-seeking, and of war. There are some emergent properties: Through the millennia man has invented *ever more powerful technologies* (Lenski 1966; Lenski and Lenski 1982; Rosenberg and Birdzell 1986). Since the Industrial Revolution, the generation of new and more powerful technologies has accelerated. In the mid-twentieth century the process seems to have speeded up again. Technology is important because it determines what people can do to nature and to each other. Technologies of destruction seem *at least* as important for the course of human history as productive technologies. Developments in military technology made the medieval city-state obsolete when it could no longer serve as a unit of protection (Herz 1957). Currently, nuclear weapons destroy the hard shell of classical European and other nation-states, including the two superpowers. There seems to be no effective substitute for the nation-state below world government, which may reestablish some meaningful degree of protection and impermeability. Neither a united Europe, nor a united Atlantic Community, nor a united Free World (nor an American empire, if you prefer this label) would be up to the task (unless SDI fulfills the wildest dreams of its proponents and more). In essence, military technologies have made the very existence of a competitive inter-state system obsolete.

There are not only technologies of destruction. Productive technologies also exist. They have permitted a multiplication of the number of human inhabitants on the globe and permitted a rising fraction of mankind to escape from the abject poverty that has been the "ordinary" existence of humanity through the ages. Nevertheless, the more benign technologies have created new problems, too. The more densely populated a region, a country, or a planet is, the more likely are externalities to be felt. Externalities may be positive or negative. Rising populations may lower transaction costs, and stimulate the division of labor and market exchanges in order to realize comparative advantages and thereby contribute to prosperity (North and Thomas 1973; with some reservations, Durkheim 1930). Simultaneously, rising populations, and more so if accompanied by rising standards of living, may contribute to the exhaustion of some raw materials, to the disappearance of free space, and to ever more pollution. In an interdependent economic system scarcities of some materials due to local disturbances may create distant, even global repercussions. By their nature, air and water pollution do not stop at national borders, but create negative externalities far beyond. In an ever more densely populated and economically interdependent world, actions within the borders of one nation may increasingly inflict costs beyond borders. Therefore, the need to internalize the externalities of productive and purely civilian activities reinforces the obsoleteness of the competitive inter-state system we know.

Technological progress may have created some need for global government or, at least, for generally accepted rules. But it has simultaneously ruled out the desirability of using *the* traditional means of expanding the geographical scope of some government—namely victory in war and annexation. Though there *may* be some rather rare instances of peaceful unification, there *certainly are many unambiguous cases of empire building by war.* Today, political unification by war risks unprecedented catastrophe.

Somehow the risk of global and nuclear war has been contained. Moreover, the multiplicity of (largely independent) political units and the benefits to be derived from a pluralistic international order have been preserved. Governmental power remained limited in the West. In the Third World, governmental control of transnational corporations in particular and of economic activities in general is limited by the existence of other states and economies, some of which are unfriendly. Many mainstream economists come close to the view (which I fully share) that only constraints deriving from the competitive international system force many Third World governments to desist from even more foolish and disastrous policies than the ones they currently pursue (Olson 1982, 175; Krauss 1983; Weede 1986c). Even in the capitalist democracies expropriatory taxation (on the Swedish model) and overregulation are made more difficult by the existence of other states and economies where capital and talent might go. In the centrally planned economies governmental powers are unlimited, the right to exit is nearly abolished, and foreign interactions are subject to tight control from above. Therefore, these nations do not reap the benefits of a pluralistic international system. But even their leaders seem to have lost their belief in their systems. Unfortunately, the benefits of a competitive international system have been preserved at the expense of a continuing risk of global or nuclear war.

The contemporary nuclear arsenals of the two superpowers amount to a doomsday machine that only waits to be triggered. Though perceptions of the damage that a nuclear exchange would cause may have been somewhat exaggerated in the early days of the nuclear age, for some decades the existence of nuclear weapons has nullified hopes for meaningful victory in a general war between the two super-powers. Without nuclear weapons at least one adversary in a conflict can always persuade itself of sufficient chances of victory.[20] In a conventional setting it happens that both adversaries look confidently forward to victory. In 1914, French troops hoped to occupy Berlin within a couple of months; German troops hoped to occupy Paris within a few months—and few soldiers, officers, or civilians foresaw the bloodbath of the trench warfare to come. With nuclear weapons the most plausible prediction is that even the winner of the war (if there should be one) will be worse off than the losers of conventional wars historically have been. Between the two superpowers the fear of war itself seems to have replaced the traditional fear of losing a war. There exists "peace through fear" (Aron 1966).

Peace through fear is precarious in at least two ways.[21] First, there are the technological instabilities in a qualitative arms race. It remains conceivable that either superpower could achieve a breakthrough in accuracy, ballistic missile defense, and antisubmarine warfare. Thereafter, a disarming strike against the adversary—before it can catch up—may look attractive. Because it is difficult to judge the battlefield performance of complex weapons systems that have been tested in peacetime only, there should still be some residual caution. But the incentive to exploit a *temporary* advantage in the qualitative arms race remains a source of serious concern.

Second, there are the linkages between the two superpowers and other nations. The superpowers are interested in or allied with many other nations. They even deploy troops on foreign soil. Therefore, they may get involved in wars that start as conflicts between lesser powers or between one superpower and a lesser power. In my view (Weede 1975, 1983a), deterrence between the two superpowers has effectively been extended to cover such contingencies. If some lesser state A is closely linked to one superpower, and another lesser state B is closely linked to the other superpower, then military conflict between A and B is regarded as dangerously escalation-prone in Moscow and Washington, and is therefore neutralized by tacit but effective imposition of the status quo. What this extended deterrence needs are two types of stability. The central balance of terror between the superpowers has to remain stable enough to rule out blueprints for victory. *And* the links between the superpowers on the one hand and lesser allies, or clients, or bloc members on the other hand have to be stable and to resemble subordination closely, at least as far as political-military decision making is concerned. The extension of deterrence from peace through fear between the superpowers to peace through fear between their blocs is paid for by the limitation and partial erosion of client-state sovereignty.[22]

Superpower control of some other states (concerning questions of war and peace, not necessarily concerning economic issues) not only prohibits war between clients of either superpower and members of the opposing bloc, but it simultaneously may reduce the risk of war between allies of the very same superpower.[23] The more tightly a superpower controls her allies or clients, the less likely these are to fight each other. Peace by subordination within blocs may complement peace through fear between blocs. Unfortunately, the links between the Western superpower and some of her clients have not been strong enough to prevent hostile military action between them. Technological instabilities may threaten the balance of terror at the central or superpower level, but social and political instabilities in superpowers and client states alike may destabilize their linkages. Instabilities due to developments in client states pose the lesser problem. At worst, they can be handled by military means—by superpower intervention. Both superpowers have applied this means in the past. Social and political instabilities within the superpowers—sometimes referred to as a loss of will or purpose, or as a "consensus lost" (Holsti and Rosenau 1986)—are a more serious matter. From the perspective of war avoidance, it is not the size of superpower blocs or the number of their commitments that is important, but the stability of the commitments and therefore the predictability of international behavior. Like civil wars in client states, foreign policy dissension within the superpowers endangers predictability between them.

The current world order based on superpower control of some other and lesser states and on extended deterrence cannot provide more than a precarious and limited peace. The peace is precarious because it rests on a precarious balance of terror and on sometimes rather tenuous control of clients by superpowers. The peace is limited, because some lesser states do not unequivocally "belong" to either the U.S. or the Soviet bloc. Such nations "enjoy" the unlimited sovereignty that most of Europe lost at the end of World War II. Most of these "sovereign" nations are located in mainland Asia and in Africa. Some of them use their sovereignty in the traditional way—to wage war against each other. Whether the geographical limitation of peace provides less than catastrophic outlets for superpower rivalry in some parts of the Third World *or* whether wars at the periphery of the international system threaten to spill over to the center, is impossible to say. But one danger to the current global security order is clear. It requires nation-states capable of behaving *as if* they were unitary actors with a well-defined set of stable preferences and capable of attempts at utility-maximization. Nations suffering from civil wars do not fit the required patterns[24]—nor do superpowers that have lost their consensus or their sense of purpose and that apply policies in haphazard ways.

Dangerous Currents in Western Development

The West has provided the world with the model of limited government and relatively safe property rights for the ruled. *Therefore,* the West became prosperous. The occidental mixture of order and rivalry, of authority and competition, has served us rather well in the past. In a very loose sense of the term, one may call this mixture pluralism. Because nuclear weapons have made the avoidance of war (at least of nuclear war or of any war that might easily escalate into nuclear war) much more urgent than any other concerns we might have, Western pluralism may serve us less well in future. Limited government within Western nations sets a ceiling to Western defense efforts that is not easily overcome and at best weakly responsive to hostile efforts.[25] If an American president or secretary of defense should dream of allocating the same percentage of GNP to the military as the Soviet Union does, then they dare not say so. And nobody has ever suggested that the United States should draft as many conscripts as the Soviets and pay them at Soviet levels in order to save the money for tanks, missiles, and bombs.

My point is not that either policy might be desirable, but that limited government implies limits to defense efforts that cannot be overcome in peacetime and that are almost unrelated to professional assessments of defense needs. The same point may be reiterated for European nations and Japan, with the only qualification being that the psychological threshold separating bearable and unbearable defense burdens is lower in Europe or Japan than in the United States. Because of limited goverment the West runs the arms race under some handicaps. If the West does well enough, it is either because the inventiveness of open societies provides us with an advantage that is at least as valuable as the fairly unlimited access of the Soviet military to its nation's resources, or because of good luck. The former proposition might have been true in the past, but its continuing validity is challenged by Olson's (1982) work on the decline of nations. The problem with luck is that it may well leave us.

Behind the ceiling on Western defense efforts are interest groups and the problem of collective goods. One may argue that mankind as a whole would be better off if both superpowers and the rest of the world did disarm—and there is little wrong with this vision, except for the difficulty of getting from here to there—but I am here concerned with a less encompassing collective good, that is, that the defense of the United States and the Western world be provided by traditional or military means. Even if every citizen of the United States or of the Western world were convinced of the desirability of military preparation for war in order to deter war, each citizen would still face strong incentives to freeride. Defense or deterrence are collective goods; Western societies are large groups. In large groups, there are strong incentives to freeride rather than to contribute to the procurement of collective goods (Olson 1965). Selective incentives (for example, better pay for volunteers) and coercion (for example, in taxation) may mitigate the problem, but they are unlikely to overcome it. The provision of the public goods of defense or deterrence is further complicated by the scarcity of another public good, that is, information about national security matters. Because the overwhelming majority of Western citizens rationally leaves thinking about national security affairs to others, politicians rarely stand to gain votes by promising better defense policies whatever "better" may mean in a specific strategic context, unless you believe that less defense effort almost always contributes to national security. Because less defense effort frees resources for at least some other projects, whether public spending or private spending made possible by lower taxation, it enjoys a natural constituency even at extremely low levels of information.

I recognize two major objections against my line of thinking. So far, I have neglected interest groups and argued as if there were no organizations between the individual and the nation. Moreover, I have neglected vested interests in "defense efforts." Concerning the first objection, I do not see how and why it may affect the recognition of a serious tendency towards the underprovision of the public goods of deterrence or defense. There are many interest groups in Western societies. Some interest groups are small and control only a minor share of national resources. Most of those small interest groups are more urgently concerned with matters other than defense, such as protection for the textile or steel industries; rights for blacks, gays, or women; Spanish-language teaching in public schools; medical services for the aged; or all kinds of public welfare benefits. The leaders of these groups have to focus on the provision of goods that are (at best) public for a subnational clientele. They rationally do not care for national public goods like defense, unless they or their clientele are asked to share in defense-related burdens. Given the logic of the situation they have to reject burdens for their clientele. They know that their cooperation hardly improves defense, but that the burden would be felt. So, freeriding still is an imperative—for democratically accountable leaders even more so than for others.

Although some interest groups are much larger and more powerful than others, most of them are not large enough to even start thinking about voluntary contributions to the procurement of the public goods of defense or deterrence. "Capitalists" or "big business" (or trade unions for that matter) are too fragmented themselves and therefore incapable of unified action. In essence, the limited size of most interest groups and the fragmentation of a few other interest groups create a situation where there is a large number of interest groups that *control* a relatively small part of national income and therefore face an incentive to freeride on deterrence and defense.

There still are those who make their living by producing tanks or missiles or by soldiering. Surely, they have an interest in a strong national defense, even in the costly overprovision of this public good. At best this widespread feeling contains a partial truth. Yes, there are vigorous special interests in favor of higher defense spending. The public good, however, is not spending per se, but defensive and/or deterrent capabilities. Many types of military spending contribute little to military readiness. Overcharging the Pentagon for spare parts is no contribution to a stronger defense. Nor does an aerospace enterprise contribute to any public good by billing all kinds of overhead and general research and development costs to the Pentagon. Nor is defense strengthened by those NCOs who prefer to spend Christmas Eve with their families rather than on some dull, but conceivably essential guard duty. The jobs and careers of some officers may depend on them withholding recently developed weapons from combat troops in order to keep the weapons on the research and development merry-go-round and themselves "usefully" employed (Luttwak 1985). Such officers are better paid than many others without providing a public good like improving defense or the deterrent posture. Upon closer inspection there are few (if any) special interests in providing a stronger defense and a better deterrent, but lots of civilian and military special interests that want to divert as much defense money for private purposes under the pretext of defense as they can get away with. Special interests in misallocating defense resources merely reinforce the tendency towards an underprovision of the public good generated by an underallocation of resources.[26]

There are ways to prevent an underallocation of resources for defense (or other public goods). If those who are more interested in defense than others (say some ruling class or nomenklatura) can force others to bear the burden, then an underallocation of resources for defense becomes rather unlikely. Coercive control from the top *may* even contain the misallocation of defensive resources for private purposes. But such policies are obviously incompatible with democracy or limited government. Unless Western societies want to mimic the least attractive traits of their opponents, we probably have to continue to run the arms race with the handicap of limited resources where the limitation derives from the nature of Western societies rather than from any interpretation of strategic necessities. To complicate Western defense efforts further, freeriding tendencies within Western societies are supplemented by freeriding tendencies within the Western alliance (Olson and Zeckhauser 1966). The smaller a Western nation is, the less deterrence and defense depend on her own efforts rather than on U.S. efforts. Therefore, the smaller countries spend *proportionately* less on defense than the larger ones. Finally, the freeriders become welfare states and the model to which others aspire.[27]

Above I have argued that the United States and the West run the arms race and the East–West confrontation under the handicap of being unable to respond to defense requests on their strategic merit. Neither the United States nor other Western societies are capable of behaving in national security matters in the same way as a unitary actor would. Conceivably, even the Soviet Union does not come as close to the model of a unitary actor in foreign and defense policies as Soviet leaders would like, but the Soviet Union certainly comes much closer than the West. The pluralist character of Western societies not only impedes defense efforts, it also burdens the deterrent communication process between East and West. There are a few and rather well-known spokesmen for the Soviets in foreign and defense policies. Many of them have served long tenures. By contrast, there is a lively debate about defense in the West, most of all in the United States. Official and unofficial points of view are heard. It is not always easy to distinguish between official and "private" arguments. Moreover, "private" arguments may become official in rather short periods of time. Given the number of voices in the debate, it is a matter of course that logical consistency even between official points of view is nothing more than a lucky coincidence. Under such circumstances it must be rather difficult for the Soviets to predict the U.S. response to policies like placing missiles into Cuba, or rearming the Syrians, or invading Afghanistan, or building some radar screens in Central Siberia that may be used for purposes forbidden by the ABM Treaty. As misunderstandings between the superpowers may be dangerous, the fragmented character of Western defense policy-making seems obsolete.

Some readers of this chapter might miss my basic point because they find my politics too disagreeable. In Holsti and Rosenau's (1986) terms, "post cold war internationalists" will tend to approve of the ceilings on U.S. and Western defense spending that I deplore. Similarly, they will approve of the lively defense debate in the West, because in their view it is at least better than the predominance of "cold war internationalism." In my view, the disadvantages of a pluralistic and fragmented system of decision making in national security matters are equally clear, if you advocate the polar opposite of cold war politics—say, unilateral disarmament by the West. Obviously, disarmament takes time. It cannot be accomplished within minutes or days. Almost certainly it would take months, if not years. For quite some time, disarmament would remain reversible. In the process of disarmament it would be unavoidable to go through some phase where the United States would be extremely vulnerable to a disarming Soviet first strike, while still being capable of rather rapid rearmament. In a pluralistic democracy, almost certainly some voices would argue in favor of rearmament instead of further disarmament. They might convince some voters. The Soviets might get scared of another cold war ahead. Wouldn't they face very strong incentives to complete U.S. or Western disarmament by a first strike? Wouldn't they feel that it is their (moral) duty to impose world government under so favorable, but temporary circumstances? (Wouldn't they even have a point?) So, my deepest worry is not that the United States and the West are incapable of professionally running an arms race and the East–West rivalry, but that the pluralistic and fragmented character of our policy-making systems makes any consistent national security policy impossible—policies I favor as well as those that I reject.

Incentives for freeriding are so strong within mass societies; thus it is difficult to procure public goods without recourse to coercive means. Freeriding cannot easily be checked without endangering the liberal and pluralistic character of Western regimes. The pervasive tendency towards an underprovision of public goods affects the maintenance of limited government and competitive economies at home in contrast to ever more regulated rent-seeking societies. It affects the defense of the Western world against the Soviet challenge. And it affects the international regime of global liberalism that the United States established after World War II and that is currently attacked by the Third World (Krasner 1985) and its allies within industrialized democracies.

Although limited government, safe property rights, and decentralized economic decision making enabled the West to overtake the most advanced Asian civilizations, most Third World governments find it difficult to accept limitations to their power, in particular concerning capitalists, entrepreneurs, and foreigners. To the detriment of the development prospects of their nations many Third World nations insist on harmful price distortions (World Bank 1983, 57–63), on an urban bias in order to exploit poor peasants (Lipton 1977), and on arbitrary overgovernment that an Indian paper once called "permit, license, quota Raj" that necessarily provides ample opportunities for corruption. In Europe trade from one jurisdiction to another first succeeded in evading traditional and governmental regulation in order to respond to supply and demand (Rosenberg and Birdzell 1986). However, the Third World wants to regulate international trade and economic cooperation by international organizations that would be capable of authoritative decision making—without much concern for efficiency, without being responsible to those who are to provide the resources (that is, Northern taxpayers), and without being responsible to a numerical majority of humanity (as repressive regimes by far outnumber democracies in the United Nations).

In accordance with Krasner (1985) I perceive a Third World assault against the Western or capitalist economic order and the related international regime. Moreover, I accept Krasner's point that the demand for a new international economic order should not be explained by the failures of the liberal regime under attack. But in contrast to Krasner (1985) I am inclined to stress a conflict of interest between ruling classes in the Third World and their subjects. Politics pays better for those at the top—if they need not respect private property, if government may be arbitrary and whimsical, and if they can impose price distortions from above in order to benefit themselves or their supporters. Moreover, a cartel of usually unelected and irresponsible governments would nicely complement their power. International organizations provide very attractive positions for Third World ruling classes. It is easy to understand why the ruling classes of the Third World believe in authoritative decision making instead of market allocation of resources.

But there is little reason to believe that the subjects of these ruling classes are well served by their ruler's preferences. According to the Western experience, limited government, safe property rights, and decentralized economic decision making improve the material well-being of the overwhelming majority of the population. There is no reason why these institutions should not serve the peoples of the Third World equally well, if they can get them. But the predatory interests of their ruling classes stand between them and a better future.

Unfortunately, price distortions and rent-seeking are by no means restricted to the Third World. Western democracies suffer from it, too, and increasingly so (Buchanan et al. 1980; Olson 1982). Rent-seeking requires some limitation of access to markets and therefore often some interference with international trade. Rent-seeking and protectionism in capitalist democracies hurt consumers at home and would-be producers in the Third World (Krauss 1983; Weede 1986c). Restrictions on rent-seeking at home and worldwide could serve the interests of huge majorities in the North as well as in the South. The attainment instead of the slow erosion of global liberalism is a public good—although it is not a perfect public good, it seems to be a fair approximation to one. Like other public goods it suffers from chronic underprovision. Again, this underprovision derives from the "logic of collective action" (Olson 1965). Small and well-organized groups, who can capture concentrated gains at the expense of much larger and less-well-organized groups who suffer thinly spread losses, are likely to prevail. One may even argue that political stability necessitates economically harmful behavior, as Lipton (1977)

242 • *Global Changes and Theoretical Challenges*

explicitly and Strange (1985, 1986) implicitly do. That is why rent-seeking is the ordinary state of affairs, why kleptocracy is older than market economies and still thriving, and why the successful institutions of capitalism are under attack.

Historically, the fragmented and pluralistic character of Western societies has served us well. Economically and technologically it still does. It is important that I attribute the positive consequences to fragmented, decentralized, and autonomous decision making—not to widespread participation or approval in collective decision making, for reasons outlined by Rosenberg and Birdzell (1986, 310): "a society which delayed innovations by the amount required to reach a political consensus would fall further and further behind a society which did not. . . . It [consensus— E.W.] implies the substantive criterion that the benefits of the innovation are sufficiently understood and predictable that they can be persuasively verbalized in advance of its adoption—that is everything is too clear to need the test of experiment." Though the economic advantages of fragmented, decentralized, and pluralistic systems with many relatively autonomous decision centers persist, the same approach seems inadequate to the maintenance of liberal capitalism at home and worldwide and to national security decision making in the nuclear age.

Notes

1. The most important kind of social change tnat I do not systematically discuss in this paper concerns the size distribution of income. According to Lenski (1966), income distributions became relatively more equal after the transition from an agrarian to an industrial society was made. Kuznets (1963) states that the equalizing trend started somewhat later, that is, early in the twentieth century in most industrialized societies.

2. A reviewer has criticized me for emphasizing the *goodness* or *badness* of public goods instead of their *publicness*. I do think that my heavy reliance on Olson's (1965) *Logic of Collective Action*, my recurring references to the freeriding problem, and even my treatment of state-making by organized criminals (who respond to the selective incentives provided by the prospect of becoming an exploitative ruling class) demonstrate an awareness of the consequences of publicness. But I admit to "establishing" the goodness or badness of goods by intuition. In my view, overwhelming majorities of people everywhere regard order, prosperity, and peace as *goods*, but anarchy, poverty, and war as *bads*. Without wishing to deny that a few people do not share these widespread preferences, I call prosperity and peace public *goods*, and disorder and war public *bads*. I am guilty of determining utility schedules by fiat in order to avoid an awkward and complicated discussion where a simpler approach seems to do.

3. This is a general point. In my view (Weede 1985, 1986a), positional goods (Hirsch 1976) are the most important kind of selective incentive for the provision of public goods. Large groups and societies procure public goods through the generation and distribution of positional goods—which, unfortunately, cannot fail to generate social conflicts.

4. This is a specific application of the more general principle that inequality of interest or resources makes the provision of public goods easier (Olson 1965). Given a very unequal distribution of resources, a resourceful (rich) person may be better off if he or she

buys the public good at his or her own expense than without it. Therefore, he or she buys it, even if everybody else freerides. Or, a small subgroup of resourceful people may procure a public good that benefits a much larger group.

5. The security dilemma has been more typical of European history than of the history of those areas that have been pacified by inclusion in a great empire, like China. As the Great Wall demonstrates, even the Chinese Empire still faced a security dilemma.

6. Although a large number of independent actors increases the difficulty of cooperation (Olson 1965; Oye 1985), single-play prisoners' dilemmas illustrate that even in two-actor situations cooperation may still be quite unlikely. In iterated prisoners' dilemmas the chances of cooperation improve dramatically. In my view, conclusions about the prospects of cooperation from the iterated prisoners' dilemma literature are more optimistic than those derived from an observation of historical facts for a number of reasons. The *perceived* payoff structures in national security affairs seem to underline the risks of cooperation. Because players may be and *have been* eliminated from the games great powers play, the shadow of the future works in a perverse way, that is, sometimes in making an iterated game into one where some move might become your last one. Finally, nations are not really unitary actors. In my view, this fact in itself increases the difficulty of international cooperation.

7. Insofar as the security dilemma was overcome, the *temporary* solution of the problem itself resulted from successful empire building by war.

8. Pax Sovietica rules out independent action of one Soviet ally against another one—an auxiliary role in a Soviet invasion of some "fraternal" country to save it from regression into capitalism is, of course, welcome—but the United States could neither prevent the football war between El Salvador and Honduras nor the Falklands war between Britain and Argentina. In addition, there have been numerous less serious clashes between U.S. allies.

9. Czempiel's (1986) views on this topic come close to being the opposite of mine. In his opinion, peace rests most safely on justice. In my view, peace is always temporary and ultimately rooted in domination and coercion. General agreements on the meaning of justice are inconceivable. Feelings of suffering from injustice are unavoidable in any conceivable type of domestic or international order. Whether such sufferings motivate violent or warlike challenges to the status quo is largely dependent on the difficulties of collective action and resource mobilization as well as on the perceived chances to prevail.

10. The purpose of this chapter is not a lengthy discussion of why Europe developed earlier and faster than the great Asian civilizations. My focus on the link between limited government (and safe property rights) on the one hand and economic growth on the other hand does not rule out other sources of growth. Similarly, my focus on the relationship between the European state system and limited government does not imply any negation of other influences that seem to have contributed to the domestication of political power in Europe, such as feudalism, the rivalries between emperor and pope or between emergent cities and territorial rulers in the Middle Ages, the Protestant Reformation and the resulting organizational fragmentation of Christendom.

11. My discussion of the establishment and safeguarding of property rights focuses on the effects of international rivalry, but the kind of trade is also important. Trade in luxury goods invites confiscation and predation to an even greater degree than trade in mass consumption goods. The early development of a regional division of labor and fairly frequent interregional exchanges of mass consumption goods in Europe resulted from the comparatively great diversity of European landscapes, soil, and climates, and the related interregional differences in comparative advantage. See Jones (1981) for a detailed treatment.

12. My focus on the positive contribution of limited government to European economic development contradicts Senghaas's (1982) account. In his view, government interference with the economy in general and protectionism in particular have exercised some positive influence on the development of most European nations. I admit that there has been quite a bit of governmental interference with the economy and protectionism in European history, but I still maintain that private enterprise was more autonomous and less often victimized by arbitrary political decision making in Europe than elsewhere. Therefore, Europe developed faster than other continents. (North America is considered to be an offspring or extension of Europe.)

13. It is no coincidence that Bismarck provided the first major push towards the development of social insurance and security systems. As a statesman Bismarck is more famous for his foreign policy achievements and for his awareness of the precarious geopolitical location of Germany than for his compassion for the lower strata of society.

14. Japan and *West* Germany after World War II provide examples of nations where government is more limited now than it was before the war. After World War I, however, defeated Russia turned communist and totalitarian and defeated Germany became Nazi and totalitarian.

15. Conceivably, the change in the impact of international rivalries and threats of war on the limitation of government (and, ultimately, on economic dynamism) is related to the widening of popular participation in war. This could first be observed after the French Revolution, thereafter declining in the relativley peaceful nineteenth century and reaching its peak in the twentieth century.

16. Tollison (1982, 577) defines rent as "a payment to a resource owner above the amount his resources could command in their next best alternative use," where the alternative use refers to a competitive market. Because excess profits are always desirable for those who can get them, there is a strong incentive for resource sellers to induce or compel buyers to pay an excessive price for the resource. Rent-seeking is competition for such contrived transfers. Where such competition and distributional struggles are on the rampage, we refer to rent-seeking societies.

17. While rivalry and nearly permanent threats of war may contribute to the establishment and protection of property rights and thereby to the limitation of government, the same international factor seems to make democracy less viable. According to Bernholz (1985, 172) less involvement in international struggles for power is correlated with democratic development.

18. My reference to Gurr, particularly to his early (1968) work, may surprise some readers. Although Gurr's theorizing focuses on relative deprivation, in the empirical analysis his strongest explanatory variable is a facilitation index that refers to a favorable terrain for insurgents, to their mode of organization, and to outside assistance.

19. Of course, domestic balances of power also determine constitutional limitations of government (Albert 1986; Chirot 1986; Ekelund and Tollison 1981; Weber 1981).

20. "Sufficient" prospects of victory need not be very persuasive. At the beginning of World War II in the Pacific, Japanese decision makers were under no illusions about U.S. military power, although they underestimated U.S. readiness to use it. Basically, the Japanese decision to attack Pearl Harbor was motivated by a comparison of the costs of doing nothing (and seeing the economic base of their empire deteriorate because of an Anglo-American embargo on oil) and the costs of attacking. The former policy provided no chance of a positive outcome at all, and the latter one was a big gamble that conceivably might have paid off. See Russett (1974) for more details.

21. I neglect the problem of accidental nuclear war, because I believe Frei (1983) that this is *not* the major threat to peace.

22. Russett (1983a; Huth and Russett 1988) is much less convinced of nuclear peace through fear than I am. Moreover, he supports his views with systematic quantitative studies. In my opinion, the results of my own quantitative studies (Weede 1975, 1983a) and those of Huth and Russett (1988) are compatible. I have investigated *general* extended deterrence and found some evidence that it contributes to the avoidance of war. They have investigated *immediate* extended deterrence. The need for immediate deterrence arises only where general deterrence does not apply or where it has collapsed. In my view, none of the Huth and Russett cases of immediate deterrence happened because of some failure of general deterrence. Therefore, I maintain the propositions that *general* extended deterrence contributes to the prevention of war and that *general* extended deterrence depends on the nuclear balance. But I can accept their argument that *immediate or short-term conventional military balances carry the main burden of deterrence in immediate deterrence situations,* that is, where general deterrence has broken down before (or where it never applied).

23. The pacifying impact of superpower control and the cold war has also been noticed by scholars who do not share my methodological and theoretical inclinations, for example by Czempiel (1971, 91–94) or Hassner (1968, 21). More recently, however, this insight seems to be in danger of being forgotten.

24. Though there seems to be no robust and general (that is, valid for all types of nations) link between internal conflict and its active externalization (for example, Rummel 1963; Tanter 1966; Eberwein et al. 1979; for a synopsis see Stohl 1980), internal conflict and civil war seem to attract foreign military interventions rather strongly (Gurr and Duvall 1973; Pearson 1974; Weede 1975).

25. According to Kahn (1960) and Taylor (1964) the lack of Western defenses against Hitler's Germany contributed to the outbreak of World War II. Conceivably, a more "hawkish" Western policy might have deterred Hitler. Kagan (1987) extends a similar argument to World War I. According to Huntington (1981, 232, 258) American values limit U.S. effectiveness in supporting liberty and democracy abroad. According to Bernholz (1985, 172), democracy is hardly compatible with being and remaining a great power.

26. Some phenomena that Rosenau (1986, 1987) notes (that is, subgroupism, defiance of governmental authority, and less governmental efficiency) seem to make the problem of an underprovision of public goods worse over time.

27. European and Japanese freeriding at the expense of the United States goes beyond defense. The United States has not only provided a nuclear umbrella to its allies, but also largely shaped the contemporary economic order. Therefore, Keohane (1984, 22) claims: "The European welfare state was built on foundations provided by American hegemony." Unfortunately, the international repercussions of recent U.S. economic policies—I think here of the deficit—seem less benign. Moreover, the openness of the international trading system might overburden the adaptive capabilities of governments and societies (see Krasner 1976; Keohane 1984; Strange 1985, 1986).

References

Albert, Hans (1986). *Freiheit und Ordnung.* Tübingen: Mohr.

Andreski, Stanislav (1964). *The Uses of Comparative Sociology.* Berkeley: University of California Press.

Andreski, Stanislav (1968a). *The African Predicament.* New York: Atherton Press.
Andreski, Stanislav (1968b). *Military Organization and Society.* Stanford: Stanford University Press.
—— (1984). *Max Weber's Insights and Errors.* London: Routledge and Keagan Paul.
Aron, Raymond (1966). "The Anarchical Order of Power." *Daedalus* 95:479–502.
Bernholz, Peter (1977). "Dominant Interest Groups and Powerless Parties." *Kyklos* 30:411–20.
—— (1985). *The International Game of Power.* Berlin-New York-Amsterdam: Mouton.
—— (1986). "Growth of Government, Economic Growth, and Individual Freedom." *Journal of Institutional and Theoretical Economics* 142:661–83.
Buchanan, James M., Robert D. Tollison, and Gordon Tullock (1980). *Toward a Theory of the Rent-Seeking Society.* College Station: Texas A&M University Press.
Chan, Steven (1984). "Mirror, Mirror on the Wall: Are Freer Countries More Pacific?" *Journal of Conflict Resolution* 28, no. 4:617–48.
Chirot, Daniel (1986). *Social Change in the Modern Era.* San Diego, Calif.: Harcourt, Brace, Jovanovich.
Choi, Kwang (1983). "A Statistical Test of Olson's Model." In Dennis C. Mueller, ed., *The Political Economy of Growth.* Pp. 57–78. New Haven: Yale University Press.
Collins, Randall (1980). "Weber's Last Theory of Capitalism." *American Sociological Review* 45:925–42.
Czempiel, Ernst-Otto (1971). "Grundzüge der Weltpolitik 1945–69." In *Bad Wildunger Beiträge zur Gemeinschaftskunde.* Vol. 4: *Internationale Politik.* Pp. 32–97. Wiesbaden: Hessische Landeszentrale für Politische Bildung.
—— (1986). *Freiedenstrategien.* Paderborn: Ferdinand Schöningh Verlag (UTB).
Dahrendorf, Ralf (1965). *Gesellschaft und Demokratie in Deutschland.* Munich: Piper.
Dixon, William J., and Bruce E. Moon (1986). "The Military Burden and Basic Human Needs." *Journal of Conflict Resolution* 30:660–84.
Doyle, Michael W. (1986). "Liberalism and World Politics." *American Political Science Review* 80, no. 4:1151–69.
Durkheim, Emile (1930). *De la division du travail social.* Paris: Presses Universitaires de France.
Eberwein, Wolf-Dieter, Gisela Hübner-Dick, Wolfgang Jagodzinski, Hans Rattinger, and Erich Weede (1979). "External and Internal Conflict Behavior among Nations." *Journal of Conflict Resolution* 23, no. 4:715–42.
Economist, The (1987). "The Emperor's New Clothes." *The Economist* 302, no. 7483 (31 January):46–48.
Ekelund, Robert B., and Robert D. Tollison (1981). *Mercantilism as a Rent-Seeking Society.* College Station: Texas A&M University Press.
Frei, Daniel (1983). *Risks of Unintentional Nuclear War.* London: Croom and Helm.
Garnier, Maurice A., and Lawrence E. Hazelrigg (1977). "Military Organization and Distributional Inequality." *Journal of Political and Military Sociology* 5:17–33.
Gilpin, Robert (1981). *War and Change in World Politics.* Cambridge: Cambridge University Press.
Gurr, Ted R. (1968). "A Causal Model of Civil Strife." *American Political Science Review* 62:1104–24.
Gurr, Ted R., and Raymond Duvall (1973). "Civil Conflict in the 1960s." *Comparative Political Studies* 6:135–69.

Hall, John A. (1985). *Power and Liberties: The Causes and Consequences of the Rise of the West.* Berkeley: University of California Press.

Hardin, Russell (1982). *Collective Action.* Baltimore: Johns Hopkins University Press.

Hassner, Pierre (1968). "Change and Security in Europe." *Adelphi Papers* 49. London: International Institute of Strategic Studies.

Hayek, Friedrich August von (1944). *The Road of Serfdom.* Chicago: University of Chicago Press.

Herz, John H. (1950). "Idealist Internationalism and the Security Dilemma." *World Politics* 2 (January):157–80.

—— (1957). "The Rise and Demise of the Territorial State." *World Politics* 9:473–93.

Hirsch, Fred (1976). *Social Limits to Growth.* Cambridge: Harvard University Press.

Holsti, Ole R., and James N. Rosenau (1986). "Consensus Lost. Consensus Regained? Foreign Policy Beliefs of American Leaders, 1976–80." *International Studies Quarterly* 30, no. 4:375–409.

Huntington, Samuel P. (1981). *American Politics: The Promise of Disharmony.* Cambridge: Harvard University Press (Belknap).

Huntington, Samuel P., and Jorge I. Dominguez (1975). "Political Development." In Fred I. Greenstein and Nelson W. Polsby, (eds., *Handbook of Political Science.* Vol. 3: *Macropolitical Theory.* Pp. 1–114. Reading, Mass.: Addison-Wesley.

Huth, Paul, and Bruce M. Russett (1988). "Deterrence Failure and Crisis Escalation." *International Studies Quarterly* 32, no. 1:29–45.

Jones, Eric L. (1981). *The European Miracle.* Cambridge: Cambridge University Press.

Kagan, Donald (1987). "World War I, World War II, World War III." *Commentary* 83, no. 3:21–40.

Kahn, Herman (1960). *On Thermonuclear War.* Princeton: Princeton University Press.

—— (1979). *World Economic Development.* London: Croom and Helm.

Keohane, Robert O. (1984). "The World Political Economy and the Crisis of Embedded Liberalism." In John H. Goldthorpe, ed., *Order and Conflict in Contemporary Capitalism.* Pp. 16–37. Oxford: Clarendon Press.

Krasner, Stephen D. (1976). "State Power and the Structure of International Trade." *World Politics* 28:317–47.

—— (1985). *Structural Conflict.* Berkeley: University of California Press.

Krauss, Melvyn B. (1983). *Development without Aid: Growth, Poverty, and Government.* New York: New Press (McGraw-Hill).

Kriesberg, Louis (1979). *Social Inequality.* Englewood Cliffs, N.J.: Prentice-Hall.

Kuznets, Simon (1963). "Quantitative Aspects of the Economic Growth of Nations. VIII: The Distribution of Income by Size." *Economic Development and Cultural Change* 11:1–80.

Lane, Jan-Erik, and Svante Errson (1986). "Political Institutions, Public Policy, and Economic Growth." *Scandinavian Political Studies* 9, no. 1:19–34.

Lasswell, Harold (1941). "The Garrison State." *American Journal of Sociology* 46:455–67.

Lenski, Gerhard (1966). *Power and Privilege.* New York: McGraw-Hill.

Lenski, Gerhard, and Jean Lenski (1982). *Human Societies.* New York: McGraw-Hill.

Lipton, Michael (1977). *Why Poor People Stay Poor.* London: Temple Smith.

Luard, Evan (1968). *Conflict and Peace in the Modern International System.* Boston: Little, Brown.

Luttwak, Edward N. (1985). *The Pentagon and the Art of War.* New York: Simon and Schuster.

McNeill, William H. (1982). *The Pursuit of Power.* Chicago: University of Chicago Press.

North, Douglass C., and Robert P. Thomas (1973). *The Rise of the Western World.* Cambridge: Cambridge University Press.

Olson, Mancur (1965). *The Logic of Collective Action.* Cambridge: Harvard University Press.

—— (1982). *The Rise and Decline of Nations.* New Haven: Yale University Press.

Olson, Mancur, and David C. Colander (1984). "Coalitions and Macroeconomics." In David C. Colander, ed., *Neoclassical Political Economy.* Pp. 115–28. Cambridge, Mass.: Ballinger.

Olson, Mancur, and Richard Zeckhauser (1966). "An Economic Theory of Alliances." *Review of Economics and Statistics* 48:266–79.

Oye, Kenneth A. (1985). "Explaining Cooperation under Anarchy." *World Politics* 38, no. 1:1–24.

Pearson, Fredric S. (1974). "Foreign Military Interventions and Domestic Disputes." *International Studies Quarterly* 18:259–90.

Rosenau, James N. (1986). "Micro Sources of Macro Global Change." Manuscript. Institute for Transnational Studies, University of Southern California, Los Angeles.

—— (1987). "Patterned Chaos in Global Life: Structure and Process in the Two Worlds of World Politics." Manuscript. Institute for Transnational Studies, University of Southern California, Los Angeles.

Rosenberg, Nathan, and L.E. Birdzell (1986). *How the West Grew Rich.* New York: Basic Books.

Ruestow, Alexander (1950). *Ortsbestimmung der Gegenwart.* Vol. 1. Erlenbach-Zürich: Rentsch.

Rummel, Rudolph J. (1963). "Dimensions of Conflict Behavior within and between Nations." *General Systems Yearbook* 8:1–50.

—— (1983). "Libertarianism and International Violence." *Journal of Conflict Resolution* 27, no. 1:27–71.

—— (1987). "On Vincent's View of Freedom and International Conflict." *International Studies Quarterly* 31, no. 1:113–17.

Russett, Bruce M. (1974). "Pearl Harbor: Deterrence Theory and Decision Theory." In Bruce M. Russett, ed., *Power and Community in World Politics.* Pp. 216–233. San Francisco: Freeman.

—— (1983a). "Away from Nuclear Mythology." In Dagobert L. Brito, Michael D. Intriligator, and Adele E. Wick, eds., *Strategies for Managing Nuclear Proliferation.* Pp. 145–55. Lexington, Mass.: Lexington Books.

—— (1983b). *The Prisoners of Insecurity.* San Francisco: Freeman.

—— (1985). "The Mysterious Case of Vanishing Hegemony; or, Is Mark Twain Really Dead?" *International Organization* 39, no. 2:207–31.

Russett, Bruce M., and Harvey Starr (1981). *World Politics.* San Francisco: Freeman.

Senghaas, Dieter (1982). *Von Europa lernen: Entwicklungsgeschichtliche Betrachtungen.* Frankfurt am Main: Suhrkamp.

Small, Melvin, and J. David Singer (1976). "The War-Proneness of Democratic Regimes." *Jerusalem Journal of International Relations* 1 (Summer):50–69.

Stohl, Michael (1980). "The Nexus of Civil and International Conflict." In Ted R. Gurr, ed., *Handbook of Political Conflict.* Pp. 297–330. New York: Free Press.

Strange, Susan (1985). "Protectionism and World Politics." *International Organization* 39, no. 1:233–59.

—— (1986). "The Bondage of Liberal Economics." *SAIS Review* 6, no. 1:25–38.

Tanter, Raymond (1966). "Dimensions of Conflict Behavior within and between Nations." *Journal of Conflict Resolution* 10:41–64.

Taylor, A.J.P. (1964). *The Origins of the Second World War*. Harmondsworth, Middlesex: Penguin.

Tilly, Charles (1985). "War-making and State-making as Organized Crime." In Peter B. Evans, Dietrich Rueschemeyer, and Theda Skocpol, eds., *Bringing the State Back In*. Pp. 169–91. Cambridge: Cambridge University Press.

Tollison, Robert D. (1982). "Rent-Seeking: A Survey." *Kyklos* 35:575–602.

Tullock, Gordon (1974). *The Social Dilemma: The Economics of War and Revolution*. Blacksburg, Va.: University Publications.

—— (1983). *Economics of Income Redistribution*. Boston, The Hague, London: Kluwer-Nijhoff.

Vedder, Richard, and Lowell Gallaway (1986). "Rent-Seeking, Distributional Coalitions, Taxes, Relative Prices, and Economic Growth." *Public Choice* 51, no. 1:93–100.

Vincent, Jack (1987). "Freedom and International Conflict: Another Look." *International Studies Quarterly* 31, no. 1:103–12.

Wallerstein, Immanuel (1974). *The Modern World System*. New York: Academic Press.

Waltz, Kenneth N. (1979). *Theory of International Politics*. Reading, Mass.: Addison-Wesley.

Weber, Max (1981). *Wirtschaftsgeschichte*. Berlin: Duncker und Humblot.

Weede, Erich (1975). *Weltpolitik und Kriegsursachen im 20. Jahrhundert*. Munich: Oldenbourg.

—— (1983a). "Extended Deterrence by Superpower Alliance." *Journal of Conflict Resolution* 27 (June):231–53; and *Journal of Conflict Resolution* 27, no. 4:739, where misprints are corrected.

—— (1983b). "Military Participation Ratios, Human Capital Formation, and Economic Growth." *Journal of Political and Military Sociology* 11 (Spring):11–19.

—— (1984a). "Democracy, Creeping Socialism, and Ideological Socialism in Rent-Seeking Societies." *Public Choice* 44:349–66.

—— (1984b). "Democracy and War Involvement." *Journal of Conflict Resolution* 28, no. 4:649–64.

—— (1985). "Dilemmas of Social Order: Collective and Positional Goods, Leadership and Political Conflicts." *Sociological Theory* 3, no. 2:46–57.

—— (1986a). *Konfliktforschung*. Opladen: Westdeutscher Verlag.

—— (1986b). "Rent-Seeking, Military Participation, and Economic Performance in LDCs." *Journal of Conflict Resolution* 30, no. 2:291–314.

—— (1986c). "Rent-Seeking or Dependency as Explanations of Why Poor People Stay Poor." *International Sociology* 1, no. 4:421–41.

—— (1986d). "Sectoral Reallocation, Distributional Coalitions, and the Welfare State as Determinants of Economic Growth Rates in Industrialized Democracies." *European Journal of Political Research* 14, nos. 5-6:501–19.

Weede, Erich, and Wolfgang Jagodzinski (1981, 1987). "National Security, Income Inequality, and Economic Growth." *Social Science and Policy Research* (Seoul, S. Korea) 3, no. 3:91–107. Reprinted in Jean H.P. Paelink and P.H. Vossen, eds., *Axiomatics and Pragmatics of Conflict Analysis*. Pp. 269–88. London: Gower.

World Bank (1983). *World Development Report*. London: Oxford University Press.

13

Imposing International Purpose: Notes on a Problematic of Governance

Richard K. Ashley

I n a recent essay, Friedrich Kratochwil and John Ruggie (1986) have sought to identify the "hard core" of the field of international organization. Using the language of Lakatos (1970), they have sought to identify the enduring set of core problems and puzzles that lend the field its coherence and identity and upon which potentially "progressive problem shifts"—from the early focus upon formal institutions through the current emphasis upon regimes—have turned. This "hard core," they contend, is to be found in the problem of international governance —governance in a sphere of conduct that lacks a central agency of rule (Kratochwil and Ruggie 1986, 754).

Taking up this "hard core" problem, James Rosenau (1987, 7) has recently asked, "How . . . can governance be a central concept when the concern is with a realm of activity in which government has yet to evolve?" In answer, he offers two concepts of governance and rule, neither of which presupposes the presence of governmental institutions. He labels these "Governance I" and "Governance II."

Governance I, for Rosenau, "consists of those determinants, nonhuman as well as human, that impel repetitive actions and sustained patterned interactions" regardless of individual actors' intentions or subjective competencies and irrespective of any authoritative directives. One refers to Governance I when one refers to regularities that are "lawful," as it were, in the natural scientific sense of the term. One refers to Governance I, in other words, when one refers to regularities that are conformed to unquestioningly as "the objective conditions of global life, those underlying, often unrecognized constraints and rules by which individuals, groups, and communities conduct their affairs" (Rosenau 1987, 8). Involving structured regularities that are always already objectively in place, prior to, and conditioning the knowledgeable actions of the agents who conform to them, Governance I is intrinsically *not* a politicized mode of rule. Certain emergent properties of an anarchic states system and the law of supply and demand in the marketplace are the principal examples that Rosenau provides (1987, 9).

Governance II, by contrast, "focuses on recurrent patterns that are developed purposively, that reflect the intervention of human will, the virtues of planning, the drawing up of constitutional charters, the organization of public affairs in such a way that goals are framed, ends realized, cooperation achieved, stable equilibria established, and order maintained" (1987, 10). As Rosenau emphasizes, "rule" here does not refer to underlying tendencies and regulating mechanisms that can be accorded a natural lawful quality. "Rule" here involves "explicit directives derived from some authority that seek to shape behavior and achieve compliance"— acts of rule and response that together make up not a static hierarchy but an interactive, always unfolding process of governance. Three features of the process of Governance II are especially important. First, in contrast to the objectivist basis of Governance I, Governance II "refers to the subjective and intersubjective bases on which actors knowingly and intentionally found their conduct, those explicit rules and constraints that are affirmed and contested as people seek to achieve or avoid compliance." Second, as this suggests, Governance II is explicitly *politicized* governance, for it is understood as such "by actors in the public arena as well as by observers who stand apart from it." As Rosenau puts it:

> People may differ sharply over how the rules should operate, and whether the order, goals, equilibria, and other outcomes thereby promoted are desirable; but they share a self-consciousness that governance is at work, that certain behaviors are appropriate while others are to be avoided, and that their compliance with the rules is sought and expected [1987, 10].

Third, Governance II is irreducible to that class of directives that might be issued by governmental institutions, grounded in claims of sovereign rights, or backed by the coercive powers of states. Countless other actors, grounding their authority claims in other ways, are involved (1987, 10–11).

There is no gainsaying the importance of Rosenau's analytic distinction. At the very least, it makes three conceptual contributions. First, it resists, and charts a workable way to escape, the thrall of what Hedley Bull (1967) has called the "domestic analogy." This is an analogy that, on Rosenau's (1987, 4) account, narrows the analysis of governance "to situations wherein compliance occurs in response to legitimate directives" and "limits attention to structures and processes that unfold in a context which accords officials exclusive authority to back their directives with coercive force." Thanks to Rosenau's distinctions, one can see that a lot of international governance, of both kinds, is done in the absence of world government. Second, by distinguishing Governance II, Rosenau invites sustained attention to aspects of international governance, involving *knowledgeable* and *intentional* conduct, that would necessarily be neglected were it supposed that all that matters in international governance is necessarily comprehensible according to models of inquiry derived from philosophical interpretations of the natural sciences.[1] Third, by making the distinction, Rosenau prepares the way for—and indeed urges—a careful analysis of the interaction between the subjective, knowledgeable, and intentional practices of politics (Governance II) and the objective, already structured, and lawlike regularities of global conduct (Governance I). As Rosenau (1987, 13) writes, "in the sense that Governance I conditions Governance II, the analyst must inquire into and integrate both forms of governance."

It seems to me, though, that for all its power, the distinction between Governance I and Governance II neglects, and to a certain extent obscures, an equally important aspect of governance in modern international life. If one wished, one might call this third aspect "Governance III." To begin to bring this third aspect of international governance into focus, one need not impose some set of restrictive assumptions. One need only be willing to make two modest turns, each involving attention to the possibilities that open up when assumptions implicit in Governance I and Governance II are *relaxed*.

First, as in Rosenau's Governance I, this third aspect involves those structured relations of global life that are taken to constitute the objective, necessary, autonomous, and even natural lawful conditions of conduct—the conditions of conduct that are themselves taken to be beyond politics. In order to understand the third aspect of international governance, though, one must be prepared to put in question an assumption, implicit in Governance I, regarding these recognizably objective structures. This is the assumption that the structures that subjects of international life normally take to be the objective conditions of their free and intentional conduct are in truth fixed, devoid of intentionality or purpose, and independent of knowledgeable practice. If one relaxes this assumption, and if one distances oneself from the normalized subjectivity of the actors of global life,[2] then another horizon of inquiry is opened up. One is able to see what the subjects of global life might not be disposed to see: that the recognizably objective structures of global life, far from being autonomous and pregiven conditions, are arbitrary and contingent *effects* that are imposed in history, through practice, and to the exclusion of other ways of structuring collective existence. Not taking these effects for granted, one is able to see that these arbitrarily imposed effects are rich in political content, though they might not be recognized as such. One is able to see that they embody a collective intentionality—an integral and integrating purpose of the social whole—though they might be perceived to be objective limits, beyond human will. And one is able to pose as a matter of serious inquiry a question that the subjects of global life might not be able to pose: How, in history, are these effects imposed and sustained, thereby to bend what people do in widely dispersed, disparate, and changing circumstances to a continuous form of social unity, a definite direction of social development, and a specific, collectively structured end overarching the local experiences and distinctive aims of individual participants?

Second, as in Rosenau's Governance II, the third aspect of governance involves knowledgeable conduct and intersubjective relations. If one is to grasp this third aspect, however, one must be ready to put in question the assumption, implicit in Governance II, that the principal effect of knowledgeable conduct is to render matters of governance explicit, subject to conscious deliberation, and open to politicized debate among the recognized subjects of global life. When this assumption is relaxed—and when, once again, one distances oneself from the normalized subjectivity of actors—one can pose a possibility that this assumption rules out. This is the possibility that knowledgeable practice also works to constitute a normalized mode of political subjectivity whose practical dispositions tend, on balance, to generate certain structures; to discipline resistances and silence competing practices; to exclude the question of the political content of those structures from serious debate; and thereby to secure recognition of those structures, not as the historical and contingent relations they are, but as necessary, objective, and self-evident limits and conditions of politics in collective life. This is the possibility, in other words, that knowledgeable practice is *productive* and that what it produces, among other things, is the recognizable structuring of subjectivity and objectivity on a global scale.

These two turns do not entail anything approaching a theory of international governance. They do, however, open up a third aspect of international governance that is best formulated as a *problematic*—one that eludes the frames of Governance I and Governance II but that merits sustained theoretical scrutiny nonetheless. I shall call it a problematic of purpose or, more exactly, a problematic of *imposing international purpose*.

Understood from the point of view of the first turn, this problematic centers on the production of an *effect* of spatial and temporal continuity and collective direction—an effect forever in jeopardy of coming undone. More specifically, it centers on the production and objectification of enduring structures that are understood to arch, differentiate, and unify the multiple local experiences and distinctive aims of individual participants and that thereby lend to global life an effect of continuity, of a direction, and of a unified collective end beyond political questioning.

Understood from the point of view of the second turn, this problematic centers on the practices that *produce* this effect. It centers on the fabrication, dissemination, and replication of knowledgeable practices across dispersed and disparate locales—especially the way in which knowledgeable practices work thereupon to effect a normalized mode of political subjectivity differentiated from, and knowing itself in opposition to, some set of necessary, objective, and extrapolitical structures that transcend time and place.

Taking the two turns together, this problematic centers on the capacities of knowledgeable practices reliably and replicably to manage all three of the tensions that preoccupy contributors to this book: the tensions between individual and collective, continuity and change, and centralizing and decentralizing dynamics. How do knowledgeable practices constitute individual subjects who are disposed and able to administer their dispersed and changing circumstances, thereby effectively to generate collective structures that they take to be objective, to exhibit a spatial and temporal continuity, and to express a unity of necessary truth *as if* authored by a single, central voice? How is this done even though there is no central origin of universal truth, no transcendental norm already in place, no unique source of power capable of imposing a homogeneous will? Here in this question one finds the problematic of imposing international purpose.

My intention in these notes is simply to pose this problematic as a proper object of theory and to outline some of the ways in which it might be theorized. I do not claim that the notes to follow amount to a grand synthesis, a theory, or even a framework—a working of framing practices, maybe, but not a framework. I am content to regard what follows as an outline of *one* coherent and generalizable way of orienting questioning into the workings of knowledge and power in the imposition of international purpose.

Poststructuralist in orientation, the notes to follow join ideas from several sources. One will find traces of Pierre Bourdieu (1977) and his writings on doxa, habitus, and the "conductorless orchestration of collective action and improvisations." One will also detect echoes of Michel Foucault (1977a, 1977b, 1978, 1984) his interpretive analytics of power, his problematization of the subject, and his notion of social "strategies without a knowing strategist." And one will catch glimpses of the influence of Jacques Derrida (1976, 1978, 1983) and his notions of difference and enframing.

Most of all, though, one should regard the notes to follow, not as an attempt to recapitulate poststructuralist themes, but as an attempt to put them suggestively to work in the service of several analytic objectives. I have eight objectives in mind:

- To supply a definite yet generalizable attitude toward the notion of "international purpose"—an attitude that respects and reconciles its simultaneous particularity and "universality," arbitrariness and "necessity," historicity and "timelessness";

- To respect the role of knowledgeable agency, especially the sovereign agency of the state, in the constitution of "international purpose," and to do so in a way that recognizes and reconciles the simultaneous essential contestedness and "essential identity" of knowledgeable agents, again including the sovereign state;

- To put forth a definite understanding of knowledgeable practice—one that does not reduce practice to a dichotomy of deliberate choice versus habitual or traditional routine, does not resort to an ahistorical partitioning of consciousness and subconsciousness, and does allow for the possibility of spontaneous, innovative collective action in the differentiation of global experience and the structuring and elaboration of collective purpose;

- To suggest how, in practice, an irony intrinsic to the problem of effecting international purpose is practically resolved (albeit never finally solved); that is, I try to suggest how, amidst a plurality of politically contesting interpretations of political identity and collective possibility generated on the surface of history, it is possible to effect international purpose by effecting the mutual recognition of a single interpretation of sovereign being and objective possibility as an extrahistorical, extrapolitical truth finally limiting the domain of political discourse;

- To come to terms with, and to illustrate, the dependence of the effect of international purpose upon knowledgeable practices of *enframing*, playing on dimensions of *time* and *space*;

- To come to terms with the role of *hegemony*, conceived as the natural and exemplary living of a self-evident paradigm of sovereign being, in the innovation of knowledgeable practices of enframing; I want to offer an interpretation that helps us not only to understand the "virtues" of hegemonic leadership but also to understand (1) why hegemonic practice *cannot* be comprehended on the model of rational action; (2) why hegemonic practice is disposed *internally* to displace potentially disabling effects transgressing international boundaries (an anomaly from the point of view of rational action models); and (3) why the "decline of hegemony" is *not* likely to occasion "beggar-thy-neighbor" struggles among core powers (another anomaly);

- To preserve sensitivity to the historicity of hegemony and of enframing practices themselves, attending in particular to the problem of constituting fields of international practice which, as a *strategic reserve* of *ambiguous* social resources, make possible innovation in the administration of global time and space; and

- To indicate why and how enframing practices might become mutually disabling, thereby generating crises of international time, space, identity, and purpose.

My notes proceed through two phases. In the first phase, presented in the immediately following section, I offer a very general overview of the problematic of imposing international purpose. I stress in particular the intrinsic irony involved in, and never finally resolved by, the problem of imposing international purpose—an irony that I take to constitute the "essential tension" chronically encountered in all aspects of international governance. I further refine my analysis of the problem by interpreting it as a problem of enframing, involving the play of knowledgeable practices drawing upon an historically constituted field of *doxa*, a "strategic reserve" of self-evident yet ambiguous knowledge.

In the second phase, presented in the section "Elaboration," I develop this initial outline by introducing a number of dimensions: the importance of international pluralism for the constitution of a "strategic reserve"; the arbitrary historical fusion of sovereignty as a naturalized mode of sovereign doing and being; the signal and contradictory role of hegemony as both a paradigm of sovereignty and a field for the "internal displacement" of boundary transgressive disturbances; the sources of potential crisis to be found in these internal displacements; and the problem of the hegemonic innovation of novel rituals for the mediation of boundary transgressive effects, thus to constitute boundaries and competencies of sovereign being that, though both new and arbitrary, are recognized as continuous with the eternal and essential truth of sovereign identity.

In the conclusion, I shall return to the question of the discipline of international organization theory and its "hard core," international governance. Reflecting upon these notes, I shall point up a dilemma to be confronted by theorists of international organization who would take up the problematic of imposing global purpose.

Some Generalities

An Essential Tension: The Problem Posed

To speak of imposing international purpose is, at a minimum, to suggest three things. First, because the expression emphasizes *international* purpose, and not, say, universal purpose, the expression immediately finds its focus in a pluralistic discourse, a discourse in which it may be supposed that there are many legitimate interpretive voices or subjects, not just one. Put negatively, one may say that the discourse of international purpose is a discourse without a central subject, without a single Archimedean point from which it becomes possible to offer a univocal, and uniquely truthful, account of history's direction, telos, or meaning (see Kratochwil and Ruggie 1986, 764). Put positively, one may say that a practical requisite of being a competent subject in any discourse on international purpose is that one's practices must recognize, and must be recognized to recognize, the legitimacy of multiple sovereign subjects in the interpretation and making of history so long as other subjects are understood to reciprocate this recognition. Pluralism, in other words, is not just an external fact, occasioned by the physical coincidence of multiple elements, each an identical voice or subject in its own right. It is not a passing condition of confused interpretation that all subjects aspire someday to overcome. Rather, respect for the intrinsic polyvocality of history's making and narration, for the dependence of any one voice upon the recognition of multiple others, for the intrinsic contestability of any one subject's interpretation, and, hence, for the inescapable ambiguity of collective experience—this respect is itself a practical requisite of having a voice that will be recognized and heard. As signified by the international construct of sovereignty, it is a never finally accomplished practical requisite of international being. It is what one must *do* in order internationally to *be*.

Second, because the expression nevertheless refers to international *purpose*, it directs attention to the questions: How is the effect of continuity and direction in social development historically produced? How does it come to pass that practices are oriented and energies concerted in such a fashion that the global life of women and men lends itself to interpretation, in both theory and in practice, as a society having some sort of collective structure? The expression thus directs attention to systemic conditions of practice that are socially recognized to be objective and whose recognition, as such, establishes the collective ends toward which political practice is concerted.

By systemic conditions I mean relations that knowing subjects take to be self-evident and objective and to which these subjects ascribe at least four attributes. *From the point of view of knowing subjects,* systemic conditions

1. exhibit a certain coherence and spatial and temporal continuity—a structured differentiation of practical domains, a pattern of interdependence, a normalized division of labor, a natural law, a rhythm of eternal return, or a narrative of the progressive development of "Western Civilization"—that arches the specific historical contexts of individual subjects and distinct events;

2. are susceptible to a unique and universally recognized interpretation, as if discernible from a single objective vantage point;

3. are apolitical, not the arbitrary impositions of some subjects in opposition to others; and

4. establish the self-evident limits of politics, the necessary conditions of meaningful social practice, and the objective and autonomous trajectory of history, to which all competent subjects will unquestioningly defer.

Socially recognized systemic conditions are, then, those effects that are usually called holistic and objective, that are taken for granted and silently affirmed as self-evident and apolitical truths of collective existence, and that, so understood, circumscribe meaningful political discourse among competent subjects. More than that, they positively fix political identity, binding recognized subjectivity to a collective purpose that is at once unspoken, unquestioned, and irreducible to some logical combination of actors' deliberate choices among visible alternatives. To be recognized as a competent subject, one must be disposed to affirm silently, and never to question, socially recognized systemic conditions. In whatever one says or does, one must be disposed to effect the collective purpose implicit in the constitution of just these systemic relationships and not some alternative set of systemic relationships that an independent analyst might take to be possible in principle.

Third, because the expression speaks of *imposing* international purpose, however, it implies that the constitution and objectification of systemic conditions and the collective purpose implicit therein is never a task that can be assumed to be already accomplished. On the contrary, to speak of imposing international purpose is to say that the production and objectification of systemic conditions, thereby to constitute a purpose of the social whole, is an irresolvably problematic, always contestable, and unceasingly political matter. This is so, in part, because it is *international* purpose that is here in question and because, as noted, competent participation in international discourse requires respect for the legitimacy of plural sovereign standpoints. In larger part, this is so because in locale after locale, and very often in wider compass, the hazardous play of history gives rise to happenings that visibly escape the limits of any one reigning interpretation of systemic conditions, thereby threatening to call into question any interpretation hitherto taken for granted as embodying the self-evident and necessary truth.

Whatever the reasons, the unceasing problematization of systemic conditions assures that the problem of imposing international purpose will always entail an irony: *a tension that may be called an "essential tension" because it is the tension chronically and unavoidably encountered in the historical production of an "essence" of international life.* On the one hand, imposing international purpose is a problem of securing that most potent form of political recognition for an arbitrarily imposed collective program: the form of recognition that comes when an arbitrary and contingent political interpretation of systemic limits of social possibility is (mis)recognized as a self-evident, politically neutral, and objective condition—a universal truth to be taken for granted and silently affirmed as a necessary limit of history (Bourdieu 1977). On the other hand, and at the same time, imposing international purpose *is* a problem precisely because no one interpretation ever stands alone, in the absence of contesting interpretations: Every interpretation exists among, and is itself a fusion of, a welter of politically contesting interpretations that emerge and potentially find voices amidst the specific times and circumstances of a history that is intrinsically irreducible to any one totalizing narrative.

The tension, then, is plain. Imposing international purpose is a problem of the *political making of the extra-political,* the *historical making of the timeless,* the *specific and arbitrary making of the universal and the necessary.* It is a problem of transforming a potentially *vocal* clash of competing interpretations into a *silently* affirmed collective truth. The problem of imposing international purpose is a thorny one, to say the least.

Imposing International Purpose as a Problem of Enframing

Just how thorny the problem is can be seen, I think, when we approach it as a problem of *enframing* political discourse and, with it, competent subjectivity itself (for a helpful introduction to enframing, see Culler 1982, 193-99). By enframing, I mean a knowledgeable practice of differentiation—a practice of differentiation that can be called knowledgeable because it presupposes subjects' abilities skillfully to call upon socially accessible symbolic resources and practical understandings to interpret circumstances, assign meaning, and get about their business in a diverse, changing, and ambiguous world. I mean, more particularly, a practice that produces a recognized boundary between competent subjectivity—the recognized sovereign subjects whose voices are to be regarded as the authentic and unproblematic origins of meaning—and the world of historical happenings and possibilities that these subjects mutually take to be the necessary and natural conditions of their experience. In effecting and elaborating this difference, knowledgeable practices of enframing simultaneously constitute both the recognized political identities of competent subjects and the shared understanding of the objective systemic conditions upon which they commonly and necessarily depend. It is this practical differentiation that effects the social recognition of systemic conditions and, in the process, collective purpose. Yet to see this is to see at once the difficulty: The very notion of enframing implicitly presupposes the absence of any absolute ground—either a commitment to an absolute subjective identity or a commitment to some necessary objective truth—upon which practices of enframing might be based. Enframing is necessary, after all, precisely because the boundaries between subject and object, and thus the content of subjectivity and objectivity, are intrinsically contested.

This, clearly, is not a difficulty that lends itself to resolution according to the classic models of legitimation, such as the models of rational-legal, traditional, and charismatic legitimation conceived by Max Weber. It is not a problem that can be resolved by appeal to a belief in the legality of a consistent system of abstract and formal rules, by appeal to the sanctity of immemorial traditions, or by appeal to the exceptional heroism or exemplary character of an individual person.[3]

The thorny problem of imposing international purpose can be answered in practice only on one condition: That knowledgeable practices of enframing are able to effect their differentiations between recognized subjectivity and objectivity *without directly confronting the problem as a political problem of arbitrarily imposing one interpretation among many and without, therefore, confronting a need to secure legitimacy by self-conscious appeal to some originary and universally acknowledged ground.* How can this condition be satisfied in practice? We may begin to glimpse an answer, I think, if we attend for a moment or two to the nature of knowledgeable practice.

Knowledgeable Practice and the Field of Doxa

Knowledgeable practice is not for the most part reducible to a matter of deliberate, theoretically informed action: the sort of action involving self-conscious appeal to some external, explicitly acknowledged rule, formal program of action, model of the good life, or norm of conduct. Although knowledgeable practice may include theoretically informed action, it also includes *practical competence*.

Practical competence involves participants' competent understandings and skillful deployments of cognitively structured practical postures or interpretive dispositions: durable, highly mobile, and always ambiguous practical attitudes that are unspoken, transferred through practice, inscribed in subjects' recognized identities and self-understandings, and replicated by them under new and changing circumstances (on practical competence, see Ashley 1987, 424–25). These ambiguous postures and dispositions are not learned through the explicit formulation and communication of concepts or formal rules. They are learned, rather, through participants' "fuzzy abstraction" (Bourdieu 1977, 82) from the no less ambiguous practices where these postures and dispositions are brought into play, sometimes artfully and sometimes ineptly. They are grasped, that is, only in the interpretation of a certain coherence of the actions they generate, in their uniting of otherwise seemingly disparate performances. These postures and dispositions are not replicated, moreover, through deliberate reflection on principles of conduct existing in some sense external to the subjects who replicate them. Their replication, instead, is simply a matter of subjects' being who, according to their experience, they understand themselves self-evidently to be.

Yet practical competence, it is important to add, is not simply a matter of habit, if by habit one means the inertial replication of the routinely performed. If this were all there were to practical competence, then the slightest change of place, circumstance, season, or tempo of life would immediately produce a disjuncture between actions performed, on the one hand, and the conditions of successful performance, on the other.

Practical competence also involves a *strategic* dimension. It involves the circulation of dispositions of interpretation and practice across dispersed and widely varied locales where they are put to work in the disciplining of an always ambiguous, always hazardous history—including the practices of others. These interpretive and practical dispositions are, as Foucault puts it, "meticulous rituals of power." For they not only orient subjects in their interpretations of novel and ambiguous circumstances. They also predispose subjects' discriminating readings of what is crucial and what is marginal; what is immediately visible and what is in the fog; what is essential to a time or a place and what can be forgotten or deferred; what is normal and necessary and what is abnormal and necessarily disciplined; to whom one should listen and to whom one should turn a deaf ear (Foucault 1977a, 1978).

In this way, these rituals administer social time and space. Put into circulation by competent subjects and replicated in dispersed and changing circumstances, they encounter new contexts where they constitute and differentiate recognized fields of objectivity and modes of conduct appropriate to them. In this way, also, they constitute and "empower" subjects who, as agents moving on the surface of history, discipline one another to replicate the rituals that constitute them and, in their replications, to recognize the boundaries of fields of practice in which they find themselves. And in this way, they reaffirm and extend the symbolic resources and practical understandings off of which their practices play.

It is thus that the equivocity of history is disciplined. Amidst the hazardous play of historical difference, the putting into play of these mobile rituals of power produces effects of univocal spaces and times of continuity, the discontinuities that separate them, and the subjects who are disposed to replicate a way of seeing, saying, and making the world and who are disposed as well to expect a lucid and precise correspondence between their subjective principles of interpretation and the objective conditions interpreted.

With this understanding of practical competence in mind, we can begin to see how the possibility condition mentioned above might be satisfied: We can begin to see how knowledgeable practices of enframing might be able to differentiate between recognized subjectivity and objectivity without directly confronting the problem as a political problem and without confronting a need to engage in self-conscious legitimation of one interpretation among many. We can begin to see, in other words, how the irony intrinsic to the problem of imposing international purpose might be kept from becoming an embarrassment that would disable practices of enframing, undo effective understandings of competent subjectivity, and undermine the social recognition of systemic relations.

The possibility condition can be satisfied, we can now say, because practices of enframing involve the exercise of practical competence to effect not a single but a *double differentiation.* As already noted, practices of enframing impose a bound-ary between subjective and objective, between the social world of competent sub-jects and the "natural" world they understand to be beyond their political discourse. As also noted, however, enframing practices could not effect this first difference, and they could not thereby impose international purpose, were the difference ever to be explicitly recognized as what it is: one arbitrarily imposed interpretation con-testing politically among many competing interpretations. This problem can be answered in practice only through the practical constitution of a second difference, a second and equally fuzzy boundary. This is the boundary between two socially recognized "regions" of knowledgeable practice itself.

• *The region of knowledgeable practice characterized by an absence of explicit for-malization.* Here is the world of *doxa,* where things "go without saying because they come without saying," as Bourdieu (1977, 89) puts it. Here knowledge is not proclaimed in self-conscious opposition to competing claims but simply and "naturally" lived and circulated through practice. Here, practice may range from monotonous routine to playful or virtuoso performance opening up new possibilities at the frontiers of collective experience, but whether routine or extraordinary, it is never subjected to formal rationalization. It is never seen to be in need of legitima-tion. For it is never set in visible contrast to alternative practices whose legitimacy might be seriously entertained. Instead, here in the region of doxa, recognition, or the denial of recognition, comes instantly, unquestioningly, as a matter of self-evident understanding. Sensitive to shared understandings of tempo and context, a social performance may adeptly put into practice socially recognized rituals of power, and it may thereby secure recognition and empowerment, even in objec-tively unfamiliar circumstances. A social performance may also be clumsy or maladroit, confusing its spheres of practice and its principles of conduct appropriate to them, in which case it will be regarded as abnormal, heretical, or meaningless, and thus subject to discipline and exclusion from the domain of serious practice. But either way, the determination is not a matter of deliberate *decision,* in which alternatives are posed. It is a matter of "living naturally"—of putting to work the ambiguous practical and interpretive dispositions that are understood, not as the arbitrary rituals of power they are, but simply as matters of living a natural order of truth (see Bourdieu 1977, chap. 2).

• *The region of knowledgeable practice characterized by explicit formalization.* Here knowledge claims regarding the objective conditions of life and the principles of conduct appropriate to them openly vie with contesting knowledge claims, and here, accordingly, *orthodoxy* is voiced in answer to *heterodoxy* (Bourdieu 1977, 164–69). Here practice is not a matter of living naturally—for how one shall live and conduct oneself, and the consequences of that conduct, are politicized by the explicit play of competing interpretations. Universalizing claims are subject to recognition, not as absolute truths, but as arbitrary interpretations, and their in-stituting in practice is recognized as a conspicuous play of power. Here, in other words, there is a radical disjunction between social truth and purpose, on the one hand, and power, on the other. The deployment of knowedgeable practices to impose interpretations in the making of history—the play of power—is deprived of the presupposition that it bespeaks an already self-evident mode of interpretation and practice embodying a collectively recognized truth. Here, as one result, the groundlessness of knowledgeable practice is always potentially exposed, and the exposure spells resistance to the interpretations any practice would impose. Here, as a second result, all knowledgeable practice is ceaselessly engaged in a self-conscious search for some ultimate ground, some foundation, some universally acknowledged objective order in which it may finally secure its claim to the self-evidence it so conspicuously lacks and without which it will never be able to silence the resistances it encounters. It is in just this region of orthodoxy and heterodoxy, then, that discourses of legitimation are perennially under way.

This second differentiation, between the region of doxa and the region of orthodoxy and heterodoxy, may be understood to correspond to a difference, mentioned earlier, between practical competence and theoretically informed action, respectively. What is important to note, though, is that this second differentiation is anything but incidental to the first.

This second differentiation makes the differentiation between subjective and objective, social and natural, possible. It makes it possible by actively preserving a domain of doxa—a domain of sometimes routine, sometimes innovative practice—that may be understood to have three overlapping characteristics. It is, first, a region of practice wherein reside the principal social resources, the practical competencies or rituals of power, by which the first differentiation is produced and transformed in history, thus to effect a normalized mode of subjectivity and a corresponding mode of objective order regarded as self-evident. It is, second, a region of *ambiguous* practice. It is this ambiguity that permits the social resources of the region of doxa to be applied innovatively, to objectively novel circumstances, while still securing recognition as but a continuation of the normal, the necessary, and the eternally true mode of existence. It is, third, a region of practice that, thanks to the second differentiation, is regarded as beyond formalization, beyond theorization, beyond politics, and, accordingly, beyond resistance or dispute.

The three characteristics tell the story. Owing to the second differentiation, the arbitrary political practices of enframing that effect the first differentiation, and thereby impose international purpose, are not subjected to critical inspection as the arbitrary and political practices they are. The irony intrinsic to the problem of imposing international purpose can be kept from view. Arbitrarily effected systemic relations can be recognized as necessary, natural, and beyond politics, and international purpose can thereby be imposed, because the subjects who effect these relations, and the arbitrary and political practices by which they effect them, can themselves be (mis)recognized as necessary, natural, and apolitical modes of being in the world.

Such an understanding of the imposing of purpose contrasts sharply with rationalist understandings, which associate the production of social purpose with overcoming ambiguity, enlightening regions of darkness, and identifying, clarifying, and discursively legitimating explicitly entertained substantive ends and principles of conduct appropriate to their achievement by conscious appeal to universal standards of truth and meaning. The present understanding suggests the perhaps disturbing conclusion that *the political imposition of purpose, in international life or in any society, is largely a matter of actively producing regions of practice characterized by ambiguity, darkness, and even mystery—regions of doxa specifically immunized from the critical gaze of formalizing discourse.* More than that, the present understanding suggests that the imposing of purpose requires the *investment* of considerable social resources in these ambiguous and uninspected regions of practice, thus to constitute them as the natural font of mysterious or even magical powers.

It is precisely by preserving regions of ambiguity, by investing social resources in these regions, and by exempting these regions from politicizing argument that a society is able to sustain a capacity to impose effects of continuity, and sustain a recognized systematicity and wholeness, despite unceasing encounters with novel historical developments that threaten to undermine these effects or expose the arbitrariness of a naturalized truth. Herein, if you will, is a *strategic reserve* for the historical and political making of extrahistorical and extrapolitical purpose.

Elaboration: Sovereignty, Hegemony, Innovation and Crisis in the Administration of Global Space and Time

My outline so far has been quite general—so much so that it might seem to apply equally to the problem of imposing purpose in almost any pluralistic social setting, the setting of international relations being only one. I want now to elaborate this general outline, refining it and putting it to work by attending to specific aspects of the problem of imposing *international* purpose. It is perhaps appropriate to begin with a proposition that might seem to fly in the face of conventional wisdom: *precisely because it is an intrinsically pluralistic domain, international politics may be a domain of modern life that is peculiarly capable of imposing social purpose in the sense I have been describing.* In this respect, the lack of an effective and recognized center of decision may be a positive political asset, not a liability.

Sovereignty, Pluralism, and a Strategic Reserve

The proposition may be introduced by setting international pluralism, in the sense given earlier, in relief against other models of political life—some domestic, some international—that presuppose the necessity of a center of decision. In domestic politics, there is the model of the state and economy in relation to its constituents.

At a global plane, there are models of world government, models of global imperium, and rationalist models of hegemonic leadership or stability.

These models are all *unicentric* in an important respect. Although they may allow for the possibility of some degree of pluralistic contest among subordinate subjects, they all presuppose the necessary *decidability* of all things political. They all assume that where interpretations of political possibility are not naturally harmonized, and where there is some conflict of interpretations, all political discourse must ultimately refer and recur to some moment of decisive and singular interpretation, some privileged focus and register of unambiguous and universal truth. Even so-called liberal-pluralistic models of the state in domestic politics presuppose such decidability, for they insist that in all things political and material, conflicts of interpretation must be brought to a point of resolution through appeal either to the decisive moment of the state (for example, through the discourse *closing* medium of the ballot) or to the state's supplement, the "impartial spectator" of the market (see Ashley 1989). All of these models additionally assume that where life is deprived of such a decisive moment, where things become intrinsically "undecidable," political life ends. Society devolves into anarchy, understood as a purely instrumental contest of opposing interpretations, each striving to subordinate others to its own. Politics, these models assume, presupposes decidability. Politics *is* nothing more than a matter of decision.

This unicentric understanding of politics is played out in familiar diagnoses of problems of governance. Because any center must ground its decisional authority in effective claims that it is the privileged focus of a universal truth, its authority threatens to unravel wherever and whenever this truth cannot be made effective. Amidst the challenges to this universal truth born of time and difference, accordingly, such a center must absorb greater and greater control over social resources, and must undertake ever more complex elaborations of its rule, if only to ever more efficiently redistribute resources so as to effect the experience of the universal truth without which its authority would soon collapse and its rule would encounter disabling resistance. Eventually, the center's "burdening of society" and "loss of innovative potential" bring it down unless extraordinary measures are taken to either acquire new resources from without, more efficiently rearrange coalitional structures within, and/or expel mounting resistances to the world beyond. Offe and Habermas on the modern state, Weber and Eisenstadt and Polanyi on historic bureaucratic-redistributive empires, Lenin against Kautsky's ultraimperialism, Gilpin and Modelski and Wallerstein on cycles of hegemony or world leadership—all speak to the tendencies toward disabling crisis built in to such unicentric models of politics (see Offe 1975, 1983; Habermas 1976, 1979; Gilpin 1981; Modelski 1978; Wallerstein 1984).

What is especially noteworthy about these unicentric models, for present purposes, is that the understanding of politics as a matter of decision tilts these models strongly against appreciating the positive role of undecidability and ambiguity as a strategic reserve for the effecting of collective purpose. Where they see ambiguity, where they see the absence of a center capable of effecting decision, and where they cannot presuppose some natural harmonization of interpretations to be at work, they can sense only anarchy. They can comprehend politics among contesting interpretations only as the absence of politics—a dangerous space of instrumental contest and instrumental cooperation, nothing more. One can therefore well understand why, when such models are instituted in historical practices of governance, they exhibit the crisis tendencies so frequently diagnosed. Deprived of access to ambiguity, and fearing rather than cultivating the indeterminate play of undecidable practices, politics instituted on such unicentric models denies itself the sort of strategic reserve that might make political innovation possible.

In considering the merits of pluralism in international politics, one must take care not to let one's interpretations be guided solely by such unicentric models of politics. International pluralism does indeed entail the absence of decidability, for sovereignty itself presupposes the absence of an overarching center of decision. But this alone should not immediately license the interpretation of international politics as a dangerous field of anarchy in the sense just considered. It should not license the interpretation of international politics as an open field of interimperial rivalry, competition among would-be hegemons, "creative destruction" and "succession crises" of systemic wars, or "freedom of maneuver" for capitalist entrepreneurs, as Wallerstein is inclined to say. Likewise, it should not license the understanding of international politics as a place where contesting interpretations undecidably collide in dangerous and mutually disabling ways, and where the dangers can be brought under control only through the deliberate and successive elaboration of regimes that function to make all meaning universally transparent and whose rules, norms, procedures, and the like are themselves susceptible to a singular, decisive reading. At least one other interpretation is possible. It is one that, like Karl Deutsch's reading of "pluralistic security communities" (Lijphart 1981), finds positive value in international pluralism, not just a dangerous problem to be solved.

The interpretation, phrased as a proposition, is this. The respect for international pluralism inscribed in the construct of sovereignty and replicated in the circulation and dissemination of sovereign practices does or might positively effect a distinctive region of ambiguous political performance: a global region of doxa that is differentiated in practice from domestic political discourse and the presumption of the necessary decidability of politics, that exhibits a distinctive mode of political subjectivity, that is invested with considerable social resources, and that thereby constitutes a strategic reserve for the innovation of practical competencies and rituals of power capable of disciplining global conduct and constituting international purpose.

Considering this possibility, one can entertain a conjecture that is, once again, remarkably at variance with unicentric interpretations of politics. The absence of an overarching center of global politics, one can conjecture, does not spell the negation of international purpose. For it is precisely through the perpetuation of a respect for international pluralism—and, with it, a field of ambiguous political conduct—that it becomes possible to undertake practices of enframing that effect international purpose by securing recognition for global systemic relations. It is precisely through the constitution of this strategic reserve that it becomes possible to concert the global and instantaneous recognition of "dangerous practices"— those practices that threaten to expose the arbitrariness and political content of socially effected systemic relations—and to orchestrate rituals of power to normalize, silence, or exclude these "dangers." It is precisely thus, one can conjecture, that it becomes possible to enframe subjective and objective, social and natural, the domain of politics and the domain of natural and necessary conditions to which all politics must ultimately bow.

Global Strategy in the Absence of a Central Strategist: The Historical "Fusion" of Sovereignty

The present understanding of the problem of imposing international purpose suggests why this point must be expressed as a conjecture: There is no necessary affinity between international pluralism as inscribed in the construct of sovereignty and any particular set of socially recognized systemic relations. There is no necessary articulation, for example, between sovereignty and international political practice, on the one hand, and bourgeois subjectivity, with its presupposition of the natural necessity of the privitization of control over social resources, with its naturalization of market structures, and with its presupposition that the state must ultimately ground its authority in the decision of possessive individuals, on the other. Far from a matter of abstract and timeless logic, the articulation of pluralistic international politics to a particular socially recognized system of relations—and, hence, to a particular international purpose—is always historical and political. It is always a historical and political matter of effecting a fusion of the construct of sovereignty, and the commitment to international pluralism contained therein, to specific, historically normalized interpretations of the state, its competencies, and the conditions and limits of its recognition and empowerment.

The effecting of such an arbitrary historical fusion is itself a matter of practice: enframing practices. It is not so much a matter of putting forth specific interpretations of the sovereign state, seeking out universal grounds for them, and positively declaring them to be the natural and necessary interpretations to which everyone must accede. This is an approach to enriching the content of sovereignty, yes, but it is always a "second-best" strategy (Bourdieu, 1977, 88) because it is always conspicuously a strategy. The "best" strategy—because it is the most effective strategy—is one of enframing. It involves the deployment of rituals of power to marginalize, forget, defer, or silence competing interpretations and the simultaneous deployment of rituals of power to exclude those perspectives and arguments that would expose these rituals for the arbitrary political strategies they are. In this way, it becomes possible to proceed from a "natural attitude" in the enframing of a "natural" meaning of sovereignty.

To the extent that such enframing practices succeed, they succeed also in inscribing in sovereignty certain practical dispositions and commitments to systemic purpose. The international practices of sovereign states will be disposed, on balance, to replicate those normalized interpretations that constitute them and to exclude or silence those practices that would challenge these constitutive interpretations. If, for instance, sovereignty is fused historically with the interpretation and legitimation of the state as the laissez-faire capitalist state, and if it is possible to ignore or marginalize those who would expose the arbitrariness of the practices by which the fusion is effected, then the ambiguous field of international politics will constitute a strategic reserve of political resources "naturally" disposed to discipline practices whenever and wherever they fail to conform to the "Natural" system of laissez-faire liberalism. If, contrariwise or at a later time, sovereignty is fused historically with the interpretation of the state as a late capitalist state, and if again evidence of the arbitrariness of the fusion can be forgotten, deferred, or pushed over the horizon and out of immediate sight, then it is the conditions and legitimations of the late capitalist interventionary state that will be naturalized and universalized by competent practitioners of international politics.

Disciplining History: Hegemony and the Enframing of Space and Time

As the examples just given should certainly remind us, the fusion of sovereignty to any specific interpretation of the state, what it does, and how one legitimates what it does is always extraordinarily problematic. A problem called to mind by Stephen Krasner in a footnote referring to John Ruggie (Krasner 1985, 106) is a chronic problem: Although one may be tempted, one cannot easily speak of an era, say, of mercantile states, an era of liberal states, and an era of "embedded liberal" states, for in every era there are exceptions—often more exceptions than states that conform to the rule. In the context of North–South relations, which Krasner specifically addresses in the book in question, the chronic problem becomes acute. For here it is manifestly the case that the practices of Northern states, undertaken consistent with their evolving domestic legitimations, facilitate the production of conditions in the South that undermine any prospect that Third World states might even approximate these domestic legitimations in their own societies. How, under these circumstances, can one seriously contemplate the notion of universal doxic understanding of a natural mode of international political being—a content-rich mode of sovereign subjectivity capable of orchestrating international practice across diverse times and places, thus to naturalize some set of systemic relations and effect global purpose? The answer has two components.

One component of an answer finds its focus in the controversial notion of hegemony. By hegemony, I do not mean an overarching ideology or cultural matrix that encloses political imagination—a notion of hegemony with which Antonio Gramsci is often associated (quite mistakenly, in my reading of him). I also do not mean a central agency possessing both the capabilities and the will to impose global purpose through its deliberate policies—a notion of hegemony that I associate with unicentric interpretations of politics. By hegemony I mean an ensemble of normalized knowledgeable practices, identified with a particular state and domestic society (or perhaps some number of states and domestic societies), that is regarded as a practical paradigm of sovereign political subjectivity and conduct. Hegemony, so understood, does several things: (1) it reliably enacts, and thus "embodies," a particular understanding of sovereign political doing and being fused to a particular interpretation of the state, its legitimations, and the objective conditions of life; (2) it lives this mode of sovereign being naturally, effortlessly, and without conscious deliberation; (3) in its normal practices, it replicates, exemplifies, and puts in circulation the rituals of power by which this mode of doing is framed as a self-evident state of being and alternative interpretations are silenced; (4) it enframes state and domestic society in a way that preserves respect for a multiplicity of other sovereign spaces and times on the condition that they, in turn, recognize and honor the boundaries of hegemonic sovereignty; and (5) it thereby stands as a living exemplar of a "normal" and "natural" mode of sovereignty to which all times and places of life are understood freely to defer and aspire, even if it is not a mode that can then and there immediately be enacted in practice.

Such an understanding of hegemony does not ascribe to a hegemonic state a conscious intention to enhance its relative power or to impose its will upon others. It would indeed lead to the quite contrary conclusion that the effect of hegemony would be diminished precisely to the extent that a state's practices are recognized as deliberately undertaken in the interest of a power it does not "naturally" have or in the interest of imposing a will not "naturally" obeyed.

The practical function of hegemony, on this account, is neither to actively construct a center of power nor to actively impose a mode of sovereign being on others. The practical function of hegemony is to exemplify what is doxically accepted as the normal and necessary mode of sovereign being. *It is to exemplify the paradigmatic "hard core" in contrast to which all anomalies of sovereignty may be practically recognized, around which puzzles for the realization of a normal political order revolve, and upon which all ritual practices of enframing pivot.* It is to serve in international life the function that an author, according to Foucault (1984), performs in a literary discourse: It is to provide "the principle of thrift" in the proliferation of meaning regarding the normal mode of sovereign doing and being and the objective systemic relations corresponding to it.

The political power of hegemony, on this same account, is neither a "power over" other actors nor a "power to" obtain some consciously deliberated future end among ends. The power of hegemony resides precisely in the capacity to inhabit a domain of doxa and to competently perform the rituals of power naturalized therein. It is the power to partake of and exercise a practically constituted strategic reserve, inscribed in the silently affirmed domain of doxa, to enframe global practices and effect international purpose.

The second component of the answer emphasizes the "elasticity" of rituals of enframing, as these take advantage of the ambiguity of doxa, as these pivot on a hegemonic interpretation of a normal mode of sovereign identity, and as these play on dimensions of space and time. On the dimension of space, it is possible to secure a recognized interpretation of political subjectivity, even in the face of mounting challenges, by putting ritual practices of enframing to work to draw and redraw the boundaries between the normal and the abnormal, the pure and the deficient, the true and the false, the Occident and the Orient, the faithful and the heretic. For example:

• The cold war is largely a matter of the ritual effecting of such spatial boundaries—a process of drawing them, erasing them, overwriting them, and drawing them anew. Thanks to the anchoring of the cold war dichotomy in a field of doxa, it is possible to interpret offending practices—practices that defy a normalized mode of political subjectivity—as emanating not from the world of the true and the normal but from the dangerous "other" world that is always properly the object of normalized subjects' severest means. It is possible thereby to excuse even hegemonic subjects' most radical departures from their own self-understandings of who and what they essentially are. By disseminating this interpretive practice, by making this doxic practice available at all times and in all places, subjects of social action circulate a ritual of power by which a normalized understanding of a natural mode of being can be secured even though, in actual conduct, it is repeatedly betrayed.
• The construct of "turbulence" in the Third World, like the construct of "terrorism," can be circulated among dispersed locales, and can thereby provide a resource with which to exclude from the space of the "normal" all of those resistant practices that threaten to embarrass or undermine the professed competencies of a normalized mode of sovereign being. These constructs need not be well defined in order to have this exclusionary effect. In fact, their utility is preserved precisely by securing recognition for these constructs as signifiers of dark and elusive forces that are intrinsically beyond rational understanding.

On the dimension of time, it is always possible to silence challenges to normalized political subjectivity by imposing boundaries between what is present and what can be deferred or forgotten, what is accomplished and what is aspiring, what is developed and what is developing. For instance:

• If the differentiation between First World and Second World plays on the spatial dimension, the differentiations between the First World and the Third World play on the temporal. Competently put to work, ritual practices of temporal differentiation, such as those contained in notions of "development" or "modernization," can be deployed to marginalize the embarrassing fact that Third World states egregiously depart from normalized modes of sovereign being: the fact can be marginalized by securing recognition for the departure, not as essential and not therefore as a challenge to normalized interpretations of sovereignty, but as a problem of development that is "only a matter of time." The practice of foreign aid, "altruistically" given, complements the ritual play on the dimension of time, even when it is of little material consequence, by expressing a hegemonic state's "gratuitous" commitment to the temporal project by which Third World states will themselves come to replicate the normal mode of sovereign being.

• In the case of North–North relations, it is possible to acknowledge state-interventionary departures from a hegemonic liberal ideal by allowing, in effect, that these departures are necessitated not only by a need to combat socialism on the spatial dimension but also by the temporal exigencies of, say, a postwar recovery.

The discriminating potential of such spatially and temporally oriented interpretive rituals can be seen to be even greater when it is remembered that, in almost all cases, it is possible to play on both dimensions at once. To illustrate:

• The differentiation between Third World and Fourth World can be made sense of, first, by deploying the ritual of "development" to situate the Third World on the dimension of time and, second, by spatially recognizing the Fourth World as a region that is deprived of access to time itself and hence to foreign aid as well.

• Jeane Kirkpatrick's distinction between authoritarian and totalitarian Third World states holds that authoritarian states are those that can be allowed their systematic exercises in terror, and can therefore be adjudged worthy of support, because they can be recognized to occupy the dimension of time and ascendance to a normalized mode of sovereign being. By the same distinction, totalitarian states are those that can be denied such recognition, and can be repudiated and rendered the proper objects of international discipline, because, according to cold war rituals, they can be spatially situated as the dangerous "other" to a normalized mode of international being.

• In liberal discourse, the differentiation between political community and economy largely turns on a spatial differentiation of two regions of time, together with the temporal mediation of effects occurring across these spaces. In this discourse, political community is that domain that is coextensive with ritual practices involving the invoking of "monumental time"—the time of diversity and change that is held to be necessarily grounded in eternal values and principles of a singular and timeless ethical order. Economy, by contrast, is understood to find its place amidst ritual practices involving the invoking of "linear time"—the time of diversity and change that is understood to occur as a progressive elaboration of material powers, produced through processes that are independent of social responsibility. The differentiation between domains of time is spatially conceived. However, because the progressive expansion of material powers, occurring in the linear time of economy, threatens to effect dislocations in the monumental time of political community, and because the ethical principles of monumental time threaten to legitimate political practices intervening in the economic space of linear time, the historical differentiation of spaces is always in jeopardy of being deprived of its natural, self-evident character. Under these circumstances, the spatial differentiation can nevertheless be naturalized in practice through the mediating ritual of invoking "cyclical time." By way of this ritual, economic disturbances in a historically effected domain of political community can be tolerated for a time, the politicization of a historically effected domain of economy can be deferred for a time, and the boundary between the two domains can continue to be honored in practice as a necessary and natural limit of social possibility, because the space of linear time is rendered as a domain of naturally periodic processes whose disturbing political effects are susceptible to correction through periodic political interventions.

The importance of these ritual practices of enframing must not be underestimated. For in combination with the construct of hegemony, they explain how a fundamental contradiction of international political life can be reconciled. It is the contradiction between *being* and *doing*: between (1) a generalized recognition that there is one paradigmatic and everywhere replicated mode of sovereign identity and (2) a diversity of state practices adapted to the diverse and discontinuous conditions and problems of global life. Thanks to hegemony, it is possible to have a socially recognized paradigm of what sovereignty *is*. Thanks to rituals of enframing, it is possible to sustain this normalized interpretation even in the face of the embarrassments potentially present in what states actually *do*.

"Handsome is as handsome does," the expression goes. In Melville's *Billy Budd,* cruel master-at-arms Claggart played on this expression with some irony when the beautiful and innocent Billy spilled his soup across Claggart's path. Billy's clumsy action would permit Claggart to call into question the beauty of Billy's being—an event that would eventually spell his undoing (see Johnson 1980). "Sovereignty is as sovereigns do" is the parallel expression in international political life. Here, though, discrepant practices that might seem to call into question what sovereignty is, and thus undo the paradigm of sovereignty itself, can be kept safely to the margins of international political discourse. Enframing practices, competently performed, make this marginalization possible.

The Ever-Present Possibility of "Crisis"

In taking note of these discriminating and normalizing rituals of power, one must not lose sight of still another point equally present in our understanding of the problem of imposing international purpose: The ambiguous region of doxa in which these rituals find their place and power is not given a priori but must be actively constituted in practice. This region, and the practices by which social purpose is imposed, must be bounded and set apart from the field whereupon the politicizing contest of orthodoxy and heterodoxy occurs. If this boundary is not sustained in practice, if totalizing and formalizing discourses encroach upon and politicize the ambiguous zone of doxa, and if, therefore, this zone of practice loses its natural, self-evident character, then the rituals of power constituted therein lose their capacities to orchestrate the enframing and discipline of collective possibility. Their arbitrariness exposed, they are deprived of instantaneous and unquestioning recognition, and they are called upon to prove their legitimacy by appeal to universal grounds. Unable to summon such grounds, they are unable to mobilize social resources in the constitution of sovereign subjectivity and the objectification of the systemic relations that this subjectivity takes as its necessary and natural ground. Political identity inscribed in the construct of sovereignty becomes politicized. Whether locally or in global compass, the systemic truths of life become themselves objects of controversy. Whether locally or in global compass, the collective purpose implicit in objectified structures becomes an issue, which is to say that it is now put in doubt. There is a crisis of political identity and a crisis of purpose.

Crisis does not occur because things suddenly change or because deeply structured contradictions erupt on the surface of history—change is *always* afoot, and deep structures *never* have a life of their own independent of the surface historical practices by which they are structured and rendered deep and mysterious. Critical "discontinuities" occur because doxic rituals of power that discipline history and impose continuity upon it begin to become mutually disabling: Enacted "naturally," and depending upon their self-evidence for their effectiveness, doxic practices begin to have effects that expose the arbitrariness of other practices, thereby denying them the status and power of doxa, exposing them to a need for legitimation, and rendering them objects of formalized and politicized discourse in which orthodoxy and heterodoxy openly contest.

Crisis, understood this way, is a crisis of enframing practice: a crisis in the decentralized administration of time and space. According to this interpretation, ritual practices of enframing differentiate space and time into naturalized domains of practice, each with its own doxic subjects who are disposed to replicate the rituals by which, in specific contexts, boundaries are produced and affirmed. However, the rituals of enframing in any one domain of space and time can in turn have *boundary transgressive effects:* effects that are *unintended, resistant,* and *disabling* in other domains, that is, in other regions of space, at some later times, or in some other contexts. These effects are "unintended" if they escape the interpretive frames of reference shared by the subjects of the domain that produces them and then find meaning from the point of subjects occupying some other place, time, or context. These effects are "resistant" if, for whatever reason, they exceed or elude the capacities of enframing rituals to normalize, silence, defer, forget, or marginalize them. These effects are "disabling" if, in other domains, they give expression to possibilities that call into question doxic modes of subjectivity and competent practice normalized therein, thereby depriving doxic rituals of the power of self-evidence and undermining their capacities to impose discipline, secure boundaries, and fix purpose in systemic relations recognized as necessary and objective.

An example of such boundary "transgressive" effects has already been alluded to: the example of the differentiation of "political community" and "economy" in liberal discourse offered just a moment ago. Here, normalized practices undertaken in the economic space of "linear time" can have effects that transgress the boundary between economics and politics, intruding upon the political space of "monumental time." These effects might be *unintended* in the sense that they have meanings in the "monumental time" of political community that are not comprehensible from the standpoint of the subjects of "economy." These effects are potentially *resistant* to the normalizing ritual practices of "political community" because, say, they might involve patterns of differential growth or social dislocations that cannot be interpreted, and hence marginalized, as normal fluctuations, as externally originating problems befalling political community as a whole, or as passing or cyclical phenomena in the natural order of things. These effects are potentially *disabling* because the continuing use of the rituals of "political community," even in the face of conspicuous resistance, only serves to make plain the arbitrariness of the rituals themselves. Even the "eternal values" of "political community," to which these rituals appeal, might begin to be recognized as arbitrary political contrivances. To the extent that this occurs—to the extent that hitherto doxic ritual practices of social discipline are politicized—they lose their capacities to normalize practice and marginalize or silence resistant interpretations of the essence and necessary boundaries of "political community." Hitherto marginalized interpretations of the boundary between politics and economics might reassert themselves, as a voice of heterodoxy, at the onetime center of political life. The time-honored boundary between politics and economics might be called into question.

Especially problematical for the practice of international governance, of course, are those transgressive effects that cannot be confined to the time and place of any one state and domestic society. Such transgressive effects may issue from the recognized domestic space and time of other sovereign states, as when one country's exports contribute to unemployment in another or when pollutants dumped into a river by one country contribute to the future ruin of the water supply of another. Or they may issue from the naturalized system of relations all states and societies "commonly inhabit," as when global "market price fluctuations" visit economic ruin upon a particular locale or when the "free flow of information" contributes to the undoing of valued cultural resources in one or another locale.

If such unintended effects are resistant, they spell a local political problem. If such unintended effects are disabling, they spell local crisis. The historically fused interpretation of sovereignty normalized and circulated among other states will then be politicized and perhaps deconstructed. Alternative interpretations—entailing different boundaries, different competencies, different practical dispositions—will be constructed, put on the agenda, and perhaps locally exemplified.

The occurrence of crisis and the politicization of sovereignty, even if occurring locally, can never be an exclusively local concern. For the event cannot be literally kept from the ears of others, and the event itself gives voice to dangerous interpretations echoing in the field of international doxa. What this voice says is that the normal interpretation of sovereign boundaries, competencies, and dispositions in circulation at any time, and exemplified by the paradigm of hegemonic sovereignty, is anything but the self-evident necessity it is widely taken to be. It is an arbitrary contrivance, contingently fused in one setting, politically imposed in another, and everywhere denying alternative ways of sovereign doing and being. This voice is right, of course. But if the strategic reserve of international doxa is to be sustained, the truth it speaks is a truth that must not be said.

One way of silencing the dangerous voice of local crisis is to be found in the deployment of ritualized practices of enframing and exclusion, playing on dimensions of time and space, to identify the sources of the dangerous interpretations and to warrant and orient the use of whatever means necessary to arrest or silence them. If these ambiguous and mobile practices are already inscribed in the normalized interpretive dispositions exemplified in the paradigm of hegemony and replicated (albeit imperfectly) elsewhere, then it can be a fairly simple matter, even a seemingly "instinctual" matter, to put these enframing practices to work. Of political resistances in Brazil, for instance, one might say that, alas, although it made "miraculous progress" toward "political and economic development" for a "time," it is now "regressing," and must now be counted among Third World states that must "necessarily" accompany their "necessary programs of economic austerity" with equally austere measures of "authoritarian political leadership" lest "turbulence" overtake them and the promise of "future progress" be forsaken. It thus becomes possible to license a special "troubled case" of normal sovereignty—a special case that is nevertheless "found" with extraordinary frequency in the Third World—in which the state is disposed to secure the "domestic truth" that emanates from *beyond* sovereign boundaries through the coercive administration of an "anarchic" domain *within* sovereign boundaries. It becomes possible internationally to license and support the local state's deployment of coercive means to arrest dangerous resistances that challenge the normal form of sovereignty.

If, however, the emergent resistances encountered defy recognition and discipline according to ambiguous and mobile practices of enframing already taken as doxa, if the rituals of enframing already inscribed in the hegemonic interpretation of sovereign dispositions prove incapable of orchestrating collective practice to silence or exclude them, then there are only two ways in which local crisis can be kept from posing a crisis in the order of sovereignty. Either local crisis must be kept from happening or new enframing rituals must be innovated, exemplified, circulated, and inscribed in sovereignty itself. Both are equally tasks of hegemonic leadership and tests of hegemonic virtue. The latter, however, is the infinitely more difficult task, and one that hegemonic subjects, most of the time, would have little inclination to perform.

The innovation of new enframing rituals is infinitely more difficult because it amounts to nothing less than the reinscription of sovereignty itself, a task that cannot be frequently performed. The circulation of novel practices of enframing takes time and occurs over space. Everywhere they are put to work, these practices must be adapted to the exigencies of locale and context, and this, too, takes time. Above all, it must be remembered that the effectiveness of ritual practices of enframing inheres in their status as doxic practices. They must be naturalized as containing an *enduring* truth. It follows, therefore, that there is some limit—not an absolute limit, to be sure—to the temporal frequency of hegemonic innovation. The acceleration of hegemonic innovation beyond this limit would mean that rituals of enframing would begin themselves to be mutually disabling. They would begin to politicize one another. If this is to be avoided, the discontinuities of innovation must be separated by periods of continuity. Crisis and the need for innovation must be deferred. Time must be spaced.

The First Virtue of Hegemony: The Internal Displacement of Resistances

This spacing of time is possible because, as I say, there is an alternative to the innovation of novel rituals of enframing. Local crisis can be kept from happening because the hegemonic subjects may *internally displace* the transgressive effects that would threaten to occasion local crisis were they directed elsewhere, to other regions having less access to the resources of an ambiguous doxa. They may willingly *absorb* within their own region of sovereign authority those unintended, resistant, and potentially disabling effects that issue from the naturalized system of relations commonly inhabited or from the normalized performance of rituals of power within other sovereign regions. They may transfer resources, extracted from their own domain, to other sovereign subjects. They may do so without regret, without politicizing the transgressions they absorb, even without apparent notice of the "costs" they disproportionately bear. From the standpoint of historically constructed hegemonic subjectivity, these transgressive effects may be regarded, not as the international political matters we may see them to be, but either as problems issuing from within the domestic domain of hegemony or as problems issuing from the natural order of things and befalling all humankind equally. They may be dealt with only in terms of the historically circumscribed domain of domestic discourse. They may be dealt with through "internal" practices of enframing.

Internal practices of enframing do not expel resistances literally beyond the geographic boundaries of a hegemonic state. They work within those geographic boundaries, once again on dimensions of space and time. Racial boundaries or gender boundaries, for example, might be deployed as spatial boundaries: A construct of a "welfare class lacking incentive" or of a "reservation Indian lacking sobriety" can be put into circulation to locate the causes of internal failures in intrinsically regressive subcultures that sociologists and educators strive to reform; or a construct of woman as maternal dependent can be circulated to naturalize women's lack of an independent role in the economic, scientific, and technological shaping of material life. Similarly, on the dimension of time, the promise of future solutions might be institutionalized in the present as an answer to the embarrassments of the present: The ritual of "public policy" can be disseminated to offer a living guarantee that this future promise is issued in good faith; an attitude of technological optimism and a faith in market-born compensations and substitutions can be disseminated and replicated to answer evidence of the despoilation of the domestic environment or of declining social welfare with a promise that future correctives are certainly assured. Or, when all else fails, these rituals can be combined, as when the discourse of public policy contemplates governmental strategies by which problems of the environment or social welfare might be resolved through the "unburdening" of technological resources or the "marketizing" of the problems themselves. Playing on the ambiguities of doxa in this way, resources can be extracted from the present for dispersal beyond, disabling effects issuing from without can be internally borne, and those who bear the costs in the present and are prone to resist—they can be marginalized and their voices can be silenced for a time.

Why would hegemonic practice exhibit this first virtue of hegemony, thus to displace events that threaten crisis in other locales? Are we to adopt a functionalist view and explain this local performance in terms of the requisites of continuity in the social whole? The answer is clearly no.

From a certain point of view, it is possible to see that a historically constituted hegemonic subjectivity will have every "interest" in displacing these transgressive effects internally. It will be disposed to do so. It will be so disposed because the alternative—always beyond imagining—is to put in question the paradigm of sovereignty and the mediating rituals that it lives naturally, that it puts in circulation, that others respect and take to be self-evident, and upon which its power depends. It will be so disposed, in other words, out of what Foucault (1978, 95) calls a "local cynicism of power." Hegemonic subjects displace transgressive effects internally, not out of conscious altruism, but out of conscious and cynical self-interest in the power of the historically normalized self as paradigmatic sovereign being.

Speaking of such a local cynicism of power, Foucault (quoted in Dreyfus and Rabinow 1983, 187) has noted that "people very often know what they do; they very often know why they do what they do; what they don't know is what what they do does." In a similar fashion, we may note that hegemonic subjects very often know that they refuse to make an international political issue of international transgressive effects, and they know that they do so because power is at stake. What they don't know is that this refusal is crucial to the spacing of international time, thus to make possible the doxic mode of sovereignty that defines international being and around which the orchestration of international purpose pivots. In effect, the refusal amounts to a taking advantage of the strategic reserve of an ambiguous international doxa—a region of doxa to which hegemonic subjects by definition have privileged access—to absorb "internally" those effects that might prove disabling were they encountered in other locales lacking similar access to social resources. It thereby permits other locales to *postpone* encounters with what is at all times the truth of the matter—that the self-evident mode of sovereign doing and being exemplified by hegemonic subjects is an arbitrary interpretation historically imposed, not the exemplary truth that all others are on the road to realizing. So long as hegemonic internal displacement is possible, this postponement is possible. So long as postponement is possible, the urgent need to innovate international rituals of enframing and inscribe them in the collectively effective meaning of sovereignty, too, can be deferred. The rituals of yesterday can be effectively put to work again today.

Yet hegemonic internal displacement is not always possible—or at least it is not always easy. The ambiguity of doxa may constitute a sort of strategic reserve disproportionately available to a hegemonic subject, it is true, but it is hardly a strategic reserve without limits. These limits are constructed through practice, yes, but that is not to say that they can be "deconstructed" at the wave of a hand.

On the contrary, the spatial and temporal enframing practices by which hegemonic internal displacements are effected themselves impose limits. On the spatial dimension, for example:

• The spatial marginalization of races and genders excludes those races and genders, and all the interpretive possibilities attached to them, from the domain of normal, acceptable, or rational meaning upon which further practices might officially draw. If being "feminine" is equated with weakness, penetrability, indecisiveness, and an unsturdy ego, and if "femininity" is set in opposition to a privileged understanding of sovereign doing and being, then the field of doxic practice is thereafter deprived of access to the richness of a feminine experience that might defy this understanding of sovereignty. It is thereafter committed to a mode of practice characterized by the strident negation of the "femininity" it subordinates to sovereignty. Having effected a discipline on femininity, hegemonic subjectivity is now subject to the discipline it effects.

Much the same can be seen to occur on the dimension of time:

• Practices of deferring the problems of the present to the future by making promises in the present entail commitments to ever more costly rituals of promising and ever less ambiguous tokens of good faith. As the rituals become more elaborate, the promises more expansive, and the tokens less ambiguous, the failures become ever more plain to see.

With the elaboration of limits, the two dimensions join:

• As the promises of the past are experienced in the present, as the failure of the future folds back upon the present, and as time seems therefore to accelerate, the only way out is to play ever more on the spatial dimension, to exclude more and more aspects of life from the domain of the normal and the true, and to thereby circumscribe the normal and the true still more than before.

Remarkably, at the very moment that domestic problems seem their greatest, domestic political imagination is most constrained. The latitude for domestic political innovation threatens to become nil. Little room for ambiguity remains.

The Second Virtue of Hegemony: The Innovation of Enframing Practices

It is at just this moment, when the latitude for hegemonic internal displacement shrinks and when domestic political imagination is confined, that a long-deferred crisis of political innovation is encountered. It is a crisis of hegemony, surely, but one must take care to understand just what this means.

In part, the crisis is *external* to the domain of hegemony. Owing to the inability of hegemonic subjects to displace transgressive effects internally, the crises long postponed in other locales begin to mount. There, in these other locales, these transgressive effects disable the rituals of power by which sovereignty is normalized, systemic relations are differentiated and objectified, and social purpose is thereby effected. They open the way for the circulation of resistant interpretations that would politicize both the hegemonic paradigm of sovereignty and global purpose itself. The failure of the strategy of internal displacement thus means mounting external challenges to the hegemonic *interpretation* of sovereignty and the commitment to international purpose implicit in it. It does *not* mean the proliferation of external challenges to the "hegemon" in the all-too-literal sense of a hegemonic territorial state.

In part, also, the crisis is *internal*. The long-time practice of internal displacement by which the crisis itself was postponed is now having its effect: Even in the space and time of the hegemonic sovereign, doxa is politicized. The hegemonic society can no longer occupy and live effortlessly a pure form of sovereign being, thus to stand for one and all as a paradigm of true sovereignty of which all other recognized states represent either specific idiomatic variants or aspiring or inferior forms. It cannot because domestic practices of enframing, by which transgressive effects have been internally displaced, have multiplied domestic resistances to the normal form of sovereign doing and being that hegemony might be purported to exemplify. Even within the bounds of a hegemonic society, the boundaries, competencies, and practical dispositions of a normalized interpretation of sovereignty are questioned. Even here, competing interpretations find a political voice. "External" challenges to the hegemonic paradigm are echoed "within."

The crisis of hegemony, then, cannot be conceived as a crisis pitting state against state in a struggle for paramountcy, a position of superordinate power that permits one state to impose its rules. *It is simply not a sort of crisis that could conceivably be resolved by war.* For the stakes of the crisis are to be found in a contest of interpretations over what the sovereign state—its boundaries, its competencies, its practical dispositions, its legitimations—shall be taken self-evidently to be. And in the moment of crisis, no one state and domestic society—not even a hegemonic society—can be regarded as a pure representation of any one interpretation, and all states and domestic societies contain traces of the several interpretations that are contesting. If the crisis may be called a crisis of hegemony, it is not because one state is losing power with respect to others. It is because doxic rituals of enframing are losing their power of self-evidence not only at the far reaches of their onetime arc of discipline but also at the paradigmatic core to which they refer and upon which they pivot. A whole world of enframing practices is losing its gravitational center.

This crisis of hegemony *is* also a crisis of political innovation. What is in need of innovation are interpretive practices of enframing that, as new rituals of power, can be put to work as highly mobile, widely replicable means of monitoring, recognizing, and deferring or redirecting global practices, thereby to effect new boundaries, a new mode of self-evident sovereign identity, a new strategic reserve of doxa, a new understanding of domesticity, and a new understanding of the objective conditions of action. What is in need of innovation, in particular, are practices of enframing that satisfy three practical constraints:

• As rituals of power, these innovated rituals of enframing must draw upon what remains of the strategic reserve of an ambiguous doxa. It is this that makes possible their recognition, not as deliberate means, but as natural, nonpolitical ways of sovereign being and doing, and it is this that makes them effective.

• As practical responses to the disablement of rituals of power in the face of boundary transgressive effects, they must appropriate interpretive resources previously marginalized or silenced to effect new boundaries, within which previously marginalized practices can now be regarded as part of the normal and natural order, and beyond which the resistant "other" to this normal order can be reliably externalized. It is this that makes possible the recognition of the space and time of each sovereign as a pure presence, devoid of internal contradictions.

• As rituals that must be replicated in diverse locales, thus to effect in each locale a recognizably normal mode of sovereign being, the boundaries effected must not define the resistant "other" in such a fashion that the resistances externalized beyond the space and time of one sovereign spell the undoing of the rituals in the space and time of another. It is this that makes it possible, over some time and among at least some number of sovereigns, to defer or marginalize the sort of mutually disabling boundary transgressive effects that occasioned the crisis in the first place.

The three practical constraints define the task. The task is to innovate, exemplify, and disseminate novel rituals of enframing adapted to historically emergent situations and capable of replicably effecting new modes of "independent sovereign being" while leaving undisturbed a generalized sense of continuity in a natural order of sovereign existence. This is a tall order. It is no wonder that it is postponed until the moment of crisis. This "tall order" defines a task whose "accomplishment," though never finally accomplished, is the second and perhaps signal historical "virtue" of hegemonic leadership. It is indeed a task whose "accomplishment" ushers in a new paradigm of sovereignty, a new (if sometimes territorially the same) hegemonic sovereign to exemplify it, and a redefined international purpose.

If it is true that no more consequential task could possibly be imagined, however, it is equally true that this task itself must not be imagined before its means of "accomplishment" are sure. It can never be directly addressed as a task in the means-ends rational sense of the word. Although it very much involves what Deutsch (1966, 251–52) might call a "strategic simplification," it cannot be contemplated as a strategy designed to accomplish some end. For once again, what is at stake are the naturalized boundaries, competencies, and practical dispositions affixed to the construct of sovereignty—the very meaning of sovereignty as a self-evident mode of international being. To regard these as problematic would be to concede that boundaries, competencies, and dispositions are anything but natural. It would be to invite their further politicization at just the time when the principal danger is that they are being politicized.

If the problem is to be solved, its solution must reside in a knowledgeable practice of innovation that refuses to acknowledge an objective need for the innovation—that refuses even to recognize the innovativeness of the innovation. It must reside in a practice of innovation that, to paraphrase Bourdieu, signifies a perfect command of the art of living; an ability to draw upon all the resources inherent in an ambiguous doxic understanding of the time and tempo of circumstances; an ability to do and signify that which others in far-flung and widely disparate times and places will immediately and unquestioningly recognize as just what *must* be done and what they, too, must do as the sovereign beings they now are, have always been, and shall always be (see Bourdieu 1977, chap. 3).

Virtuous practice of hegemonic innovation is, then, a practice of international savoir faire. Three things it is not. First, it is not a *heroic* practice, if heroism is taken to betoken the possession of distinctive attributes or powers intrinsically beyond the reach or emulation of others. It is an extraordinary practice of signifying what is recognized as necessarily ordinary, a mode of being and doing to which others can reasonably claim to aspire.

Second, it is also not a practice of a mysterious *charisma*, whose roots, for Weber, lie intrinsically beyond analysis. The "roots" of hegemonic virtue are eminently susceptible to analysis, albeit not a form of analysis, that is predicated upon the existence of unproblematic choice-making actors and that refuses to acknowledge the importance of ambiguity in politics. The "roots" of hegemonic virtue, and the possibility condition of the historical innovation of rituals of enframing, lie in the constitution of the strategic reserve of an ambiguous doxa and in the mobility of knowledgeable rituals by which this ambiguous region of practice is itself constituted and enframed. The sources of innovation, ironically enough, are to be found in the play of knowledgeable practices by which effects of continuity are made.

Third, the virtuous practice of hegemonic innovation is least of all a *lonely* practice. It is not a practice undertaken through the solitary creative genius of hegemonic statesmen and then projected onto a world of indifferent or resistant others.

It is not a source of significations. It is not even an originary practice, preceding the social effects it produces and to which all effects might ultimately be traced. It is indeed just the opposite. "Hegemonic innovation" is an effect that is socially produced. To be sure, "the originary moment of hegemonic leadership," the "virtuoso performance of system renewal," "the act of creative genius in statecraft"—all of these locutions *signify* a lonely act of invention that solves a problem, answers a crisis, shows a way, casts a light, or serves a need. In point of fact, however, innovation does not consist in some pure moment of invention signified. It consists in the social construction and valorization of the *signifier* itself. It consists in the collaborative production of the signifier of the "hegemonic leader" whose "act of creative genius" solves a "crisis" as a socially recognized, widely disseminable principle of interpretation—a functional principle by which, in times of a dangerous proliferation of interpretations, it becomes possible to enframe practices and recognize and exclude dangers. In short, one cannot say that the virtuous hegemonic leader innovates rituals of enframing; one can say that "virtuous hegemonic leadership" is a ritual of enframing socially innovated.[4]

The social innovation of new enframing practices, recognized as hegemonic innovation, might of course seem quite unlikely in view of the "anarchy" of international political life. It might seem especially unlikely in a time of crisis. There is, though, a reason to think collaboration possible and a reason to think that the subjects of international politics might be favorably disposed. Collaborative innovation is possible, even at a distance, because crisis is a crisis of interpretations first and primarily—only secondarily is it an "inter-state" crisis—and because, as noted earlier, traces of the contesting interpretations are to be found within the times and spaces of all sovereign states. With different inflections, with different priorities, with different arrangements and dispersals of terms and meanings, the tensions at work within any one are at work in all. As a result, it is most unlikely that a practice of innovation in one locale would lack significance in others. It is most unlikely that a deconstruction, inversion, and reinscription of terms of discourse in one place and time would be without its strategic implications for the deconstruction of discourses going on elsewhere. In fact, it is only through practices of enframing that this proliferation and circulation of meanings is contained. When there is a crisis of enframing practices, it is quite true that boundaries are proclaimed in ever louder voices, but it is equally true that the boundaries are less effective, the dissemination more likely, the cross-boundary connections more probable. In every locale, each interpretation finds a possible voice, whether in the center of the political stage, the museum, the asylum, or the jails. The resources out of which novel enframing practices will be constructed are susceptible to being alienated, but they are nowhere purely alien.

The subjects of international relations are disposed to collaborate for the same reason that members of an audience, upon witnessing the performance of a sincere but inept comedian, nervously squirm and titter in antipation of the too long delayed moment in which their voices may echo in a chorus of collective laughter. The ritual practices associated with the moment are failing, and identity is unaffirmed. All manner of interpretive possibilities that would be silenced were the comedian successful now threaten to find a voice. Will the comedian choke up or break down, turning comedy into tragedy? Will the audience contribute to the embarrassment by prompting the comedian—"What about your wife?!"—only to have the prompts misunderstood? Will hecklers heckle? Will the comedian's repartee succeed or fail? Will the audience be confronted with the choice of reproaching the heckler for his boorishness or admiring his jeers? Will the busboy leap to the stage, there to try out the awful routine practiced before his bedroom mirror? Will the nightclub manager whisper something to the comedian and then offer one of those dreadful apologies that only make matters worse? What will the room become? Who, each member of the audience asks, am I to become? In not dissimilar fashion, a crisis of political identity is understood, by all sovereign subjects, as a failure of interpretation in which they themselves are mutually in question, in which being in question means being at risk of discipline, and to which the only answer is to exercise the practiced rituals by which recognition might be mutually restored.

One example of the innovation of a ritual of enframing is to be found in the nineteenth-century innovation of what might be called a ritual of "imperial displacement." Occasioned by crisis, the ritual involved the enframing of international community by appeal to, for example, racial criteria, European heritage, the unity of Christendom, and long-standing diplomatic tradition—a practice of enframing that made it possible to recognize vast regions of the world as occupying an "unspeakable" domain "beyond the line." By summoning the European remembrances of the glory of ancient empires, by recalling European imperialism of previous centuries, by circulating the notion that imperial conquest beyond the line is self-evidently a source and emblem of power and prestige among sovereign states themselves, and by affixing this interpretation especially upon British imperialism, this practice made it possible to construct British imperial practice as an exemplar worthy of emulation, indeed, an exemplar that must be replicated if the normal form of sovereign being is to be fulfilled. This enframing practice thus created a field of imperial practice and a set of dispositions toward it that permitted sovereign states to displace their domestic resistances (from those stressed by Schumpeter to those stressed by Lenin). It made possible the coordination of the displacement of resistance in such a fashion that the resistances displaced did not, for a time, become mutually disabling effects among mutually recognizing sovereign states themselves. The innovation of this enframing practice made this coordinated displacement possible, importantly, without acknowledging the problem solved and without contemplating imperial practice as a means of solving it; indeed, the coordination of displacement was officially recognized as imperial rivalry. The boundaries and content of sovereign being could continue to be recognized as unproblematic even though, in fact, they were then, as they are now, problematic through and through.

A second example is to be found in a prior enframing ritual, of which the ritual of imperial displacement could be considered a crisis-born refinement. The prior innovation is the enframing ritual of "free trade." Here it can again be noted that the ritual involves a certain form of spacing—now, though, more social and "vertical" than geographic and "horizontal." It inheres, in part, in a recognition of a difference between state (politics) and market (economy), the former territorial and the latter a domain of universal mobility. It necessarily inheres also in a recognition of the limited permeability of territorial boundaries: open to the movement of some socially recognizable practices, and closed to others. These were innovations that came to be identified with British statecraft and that were pronounced natural. Yet it is clear that this innovation could not have been possible had it not (1) been susceptible to normalization by appeal to the mutually accessible cognitive resources of European experience (see, for example, Hirschman 1977) and (2) been founded on a critical deconstruction (a decomposition, partial reversal, and reinscription) of hierarchies of understanding already at work and naturalized in mercantile doxa of European state practice.

Many other examples of strategic innovations could be given. The cold war—with its implications for the stigmatization of socialism as the "other" to Western sovereignty, for the legitimation of global surveillance and "power projection" vis-à-vis the Third World, and for the legitimation of a militaristic "industrial policy" in the West—is certainly one. Programs of political and economic development, especially the international institutionalization thereof, provide other examples. Still other examples are explored in Janice Thomson's recent work with Stephen Krasner (Thomson and Krasner 1989, chapter 11 in this book): work that can be regarded as a concentrated analysis of just this problem of innovating rituals of enframing and, with them, new modes of sovereign doing and being. Where did all the privateers go? Why is the mercenary no longer the norm? Why does "intervention" have one normalized content in one period, another content in another? Asking these questions, as Thomson and Krasner do, one directs attention to just this innovative practice.

That examples of such strategic innovations are to be found does not mean that in every crisis strategic innovations will be made and exemplified in practice. Crisis can be long protracted. Attempted innovations can fail. Practices can misfire. As crisis protracts, several themes are likely to be echoed: growing complexity, dwindling resources, mounting interdependence, the acceleration of time, the shrinking of space, the decline of hegemony, the waning of the principle of sovereignty, and emerging turbulence or disorder. The constellation of themes reflects several sides of one phenomenon: the failure of ritual enframing practices and a resulting crisis of political identity and international purpose.

• "Growing complexity" reflects the fact that ever more refined practices of enframing, undertaken to marginalize resistances, produce more resistances and require ever more elaborate rituals of enframing.

• "Dwindling resources" reflects the fact that, with the complication and elaboration of resistances, and with the corresponding imposition of limits on the ambiguity of doxa itself, it becomes more and more difficult to generate new rituals capable of arresting the heightening dangers.

• "Mounting interdependence" reflects the fact that practices undertaken within any one sovereign "field" have effects that are unintended, resistant, and disabling of the rituals of power in other sovereign fields.

• "The acceleration of time" and the "shrinking of space" reflect the fact that resistances that have hitherto been excluded over the line, forgotten into the past, or deferred into the future now fold back upon the immediate and the present to expose the arbitrariness of the enframing practices themselves.

• "The decline of hegemony" reflects the fact that these unintended, resistant, and disabling effects are now experienced even in the onetime "hegemonic field," where the normalized mode of sovereign being was once most naturally and effortlessly lived and exemplified for all to see. Owing to this, instances of departures from a norm of sovereign being can no longer be marginalized by way of enframing practices playing on dimensions of time and space, for the norm itself is deprived of a place or a time of its paradigmatic being.

• "The waning of the principle of sovereignty" reflects the fact that the practices of enframing, by which a normalized mode of international political identity is constituted, are no longer so effective as they once were, with the result that the normalized meaning of sovereignty and of the practical competencies affixed to it are now largely politicized, not doxically accepted.

• "Emerging turbulence and disorder" reflect nothing more, but certainly nothing less, than a resulting fear—fear that the world is entering an abyss where anarchy reigns, meaning proliferates beyond control, identity is never sure.

Conclusion: A Dilemma for Theory of International Governance

The dangers inherent in such a situation are no doubt real, and it is perhaps understandable that theorists of international governance, confronting these dangers, would want to pose the question of control: How, by way of what practices, might it be possible to establish unambiguous voices of authority, stabilize meanings, secure boundaries, and effect a lucid understanding of the objective conditions and necessary limits of responsible social action in world affairs? The question is a perfectly valid one for theorists of international governance to ask. In fact, it is the force of these notes to suggest that this is precisely the question to be asked. It is, after all, a question that goes to the heart of the problematic of international governance outlined here: a problematic of imposing international purpose.

Yet these notes also point to something of a dilemma encountered by theorists who would take this question seriously and make this problematic of governance the object of sustained and critical scrutiny. In order to take up this problematic as a focus of theory, one must be prepared to give up something that many take to be virtually constitutive of doing theory. One must be prepared to give up the time-honored dream that theory, in constructing knowledge, can plant its feet in some absolute foundation, some "hard bottom" already in place, beyond history and independent of politics. This dream of "hard bottom" is well encapsulated in a famous snippet from Henry David Thoreau's *Walden:*

> Let us settle ourselves, and work and wedge our feet downward through the mud and slush of opinion, and prejudice, and tradition, and delusion, and appearance, that alluvion which covers the globe, . . . through church and state, through poetry and philosophy and religion, till we come to hard bottom and rocks in place, which we can call *reality*, and say, This is, and no mistake; and then begin, having *point d'appui*, below freshet and frost and fire, a place where you might found a wall or a state, or set a lamp-post safely, or perhaps a gauge, not a Nilometer, but a Realometer, that future ages might know how deep a freshet of shams and appearances had gathered from time to time [quoted in Michaels 1977, 133].

Why must the theorist interested in the problem of imposing global purpose renounce this foundationalist dream? The answer, it seems to me, is plain. The claim that the conduct of theory is grounded in some secure foundation, independent of history and politics, is itself a ritual practice of enframing intimately involved in the imposition of purpose in the sense considered here. Like all such rituals, the claim of some absolute foundation depends upon the ability skillfully to deploy the doxic knowledge of a culture, thus to define some set of historical limitations as a necessary, timeless, and universal ground, intrinsic to human beings as they are and must be. Like all such rituals, too, it depends for its force upon a systematic refusal to see that it is an arbitrary political practice and that imposing purpose is just what it does. If theory is to take up the problem of imposing international purpose, it must take its distance from ritual practices such as these. It must renounce the claim that it speaks from some absolute foundation.

True, such a conclusion will encounter objections. In the absence of a secure foundation, many might say, theory would be unable to speak clearly, reliably, and decisively in answer to the dangers that we confront in world politics today. We have produced a worldwide web of instantaneous communications, and as a result, we can no longer be deaf to the problems occurring anywhere in the world. We have constructed a world economy upon which our material well-being depends, and we cannot extricate ourselves from the world's terrors. We have created nuclear weapons, and we have put our very being, as species, in doubt. In the face of these dangers, many might conclude it would be the height of irresponsibility for theorists to give up upon the ideal of the absolute foundation. In the absence of a foundation, theory would have no basis upon which to discriminate truth from ideology, to separate necessity from contingency, to distinguish the fearsome from the benign, or even to decide what we must do. We would be lacking the "hard bottom" upon which to set the "lamp-post" by which we cast our light, the "Realometers" by which we measure difference and change in history. And we would be unable to give advice to the "state," itself in need of a secure foundation, as to how it might reasonably secure our freedoms, focus our collective aims, and bring what endangers us under control.

The objection on behalf of "foundationalist" theory is familiar, of course, and it might even be persuasive in those places where people might still cling to the ideal of hegemony in the sense of the term presented earlier. It is primarily here, after all, that subjects readily know themselves as part of the universal "we" of the sort that the objection repeatedly invokes and on whose behalf it would have theory speak. It is primarily here, too, that subjects are disposed to acknowledge an equally universal "objectivity" in which theory might secure its foundations. And it is primarily here that subjects are likely to be persuaded by arguments that invoke terrifying dangers that "we" confront, as if all people everywhere would necessarily agree as to what their real dangers are. For these hegemonic subjects, identity and purpose can hardly be in question. We know who we are, these subjects might claim, and we know the objective conditions of our lives. Our purpose is to survive. Accepting this, theory must dedicate itself to the survival of this hegemonic subjectivity, whatever the dangers to it might be. It would be irresponsible for theory to do otherwise.

When, however, one moves beyond the reaches of hegemonic certainty, the objection that is founded upon "dangers to man" loses its force. For what one hears when one turns an ear to the margins of hegemonic culture is anything but an eagerness to affirm a universal "we" or to worry about threats to it. What one hears, instead, is an insistent echoing of the question, "Who are we?" (Foucault's afterword to Dreyfus and Rabinow 1983). This question is not asked in yearning for a return to a traditional being or a pure and universal self. It is a question that reverberates in a vast series of immediate struggles going on in all parts of the world—wherever and whenever boundaries are blurred, fields of practice intersect in mutually destabilizing ways, ambiguities reign, and identity is undecidable. These are struggles against forms and techniques of knowledge and power that would control ambiguity, effect boundaries, regiment subjects, define what their identities must be, determine how they must be joined to and separated from others, and impose upon them a law of truth that they are obliged to recognize and that others have to recognize in them (Foucault's afterword to Dreyfus and Rabinow 1983). Here, in the marginal places and times, the primary dangers are not those abstract dangers seen from the totalizing standpoint of a hegemonic "we." The primary dangers to be resisted—immediately and practically—are to be found in the knowledgeable practices of enframing that would intrude upon a space, a time, an individual, there to impose what must be. Theory that participates in these knowledgeable practices of enframing, as "foundationalist" theory does, is likely to be counted among the dangers to be resisted.

As it happens, these marginal struggles of resistance against knowledgeable rituals of enframing do more than give the lie to the universalist conceits implicit in familiar defenses of "foundationalist" theory. They also provide something of a model for a kind of "foundation-less" theorizing appropriate to the problematic of imposing international purpose. To learn how to theorize the problematic of international purpose, one might do well to watch these marginal struggles at work.

Notes

1. In this respect, Rosenau's distinction accommodates without entirely bowing to Kratochwil and Ruggie's provocative claim (1986, 763–68) that in the study of international governance—and most especially in the study of international regimes—methodology and epistemology need to be squared with subjectivist ontology.

2. "Governance I," Rosenau writes (1987, 13), "can be seen as the objective conditions of global life, those underlying, often unrecognized constraints and rules by which individuals, groups, and communities conduct their affairs." Implicit in this interpretation of "objective conditions" is the assumption that their objectivity obtains, not in any absolute sense, but only from the point of view of historical subjects (individuals, groups, and communities). The analyst may therefore join in calling them objective, for analytic purposes, only by refusing to distance himself from this normalized subjectivity. When this subjectivity is put in question and analytic distance is effected, objectivity becomes problematic.

3. Weber's models are models for the legitimation of the investment of power in a single center of domination, where power is taken to consist in an ability to issue *visible* commands to which others have a duty to conform in practice, and where power is made visible because it is set in relief against the socially recognized possibility that other centers might issue the commands, that other commands might be issued, or that practice might, in the absence of the commands, depart from the practices commanded. These models speak not at all to the problem at hand. They do not speak to the problem of differentiating subjective and objective, thereby to fix political identity and practical dispositions, naturalize systemic relations, circumscribe meaningful political discourse, and effect a commitment to a collective purpose that is not a visible commitment because no other interpretations of collective possibility are seriously entertained. Besides, these models presuppose as given what the problem of imposing purpose puts in question: the existence of some well-bounded community of subjects who are competent and mutually disposed to recognize a universally applicable legal formalism, to acknowledge the communal sanctity of an eternal yesterday, or to bear concerted witness to the miraculous proof of a hero's exemplary powers. See Weber (1978, vol. 1, 36–38; vol. 2, 921–26).

4. If one can detect in these words echoes of Foucault's writings on the "author function," it is not by coincidence. Hear Foucault (1984, 118–19):

> [W]e must entirely reverse the traditional idea of the author. We are accustomed . . . to saying that the author is the genial creator of a work in which he deposits, with infinite wealth and generosity, an inexhaustible world of significations. . . .
>
> The truth is quite the contrary: the author is not an infinite source of significations which fill a work; the author does not precede the works; he is a certain functional principle by which, in our culture, one limits, excludes, and chooses; in short, by which one impedes the free circulation, the free manipulation, the free composition, decomposition, and recomposition of fiction. In fact, if we are accustomed to presenting the author as a genius, as a perpetual surging of invention,

it is because, in reality, we make him function in exactly the opposite fashion. One can say that the author is an ideological product, since we represent him as the opposite of his real function. . . . The author is therefore the ideological figure by which one marks the manner in which we fear the proliferation of meaning.

References

Ashley, R.K. (1987). "The Geopolitics of Geopolitical Space: Toward a Critical Theory of International Politics." *Alternatives* 12, no. 2.

—— (1989). "Living on Border Lines: Man, Poststructuralism, and War." In J. Der Derian and M. Shapiro, eds., *International/Intertextual Relations: Boundaries of Knowledge and Practice in International Politics.* Lexington, Mass.: Lexington Books.

—— (Forthcoming). "The Powers of Anarchy." In H.R. Alker, Jr., and R.K. Ashley, eds., *After Neorealism: Anarchy, Power, and Community in International Collaboration.*

Bourdieu, P. (1977). *Outline of a Theory of Practice.* Cambridge: Cambridge University Press.

Bull, H. (1967). "Society and Anarchy in International Relations." In H. Butterfield and M. Wight, eds., *Diplomatic Investigation.* London: Allen and Unwin.

Culler, J. (1982). *On Deconstruction: Theory and Criticism after Structuralism.* Ithaca: Cornell University Press.

Derrida, J. (1976). *Of Grammatology.* Baltimore: Johns Hopkins University Press.

—— (1978). *Writing and Difference.* Chicago: University of Chicago Press.

—— (1983). *Margins of Philosophy.* Chicago: University of Chicago Press.

Deutsch, K.W. (1966). *The Nerves of Government: Models of Political Communication and Control.* New York: Free Press.

Dreyfus, H., and P. Rabinow (1983). *Michel Foucault: Beyond Structuralism and Hermeneutics.* 2d ed. Chicago: University of Chicago Press.

Foucault, M. (1977a). *Discipline and Punish: The Birth of the Prison.* Translated by Alan Sheridan. New York: Pantheon.

—— (1977b). *Power/Knowledge: Selected Interviews and Other Writings, 1972–77.* Edited by Colin Gordon. New York: Random House.

—— (1978). *The History of Sexuality.* Vol. 1. *An Introduction.* Translated by Robert Hurley. New York: Random House.

—— (1984). "What Is an Author?" In P. Rabinow, ed., *The Foucault Reader.* New York: Pantheon.

Gilpin, R. (1981). *War and Change in World Politics.* Cambridge: Cambridge University Press.

Habermas, J. (1976). *Legitimation Crisis.* London: Heinemann.

—— (1979). *Communication and the Evolution of Society.* London: Heinemann.

Hirschman, A. (1977). *The Passions and the Interests: Political Arguments for Capitalism before Its Triumph.* Princeton: Princeton University Press.

Johnson, B. (1980). "Melville's Fist: The Execution of *Billy Budd.*" In B. Johnson, ed., *The Critical Difference: Essays in the Contemporary Rhetoric of Reading.* Baltimore: Johns Hopkins University Press.

Krasner, S. (1985). *Structural Conflict: The Third World against Global Liberalism.* Berkeley: University of California Press.

Kratochwil, F., and J.G. Ruggie (1986). "International Organization: A State of the Art of an Art of the State." *International Organization* 40, no. 4.

Lakatos, I. (1970). "Falsification and the Methodology of Scientific Research Programmes." In I. Lakatos and A. Musgrave, eds., *Criticism and the Growth of Knowledge.* Cambridge: Cambridge University Press.

Lijphart, A. (1981). "Karl W. Deutsch and the New Paradigm in International Relations." In R.L. Merritt and B.M. Russett, eds., *From National Development to Global Community: Essays in Honor of Karl W. Deutsch.* London: Allen and Unwin.

Michaels, W.B. (1977). "*Walden*'s False Bottoms." *Glyph* 1, no. 1.

Modelski, G. (1978). "The Long Cycle of Global Politics and the Nation-State." *Comparative Studies in Society and History* 20, no. 2.

Offe, C. (1975). "The Theory of the Capitalist State and the Problem of Policy Formation." In L. Lindberg, R. Alford, C. Crouch, and C. Offe, eds., *Stress and Contradiction in Modern Capitalism.* Lexington, Mass.: Lexington Books.

—— (1983). *Contradictions of the Welfare State.* London: Hutchinson.

Rosenau, J.N. (1987). "Governance without Government: Systems of Rule in World Politics." Unpublished notes for a research collaboration. Los Angeles: Institute of Transnational Studies, University of Southern California.

Thomson, Janice E., and Stephen D. Krasner (1989). "Global Transactions and the Consolidation of Sovereignty." In Ernst-Otto Czempiel and James N. Rosenau, eds., *Global Changes and Theoretical Challenges: Approaches to World Politics for the 1990s.* Lexington, Mass.: Lexington Books.

Wallerstein, I. (1984). "The Three Instances of Hegemony in the Capitalist World Economy." *International Journal of Comparative Sociology* 24, nos. 1 and 2.

Weber, M. (1978). *Economy and Society.* Vols. 1 and 2. Berkeley: University of California Press.

14
International Relations Theory and the Analysis of Change

Peter J. Katzenstein

T he 1980s are noteworthy for many changes. Secular changes in the spread of information technologies and international interdependence are continuing apace. Cyclical changes that attend the rise and fall of great powers in the international system are also noteworthy, as is illustrated by the shift of financial power from the United States to Japan and the decline of U.S. competitiveness. And the interaction of secular and cyclical changes is creating substantial changes in the character of major states and regions. This is noteworthy, for example, among socialist states. China, the Soviet Union, and the Eastern European states are experiencing change of crisis proportions. The most basic principles of socialism are being contested. Capitalist states also deal with a set of stern challenges requiring sharp reversals in policy (as for example in the United States, Britain, or France) or cautious experimentation (as for example in Japan, West Germany, and the small Western European states). Latin America struggles at the brink of bankruptcy. The ethnic and religious conflicts in the Middle East are a continuous source of military conflicts. And Africa is facing a monumental crisis of social disintegration. In short, wherever international relations scholars look their analyses are expected to account for change.

Yet the core paradigm of international relations theory, neorealism, emphasizes not change but continuity. In his celebrated *Theory of International Politics*, which quickly established itself as the central text of the neorealists, Kenneth Waltz espoused the cause of a parsimonious theory of the international state system centered around three features (Waltz 1979): the anarchic arrangement of the international state system, the low degree of functional differentiation between states as the system's central actors, and the relative distribution of capabilities as a defining characteristic of the system's structure. Neorealism predicts balancing as the central tendency of the competitive pressures of the international state system. It emphasizes stability and continuity. And it relegates change to something beyond the

I would like to thank David Baldwin, Robert Keohane, James N. Rosenau, and John Ruggie as well as the members of the Workshop on International Political Economy at Columbia University for their helpful comments on an earlier draft.

purview of systemic level analysis. "Changes in, and transformation of, systems originate not in the structure of a system," writes Waltz, in answering his critics, "but in its parts. Through selection, structures promote the continuity of systems in form; through variation, unit-level forces contain the possibilities of systemic changes. . . . Systems change, or are transformed, depending on the resources and aims of their units and on the fates that befall them" (Waltz 1986, 343).

When E.-O. Czempiel and James Rosenau invited the contributors in this book to attend a workshop on international relations theory they pointed to the pervasiveness of change that was grasped inadequately by the state-centric view of neorealism. My assigned role was to summarize the proceedings. The papers prepared for the workshop and published here in revised form express the pervasive unease that marks the field. Neorealism, it seems, provides a parsimonious explanation of *stability*. Yet much of what we need to understand is *change*. This disjunction between the world of international relations scholarship and the world of international politics is an underlying theme that motivates all the chapters in this book.

Admittedly, the chapters are of a bewildering scope. They emphasize different kinds of theories and different kinds of methods. At the level of theory the book exhibits philosophical, conceptual, empirical, and experimental approaches to theory. At the level of methodology one encounters discussions of rational choice, simulation, the general linear model, poststructuralism, macro theory and case studies.

After perusing these chapters the sympathetic reader is reminded of the world's largest hand-cast iron cannon, which is in the fort above the royal palace of Jaipur. Because the Indians are prone to hyperbole, I lack full confidence in their claim about the size of the gun. But it is a very large gun indeed, cast in the middle of the eighteenth century. It took thirty men eight hours to load it and to prepare it for firing. It was fired only once. The reason for the lack of use was not the scarcity of labor. It was the dearth of a target.

This, I surmise, is the overwhelming impression anyone will carry away from reading these chapters. Change is an elusive topic, but the purpose of the conference, and the chapters that are assembled here, was not to have a clear empirical target. Rather the intent was to survey diverse and far-ranging theoretical perspectives. When the emperor's clothes are tattered many a tailor will be found working on new robes.

Compared to the late 1960s (with its great debate between "traditionalist" and "behavioralist" international relations scholars) the tone of the theoretical discourse in the 1980s is less acrimonious. The main reason, as I shall argue below, lies in this recognition, shared by theorists of all stripes: Without a puzzle that disciplines our thinking most theoretical debates remain empty speculation. Hans Morgenthau is reported to have muttered in bewilderment in the 1960s that the behavioralists were always sharpening their tools but rarely cutting anything. Today we have all become cutters in the forest. We disagree on what we are cutting—weeds or oak trees. But only very few of us are simply sitting still and sharpening our tools.

Though these chapters may lack a common target they do not lack common themes. First, they take different approaches to the analysis of change. Second, they have distinctive views on the role of the state. Third, they express a noteworthy interest in history. And, finally, they link particular political developments to general theories in distinctive ways. But before developing these four themes I want to briefly sketch one particular development that has taken place in the field of international relations theory during the last two decades.

Cycles of Theory

During the last generation theories of international relations have moved in opposite directions in security studies and political economy. Based on Thomas Schelling's path-breaking applications of game theory to international relations (Schelling 1963, 1966), security studies in the 1960s proceeded to develop models, for example, of strategic bargaining, arms races, and crisis decision making that were based on the assumption of rationality. States were viewed as unitary actors rationally pursuing their preferred strategies. Although successive generations of weapon technologies and alternative strategic scenarios provided new data, the central task remained to develop parsimonious models based on the strong assumption about the rationality of governments engaged, for example in the area of deterrence, in calculated, competitive risk taking.

Meanwhile the field of international political economy was very much in a nascent state. But to the extent that, in the 1960s, international economic issues were seen as creating both distinctive political problems and the need for sustained analysis (for example, in the works of Klaus Knorr and a small number of other scholars), the mode of inquiry was historical and descriptive (Knorr 1975). No strong prior assumptions about the rationality of actors or the dynamics of systems informed these studies. There was virtually no attempt to build models. The difference in theoretical orientation between the two fields was very marked.

The rapid growth of historically informed and often descriptive studies in international political economy by the early 1980s encouraged a new trend. The application of economic and game-theoretic approaches spread rapidly. This development was no doubt spurred by advances of public choice theories in political science and in other parts of the social sciences. But it probably came also from the understandable desire to apply some economic styles of analysis to political phenomena linked intimately to the economy. Virtually all of the new styles of analysis were now based on variants of the rationality assumption that had been embraced by the security literature in the 1960s. It remains to be seen whether future theoretical developments will view rationality primarily as a baseline of expectations which, if disappointed, will drive analysis to encompass other theoretical traditions to account for particular developments in international politics; or whether future work will try to build rigorously deductive models of international politics based on the assumption of national state actors.

In security studies this tension has in fact become very evident in the 1980s. One strand of work, based on strong assumptions, is rigorously deductive (de Mesquita 1981; de Mesquita and Lalman 1986). At the same time the growing prominence of the cognitive model and a sharp turn to intensive historical studies, especially of crisis decision making, led to a fundamental assault on the rationality assumption. States were no longer viewed as unitary actors and governments were no longer viewed as rational. Instead the rare conditions under which rational decisionmaking is possible and the reasons for the pervasiveness of misperceptions and motivational biases have become the focus of an entire new line of research (Jervis 1976; Lebow 1981).

Both in the 1960s and in the 1980s theorists of international relations have chosen not to take a unified approach to the pressing questions in the field. This I do not expect to change in the coming years. But the sharp demarcation line between security and political economy studies is likely to be eroded. Substantive political problems are no longer as neatly separated between these two subfields as was true when specialists distinguished between "high" and "low" politics in the 1970s. The discrepancy between theoretical orientations is sufficiently great to invite the borrowing of approaches from one subspecialty for the benefit of the other. And the need to think creatively about change makes this cross-fertilization highly desirable.

Different Conceptions of Change

The theoretical approaches that find expression in these chapters conceive of change differently. Table 14–1 adapts categories proposed by Robert Gilpin for the purpose of thinking about these chapters. Because most theories of international relations focus on different factors (for example, the international state system or the character of the main actors), unsurprisingly they record different types as well as consequences of change. Neorealism, I argued above, emphasizes continuity.

Table 14–1
Different Conceptions of Change

Type of Change Affecting	Factors that Change	Consequence of Change
Systems	International state system	Revolutionary
Actors	Character of main actors (empires, states, etc.)	Major
Systemic rules	Governance	Moderate
Interaction	Processes	Incremental

Note: Adapted from Robert Gilpin, *War and Change in World Politics.* Cambridge: Cambridge University Press, 1981, p. 40.

In Waltz's structural theory there exists a sharp conceptual break between the structure of the international system on the one hand and the attributes of the states as the major actors on the other. In the terms of table 14-1 this version of systemic theory thus focuses exclusively on the relative position of states, a defining characteristic of structure, while neglecting altogether the role of systemic rules and processes of interaction. Through competition or socialization, system structure and the relative position of the actors have a strong effect on actor behavior. But systemic theory is static. It predicts balancing. Stability is defined as system maintenance. Change is exclusively an attribute of the actors rather than the international system.

Although this sparse and elegant formulation of neorealism has many attractive features, it fails to deal with the changes that brought together the authors of this book. Some scholars have tried to extend neorealism, but John Ruggie has offered the most trenchant critical discussion of Waltz's conception of stability and change (Ruggie 1986). For Ruggie a major virtue of Waltz's structural perspective is the fact that the generative aspects of the international structure are seen to operate at different levels. The three defining characteristics of structure—anarchy, low differentiation, and relative capabilities—can be thought of as operating at successive levels of causation. Ruggie holds that Waltz misses some of the systemic attributes of his own model. Sovereignty is the principle that differentiates actors in the modern state system. It is an attribute of the system as well as of individual states. At the same time Ruggie also argues that Waltz misses the systemic significance of actor attributes. Even at the risk of losing parsimony, the low differentiation of actors must include attributes of actors if a modified systemic theory is to help us in understanding change.

Building in part on the foundation of what Alexander Wendt and Raymond Duvall (chapter 4) call the "old" institutionalism, "poststructural" theorizing, exemplified in this book by Ashley's contribution, emphasizes change rather than continuity (Bull 1977; Ashley 1984; Alker 1986). It criticizes the narrow, economic perspective of structural theory as well as various game-theoretic approaches to the study of international relations. Structural, neorealist theories narrow the theoretical as well as political agenda. They discount or conceal altogether processes of change occurring below the level of the international system. Poststructural theories seek to overcome this static and conservative character by insisting that societies are always engaged in a process of self-reflection on their own historicity. Change is never-ending. Self-reflection is shared and interpretative. It is a consensual rewriting of institutional arrangements and political praxis. And this process of self-reflection is communicated to other societies. International conflict or cooperation do not result from a process open to a reductionist logic of analysis that takes actors and interests as a given. Conflict and cooperation emerge instead from the never-ending process of redefining social and political identities that generates consensually shared and contextually appropriate standards of action. In international society these standards are called regimes. In brief, this theoretical perspective insists on the pervasiveness of change especially at the margins of society and politics and at the intersections and crosscurrents of social and political developments.

Between these two theoretical positions there exists a third to which, I believe, a majority of international relations scholars subscribe today. This third position argues that change and continuity blend together in historically shaped, specific structures. This invocation of historicity and the importance of historical context reverberated throughout the discussions the authors had. But the discussions showed two distinct theoretical orientations. First, some view history as a storehouse of facts. The availability of machine-readable, longitudinal data of attributes, of events, of interactions, and of images has given scholars the means for investigating the past, for delineating patterns while remaining agnostic about the relative importance of change and continuity. Alternatively, there is the view of history as a sequence of irregular big bangs. Here the focus is on infrequent major discontinuities that rearrange all aspects of international politics—systems, actors, systemic rules and interactions—followed by long periods of relative calm. To date we have no social science equivalent to chaos theory, no concepts or models that help us to discriminate between incremental and discontinuous changes. Incremental or large-scale change thus can be interpreted only after the fact. But once our hunch tells us that we are living in a period of relative normalcy or great turbulence, something that we must judge ourselves, then we can make contingent generalizations about systems, actors, rules, and interactions. Our discussions suggested that international relations theory relies on intuition and historically informed analogies to guess about the magnitude and character of present-day change.

If this conception of change in current international relations theory is anywhere close to the truth, I think that we shall not be able to prove conclusively whether change or continuity is the dominant characteristic of international politics. The owl of Minerva always flies in twilight. But we do not know whether it flies at dawn or dusk. Scholars must bring their own philosophy of history to this important question. Our theories will not help us further. Indeed, I don't see any reason why international relations theory should be called upon to answer questions in the philosophy of history.

The Role of the State

These chapters appear to diverge greatly on the approach they take to the study of the state. Janice Thompson and Stephen Krasner, for example, for a variety of reasons in chapter 11 adhere to the state-as-an-actor model. E.-O. Czempiel (chapter 7), on the other hand, wants to abolish the state altogether, at least as an analytical category for the study of international relations. Between these two extreme positions the chapters, and the discussions that preceded them, are groping toward a third position that views the state as a structure—a beguiling and opaque concept.

Raymond Duvall and Alexander Wendt have done all of us a great service in clarifying this state-as-structure concept (Duvall and Wendt 1987, 32–36; Wendt 1987). Building on analytical distinctions made by neo-Marxist and neo-Weberian scholars, they argue that the state should be thought of both in terms of its internal relations and the social structures that embed it. The state is a structure of governance and rule that defines, institutionally and legally, political authority in society. States do not act—governments do. This relation between states as structures and governments as agents is complex. States shape both the interests and the powers of governments. But states exist only insofar as their existence finds expression in government practices and the norms that sustain them. Government practices are conditioned (but not determined) by the state and social structures of which they are a part.

This state-as-structure concept is fundamentally different from the view of neorealism and game-theoretic approaches to international politics. The state is not equated with government. The state is not viewed as divorced from its social context. State interest and power are not stipulated. The state is not used as an ahistorical category that leads to an atomistic and voluntarist view of politics. Instead the state-as-structure conception separates structure and agent analytically. It views the state as in part, but not solely, constituted by social structures. State interests and powers become the subjects of sustained inquiry. And the state is viewed in the context that makes atomism and voluntarism a historically conditioned outcome. In brief a basic category of analysis in neorealism is no longer accepted at face value but becomes itself a subject of study.

This conception of the state-as-structure shows up, under the label of "constraint," in several of the chapters. Territoriality (discussed by Susan Strange in chapter 9, as well as by Thompson and Krasner in chapter 11), transnationalism (discussed by Werner Link in chapter 6), and interdependence (as discussed by Wolf-Dieter Eberwein in chapter 5), are but three examples. And the concepts of sovereignty or autonomy are undercurrents in virtually all of the chapters.

The category of transnational relations appears with a frequency in this book that, at first glance, must be astonishing at least to the U.S. reader. The transnational paradigm after all dates back to the 1970s. Because U.S. international relations theorists produce new concepts and paradigms at least once every decade, the reappearance of this category in this book may be a source of concern to some interested readers. Is U.S. faddishness on the decline? Or is the surprising reappearance of the concept of transnationalism in these chapters merely another instance of cultural lag? Has the concept of transnationalism finally penetrated the dense cultural hinterland on the European continent?

I think that the reason for the reappearance of the category of transnational relations taps a deeper intellectual root. States and transnational relations are instances of viewing international politics from the vantage point of states-as-structures, thus making the category of an atomistic, voluntarist, and state-as-an-actor model problematic. The invocation of transnationalism touches on the same analytical point that motivates the chapters by Cox (chapter 3), Czempiel (chapter 7), and

Ruggie (chapter 2). All of these authors talk about the relations between states and various kinds of structures: economic, social, and domestic. The intellectual enterprise in these chapters is the same as for the transnationalists. What differs is the structure to which the state is linked.

I do not wish to minimize the theoretical difficulties that derive from the fact that different kinds of structures—conceptualized and defined differently in different theoretical frameworks—are thought central to the study of international relations. In their chapters Ruggie, as well as Wendt and Duvall, have discussed these difficulties in depth. But one of Waltz's most important contributions has in fact been to alert the international relations theorists among us, by the very sparseness and parsimony of his analysis, to the need of rethinking the category of the state, an enterprise fueled also by other currents in the social sciences. The substantial theoretical disagreements to which this process of reconsideration leads, this book suggests, does not undermine the shared critique of neorealism.

Despite the differences in the structure deemed central and the particular ways of linking the concept of the state to specific social structures in individual research projects, this book signals an important change in direction. Significant, new theoretical approaches inquire into the very nature of the state rather than taking the nature of the state as a given. It would be wrong to argue that the state-as-actor view has been replaced by the state-as-structure approach. Microeconomic and game-theoretic approaches, represented in this book by Erich Weede (chapter 12), enjoy a growing currency in certain fields of international relations theorizing. And because this paradigm is increasingly aware of some of its obvious shortcomings (for example, in the specification of the origins of preferences) we can look forward to further progress. At the same time though developments in the analysis of comparative politics, sociology, and history have also influenced international relations scholarship. Here structural approaches to the study of state are of growing importance.

We have no way of knowing how these different analytical traditions will influence one another. But it seems almost unavoidable that the basic category of international relations theory—the state, its interests, and powers—will become a subject of inquiry rather than an analytical assumption. And this shift in perspective may open up new insights into the processes of change that are affecting world politics.

The Role of History

A third area of substantive agreements, both in the discussion and in the chapters, is the invocation of the importance of history and context-specific propositions. "Historically informed" theorizing appears to have gained ground on "pure" theorizing. The chapters by Cox, Thompson and Krasner, Link, Ruggie, and Weede (chapters 3, 11, 6, 2, and 12, respectively), for example, refer explicitly to general European history. If I called it "Wallersteinian history," all of the authors and most of the readers of this book would understand the terms of debate: political polycentrism in an integrated global economy. Since the mid-1970s, most of the theorists published in this book have made it a habit to read history. In this they are perhaps not altogether atypical. International relations theory does not keep abreast of changes in historiography. But it wants to be aware of the major books, especially in the area of macrohistory. This strikes me as a very considerable change from the process of "scientific" theory building in the 1950s and 1960s.

The reasons for this change are not simple. Developments in security studies, I argued above, have made it imperative to take history seriously again. Theoretically informed empirical work increasingly is going back to primary sources to reconstruct as precisely as possible the context in which particular policy choices were made. Furthermore many of the authors in this book are driven toward history because they seek a better understanding of the present. Scholars of international political economy, for example, have sought to identify the distinctive elements in the decline of America's position in the world. Comparisons with other modern empires, British, Dutch, Spanish, or French, may help. Finally, theorists of international relations are also reading history because, let's face it, reading history is fun.

The synthesis of theory and history that is emerging extends the approach of historical sociology that Stanley Hoffmann was advocating vigorously in the 1960s (Hoffmann 1965). Immanuel Wallerstein and Paul Kennedy, to name but two examples, do not represent conventional historiography (Wallerstein 1974, 1980; Kennedy 1987). Their work is theoretically informed. It is macroscopic. It deals with large questions and big slices of history. Macrohistory, in short, provides a useful referent for the big theoretical or political questions that drive much of the current international relations work. What is the nature of the state? What is the character of the decline in U.S. power?

Significantly the convergence of macrohistory with macrotheory does not lead to the quest for general theory. Theorists of international relations are now willing to entertain, for example, the distinctive claims, strengths, and weaknesses of historical and functional explanations of international politics. Historical explanations are offered for the big and discontinuous changes in history—for example, major wars or social transformations. These explanations are context-specific and do not, at least as of today, tell us much that is systematic about breakpoints in history. Theorizing about periods of relative stability, a disconcertingly amorphous and stretchable concept, proceeds quite differently. It is based on contingent generalizations about the consequences of the interrelation of different variables or clusters of variables. Still informed by history, the enterprise resembles more closely the business of social science. There exist, to be sure, strands of theorizing that take other approaches to history, improved for example by the theoretical question of a particular research project or driven by the availability of specific types of historical data. But awareness has spread of the dangers of homogenizing history, of taking what some of my historian friends deride as the big-blender approach of political scientists to the study of history.

As discussed here by James Caporaso (chapter 8), developments in economic history that are theoretically informed by the neoclassical paradigm, transaction cost analysis, and public goods theories point in my opinion in the same direction. They combine theory with history and have reduced sharply their expectations about formulating a general theory of economic history. This is nowhere clearer than in the widely noted work of Douglass North (Davis and North 1971; North and Thomas 1973; North 1981). In the early 1970s his aim had been to explain all institutions, including the state, as the result of changes in relative market prices that in turn reflected individual or group preferences. By the early 1980s North had reformulated his approach quite dramatically. Institutional developments in military technology, political conflicts within the modern pluralist state, and the supply function of institutional innovation lack adequate theories. Furthermore the theory of economic history that North is seeking to develop is also held back by the lack of a theory of demographic change and a positive theory of the sociology of knowledge (North 1981, 68). The obstacles to general theory have proven formidable indeed without, however, discouraging the convergence between history and theory.

The renewed relevance of history to international relations theory is laudable. But it is open to one serious change. It is largely European-centric. The canon of historical books that international relations scholars read and cite excludes Latin America, Africa, Near Eastern, and Asian history. Consider the putative decline of American hegemony that has attracted so much attention and work in recent years. We have viewed the process through realist lenses trained on the Westphalian state system, based on the assumption of separate and exclusive spheres of sovereign state authority. The picture changes dramatically if we view it from the standpoint of Asian empires (Ottoman, Indian, or Chinese) with their complex welter of overlapping jurisdictional claims, interlacing norms, and complex military and taxation arrangements. The role of medium-sized, supporter states, such as Japan and West Germany, has apparently much to do with the stability of international arrangements despite the dramatic decline of America's relative power in several issue areas (Snidal 1985; Lake 1984). These supporter states are penetrated political systems on questions of national security but relatively more self-contained on other issues. Asian history may help us to discern elements in the Western state systems that are of growing relevance since 1945. And in so doing the study of history may reinforce theoretical currents that question the billiard ball view of the state central to the neorealist theory of international politics.

Levels of Analysis and Issue Areas

The chapters in this book are united by a common concern for narrowing the gap between macrotheory and particular political developments. By and large though they do not follow the analytical stance of a recent collection of essays that combined an "upward" looking game theory with a "downward" looking regime analysis (Oye 1986). One group of chapters is organized around the traditional distinction between international, national, and subnational levels of analysis. In the course of our discussions it became clear that many authors sought, in one way or another, to break "up" or break "down" the state. Whether analysis moves "up" or "down" depends evidently on the particular synthesis of national and international determinants of political strategies or structures. Cox's chapter (3), for example, is organized around this vertical notion of how to relate the state to both the process of material production "below" and the global order "above," and helps us to develop categories of analysis that for a given piece of empirical research need to be brought together in specific ways that suit particular theoretical formulations. Distinguishing by levels of analysis is also found in other chapters. Caporaso (chapter 8), for example, explores what can be learned from neoclassical economics at different levels of analysis. Both Russett (chapter 10) and Weede (chapter 12) look at national as well as international determinants of state action. And Link (chapter 6) distinguishes between national, international, and transnational determinants of policy.

A second group of authors seeks to narrow the gap between theory and politics by investigating particular arenas of politics or issue areas. This approach is very common in the analysis of public policy. And it has become a standard research procedure in the field of international political economy. Power is not necessarily fungible across different issue areas. And international regimes vary by policy sectors. Thompson and Krasner (chapter 11) as well as Strange (chapter 9) rely on this distinction. It serves the same analytical purpose as distinguishing by levels of analysis, narrowing the gap between theoretical constructs and particular empirical applications.

Narrowing that gap surely is an important task for new theoretical formulations of international relations. Macro theories such as world systems or long-cycle analysis are by their very nature weak at helping us understand political processes at the micro level or over shorter time periods (Wallerstein 1974, 1980; Modelski 1978). Conversely, theorizing from the micro level upward often leaves opaque how particular processes generate new macro structures in international relations (Axelrod 1984). The theoretical approaches reflected in these chapters point to the usefulness of bridging the gap between macro and micro structures and processes.

I believe that a good deal of evidence concerning these central arenas and actors in global politics suggests not a reinforcing but a cross-cutting pattern of change. To extend the metaphor in one of James Rosenau's background papers, we are dealing not with a pattern of "cascades" but of "circuit breakers." I see little evidence in the political architecture of global politics that points in the 1980s to the rearrangements of interlocking structures of politics through a simultaneous throwing of all switches. Instead strategy and statecraft will remain an essential tool for navigating political currents.

Conclusion

I have argued in this chapter that international relations theorizing is infused by a number of intellectual crosscurrents: a likely narrowing between the subfields of international security and international political economy; an emphasis on continuity and change that differs in different analytical traditions; a reconsideration of the state as the basic actor in international relations and a further development of game-theoretic approaches; a reconceptualization of the relation between history and theory; and renewed attempts to bridge the gap between macro theories and micro phenomena through either vertical (level of analysis) or horizontal (sector or issue approaches) conceptual distinctions. The intellectual stakes in these theoretical debates are high and the consequences of theoretical choices for particular research programs or concrete projects are very noticeable.

Yet though the theoretical stakes are high, this book and the discussions that led up to it offer little evidence that we are heading toward another great debate, 1960s-style. The discussion is being conducted in muted tones. Claims of the superiority of one's preferred paradigm are not made, and the opposition is not hooted, at least not publicly. We are all simply too aware of the imperfections of all analytical traditions, including our preferred ones. I am not saying that the field is altogether bereft of zealots. But there is a world of difference between the content and the tone of theoretical debates in the late 1980s compared to those in the late 1960s.

There exist two plausible reasons that account for this civility and tolerance. First, the debate of the 1960s has taught us all one very important lesson. Discussion about the advantages or disadvantages of particular theories or analytical traditions are fruitless without a clear problem focus. This lesson we have all learned. And we are likely to be focused more on questions than approaches. But in this common attempt to sidestep any new grand debate, we remain divided into two scientific cultures that sustain each other not through debate and sparring but through mutual indifference.

In preparation for attending the conference and writing this chapter I asked about two dozen prominent international relations theorists, including many who have written chapters for this book, for copies of their graduate reading lists. Although I have not made a detailed study of it, the deep divide in how we are training our students (as indicated by what we expect them to read) was very surprising indeed. Call it the tit-for-tat of graduate education. The places where international relations theorists prefer to publish give us only a weak sense of the schism that divides the field: the *American Political Science Review* and the *Journal of Conflict Resolution* versus *International Security* and *World Politics*, with *International Organization* and the *International Studies Quarterly* holding a very tenuous middle ground. The training we give our students is eloquent testimony to the fact that the conflict of the 1960s has divided the field deeply.

Problem focus and mutual indifference are the two major reasons why the analysis of change is unlikely to generate a new grand debate among international relations scholars. It did not happen in the meetings that led to this book. And it did not occur, as I argued, in the broader evolution of the fields of international security and international political economy that have led to the current array of analytical approaches. This is only to the good. I for one am convinced that in this case less heat will lead to more light.

References

Alker, Hayward, R., Jr. (1986). "The Presumption of Anarchy in World Politics." Unpublished paper.

Ashley, Richard K. (1984). "The Poverty of Neorealism." *International Organization* 38, no. 2 (Spring):225–86.

Axelrod, Robert (1984). *The Evolution of Cooperation.* New York: Basic Books.

Bull, Hedley (1977). *The Anarchical Society: A Study of Order in World Politics.* New York: Columbia University Press.

Davis, Lance E., and Douglass C. North (1971). *Institutional Change and American Economic Growth.* Cambridge: Cambridge University Press.

Duvall, Raymond, and Alexander Wendt (1987). "The International Capital Regime and the Internationalization of the State." Unpublished paper, May.

Hoffmann, Stanley (1965). *The State of War: Essays on the Theory and Practice of International Politics* New York: Praeger.

Jervis, Robert (1976). *Perception and Misperception in International Politics.* Princeton: Princeton University Press.

Kennedy, Paul (1987). *The Rise and Fall of the Great Powers: Economic Change and Military Conflict from 1500 to 2000.* New York: Random House.

Knorr, Klaus (1975). *The Power of Nations: The Political Economy of International Relations.* New York: Basic Books.

Lake, David A. (1984). "Beneath the Commerce of Nations: A Theory of International Economic Structures." *International Studies Quarterly* 28, no. 2 (June):143–70.

Lebow, Richard N. (1981). *Between Peace and War: The Nature of International Crisis.* Baltimore: Johns Hopkins University Press.

de Mesquita, Bruce Bueno (1981). *The War Trap.* New Haven: Yale University Press.

de Mesquita, Bruce Bueno, and D. Lalman. (1986). "Reason and War." *American Political Science Review* 80, no. 4 (December):1113–30.

Modelski, George (1978). "The Long Cycle of Global Politics and the Nation-State." *Comparative Studies in Society and History* 20, no. 2 (April):214–35.

North, Douglass C. (1981). *Structure and Change in Economic History.* New York: Norton.

North, Douglass C., and Robert Thomas (1973). *The Rise of the Western World: A New Economic History.* Cambridge: Cambridge University Press.

Oye, Kenneth A., ed. (1986). *Cooperation under Anarchy.* Princeton: Princeton University Press.

Ruggie, John Gerard (1986). "Continuity and Transformation in the World Polity: Toward a Neorealist Synthesis." In Robert O. Keohane, ed., *Neorealism and Its Critics.* Pp. 131–57. New York: Columbia University Press.

Schelling, Thomas C. (1963). *The Strategy of Conflict.* New York: Oxford University Press.

Schelling, Thomas C. (1966). *Arms and Influence.* New Haven: Yale University Press.

Snidal, Duncan (1985). "The Limits of Hegemonic Stability Theory." *International Organization* 39, no. 4 (Autumn):579–614.

Wallerstein, Immanuel (1974). *The Modern World System: Capitalist Agriculture and the Origins of the European World-Economy in the Sixteenth Century.* New York: Academic Press.

—— (1980). *The Modern World System: Mercantilism and the Consolidation of the European World-Economy, 1600–1750.* New York: Academic Press.

Waltz, Kenneth N. (1979). *Theory of International Politics.* Reading, Mass.: Addison-Wesley.

—— (1986). "Reflections on *Theory of International Politics*: A Response to My Critics." In Robert O. Keohane, ed., *Neorealism and Its Critics.* Pp. 322–45. New York: Columbia University Press.

Wendt, Alexander E. (1987). "The Agent-Structure Problem in International Relations Theory." *International Organization* 41, no. 3 (Summer):335–70.

Index

About the Contributors

Richard K. Ashley is associate professor of political science at the Arizona State University. An editor of the *International Studies Quarterly,* he is a leader in the application of European social theory to the critical analysis of global politics.

James A. Caporaso is professor of political science at the University of Washington. The editor of *Comparative Political Studies* since 1974, his work has been distinguished by efforts to achieve theoretical coherence among political and economic dynamics as well as those that transgress the boundaries between domestic and international politics.

Robert W. Cox is professor of political science at York University in Canada. A former official of the International Labor Organization, his research focuses on theoretical problems in the field of international political economy and international organization.

Ernst-Otto Czempiel is professor of international relations at the University of Frankfurt. The codirector of the Frankfurt Peace Research Institute, his research program includes a concern with the dynamics of U.S. foreign policy as well as the general challenge of theorizing about world politics.

Raymond D. Duvall is professor of political science at the University of Minnesota. Previously a consultant to the World Bank and editor of *International Studies Quarterly,* his research program focuses on the political-economic transformation of dependent societies.

Wolf-Dieter Eberwein is an associate of the Science Center for Social Research (Berlin) and its long-range computer simulation project, GLOBUS. His work combines an empirical interest in problems of domestic political instability in world politics and a methodological concern with the tasks of generating comprehension through the use of computer simulations.

Peter J. Katzenstein is professor of government at Cornell University. A former editor of *International Organization*, his research ranges widely across the fields of international relations, comparative politics, political economy, public policy, and history.

Stephen D. Krasner is professor of political science at Stanford University. The present editor of *International Organization*, he is a leading theorist in the field of political economy, especially with respect to the role of the state, the concept of international regimes, and the dynamics of North–South relations.

Werner Link is professor of political science (international relations) at the University of Trier. His research has revolved around a number of topics, including German-American relations, the East–West conflict, North–South tensions, and transnational relations involving trade unionists and business executives.

James N. Rosenau is professor of international relations and political science at the University of Southern California. His research program combines theoretical and empirical inquiries into the various facets of the boundaries that divide national and international political systems.

John Gerard Ruggie is professor of international relations and Pacific studies at the University of California, San Diego. His work reflects a continuing concern with various theoretical and empirical aspects of change and continuity in the world political system, the impact of international institutions, and the ecological challenges now confronting humankind.

Bruce M. Russett is Dean Acheson Professor of International Relations and Political Science at Yale University. The editor of the *Journal of Conflict Resolution* since 1972, his work probes deeply into a number of aspects of international politics, from strategic affairs to international political economy to foreign policy analysis.

Susan Strange recently retired as Montague Burton Professor of International Relations at the London School of Economics and Political Science. She has been a pioneer in the development of the field of international political economy, giving due emphasis to both its theoretical and empirical sides.

Janice E. Thomson is assistant professor of political science at the University of Washington, having recently been awarded a doctorate by Stanford University.

Erich Weede is associate professor of sociology at the University of Cologne. He has done research on deterrence and causes of war, domestic conflicts and violence, economic growth, and income inequality. Since 1988 he has been the European editor of *International Interactions*.

Alexander Wendt is assistant professor of political science at Yale University. His research interests include global militarization, national security theory and policy, and the application of social theory to the study of international relations.

Issues in World Politics

James N. Rosenau and *William C. Potter,* consulting editors

Other Publications in the Series